Aging and Work
in the
21st Century

SERIES IN APPLIED PSYCHOLOGY

Edwin A. Fleishmann, (formerly) George Mason University
Jeanette N. Cleveland, Pennsylvania State University
Series Editors

Gregory Bedny and David Meister
The Russian Theory of Activity: Current Applications to Design and Learning

Winston Bennett, David Woehr, and Charles Lance
Performance Measurement: Current Perspectives and Future Challenges

Michael T. Brannick, Eduardo Salas, and Carolyn Prince
Team Performance Assessment and Measurement: Theory, Research, and Applications

Jeanette N. Cleveland, Margaret Stockdale, and Kevin R. Murphy
Women and Men in Organizations: Sex and Gender Issues at Work

Aaron Cohen
Multiple Commitments in the Workplace: An Integrative Approach

Russell Cropanzano
Justice in the Workplace: Approaching Fairness in Human Resource Management, Volume 1

Russell Cropanzano
Justice in the Workplace: From Theory to Practice, Volume 2

David V. Day, Stephen Zaccaro, Stanley M. Halpin
Leader Development for Transforming Organizations: Growing Leaders for Tomorrow's Teams and Organizations

James E. Driskell and Eduardo Salas
Stress and Human Performance

Sidney A. Fine and Steven F. Cronshaw
Functional Job Analysis: A Foundation for Human Resources Management

Sidney A. Fine and Maury Getkate
Benchmark Tasks for Job Analysis: A Guide for Functional Job Analysis (FJA) Scales

J. Kevin Ford, Steve W. J. Kozlowski, Kurt Kraiger, Eduardo Salas, and Mark S. Teachout
Improving Training Effectiveness in Work Organizations

Jerald Greenberg
Organizational Behavior: The State of the Science, Second Edition

Uwe E. Kleinbeck, HansHenning Quast, Henk Thierry, and Hartmut Häcker
Work Motivation

Laura Koppes
Historical Perspectives in Industrial and Organizational Psychology

Ellen Kossek and Susan Lambert
Work and Life Integration: Organizational, Cultural, and Individual Perspectives

Martin I. Kurke and Ellen M. Scrivner
Police Psychology into the 21st Century

Joel Lefkowitz
Ethics and Values in Industrial Organizational Psychology

Manuel London
Job Feedback: Giving, Seeking, and Using Feedback for Performance Improvement, Second Edition

Manuel London
How People Evaluate Others in Organizations

Manuel London
Leadership Development: Paths to Self-Insight and Professional Growth

Robert F. Morrison and Jerome Adams
Contemporary Career Development Issues

Michael D. Mumford, Garnett Stokes, and William A. Owens
Patterns of Life History: The Ecology of Human Individuality

Michael D. Mumford
Pathways to Outstanding Leadership: A Comparative Analysis of Charismatic, Ideological, and Pragmatic Leaders

Kevin R. Murphy
Validity Generalization: A Critical Review

Kevin R. Murphy and Frank E. Saal
Psychology in Organizations: Integrating Science and Practice

Kevin R. Murphy
A Critique of Emotional Intelligence: What Are the Problems and How Can They Be Fixed?

Susan E. Murphy and Ronald E. Riggio
The Future of Leadership Development

Margaret A. Neal and Leslie Brett Hammer
Working Couples Caring for Children, Aging Parents: Effects on Work and Well-Being

Steven A. Y. Poelmans
Work and Family: An International Research Perspective

Robert E. Ployhart, Benjamin Schneider, and Neal Schmitt
Staffing Organizations: Contemporary Practice and Theory, Third Edition

Erich P. Prien, Jeffrey S. Schippmann, and Kristin O. Prien
Individual Assessment: As Practiced in Industry and Consulting

Ned Rosen
Teamwork and the Bottom Line: Groups Make a Difference

Heinz Schuler, James L. Farr, and Mike Smith
Personnel Selection and Assessment: Individual and Organizational Perspectives

Kenneth S. Shultz and Gary A. Adams
Aging and Work in the 21st Century

John W. Senders and Neville P. Moray
Human Error: Cause, Prediction, and Reduction

Frank J. Smith
Organizational Surveys: The Diagnosis and Betterment of Organizations Through Their Members

George C. Thornton III and Rose Mueller-Hanson
Developing Organizational Simulations: A Guide for Practitioners and Students

George C. Thornton III and Deborah Rupp
Assessment Centers in Human Resource Management: Strategies for Prediction, Diagnosis, and Development

Yoav Vardi and Ely Weitz
Misbehavior in Organizations: Theory, Research, and Management

Patricia Voydanoff
Work, Family, and Community

Aging and Work in the 21st Century

Edited by

Kenneth S. Shultz
California State University, San Bernardino

Gary A. Adams
University of Wisconsin, Oshkosh

Psychology Press
Taylor & Francis Group

New York   London

Senior Acquisitions Editor: Anne C. Duffy
Editorial Assistant: Rebecca Larsen
Cover Design: Tomai Maridou
Full-Service Compositor: MidAtlantic Books and Journals, Inc.

Reprinted 2009 by Psychology Press

This book was typeset in 10.5/12 pt. Goudy Old Style, Italic, Bold, and Bold Italic. Headings were typeset in Americana Bold and Italic.

First Published by Lawrence Erlbaum Associates, Inc., Publishers
10 Industrial Avenue
Mahwah, New Jersey 07430

CIP information for this volume can be obtained by contacting the
Library of Congress

ISBN 978-0-8058-5726-9—0-8058-5726-5 (case)
ISBN 978-0-8058-5727-6—0-8058-5727-3 (paper)
ISBN 978-1-4106-1617-3—1-4106-1617-7 (e-book)

10   9   8   7   6   5   4   3   2

Contents

Series Foreword   xi

Preface   xv

Contributors   xvii

1. Editors' Overview   1
    Gary A. Adams and Kenneth S. Shultz

2. The Demography of Aging and Work   7
    Dawn Alley and Eileen Crimmins

3. Low-Income Older Workers   25
    Mary Anne Taylor and Holly A. Geldhauser

4. Diversity Issues for an Aging Workforce   51
    Caren Goldberg

5. An Expanded View of Age Bias in the Workplace   73
    Lisa M. Finkelstein and Sara K. Farrell

6. Employee Age and Performance in Organizations   109
    Jeanette N. Cleveland and Audrey S. Lim

7. Age and Work Attitudes   139
    Janet Barnes-Farrell and Russell A. Matthews

8. Employee Development and Training Issues Related
    to the Aging Workforce   163
    Todd J. Maurer

9. Career Mobility and Career Stability Among Older Workers   179
    Daniel C. Feldman

10. Aging and Occupational Health   199
    Steve M. Jex, Mo Wang, and Anna Zarubin

11. Age and Technology for Work   225
    Neil Charness, Sara Czaja, and Joseph Sharit

12.   Aging and Work/Family Issues   251
       Boris B. Baltes and Lindsey M. Young

13.   Examining Retirement from a Multi-level Perspective   277
       Terry A. Beehr and Misty M. Bennett

14.   In Search of a Unifying Paradigm for Understanding Aging
       and Work in the 21st Century   303
       Kenneth S. Shultz and Gary A. Adams

Author Index   *321*
Subject Index   *373*

Series Foreword

Jeanette N. Cleveland
The Pennsylvania State University

Edwin A. Fleishman
George Mason University
Series Editors

There is a compelling need for innovative approaches to the solution of many pressing problems involving human relationships in today's society. Such approaches are more likely to be successful when they are based on sound research and application. This Series in Applied Psychology offers publications that emphasize state-of-the-art research and its applications to important issues of human behavior in a variety of social settings. The objective is to bridge both academic and applied interests.

One of the most important social issues facing the United States within a global community is the rapidly aging population. During the next decade, as baby boomers approach age 60, the U.S. workforce will begin to lose millions of highly skilled and experienced workers due to retirement. This, coupled with the next generation's drop in birthrates, could lead to labor shortages of younger entrants. At the same time, these generational circumstances could also provide opportunities to transform the workplace. We are pleased to welcome the book, *Aging and Work in the 21st Century*, edited by Kenneth S. Shultz and Gary A. Adams into our Series in Applied Psychology. The book joins a number of Erlbaum books that address the increasing diversity within our workforce.

In 1983, Susan R. Rhodes published a classic review of work attitudes and older workers in the *Psychological Bulletin*. Her article was followed by a comprehensive 1983 textbook by Mildred Doering, Susan Rhodes and Michael Schuster, The *Aging Worker: Research and Recommendations*. In the present book, Shultz and Adams address some significant gaps that still exist in the research literature on older workers. They have enlisted an impressive group of authors from a variety of disciplines including industrial and organizational psychology, gerontology, management, and industrial engineering to summarize the key issues surrounding the work and non- work issues concerning older employees.

This cutting edge text will be an invaluable resource for both organizational researchers and practitioners. It represents a contribution in at least four ways. First, each chapter provides a comprehensive, innovative and much needed, update of current research on core organizational topics. These include age stereotypes and bias, work attitudes, work performance, training and development, career mobility and stability, and retirement. In addition to presenting updated research reviews, each chapter topic is discussed thoughtfully in light of emerging theories and within broader, more interdisciplinary frameworks. For example, in the chapter on age stereotypes, bias and decisions, Lisa Finkelstein and Sara Farrell review the current research and theoretical literatures concerning stereotypic perceptions of older worker held by others. This chapter also describes a second perspective: that of target perceptions of their *own* aging. The chapter by Janet Barnes-Farrell and Russell Matthews on work attitudes reviews the perceptions of older worker on job involvement and the attitudes that aging workers themselves hold toward their jobs and organization. Jeanette Cleveland and Audrey Lim review the current literature comparing older and younger workers on traditional indices of task performance, and the expansion of the performance construct itself in relation to age (e.g., citizenship behaviors, adaptability, and counterproductive work behavior). Todd Maurer presents current data on the training performance and developmental experiences of older employees and argues that these differences may be the result, in part, of discriminatory treatment as well as a number of situational factors. Daniel Feldman introduces the concept of "career embeddedness" as it concerns career stability and mobility among older employees. He explores both motivational and ability factors that contribute to shaping careers among older workers. Next, Terry Beehr and Misty Bennett take a multilevel perspective on retirement.

Second, the text introduces cutting edge topics in relation to aging workers including technology, occupational health, and work-family issues. Neil Charness, Sara Czaja and Joseph Sharit present a much needed discussion of technology and aging. These authors review statistics on age and technology use and they outline the factors to consider in order to understand how older workers interact with a range of technologies. For example, telework is discussed in relation to the aging workforce. We know of no other text that includes a discussion of the aging workforce in terms of the emerging interdisciplinary field of occupational health. Steve Jex, Mo Wang and Anna Zarubin discuss the relationships among age, job, and organizational conditions that predict employee health.

Third, we know of no single resource that addresses aging across such a wide diversity spectrum. Specifically in the first chapter, Dawn Alley and

Eileen Crimmins describe the demography of the aging workforce within the global context and within the larger context of labor force participation rates, health status of work, educational trend and economic conditions. In subsequent chapters, Mary Anne Taylor and Holly Geldhauser deal with low income older workers while Caren Goldberg addresses race and gender diversity among older workers. Finally, in the last chapter, the editors Ken Shultz and Gary Adams discuss common theoretical, methodological and practice themes across the chapters. They provide a research agenda encompassing the scientific and applied issues identified in this ground-breaking book.

This book is appropriate for students in industrial and organizational psychology, human resources management, gerontology, and education. It's appropriate for courses on selection, training and development, performance feedback, and aging and diversity in the workplace. Professionals who are engaged in the development of employees and leaders in organizational and academic settings will find this book essential to their work.

REFERENCES

Doering, M., Rhodes, S. R. & Schuster, M. (1983). *The aging worker: Research and recommendations.* Sege Publications.

Rhodes, S. R. (1983). Age-related differences in work attitudes and behavior: A review and conceptual analysis. *Phychological Bulletin 93*, 328–367.

Preface

A rapid aging of the workforce will take place during the 21st century across most of the developed countries of the world, bringing with it many issues. Some of the more obvious issues center on understanding the relationship of aging to work-related attitudes and job performance. Some of the less obvious issues include maintaining older workers' competence and occupational health, as well as facilitating their adaptation to new technologies and their management of the boundaries between work and nonwork. Thus, the purpose of this edited book is to review, summarize, and integrate the extant literature on a wide variety of issues related to aging and work. To begin, trends and implications related to the demography, income, and diversity of the aging workforce are reviewed. Then, the issue of age bias in the workplace is examined. Next, the job performance, work-related attitudes, training and development, and career issues of older workers are addressed. Following these are the topics of age and occupational health, technology, work and family issues, and retirement. We conclude with a chapter aimed at identifying and integrating the key themes and ideas developed across all of these various topics. A more detailed overview of each chapter in the book is provided in chapter 1.

APPROACH

Rather than adopt a particular theoretical or disciplinary approach, the authors of each chapter focus on a specific topic related to aging and work, integrating theory and the various interdisciplinary literatures as appropriate, related to that given topic. Additionally, the issues involving aging and work revolve around not only the individual worker, but also the employing organizations and society in general. Therefore, each chapter addresses and incorporates material relevant to each of these major constituents. While each of the chapter authors describe what we do know, and offer practical suggestions to address the issues that are identified, they also highlight some as yet unanswered questions and directions for future research. Many of the authors also provide cases, exercises, or examples, in order to more fully illustrate the issues discussed in their chapter. We hope that inclusion of these additional materials in the chapters will help the reader gain an even better appreciation for the issues related to aging and work espoused in each chapter.

AUDIENCE

The primary audience for this book is advanced undergraduate and graduate students, as well as scholars in both academic and applied settings. The disciplines of industrial and organizational psychology, developmental psychology, gerontology, sociology, economics, and social work (that study aging work force issues) serve as the primary audience. However, while the book is intended primarily as a reference text for students and scholars, organizational decision makers, public policy makers, and older worker advocates (e.g., AARP) will also have a keen interest in the various topics discussed in this book.

ACKNOWLEDGMENTS

We would like to thank numerous individuals who provided assistance in various phases of the development and completion of this book. First, we thank Stan Wakefield, our independent acquisitions editor, who shopped our book prospectus to numerous publishers in search of a home. He introduced us to Anne Duffy, our acquisitions editor at Lawrence Erlbaum Associates (LEA). Anne, and Applied Psychology series co-editor Jeanette Cleveland, provided assistance in finalizing the topics and authors that appear in this work. They also graciously answered our various questions that arose throughout the project. We are, of course, first and foremost indebted to the authors who agreed to write chapters for this edited volume and are appreciative of their timeliness in submitting drafts and the final versions of their chapters. Most chapter authors also provided a review of at least one other chapter in this book. Thus, this book would obviously not be possible without their fine work. We also thank Jennica Webster and Nicole Krause for their assistance in checking references and citations. Thanks also go out to those who reviewed the prospectus for this book and/or the final manuscript providing helpful suggestions for improvement. Our colleagues Helen Dennis, William Gallo, Robert Hansson, Susan McFadden, and Sara Rix also provided reviewers of various chapters in this work. Last, but certainly not least, we thank our respective families and friends for their support and encouragement as we completed this book.

Kenneth S. Shultz
Gary A. Adams

Contributors

EDITORS

Kenneth S. Shultz, PhD, is a professor in the psychology department at California State University, San Bernardino. His degree is in industrial and organizational psychology from Wayne State University in Detroit, Michigan. He also completed postdoctoral work as a National Institute on Aging Postdoctoral Fellow in gerontology at the Andrus Gerontology Center at the University of Southern California. He has more than 30 publications (including two book chapters and several encyclopedia entries) and more than 50 presentations on a variety of topics, most recently focusing on aging workforce and retirement issues. He also recently coauthored, with David J. Whitney, a book on psychometrics, titled *Measurement Theory in Action: Case Studies and Exercises*, published by Sage Publications.

Gary A. Adams, PhD, is an associate professor and the director of the MS I/O Program at the University of Wisconsin Oshkosh. His degree is in industrial and organizational psychology from Central Michigan University in Mount Pleasant, Michigan. He has edited a book on the topic of retirement, written several book chapters, and published more than 25 articles in journals such as *Personnel Psychology*, *Journal of Applied Psychology*, *Journal of Occupational Health Psychology*, *Journal of Organizational Behavior*, and *Journal of Vocational Behavior*. He has also made over 50 professional presentations.

CONTRIBUTING AUTHORS

Dawn Alley, BA, is a doctoral candidate in gerontology and National Institute on Aging trainee at the University of Southern California. Her research focuses on late-life socioeconomic disparities in physical and cognitive health, including differences by education, occupation, and income, and on theories of aging and the life course.

Boris B. Baltes, PhD, is an associate professor in the psychology department at Wayne State University in Detroit. He received his degree in industrial and organizational psychology from Northern Illinois University. He also has an MBA in international business from the University of Wisconsin. His research interests include the following areas: biases in performance appraisal, organizational climate, and work/family balance. His work has appeared in many journals including the *Journal of Applied Psychology*, *Organizational Behavior and Human Decision Processes*, and the *Journal of Organizational Behavior*. He is a consulting editor for the *Journal of Organizational Behavior* and is on the editorial board of various journals.

Janet Barnes-Farrell, PhD, is director of the graduate program in industrial and organizational psychology at the University of Connecticut. Her primary fields of expertise include aging and work, performance appraisal, and work-life balance. She is the author of over 30 papers and presentations on the workplace concerns of older workers, on topics ranging from age discrimination to retirement decision processes. Dr. Barnes-Farrell is a member of the editorial board for the *Journal of Applied Psychology* and the Senior Editorial Advisory Board for *The Encyclopedia of Industrial and Organizational Psychology*, and she recently served as coeditor of a special issue on aging and work for the journal *Experimental Aging Research*.

Terry A. Beehr, PhD, is a professor in the psychology department at Central Michigan University. His degree is in organizational psychology from the University of Michigan, Ann Arbor. He also completed postdoctoral work at the Institute for Social Research in Ann Arbor and at Illinois State University. He has published recently on the topics of occupational stress, retirement, and careers, among others.

Misty M. Bennett, BS, is a doctoral student in the Industrial and Organizational Psychology Program at Central Michigan University. Her research interests include retirement, work/family conflict, occupational stress, psychometrics and testing, and women's issues.

Neil Charness, PhD, is Professor of Psychology and Associate of the Pepper Institute on Aging and Public Policy at Florida State University. He received his BA degree at McGill University in 1965 and his MSc (1971) and PhD (1974) from Carnegie Mellon University. Current research interests include age and technology use, and age and expert performance. He has published over 85 journal articles and book chapters. Recent books include *Impact of Technology on Successful Aging* (coedited with K. W. Schaie, 2003) and *Designing for Older Adults: Principles and Creative Human Factors Approaches* (coauthored with Fisk, Rogers, Czaja & Sharit, 2004).

Jeanette N. Cleveland, PhD, is Professor of Industrial and Organizational Psychology at The Pennsylvania State University. Her research interests include personal and contextual variables in performance appraisal, workforce diversity issues, work and family issues, and international human resources. She was consulting editor for the *Journal of Organizational Behavior* and has served or is currently serving on the editorial boards of the *Journal of Applied Psychology*, *Personnel Psychology*, *Journal of Management*, *Academy of Management Journal*, *Journal of Vocational Behavior*, *Human Resource Management Review*, *Journal of Organizational Behavior*, and *International Journal of Management Reviews*. She is the coeditor for the Applied Psychology Series for Lawrence Erlbaum and Associates. She is the author of numerous research articles and books including: *Understanding Performance Appraisal: Social, Organizational and Goal Perspectives* (with K. Murphy) and most recently, *Women and Men in Organizations: Sex and Gender Issues* (with M. Stockdale & K. Murphy, 2000). She is also a fellow of SIOP (Division 14) and the American Psychological Association.

Eileen M. Crimmins, PhD, is Edna M. Jones Professor of Gerontology and Sociology at the University of Southern California and director of the USC/UCLA Center on Biodemography and Population Health, which is supported by the National Institute on Aging. Her current work is on the role of biological factors as mediators of educational and income differentials in health, and on active life expectancy in the older population. She holds a PhD in demography from the University of Pennsylvania.

Sara J. Czaja, PhD, is a professor in the Department of Psychiatry and Behavioral Sciences and the Department of Industrial Engineering at the University of Miami. She is also the Director of the Center on Research and Education for Aging and Technology Enhancement (CREATE) and the Codirector of the Center on Aging at the University of Miami Miller School of Medicine. Her research interests include: aging and cognition, employment, caregiving, human-computer interaction, training, and functional assessment. She is a fellow of the American Psychological Association, the Human Factors and Ergonomics Society, and the Gerontological Society of America.

Sara K. Farrell, PhD, is an assistant professor at Coe College in Cedar Rapids, Iowa. She received her MA from Minnesota State University, Mankato, in industrial and organizational psychology and her PhD from Northern Illinois University in social and industrial/organizational psychology. Her research interests include applicants' fairness perceptions of recruitment procedures and employees' fairness perceptions of organizational decisions.

Daniel C. Feldman, PhD, is the Synovus Chair of Servant Leadership at the University of Georgia and Associate Dean for Research in the Terry College of

Business. He recently served as the editor-in-chief of the *Journal of Management* and has been chair of the Careers Division of the Academy of Management. Dr. Feldman has written six books and over 100 articles on career development on such topics as organizational socialization, contingent employment, bridge employment, early retirement incentives, and career change. He received his PhD in organizational behavior from Yale University.

Lisa M. Finkelstein, PhD, is an associate professor and Coordinator of the Social-I/O Psychology Area at Northern Illinois University. She received her doctorate in 1996 in industrial and organizational psychology from Tulane University. Her current research interests focus on age stereotyping and discrimination, generation identification, intergenerational relations, mentoring relationships, newcomer socialization, obesity discrimination, and humor in the workplace. She is also a Gerontology Faculty Associate for the interdisciplinary gerontology program at Northern Illinois University. She served as program chair for the 20th Annual Meeting of the Society for Industrial and Organizational Psychology (SIOP), and has recently been elected Secretary of the Executive Committee of SIOP.

Holly A. Geldhauser, BA, is a doctoral candidate in industrial and organizational psychology at Clemson University. She is currently researching organizational policies that influence recruitment and retention of older workers. She has an interest in occupational health, which has lead to current research on sleep deprivation and cognitive impacts of work performance. She has also conducted research on perceptions of work/family fairness.

Caren Goldberg, PhD, is a faculty member at American University. Her research, which focuses primarily on relational demography, has appeared in such journals as the *Journal of Applied Psychology*, *Sex Roles*, *Journal of Organizational Behavior*, and *Group and Organization Management*. She recently coauthored a chapter on age discrimination in the SIOP Frontiers book, *Psychological and Organizational Bases of Discrimination at Work*. Dr. Goldberg is currently an associate editor at *Group and Organization Management* and serves on the editorial boards of the *Journal of Management* and *Human Resource Management Journal*. Dr. Goldberg has also appeared on *Dateline, NBC*, to discuss age discrimination.

Steve M. Jex, PhD, is currently Associate Professor of Industrial and Organizational Psychology at Bowling Green State University and Guest Scientist at Walter Reed Army Institute of Research. He has also held faculty positions at Central Michigan University and the University of Wisconsin Oshkosh. Dr. Jex received his PhD in industrial and organizational psychology from the University of South Florida and has spent most of his postdoctoral career conducting research on occupational stress. His research has appeared in a number of scholarly journals including the *Journal of Applied Psychology*, *Journal of Organizational Behavior*, *Journal of Occupational Health Psychology*, *Journal of Applied Social Psychology*, and *Work & Stress*. His also serves on two editorial boards and is Associate Editor of the *Journal of Occupational and Organizational Psychology*. In addition to his research and editorial activities, Dr. Jex is the author of two books, *Stress and Job Performance: Theory, Research, and Implications for Managerial Practice* and *Organizational Psychology: A Scientist-Practitioner Approach*.

Audrey S. Lim, MSc, is currently a graduate student in industrial and organizational psychology at The Pennsylvania State University. Her research interests include issues relevant to selection and performance evaluation. She is also interested in dynamic performance and multilevel modeling. Having worked in public service in Singapore, Ms. Lim also has research interests in program evaluation. She is a student affiliate of SIOP and a graduate member of the British Psychological Society.

Russell A. Matthews, BA, is a PhD candidate in industrial and organizational psychology at the University of Connecticut. His primary research interests include examining the work/family interface from a systems perspective, with an emphasis on worker wellbeing. He has also conducted research on workplace concerns of older workers, work motivation, and participatory ergonomics.

Todd J. Maurer, PhD, is a professor and Chair of the Department of Managerial Sciences at Georgia State University. His research has addressed issues in aging and employee development, leadership development, and human resource selection. His work has been supported by various organizations, including the National Science Foundation, the National Institutes of Health, the U.S. Army Research Institute, and the Society for Industrial and Organizational Psychology (SIOP). He is a winner of the Outstanding Human Resource Development Scholar Award from the Academy of Human Resource Development and a fellow of SIOP and of the American Psychological Association.

Joseph Sharit, PhD, is a professor in the Department of Industrial Engineering at the University of Miami and has secondary appointments in the Department of Psychiatry and Behavioral Science and the Department of Anesthesiology at the University of Miami Miller School of Medicine. He is an investigator at the Center on Research and Education for Aging and Technology Enhancement (CREATE) and is also involved with the Miami Patient Safety Center. Professor Sharit's research interests include human-machine interaction, aging, and performance in interacting with technology, cognitive work analysis, human error and system safety, and human decision-making.

Mary Anne Taylor, PhD, is a professor in the psychology department at Clemson University in Clemson, South Carolina and a member of a cross-disciplinary Gerontology Research Team at that institution. She earned her doctorate in industrial and organizational psychology from the University of Akron. She has a number of publications, presentations, and two book chapters in areas related to retirement, including the retirement planning-adjustment relationship and the recruitment of older workers. Her current work focuses on the factors in retirement planning that facilitate later life satisfaction and on exploring the planning needs of the diverse baby boomer generation.

Mo Wang, PhD, is an assistant professor at Portland State University. He received his doctorate from Bowling Green State University in Bowling Green, Ohio, majoring in both industrial and organizational psychology and developmental psychology and minoring in quantitative methods,. His research interests include four broad areas of investigation: older worker employment and retirement; social cognition and aging; expatriate management and global/cross-cultural HR practice; and application of advanced quantitative methodology. His research in some of these areas closely ties to the research field of occupational health psychology, such as safety and health concerns for older workers. He has published his work in *Psychology and Aging, Personnel Psychology,* the *Journal of Applied Psychology,* and *Educational and Psychological Measurement.*

Lindsey M. Young, BA, is a graduate student working on her PhD in industrial and organizational psychology at Wayne State University. Her research interests center around work/family conflict and measurement and statistical applications. Within work/family conflict, she is primarily interested in better understanding the antecedents of work/family conflict, and the coping strategies that individuals may use in order to reduce work/family conflict. Her interest in statistics and measurement centers primarily on studying the proper use of relative importance statistics such as dominance analysis as well as the general use of Monte Carlo simulations.

Anna Zarubin, BA, is a graduate student in the Psychology Department at Bowling Green State University, Bowling Green, OH. She is working toward her master's and doctoral degrees in industrial and organizational psychology. Her bachelor's degree in psychology is from DePaul University in Chicago. Anna's current research interests include topics in occupational health psychology, as well as diversity training.

Aging and Work
in the
21st Century

1

Editors' Overview

Gary A. Adams and Kenneth S. Shultz

> In this chapter we provide an introduction and overview of the topic of aging and work in the 21st century. To accomplish this we describe how the text unfolds by highlighting some of the key findings and issues raised by each chapter. In doing so, we provide the reader with a broad view of aging and work in the 21st century and a sense of the interconnectedness of the topics covered. We hope that by including such a chapter, the reader will come to see the whole of this text as something more than a collection of individual chapters.

Most developed countries are experiencing rapid aging of their populations, while those countries that have not yet begun experiencing population aging will do so during the first half of the 21st century. Along with this population aging, the workforces of these countries will also, on average, grow older. Given the sheer size of this phenomenon and the centrality of work to people's lives and livelihoods, as well the importance of the workforce to organizations and the economy, researchers, organizational decision-makers, those interested in public policy, and even the general public, have shown an interest in better understanding the aging workforce. Our contention is that a better understanding requires a comprehensive review of the theoretical and empirical literature with an eye toward identifying both recommendations for applied practice and future research needs. Thus, we set out to do just that with this edited volume by bringing together the top scholars in the various areas of aging and work to provide chapters that review and summarize their respective areas.

To better understand the size and nature of the aging workforce, Dawn Alley and Eileen Crimmins introduce both population aging and labor force participation as the key trends that lead to an aging workforce. They discuss what is known about population aging and the trends in fertility and mortality rates that underlie it. Then they discuss current projections surrounding labor force participation of older workers. They next point out that although much is known about population aging, labor force participation is somewhat less certain. They identify factors such as diversity, technology, health, and retirement patterns that will help determine labor force participation of an aging population. Their discussion of these issues sets the stage and foreshadows many of the topics that are covered in subsequent chapters.

The chapter by Mary Anne Taylor and Holly Geldhauser, as well as that of Caren Goldberg, takes a closer look at specific demographic groups. Taylor and Geldhauser focus on aging among low-income workers. They discuss the negative impact of poverty on psychological and economic wellbeing and also point out that some groups, such as women and certain ethnic groups, are at even more risk of poverty as they become older. As their discussion unfolds, a strong case for active efforts to ameliorate poverty among low-income older workers emerges. They suggest a number of approaches to financial planning programs and programs aimed at increasing the employability of low-income older workers.

Meanwhile, Caren Goldberg directly addresses issues surrounding aging women and minorities in her chapter. She describes trends in labor force participation of these groups and discusses how being a member of these groups, separately and in combination with one another, may be negatively related to employment decisions such as those surrounding hiring, performance appraisal, training, and compensation—that is, how being older and belonging to one or more of these other groups might be related to a wide variety of work-related outcomes. Beyond this, however, she discusses not only the demographic characteristics and person-based stereotypes prevalent in the workplace, but also the nature of the labor market and stereotypes associated with jobs as well. She develops a model linking these individual and contextual constructs to organizational decision-making regarding work outcomes.

A key point from these two chapters is a reminder that decisions made about work-related outcomes such as who gets hired, promoted, offered training and the like, are fundamentally decisions made by people about other people within the context of the work and social environment. They argue that such decisions are based on perceptions that may or may not be accurate. This point is taken up in considerable depth in Lisa Finkelstein and Sara Farrell's chapter on age bias. However, these authors go a step further by disentangling perceptions from feelings and evaluations, and from decisions about older workers. They use this tripartite framework to review the literature on age bias. In doing so, Finkelstein and Farrell identify, (1) the motives that may initiate age biases, (2) the possible mechanisms that lead to age bias incidents, (3) the conditions under which these are more or less likely to occur, and (4) what might be done to prevent age bias.

The next two chapters deal with aging and two of the most popular variables in the human resources (HR), organizational behavior (OB), and industrial/organizational (I/O) psychology literatures. These are employee performance and work-related attitudes. First, Jeanette Cleveland and Audrey Lim begin their chapter on job performance by discussing the various ways in which age and performance have been conceptualized. They distinguish between person-based measures of age, such as chronological age and subjective or personal age, and context-based measures of age, such as age status and perceived age as evaluated by others. They also distinguish task performance as measured by objective, subjective, and interestingly, health-related indicators, from contextual performance, counterproductive, and adaptive behaviors. These distinctions allow for a nuanced discussion of the relationships between the age and performance. They conclude that while much research has focused on chronological age and task performance, relatively little research has focused on these alternative ways to conceptualize these two constructs. They also recognize that performance is not just determined by ability, but also motivation. They encourage practitioners to be mindful of the effects of age when designing and implementing traditional performance appraisals, as well as more recent multisource feedback systems.

In their chapter on aging, worker attitudes, and motivation, Janet Barnes-Farrell and Russell Matthews begin by reviewing the literature on aging and employee attitudes, and concluding that there is a generally positive relationship between age and global job satisfaction, albeit not always linear. They then examine the relationship between specific attitudes such as the various facets of satisfaction, job involvement, and commitment. Next they turn their attention to both motivation and motives of aging workers. They conclude that while much is known about aging and work attitudes, as well as the "what's and why's" of aging and work motivation, there is still much more to learn. They suggest researchers begin treating age as a focal variable in their theorizing and empirical research. They also suggest practitioners be aware of the differing and changing needs and motives of workers as they age and provide opportunities for workers to meet these needs and motives.

The discussion of job performance and work attitudes provided in the preceding chapters leads nicely to the next two chapters, which address aging related to training and development, and older workers' careers. Todd Maurer, in his chapter on training and development, points out that, like the research and theorizing on the topic of motivation, age is often included in research on training and development, but is rarely of primary or substantive concern. That is, age is treated as a predictor of outcomes surrounding training and development, but not in relation to the other individual and situational antecedents often included in various models of training and development. Rejecting this approach, he reviews not only the relationship between age and outcomes, such as participation and performance in training, but also how age is substantively related to a number of situational and individual characteristics that influence these outcomes. In doing so, he more fully captures age-related effects in the training and development process.

Next, Daniel Feldman's chapter addresses the topic of career change among older workers. In his chapter he describes the individual, job, and organizational-level factors that influence the decision of those over the age of 50 to change careers. Based on the notion of job embeddedness, he develops a parallel construct called career embeddedness. Career embeddedness refers to a multidimensional construct that is composed of a collection of variables that tend to tie individuals to their career. These variables are described along three subdimensions (links, fit, and sacrifices) with each arising from two sources (work and community). This new construct of career embeddedness has the potential for furthering our understanding of career change by moving our attention from strictly time-based variables (e.g., age, organizational tenure) to the underlying mechanisms for which these other variables tend to serve as proxies (e.g., involvement, personal investment, and maintaining important relationships).

The chapter by Steve Jex, Mo Wang, and Anna Zarubin tackles the issue of age and occupational health. They begin by reviewing the various perspectives on health and settle on the idea that health is a state of physical, psychological, and social wellbeing. In doing so, they move away from the narrow focus on physical health and the absence of disease. They then review the physical and cognitive changes that come with increasing age and their relationship to this expanded view of occupational health. They offer a number of suggestions for improving the health of aging workers, such as job redesign and health promotions programs. They also offer a number of suggestions for future research, such as those aimed at identifying those factors that may make aging workers more resilient to poor occupational health than younger workers.

Perhaps the single biggest factor that has brought about changes in the basic nature of work itself is the accelerated use of technology, particularly computer technology. Recognizing this, and the unique issues it presents to an aging workforce, Neil Charness, Sara Czaja, and Joseph Sharit describe the age-related changes in attention, perception, cognitive, and psychomotor abilities that influence the use of technology. An important conclusion in their chapter is that aging workers are both willing and able to use technology, but there are steps that can be taken to enhance this willingness and ability. Accordingly, they provide a series of recommendations for the design of training programs and the computer software that are aimed at increasing aging workers' effective use of technology.

At first glance it may seem odd to include a chapter on aging and work/family issues in a book on aging and work. However, as Boris Baltes and Lindsey Young point out, the basic issue of balancing the competing demands of the two most influential spheres of adult life is no less salient for aging workers than it is for younger workers. In their review, they note some of the different priorities and demands faced by older, as opposed to younger, workers. They also discuss differences in coping strategies and resources that aging workers use to meet work and nonwork demands. They then focus on the issue of eldercare. They describe its potentially negative consequences for individuals and organizations, and offer practical suggestions about how to mitigate these consequences.

The chapter by Terry Beehr and Misty Bennett addresses the topic of retirement. These authors point out that while at one time retirement meant an end to involvement in paid work, this is no longer the case for many retirees. They organize their review by examining the predictors and outcomes of retirement at three levels, (1) individual and family, (2) organizational, and (3) societal. They also discuss bridge employment and volunteer work. In doing so, they provide a coherent and comprehensive review of what is known about the topic of retirement, and identify some important, yet unanswered, questions. A key take away point is that retirement in the 21st century will be different from what it was in the past.

In the concluding chapter, we (the editors) weave together the common themes from across the various chapters in an attempt to begin the process of creating a unifying framework or paradigm for studying aging and work in the 21st century. We discuss theoretical, methodological, as well as practice issues. In the theoretical section we highlight the common themes of successful aging, perceptions matter, diversity issues, and contextual factors. Next, in the methodological section, we discuss measurement, statistical, and research design issues related to aging and work. Finally, in the concluding section on practice issues, we discuss individual, organizational, and societal level issues that span the chapters in this book. We conclude the final chapter with a brief discussion, and a series of questions, related to the concept of creating a unifying paradigm for studying aging and work in the 21st century.

Taken together, the various chapters provide a comprehensive summary and integration of the literature on aging and work. They identify gaps in the existing knowledge base and offer recommendations to address those gaps. They also make substantive suggestions for public policy and organizational decision-makers to consider as they confront the issues associated with managing an aging workforce. In doing so, the chapters that comprise this text tell us not only where we have already been, but also provide a roadmap useful for charting a course into the domain of aging and work in the 21st century.

2

The Demography of Aging and Work

Dawn Alley and Eileen Crimmins

The workforce is growing older as the population ages, and in particular, as baby boomers age; by 2012, the number of workers over 55 is projected to grow at nearly four times the rate of the overall labor force. The speed of workforce aging in the future will depend on trends in labor force participation. For example, if older adults choose to remain in the labor force and delay retirement, workforce aging will accelerate. Labor force participation in the future will depend on trends in education, female labor force participation, the health status of the aging workforce, economic conditions, and pension availability. Future research should address how emerging issues, such as the diversity of the older population, the growth of defined contribution pension programs, the development of bridge jobs, emerging technologies, and changing markets will affect retirement age, and how the policy environment can modify these trends.

The population is aging, and with it the workforce is "graying." By 2030, the elderly population will nearly double; the U.S. will be home to more than 70 million people ages 65 and over who will make up more than 20 percent of the population (U.S. Census Bureau, 1996). Population aging will increase the potential supply of older workers and the number of retirees, raising a variety of questions about the value of older workers, the structure of retirement benefits, and the solvency of pension programs. This chapter will provide a demographic framework for addressing these issues, as well as the many issues discussed throughout the rest of this book.

POPULATION AGING

Changes in population composition are the result of changes in fertility, mortality, and migration. The fertility rate refers to the number of live births per woman ages 15–44 years in a population. When the fertility rate is equal to 2.1, or the replacement rate, the population stabilizes. When the fertility rate is higher than 2.1, as it was during the baby boom of 1946–1964, the population grows as the number of young people increases. When the fertility rate drops, the number of children declines in successive cohorts.

Population aging generally occurs due to a combination of fertility and mortality decline known as the demographic transition. Fertility decline reduces family size and produces smaller cohorts at younger ages, while mortality decline increases life expectancy. This combination of smaller young cohorts and larger, more long-lived older cohorts results in population aging. The demographic transition has already occurred in most developed nations and is rapidly underway in many developing nations (see Table 2.1). Europe has the highest proportion of elderly residents and is likely to remain the oldest region for decades (Waite, 2004). Although the proportion of the population over 65 is highest in industrialized countries (as high as 19 percent in Japan and Italy), 59 percent of the world's elderly now live in developing nations (Kinsella & Velkoff, 2001).

Figure 2–1 shows population pyramids for the U.S. population from 2000 to 2050. These figures illustrate three important points. First, the population at older age groups is increasing, and the largest increases are related to the aging of the baby boomers. Second, due to fertility declines, there are actually reductions in the number of people among younger age groups. The baby boomers (the large cohort born between 1946 and 1964) are larger than any of

TABLE 2.1.
Percent of Population Aged 65 and Over in Selected Countries in 2005 and 2025

	2005	2025
Developed Countries		
Australia	12.9%	19.5%
France	16.4%	22.2%
Italy	19.4%	24.7%
Japan	19.5%	28.0%
United States	12.4%	18.2%
Developing Countries		
Bolivia	4.5%	7.1%
Brazil	5.9%	11.0%
China	7.6%	13.7%
Ghana	3.5%	4.7%
India	4.9%	7.8%

Source: U.S. Census Bureau, International Data Base, April 2005 version.

2000

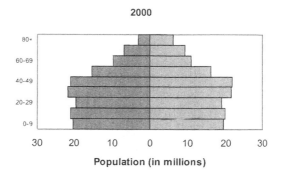

2025

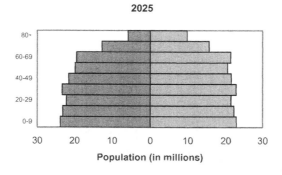

2050

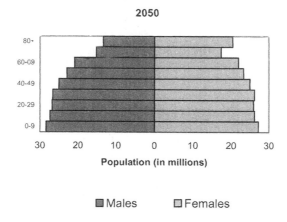

■ Males ▢ Females

Source: U.S. Census Bureau, International Data Base, April 2005 version.

FIGURE 2-1.   Population pyramids for U.S. population distribution by age and gender: 2000, 2025, and 2050.

the cohorts following them and are visible as a bulge in the pyramid in the 35–54 age groups. This relatively large cohort is sometimes described as "the pig in the python," an allusion to its large size relative to the cohorts both before and after it. Because fertility after the baby boom declined to near replacement rates, the population age structure begins to look more like a rectangle after the baby boom. Finally, not only is the proportion of the population over 65 increasing, but the older population is aging, as well. In fact, the population over age 80 is the fastest growing segment of the U.S. population.

Another way to think about population aging is by looking at dependency ratios. Workers typically provide for individuals not in the labor force, whether through private savings, family transfers, or government programs. Dependency ratios provide an indicator of the number of persons at older and younger ages that may need to be supported by the working population. The elderly dependency ratio offers a rough approximation of the number of retirees per worker by comparing the number of individuals ages 65 and over to those ages 20–64 in the population. Similarly, the youth dependency ratio compares the number of children and young adults under 20 to the number of workers, and the total dependency ratio compares the number of children and elderly to the working population. Of course, these are only estimates; many working age people are not in the labor force and many people over 65 continue to work. Nonetheless, they provide a measure of the relative size of the working population to other age groups. Figure 2–2 shows the dependency ratio predicted using census bureau projections through 2050. In 2000, there were approximately 0.21 retirees per person of working age, but this number increases to 0.39 by 2050.

Increasing elderly dependency ratios have caused major concerns about how to fund "pay-as-you-go" old-age entitlement programs, like Social Security and Medicare, in which current workers finance the benefits of current retirees. Projections of fewer workers to support these programs and greater numbers of retirees entitled to benefits have prompted concern regarding program financing and discussions about ways to encourage older workers to remain in the labor force (Burkhauser & Quinn, 1997; Lee, 2004). However, elderly dependency ratios are only part of the picture and may paint an overly pessimistic view of the future; total dependency ratios that account for the costs of children are also important. The youth dependency ratio is projected to remain relatively constant around 0.48, due to assumptions that fertility rates will continue to approximate replacement rates. Thus, change in the total dependency ratio is not that large. In 2000, there were 0.7 workers per dependent (including youth and elderly), and this number is projected to increase to 0.9 workers per dependent by 2050. Although there are large changes in the number of older people relative to the working population, changes in the total proportion of those in working ages to those outside working ages

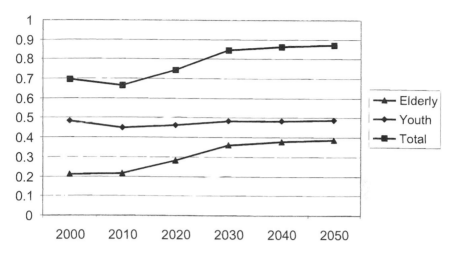

Source: Calculated from data in U.S. Census Bureau (2004). U.S. Interim Projections by Age, Sex, Race, and Hispanic Origin.

FIGURE 2-2. Elderly, youth, and total dependency ratios: 2000 to 2050.

are not as great. Nonetheless, children and older people reflect somewhat different types of dependents. The majority of costs associated with children are borne by families and local governments, while many programs designed to support older people are financed by federal taxes. Even if the overall cost of nonworkers does not change dramatically, the distribution of costs between families and the government is likely to change as the number of retirees increases.

THE AGING WORKFORCE

As the population is aging, so too is the workforce, yet the age structure of the workforce is determined by factors beyond those associated with population aging. Our discussion about changes in population aging is based on reliable demographic projections about the number of births and deaths in the population. All those who will be age 45 in 2050 are alive today. What is harder to predict is labor force participation: How many people of different ages will choose to work? At what ages will people enter and exit the labor force? These two forces, population aging and changes in labor force participation, contribute to an aging workforce.

The population pyramids in Figure 2-3 show the age structure of the workforce based on data from the Bureau of Labor Statistics (Jacobs & Ryan,

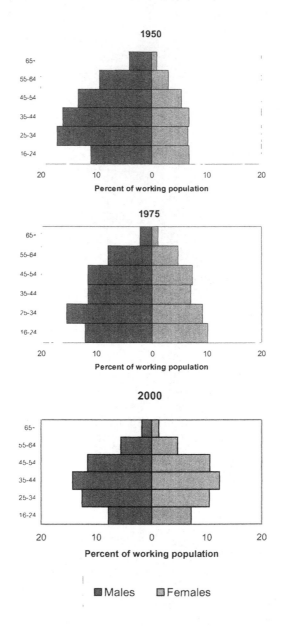

Source: This figure was created based on data from Jacobs, E., & Ryan, M. M. (2004). *Handbook of U.S. Labor Statistics: Employment, Earnings, Prices, Productivity.* Lanham, MD: Bernan Press.

FIGURE 2-3.   Population pyramids for U.S. working population by age and gender: 1950, 1975, and 2000.

2004). This figure reflects an important trend: the aging of the workforce is really a *middle-aging*. The largest group of workers in 1975 was made up of young males ages 25–34. By 2000, the largest group was the 35–44 age group, and it was nearly evenly divided between men and women. By 2012, the number of workers over age 55 is expected to grow at nearly four times the rate of the overall labor force, and the median age of the labor force is projected to rise to 41.4 years (Toossi, 2004), compared to just 34.6 years in 1982. These pyramids also illustrate two other important trends. First, there has been a decline in the proportion of workers ages 65 and over, further supporting the argument that the aging of the workforce is occurring in the middle, rather than the older, age groups. In 1950, workers 65 and over made up 5 percent of the labor force, but these older workers were only 3 percent of the workforce in 2000. Second, women have become increasingly important in the labor force. In 1950, women made up less than 30 percent of the labor force, but by 2000, women were 46 percent of the workforce.

Clearly, population aging has contributed to aging of the workforce, but trends in labor force participation across age and gender groups have been equally important. If the population is aging but workers are retiring at younger ages, as has been the recent trend, workforce aging is limited by high levels of retirement above age 60. If, however, workers remain in the labor force at or beyond the normal retirement age, workforce aging will be greatly accelerated.

Historical Trends In Workforce Participation

Declines in labor force participation among men over age 60 began early in this century, as men moved from agricultural to industrial employment (Easterlin, Crimmins, & Ohanian, 1984; Levine & Mitchell, 1993). Declines accelerated after the establishment of the Social Security system in 1935 and expanding eligibility for private pensions in the 1950s and 60s. The normal or median retirement age (the age at which half the males in the workforce have retired) in the early twentieth century was around age 70 (Burkhauser & Quinn, 1997), although many workers did not survive to retirement. One half of all men ages 65 and over were in the labor force in 1950; by 1985, this number declined to one in six and the normal retirement age fell to age 62 (Clark, Burkhauser, Moon, Quinn, & Smeeding, 2004). Since then, labor force participation of older men has remained relatively stable; in 2000, 17 percent of men 65 and over were in the labor force. This downward trend occurred even in middle-aged workers; between 1960 and 1985, the labor force participation of men ages 62 and over fell by a third, from 80 to 51 percent, and the labor force participation of middle-aged men also declined. Since the mid-1980s, participation rates for men ages 65 and over appeared to stabilize, but labor force participation of men ages 55–64 continued to decline until the late 1990s (Figure 2–4).

Recent analyses confirm that this trend toward declining labor force participation appears to be leveling out and even reversing (Burkhauser & Quinn, 1997; Quinn, 1997, 1999). Quinn (1999) and Rix (1999) both suggest a number of reasons for stabilizing rates of male late-life labor force participation, including: changes in social security and employer-sponsored pensions; an end to mandatory retirement rules; favorable labor market due to expanding economy in the 1990s; the emergence of *bridge jobs* and employment after traditional retirement; and a new social attitude toward work late in life. Others have suggested that the expanding economy in the late 1980s resulted in a shortage of younger workers and an increased demand for older workers, driving up wages and workforce participation (U.S. Census Bureau, 1996).

Trends in women's participation in the paid labor force have been different from those in men. Women's labor force participation has increased continuously in the latter half of the 20th century (Figure 2–5). Female labor force participation at younger ages has increased dramatically, more than doubling in the last 50 years. Only 37 percent of women ages 25–54 participated in the labor force in 1950, while 74 percent of these women were in the labor force in 2000; this number is expected to increase to 80 percent by 2008 (Purcell, 2000). Labor force participation among middle-aged women ages 55–64 has also increased dramatically, from less than 30 percent in 1950 to more

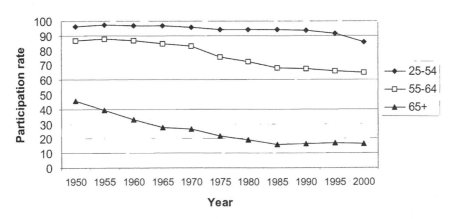

Sources: This figure was created based on data from Purcell, P. J. (2000). Older workers: employment and retirement trends. *Monthly Labor Review, 123,* p. 21; Jacobs, E. & Ryan, M. M. (2004). *Handbook of U.S. Labor Statistics: Employment, Earnings, Prices, Productivity.* Landham, MD: Bernan Press.

FIGURE 2–4.   Male labor force participation rates by age: 1950 to 2000.

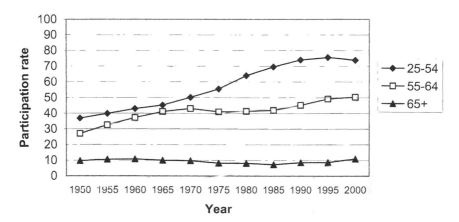

Sources: This figure was created based on data from Purcell, P. J. (2000). Older workers: employment and retirement trends. *Monthly Labor Review, 123,* p. 21; Jacobs, E. & Ryan, M. M. (2004). *Handbook of U.S. Labor Statistics: Employment, Earnings, Prices, Productivity.* Landham, MD: Bernan Press.

FIGURE 2-5.   Female labor force participation rates by age: 1950 to 2000.

than 50 percent in 1999. Labor force participation among women ages 65 and older has remained relatively constant, with about 1 in 10 older women in the labor force.

Together with population aging, retirement timing is perhaps the most important factor affecting the number of older workers. In the past, life expectancy has increased but the median retirement age has decreased, so that the average worker spends fewer years working and more years in retirement. For example, between 1965 and 1990, the average length of retirement among U.S. male workers increased by 4 years, from 13.5 to 17.4 years spent in retirement (Gendell, 1998). It remains to be seen whether this trend will continue in the future.

INFLUENCES ON THE AGE STRUCTURE OF THE WORKFORCE

What will the workforce look like in the future? This seems like a straightforward question, given that everyone who will be old in 2050 is alive today. But, while we know their numbers, we can only make educated guesses about how long older people in the future will work, how long they will live, and what their needs and resources will be (Waite, 2004). We could extrapolate based on past trends, but predictions of future labor force participation rates based on past trends may not be useful in the context of a changing world (Quinn, 1993). Given rapid changes in education, health, and other factors, it may be useful to consider how changes in these contextual factors may affect the age composition of the workforce of the future.

Education

The average education level in the U.S. is increasing, primarily due to increases in higher education. Between 1971 and 2004, the percentage of young adults ages 25 to 29 with a college degree increased from 17 percent to 29 percent (Child Trends Data Bank, 2005). Higher levels of education affect workforce participation at both the beginning and end of working life. Higher education delays entry into the workforce and may also delay retirement. Quinn and colleagues (1998) demonstrate that higher education results in delayed retirement, perhaps because of higher job satisfaction among well-educated workers and higher costs associated with leaving a job. Furthermore, there is an increasing trend toward additional education at later ages. Nontraditional students, students over the age of 25, now make up almost 40 percent of college enrollment in the U.S. (National Center for Education Statistics, 2002). An increasing amount of later life education may increase working life, as people seek to recoup their educational investment and make up for lost years of labor force participation.

Female labor force participation

In 1960, 38 percent of adult women participated in the labor force; by the year 2000, more than 60 percent of women were participating in the labor force (Szafran, 2002). As shown in Figure 2–5, the largest increases have been among women ages 25–54. This suggests a potential increase in female labor force participation at older ages in the future, because women with a lifetime of labor force attachment typically continue strong attachment at older ages. Hill (2002) has shown that the percentage of years a woman has worked in her adult life is strongly associated with labor force participation at all age groups, even after age 70.

Health

Poor health is one of the most important factors encouraging early retirement (Quinn, 1999). Disability rates, and health status more generally, are important determinants of the age distribution of the labor force, because rates of chronic disease and disability typically increase with age. The main causes of inability to work are heart disease and arthritis, potentially disabling diseases that often affect people as early as their 50s (Crimmins, Reynolds, & Saito,

1999). Persons with disabilities have lower employment rates, higher rates of job loss, and earlier labor force withdrawal than those without disabilities (Yelin & Trupin, 2003). In the 2000 census, nearly 12 percent of the U.S. working age population (ages 16 to 64) reported having a disability that made working difficult (Waldrop & Stern, 2003). Unfortunately, research suggests that recent cohorts, including many baby boomers, have higher levels of musculoskeletal conditions than previous cohorts, potentially placing them at increased risk of disability (Reynolds, Crimmins, & Saito, 1998). This calls into question assumptions that the workforce of the future will be healthier than previous cohorts and raises concerns about potential early labor force withdrawal among baby boomers due to health problems.

Economic conditions

Older workers tend to experience higher demand during periods of economic growth, when younger workers cannot supply enough labor to meet employer demands. Conversely, older workers are more likely than middle-aged workers to be laid off in periods of job cutbacks and experience longer periods of unemployment after job loss (Chan & Stevens, 2001). In future economic expansions occurring in the context of an aging workforce, businesses may not be able to rely on a young cohort of unemployed to fill new positions. Although a variety of strategies, including increased immigration and female labor force participation, have been used to compensate for a shortage of workers in the past, displaced older workers may become the new recruits (Burkhauser & Quinn, 1997; Levine & Mitchell, 1993).

Pension availability

The availability of pensions, including employer-based pensions and public pensions, is an important determinant of timing of withdrawal from the labor force. Pension availability is essentially a measure of access to assets, which can finance consumption for a person no longer in the labor force. In other words, pensions provide an alternative source of income, allowing an individual the option to retire. Cross-national comparisons show that almost all industrialized countries have seen a notable decline in labor force participation since the adoption of employer-based pension plans and government-supported social security plans (Wise, 2004). Using data from 12 industrialized countries, Gruber and Wise (1999) found a marked correspondence between the age at which retirement benefits first become available and workers' departure from the labor force.

In the past, early Social Security benefits available at age 62 encouraged early retirement. However, recent changes in Social Security benefit calculations have made the system actuarially fair, which reduces the incentive for retirement. Changes in private pension plans are also likely to lead to changes in the retirement age. Because of growing concern about the cost of providing pension benefits, older workers are increasingly less likely to be covered by a traditional defined benefit pension plan, which provides a set monthly benefit over the lifetime of the retired worker. Instead, older workers of today are more likely to be covered by a defined contribution plan, such as a 401k, in which workers and employers may contribute to a retirement fund that then must be distributed over the retirement years. Data from the Employee Benefits Survey show that the proportion of full-time employees in medium-to-large private firms who were covered by a defined-benefit pension plan fell from 56 percent in 1993 to 50 percent in 1997 (Purcell, 2000). At the same time, the proportion of employees covered by defined-contribution plans increased from 49 percent to 57 percent. Similar trends were observed in smaller companies with fewer than 100 employees. This has important implications for labor force participation at older ages, because defined benefit pension plans encourage early withdrawal from the labor force (Quinn & Burkhauser, 1994). It is unclear how defined contribution plans, which are age neutral in design and reward additional years of labor force participation, will be related to retirement age.

Emerging Issues

Diversity

As the labor force ages, it is also becoming more diverse in terms of age, gender, and racial and ethnic background. Although labor force participation drops sharply after age 62, many individuals continue to work, especially in flexible or part-time work, through their 70s. Given the large growth expected in this group, the older workforce in the future is likely to include larger numbers of workers past traditional retirement ages, increasing the age diversity of the labor force. At the same time, the older workforce is becoming more diverse in terms of gender, for reasons already described, including larger numbers of women in the workforce and women's propensity to continue work at older ages. Finally, due largely to the aging of immigrant populations, the workforce is rapidly become more racially and ethnically diverse. For example, the Hispanic proportion of the workforce is likely to exceed the African-American proportion by 2006, and the Asian group is the most rapidly increasing ethnic group in the labor force (Fullerton, 1997). Thus, non-Whites will comprise a significant proportion of the older workers in the labor force in the future. Research has demonstrated that African Americans are more likely to retire early, primarily because of poor health (Bound, Schoenbaum, & Waidmann, 1995), and to experience involuntary retirement (Hayward, Friedman, &

Chen, 1996). However, relatively little is known about retirement behavior of other minority groups. Hispanic and Asian older adults include extremely diverse populations with widely varying work history and health status, making it difficult to generalize about the effects of increases in the minority older population on the number of older workers.

Bridge employment

Bridge employment refers to labor force participation in older workers between their career jobs (e.g., jobs held 10 or more years) and complete labor force withdrawal in full retirement (Shultz, 2003). In recent years, there has been an increase in the frequency of labor force reentry, mostly among younger retirees (under 65) (Hayward, Crimmins, & Wray, 1994). Several changes in common labor force practices are driving an increase in the prevalence of bridge employment among older workers (Henretta, 2001). For example, workers are less likely to have one employer for an entire career, and, as a result, are less likely to build sufficient pension wealth to retire early. At the same time, employers have encouraged early retirement through pension structures, allowing employees to reenter the labor force while simultaneously receiving retirement income. Finally, variability in retirement wealth means that many workers may need to remain in the labor force, at least part-time, to maintain sufficient retirement income, reducing the likelihood of a typical retirement transition (O'Rand, 1996).

Survey data suggest that by age 60 over half of all older adults have left their career jobs and are engaging in bridge employment (Ruhm, 1990). Fewer than 40 percent of household heads retire directly from career jobs, over half partially retire at some point in their working lives, and a quarter reenter the labor force after initially retiring. Partial retirement is rare prior to age 62, increases rapidly from 62 through 67, and then gradually declines. Although many people do hold *career jobs* at some point, over the working life the average American worker holds ten jobs, and this number is likely to increase in the future (Bureau of Labor Statistics, 2004). More fluid employment throughout working life may increase desire to continue working at older ages and increase flexibility in the types of work in which older workers can and will participate.

Technology

Technological innovations in the last 20 years have rapidly changed the workplace, leading to concerns about the ability of older workers to adapt to changing work environments. Research suggests that high rates of technological change can actually lead workers to retire later, if this technology is related to greater on-the-job training (Bartel & Sicherman, 1993). When technological change requires all workers to have regularly updated training, there are fewer costs associated with training older workers. However, a rapid increase in technological change may lead older workers to retire sooner, because the required amount of retraining required may be perceived as an unattractive investment by either the worker or the employer. New cohorts of older workers may respond differently to technological changes than past cohorts, as they have experienced change throughout their working lives.

Changing markets

Broad changes in the U.S. economy, including the transition to a service- and information-based economy and increasing globalization, may contribute to a higher rate of labor force participation among older workers. Professional occupations typically have a disproportionate number of older workers, especially in positions that require postgraduate degrees. The opportunity costs associated with leaving the labor force for these high wage earners may be higher than for workers in other occupations (Dohm, 2000). Conversely, blue-collar workers are more likely to leave the labor force at age 55 than more highly educated workers, possibly due to the physically demanding nature of these jobs (U.S. Census Bureau, 1996). Thus, the economic transition away from more manual labor, in which workers tend to retire earlier, to more professional labor, in which workers tend to remain in the labor force, may accelerate the aging of the labor force. A parallel trend is the increasing globalization of labor markets. Some researchers have suggested that increased global competition is likely to lead to a reduction in health and pension benefits for American workers, causing older workers to remain in the labor force longer (Wilson, 2002).

The policy environment

Burkhauser and Quinn (1997) trace the historical progression from policies that actively discouraged older workers from remaining in the labor force to more neutral policies. Important steps include the passage of the Age Discrimination in Employment Act, which prohibits mandatory retirement for nearly all workers, the increase in the Social Security retirement age, and changes to Social Security benefits allowing workers to withdraw benefits while remaining in the labor force. Recently, however, concern about the financing of entitlement programs has prompted a great deal of interest in crafting policies which would actively promote labor force participation at older ages (Burkhauser & Quinn, 1997; Van Dalen & Henkens, 2002). The policy environment is a uniquely adaptable way to address issues related to the aging of the workforce, because it is one of few factors amenable to intervention.

DIRECTIONS FOR FUTURE RESEARCH

Future research must address how changes in the workplace environment and changes in the working population interact to affect labor force participation. Will the baby boomers, with a different history of education and different attitudes about work than previous cohorts, continue current retirement trends? What will be the impact of macro-level processes, including changes in markets, technology, and family structure, on the retirement age? How will employers respond to an increase in the number of older workers, and how can policymakers affect employer attitudes and policies toward older workers? How will employees respond to changing incentives in public and private pension programs? Will future older workers be healthier, and if they are, will they choose to remain in the labor force?

As shown here, the aging of the workforce is related to both the aging of the population and changes in workforce participation patterns. While we can make reliable predictions about the numbers of potential workers in the population, it is much harder to predict who will be able to work and who will choose to work in the future. Understanding the ways in which social trends interact with individual's work preferences to affect labor force participation now and in the future has important implications for government, employers, and families.

CONCLUSION

The workforce is aging. By 2012, more than half of all workers will be over age 40. Older workers will be more diverse in terms of age, gender, and race/ethnic backgrounds than ever before. However, the number of older workers in the future will depend upon how long workers choose to remain in the labor force or postpone retirement. Rising levels of education and larger numbers of women in the labor force are likely to accelerate workforce aging. The effects of changing technology, economic conditions, and the rise of defined contribution pensions are less certain. Policies have begun to respond to the needs of aging workers and represent a tool to respond to changing labor force demands.

REFERENCES

Bartel, A. P., & Sicherman, N. (1993). Technological change and retirement decisions of older workers. *Journal of Labor Economics, 11*, 162–183.

Bound, J., Schoenbaum, M., & Waidmann, T. (1995). Race and education differences in disability status and labor force attachment. *NBER Working Paper No. W5159.*

Bureau of Labor Statistics. (2004). *Number of jobs held, labor market activity, and earnings growth among younger baby boomers: Recent results from a longitudinal survey.* Washington, DC: U.S. Department of Labor.

Burkhauser, R. V., & Quinn, J. F. (1997). *Pro-work Policy Proposals for Older Americans in the 21st Century*. Syracuse, NY: Syracuse University.

Chan, S., & Stevens, A. H. (2001). Job loss and employment patterns of older workers. *Journal of Labor Economics, 19*, 484–521.

Child Trends Data Bank. (2005). *Educational Attainment*. Washington, DC: Child Trends Data Bank.

Clark, R. L., Burkhauser, R. V., Moon, M., Quinn, J. F., & Smeeding, T. M. (2004). *The Economics of an Aging Society*. Malden, MA: Blackwell Publishing.

Crimmins, E. M., Reynolds, S. L., & Saito, Y. (1999). Trends and differences in health and ability to work among the older working-age population. *Journals of Gerontology: Social Sciences. 54B*, 31–40.

Dohm, A. (2000). Gauging the labor force effects of retiring baby boomers. *Monthly Labor Review, 123*, 17–25.

Easterlin, R. A., Crimmins, E. M., & Ohanian, L. (1984). Changes in labor force participation of persons 55 and over since World War II: Their nature and causes. In P. Robinson & J. Birren (Eds.), *Aging and Technological Advances* (pp. 89–97). New York: Plenum Publishing.

Fullerton, H. N. (1997). Labor Force 2006: Slowing Down and Changing Composition. *Monthly Labor Review, 120*, 23–38.

Gendell, M. (1998). Trends in retirement age in four countries: 1965–1995. *Monthly Labor Review, 121*, 20–30.

Gruber, J., & Wise, D. A. (1999). *Social Security and Retirement Around the World*. Chicago: University of Chicago Press

Hayward, M. D., Crimmins, E. M., & Wray, L. A. (1994). The relationship between retirement life cycle changes and older men's labor force participation rates. *Journal of Gerontology: Social Sciences, 49B*, S219–S230.

Hayward, M. D., Friedman, S., & Chen, H. (1996). Race inequalities in men's retirement. *Journal of Gerontology, 51B*: S1–S10.

Henretta, J. C. (2001). Work and retirement. In R. H. Binstock & L. K. George (Eds.), *Handbook of Aging and the Social Sciences, 5th ed.* (pp. 255–271). San Diego, CA: Academic Press.

Hill, E. T. (2002). The labor force participation of older women: Retired? Working? Both? *Monthly Labor Review, 125*, 39–48.

Jacobs, E. E., & Ryan, M. M. (2004). *Handbook of U.S. Labor Statistics: Employment, Earnings, Prices, Productivity*. Lanham, MD: Bernan Press.

Kinsella, K., & Velkoff, V. A. (2001). *An Aging World: 2001*. U.S. Census Bureau, Series P95/01-1. Washington DC: U.S. Government Printing Office.

Lee, R. (2004). Quantifying our ignorance: Stochastic forecasts of population and public budgets. *Population and Development Review, 30*, 153–175.

Levine, P. B., & Mitchell, O. S. (1993). Expected changes in the workforce and implications for labor markets. In A. M. Rappaport & S. J. Schieber (Eds.), *Demography and Retirement: The Twenty-first Century*. Westport, CT: Praeger.

National Center for Education Statistics. (2002). *Findings from the Condition of Education 2002: Nontraditional Undergraduates*. Washington, DC: U.S. Department of Education.

O'Rand, A. M. (1996). The cumulative stratification of the life course. In R. H. Binstock & L. K. George (Eds.), *Handbook of Aging and the Social Sciences 4th ed.*, (pp. 188–207). San Diego, CA: Academic Press.

Purcell, P. J. (2000). Older workers: Employment and retirement trends. *Monthly Labor Review, 123,* 19–30.

Quinn, J. F. (1993). Discussion—Expected changes in the workforce. In A. M. Rappaport & S. J. Schieber (Eds.), *Demography and Retirement: The Twenty-first Century.* Westport, CT: Praeger.

Quinn, J. F. (1997). Retirement trends and patterns in the 1990s: The end of an era? *The Public Policy and Aging Report, 8*(3), 10–14, 19.

Quinn, J. F. (1999). Retirement patterns and bridge jobs in the 1990s. Employee Benefit Research Institute (EBRI) Issue Brief Number 206. Washington, DC: EBRI.

Quinn, J. F., & Burkhauser, R. V. (1994). Retirement and the labor force: Behavior of the elderly. In L. G. Martin & S. H. Preston (Eds.), *The Demography of Aging* (pp. 50–101). Washington, DC: National Academy Press.

Quinn, J., Burkhauser, R., Cahill, K., & Weathers, R. (1998). Microeconometric analysis of the retirement decision. Economics Department Working Papers No. 203. Organisation for Economic Co-operation and Development (OECD).

Reynolds, S. L., Crimmins, E. M., & Saito, Y. (1998). Cohort differences in disability and disease presence. *The Gerontologist, 38,* 578–590.

Rix, S. E. (1999). The older worker in a graying America. In R. N. Butler, L. K. George, & M. R. Oberlink (Eds.), *Life in an older America* (pp. 187–216). New York: Century Foundation Press.

Ruhm, C. J. (1990). Bridge jobs and partial retirement. *Journal of Labor Economics, 8,* 582–601.

Shultz, K. S. (2003). Bridge employment: Work after retirement. In G. A. Adams & T. A. Beehr (Eds.), *Retirement: Reasons, processes, and results* (pp. 214–241). New York: Springer.

Szafran, R. F. (2002). Age-adjusted labor force participation rates, 1960–2045. *Monthly Labor Review, 125,* 25–38.

Toossi, M. (2004). Labor force projections to 2012: The graying of the U.S. workforce. *Monthly Labor Review, 127,* 37–57.

U.S. Census Bureau. (1996). *65+ in the United States.* Current Population Reports, Special Studies, P23–190. Washington, DC: U.S. Government Printing Office.

Van Dalen, H. P., & Henkens, K. (2002). Early retirement reform: Can it and will it work? *Ageing and Society, 22,* 209–231.

Waite, L. J. (2004). The demographic faces of the elderly. *Population and Development Review, 30,* 3–16.

Waldrop, J., & Stern, S. M. (2003). *Disability status: 2000.* U.S. Census Bureau Brief C2KBR-17. Washington, DC: U.S. Government Printing Office.

Wilson, G. (2002). Globalisation and older people: Effects of markets and migration. *Ageing & Society, 22,* 647–663.

Wise, D. A. (2004). Social Security provisions and the labor force participation of older workers. *Population and Development Review, 30*(Supplement), 176–205.

Yelin, E. H., & Trupin, L. (2003). Disability and the characteristics of employment. *Monthly Labor Review, 126,* 20–31.

3

Low-Income Older Workers

Mary Anne Taylor and Holly A. Geldhauser

This chapter begins with a discussion of the economic and psychological challenges faced by low-income workers, providing a rationale for increasing the investment of research and applied resources to this group. We focus on two paths for enhancing their status: financial planning and mobility into better jobs. Obstacles associated with each path are described in detail. Recommendations for facilitating financial planning behavior and improving the job search process for low-income older workers are discussed. Within each segment, gender and ethnic issues relevant to low-income older workers are described, since women and minorities are overrepresented in this group. We end with recommendations for those who are interested in research on this disadvantaged population of employees.

There are a number of compelling reasons to understand the issues facing low-income older workers and their financial future. Some of these stem from economic pressures from an overextended Social Security system, coupled with the sheer prevalence of poverty among older people. Another critical reason for enhancing finances of older workers is based on our knowledge of the importance of financial stability in psychological wellbeing. Whether one is interested in low-income older workers because of public policy implications or because of humanitarian concern regarding their post-retirement adjustment, it is clearly beneficial to explore the challenges they face and to attempt to remedy some of the obstacles that will confront this population in retirement.

Therefore, in this chapter we first provide an overview of the prevalence of low-income and poverty among older people and older workers, and the insufficiency of the Social Security system to meet their needs. Next, we examine the relationship of economic wellbeing to adjustment, providing a psychologically based rationale for improving the financial status of older workers.

Our next segments turn to two major means of remedying the long-term effects of low-income: financial planning and finding either higher-income jobs or
continued employment. We identify obstacles associated with each path, as well
as potential solutions for some of the issues identified. While these suggestions
are not sufficient for overcoming the problems faced by this economically depressed group, they are intended to provide some basic strategies for improving the financial planning and job search success of these older workers.

DEFINING LOW-INCOME OLDER WORKERS

As a first step in this discussion, we need to define what we mean by *low-income*
and to examine the prevalence of low-income older workers. Many of us who
are fortunate enough to have our financial needs met underestimate the extent
of poverty in this nation among those who are working. Almost a quarter of the
nation's workforce in 2001 earned less than $8.70 an hour, which would place
a family of four close to the official poverty line (Ferguson, 2005). This has
led researchers to identify a new group of *working poor*, with their own unique
challenges.

The very terms *poverty* and *low-income worker* are difficult to define.
Poverty is generally described as the state of having little or no money and
few or no material possessions, yet the precise definition of the term is somewhat controversial. The Census Bureau uses a set of income thresholds that
vary by family size and composition to define poverty. For a single person under
65 years of age, the 2004 poverty threshold was $9,827, and was $9,060 for
those over 65 years of age (U.S. Census Bureau, 2004).

The Census Bureau definition of poverty is considered to be conservative, since it was developed at a time when the average family spent one-third
of their income on food (Cozzarelli, Wilkinson, & Tagler, 2001). Now the relative percentage of income spent on food is smaller than other expenses such
as rent that contribute more to family costs (Leavitt & Lingafelter, 2005;
Loewentheil & Weller, 2005). Based on this issue, a consortium formed of the
Panel on Poverty and Family Assistance, the Committee on National Statistics,
the Commission on Behavioral and Social Sciences and Education, and the
National Research Council (1995) made suggestions on how to revise this
poverty index. The new standards incorporated the basic categories of food,
clothing, shelter, and other needs, and made adjustments based on regional differences in costs of covering these needs. While a detailed discussion of the
issues involved in the definition of poverty are beyond the scope of this chapter, it is certainly worth noting that there is some controversy about the existing Census Bureau definition, and the new definition, if adopted, could change
the poverty thresholds.

While the definition of poverty is controversial, there is a similar lack of consensus among economists regarding what is meant by *low wage* work. The most common definitions involve one absolute measure based on the number of total hours that are worked in a job that fits a low wage profile. This was below $8/hour in 2001. Two other definitions of low wage are based on relative measures; one classifies low wage work as falling below two-thirds of the median rate of pay ($8.67 in 2001) and a second defines low wages as those that fall in the bottom quintile of the wage distribution (Bernstein & Gittleman, 2003).

In the research literature, it is probable that definitions of *poverty*, *low-income*, and *low wage* workers vary across different researchers. Despite this fact, when one examines the participants chosen by researchers, few of us would argue that the people under investigation were inaccurately labeled.

PREVALENCE OF POVERTY

According to the Census Bureau, there were 37.0 million people in poverty (12.7 percent of the population) in 2004, up from 35.9 million (12.5 percent) in 2003. There were 7.9 million families in poverty in 2004, up from 7.6 million in 2003. This poverty rate for families is at 10.2 percent for both years.

One of the more disturbing aspects of poverty is that older individuals tend to become trapped in that income level. For those older Americans who spend over three consecutive years in poverty, 21.3 percent will not escape it (Wu, 2001). This is consistent with what has been called "the hypothesis of cumulative advantage" (O'Rand, 1999). That is, those groups who are in poverty have less access to resources that free them from poverty. This is particularly relevant for the low-income elderly. Those in poverty are less likely to have access to the financial planning resources, the discretionary income, and the job skills that could potentially free them from their situation. These obstacles will be discussed in the upcoming segments on financial planning and job search issues.

The sheer number of those living at or near poverty, especially among women and minorities, is overwhelming. Historically, the number of women in poverty has outnumbered the number of men. The median income for women 65 and older is only $3,000 over the Census Bureau standard for poverty (Beedon & Wu, 2005). Thus, there is a substantial economic burden on elderly women, who typically live three years longer than men and receive less income throughout their entire lives. Almost 5 million women at midlife and older fall below the poverty line, and many of these women have not received pensions because of shorter job tenure and segregation into jobs without pension coverage (Perkins, 1992). As a result, fewer women than men are able to escape from poverty (Wu, 2001).

Further data show that working women comprise more than 50 percent of those employed in the lowest wage occupations in 71 percent of the largest U.S. cities. They comprise 50 percent of those in the highest wage jobs in only 3 percent of U.S. cities (Lichtenwalter, 2005). Not surprisingly, many advocates have suggested wage adjustments for female dominated occupations as a way to reduce the gender-poverty gap (Elman & O'Rand, 2004).

Similar statistics characterize the economic status of minorities. Poverty rates for minorities are greater than that for nonminorities. For example, for non-Hispanic Whites the overall poverty rate is 8.6 percent. In 2004, the poverty rate for Hispanics was 21.9 percent and for African Americans it was 24.7 percent. African Americans age 65 and older have a poverty rate twice that of all older people (23.9 percent). The proportion of African American and Hispanic women in poverty is similarly dismal, with 28 percent and 22 percent, respectively, living below the poverty line (Wu & Beedon, 2004; Wu, 2004).

The overall poverty rate for Asians in 2004 was 9.8 percent (U.S. Census Bureau, 2004). A study released by the Asian Pacific American Public Policy Institute revealed that the economic status of Asian Americans has a barbell or hourglass shape; for every family with an income greater than $75,000, there is another Asian American family with an income of less than $10,000 (Dunn, 1994). While 80 percent of older Asian Americans live above the poverty level, many live close to the poverty line. In addition, the percentage in poverty varies greatly by the particular ethnic group studied; 22 percent of Indochinese, 15 percent of Koreans, and 14 percent of Chinese are near this level (McNally, Voon, & Park, 2004).

Given this prevalence of poverty and low income in the United States among employed and unemployed older people, one would hope that Social Security would provide a safety net for them as they age. However, Social Security is not a secure social system. In the next segment, we analyze the future of the system as a means of supporting older workers and older people in general. Then we turn to financial planning and employment as more promising alternatives for improving the status of low-income workers.

An Economic Imperative for Studying Low-Income Older Workers: Inadequacy of Social Security

Recently, there has been much discussion of the limitations of Social Security as a means to meet the needs of the growing population of retirees. Those 65 and older comprise 17 percent of the population at this time. By 2030, the percentage at this traditional retirement age will rise to 26 percent. Given current retirement rates, the ratio of workers to the total population will shrink by

7 percent by 2030, increasing pressure on the system that provides critical support for low-income retirees (Greenspan, 2005).

Statistics regarding the ability of the Social Security system to meet the upcoming demands are not encouraging. Current Social Security obligations exceed revenues by 10.4 trillion dollars. Low-income workers may be particularly hard hit by these significant changes. In a report to the Senate Committee on Aging in 2005, Alan Greenspan, Chairman of the Federal Reserve Board, noted that the Social Security income replacement rate of 56 percent for low-income workers is projected to drop to 40 percent, and the average worker should be prepared to replace 45 percent of their income rather than the current 33 percent as a consequence of this change.

Are baby boomers realistic about the future of Social Security? Research suggests that they may be overly optimistic about the financial benefits they can expect from this system. In a Roper survey conducted for the American Association of Retired Persons (AARP) in 2004, 63 percent of respondents believed they could count on Social Security in retirement. In addition, more than a third of respondents believed that Social Security would meet their needs as well as it had met their parents' needs.

This over reliance on Social Security is a particularly serious error for low-income groups. This group has a disproportionate number of females, Hispanics, and African Americans, and these minorities are heavily dependent on Social Security. Currently, social security is the major source of income for older women and is particularly important for older minority women, who are less likely to have private pensions or assets (Rix & Beedon, 2003). Hispanics and African Americans are particularly dependent on this system as well; over 75 percent of older Hispanics rely on Social Security for 50 percent or more of their total income. Without it, 33 percent of older Hispanics would fall into poverty (Beedon & Wu, 2003). Similarly, African Americans' poverty rate would rise from 23.9 percent to 58.2 percent without the aid of Social Security (Beedon & Wu, 2004). As will be seen in the segment on financial planning, many older people believe they will be able to rely on Social Security as a source of income in the future, and are overconfident in the system.

Clearly the statistics reviewed emphasize the need to encourage low-income workers to develop alternative means of support. The overextension of the Social Security system, and continued stress on the system as baby boomers retire in large numbers, is a financially compelling reason to explore options to help low-income workers develop more financial security. There are other persuasive psychologically based reasons why we should encourage low-income workers to invest in ways to increase their income. Namely, there is a relationship between financial wellbeing and adjustment, which will be briefly reviewed in the next segment.

A Psychological Imperative for Studying Low-Income Older Workers: The Importance of Income In Wellbeing

It would be overly simplistic to say that those who are rich are better off than those who are poor. However, research suggests that finances impact a broad range of indicators of both overall adjustment and retirement adjustment. In general, income is positively related to psychological wellbeing and health, and is inversely related to stress, depression, and anxiety (Austrom, Perking, Damush & Hendrie, 2003; Ettner & Grzywacz, 2003; Rosenkoetter & Garris, 2001).

Proxies for income such as pension eligibility are also generally associated with adjustment and attitudes toward retirement (Hershey, Jacobs-Lawson, & Neukam, 2002). Some research suggests that these effects of income are long-lasting, and are significantly related to retirement attitudes 6, 12, and even 24 months after leaving the workforce (Reitzes & Mutran, 2004). Researchers have found that expectations regarding finances impacted post-retirement satisfaction as long as 6 to 7 years post retirement (Gall & Evans, 2000).

An important distinction for practitioners and researchers is that affectively loaded measures that tap into financial stress may be more strongly associated with adjustment than simple income measures (Danigelis & McIntosh, 2001). For example, Stoller and Stoller (2003) found that low-income elderly were relatively satisfied with their income as long as their health was adequate. While income was significantly related to the ability to meet ones' financial needs, the effect was weaker than anticipated. Stoller and Stoller caution that one explanation of this finding is that people may not be very proficient at estimating their financial needs and at assessing their financial situation, and this can create unrealistic financial optimism.

Freedom from financial stress, a more emotion-based indicator of financial wellbeing than simple income, is related to post-retirement adjustment across professions ranging from physicians (Guerriero-Austrom, Perkins, Damush, & Hendrie, 2003) to rural farm workers (Armstrong & Schulman, 1990). Financial status and strain is associated with many measures of adjustment after leaving the workforce, including post-retirement quality of life (Gall & Evans, 2000) and post-retirement satisfaction (Quick & Moen, 1998). This relationship has been found to hold for women as well as men (Choi, 2001). One study found that for both men and women, those who reported greater income adequacy were more than twice as likely to be satisfied in retirement as those who felt they had an inadequate income (Smith & Moen, 2004).

These findings emphasize the important distinction between objective and subjective measurements of finances. There are critical differences in the predictive validity of a measure of *income*, a measure of *perceived adequacy of income* and affectively loaded measures such as *financial stress*, depending on the dependent variable of interest. Nonincome measures such as financial stress may be influenced by factors such as health and family demands. Thus, two families with the same income may have very different levels of financial stress. Such affective measures may have a stronger relationship to dependent variables such as adjustment and wellbeing than simple income. A further distinction between income and more subjective measures, such as perceived adequacy of income, worth noting is that people tend be overly optimistic about the availability of resources postretirement and adequacy of income postretirement, as will be discussed in the segment on financial planning (Hershey, Walsh, Brougham, Carter, & Farrell, 1998). Thus, objective measures of income may serve as a better predictor of ability to meet postretirement costs after retirement than subjective projections of financial comfort. Matching subjective financial predictors with affective dependent variables and more objective indices of finances with objective dependent variables may be one way of improving our understanding of the role of finances in psychological and financial wellbeing of low-income workers.

Understanding the relationship between finances and wellbeing depends not just on an appreciation of these measurement issues but also on a consideration of moderators of the income-adjustment relationship. Individual difference variables and environmental characteristics both moderate the relationship between financial indices and adjustment. Many individual difference variables such as positive perceptions of control are associated with more favorable retirement experiences for both men and women (Kim & Moen, 2002), and management of financial stress is no exception. These dispositional factors such as locus of control and positive coping strategies with regard to income problems are related to more favorable adjustment outcomes for those facing financial stress (Armstrong & Schulman, 1990; Chou & Chi, 2001; Wrosch, Heckhausen, & Lachman, 2000). To the extent that financial planning can enhance perceptions of control, this may be one way to increase adjustment and satisfaction of low-income older workers.

An environmental variable, social support, has also been found to moderate the relationship between financial hardship and depression in older adults (Krause, 1987; Tower & Kasl, 1995). Social support appears to reduce the negative impact of financial stress. Thus, while it is logical to expect that inadequate resources are associated with lowered psychological wellbeing, consideration of individual and environmental moderators will help us improve our theoretical models and our applied interventions targeted toward low-income workers.

While it is clear that low income and financial stress have direct effects on wellbeing, we are starting to understand that income also has indirect effects on adjustment. Income is a gatekeeper for access to important predictors of postretirement wellbeing, such as health care and leisure activities. Health is lower among low-income individuals and particularly among African Americans (Johnson, 2005). While poor health may impose costs that limit one's ability to save for retirement (Lum & Lightfoot, 2003), there is a reciprocal relationship as well. Income limits access to quality health care and health aids (Bond-Huie, Krueger, Rogers, & Hummer, 2003).

Other potential indirect effects of income stem from the limits it may impose on access to leisure and other social activities, which are important in postretirement adjustment (Dittmann, 2004). While there are low cost leisure activities, the economic restrictions imposed by very low-income would logically limit access to resources that require transportation or require more financial expenditures.

Given the importance of finances in wellbeing, exploring options for enhancing finances for low-income workers is critical. Within this domain, we first turn to the financial planning literature, and discuss why this is so important for low-income individuals and how to best encourage financial planning. Next, we explore continued full- or part-time employment as an option to enhance financial status, and we discuss some of the obstacles within this area.

FINANCIAL PLANNING BEHAVIOR OF BOOMERS

Given the relationship between finances and wellbeing discussed in the previous segment, it is not surprising that there is a similar positive relationship between financial planning and adjustment for older workers. While financial planning is most closely tied to financial adjustment postretirement (MacEwen, Barling, Kelloway, & Higginbottom, 2001), there are more generalized effects of retirement planning that have been documented in the literature. Retirement planning, which typically contains a financial component, is associated with more positive affect toward retirement, more favorable levels of postretirement adjustment, and with greater postretirement satisfaction (Spiegel & Shultz, 2003; Taylor & Doverspike, 2003). Research suggests that those who have retired show a sharp increase in their perceptions of the importance of financial planning relative to their ratings before retirement (Rosenkoetter & Garris, 2001).

This relationship holds for both men and women, in that retirement planning is a strong predictor of retirement adjustment for both groups (Quick & Moen, 1998). Planning may help those who are entering this new phase of their life form realistic expectations about their financial needs, and may encourage investment behaviors that increase financial wellbeing.

FINANCIAL PLANNING WITHIN
THE LOW-INCOME GROUPS

There are clear distinctions in planning behavior when one contrasts the "haves," or those with $100K and over incomes, with the "have-nots," or $40K and under incomes (AARP, 2004). Those with low incomes are less likely to engage in both formal and informal planning. For example, 58 percent of the "haves" have given great thought to retirement, while only 28 percent of "have nots" have done so. Low-income groups are also less likely to even informally discuss retirement plans with others. These low-income groups have high proportions of women and ethnic minorities. Thus, it is useful to examine the data on these individual groups, although little research exists in this area relative to research on high-income White males.

A fairly consistent gender difference emerges when one examines retirement planning behavior. While the factors that predict financial planning are similar across gender (e.g., higher income is associated with planning for both groups), men are more likely to engage in planning strategies that optimize their retirement incomes (Glass & Kilpatrick, 1998). Given differences in planning behavior, it is not surprising that the retirement goals set by women are, in general, more abstract than those set by men (Hershey, Jacobs-Lawson, & Neukam, 2002). Unfortunately, women may be less able to set aside money than men. The balance for women's retirement savings is, on average, only 20 percent of the balance set aside by men (Goodman, 2004). Given the overrepresentation of women in low-income brackets, this failure to plan and set aside adequate funds may lead to later financial distress.

Similarly, ethnic minorities such as African Americans and Hispanics are less likely to plan financially for retirement. Attitudes about the futility of planning may exacerbate this problem. For example, Hispanics are significantly more likely than non-Hispanic Whites to believe the future will take care of itself (20 percent of Whites versus 32 percent of Hispanics). This attitude is likely to discourage retirement planning.

UNDERSTANDING IMPEDIMENTS TO PLANNING

Understanding why people do not set aside funds and why they do not engage in planning is a necessary first step in designing interventions to encourage financial preparation. The first impediment in financial planning is unrealistic views of the money needed for retirement and the availability of Social Security supplements postretirement. This set of beliefs shapes satisfaction with current levels of savings as well as future investments in retirement funds.

Given the importance of finances, it is discouraging to note that personal savings rates are at a historic low, and retirement savings are inadequate for much of the population. One study found that one of three adults ages 45–54 and one out of four of those 55–64 report that they have not set aside savings for retirement (Committee for Economic Development, 1999). A more recent study found that 53 percent of those ages 55–64 have not set aside a formal retirement savings account, and for those who do have savings, the median amount of funds is only $25,000. Unfortunately, those who are most in need of financial planning, low-income workers, are least likely to plan and least likely to have set money aside as part of a formal plan (Kim & Moen, 2002; Turner, Bailey, & Scott, 1994).

There is some suggestion that low-income workers may be aware that they may not have enough income in retirement, although research is mixed in this area. Eighty percent of affluent Baby Boomers are satisfied with savings, while only 52 percent of those earning less than $50K per year show this level of satisfaction with retirement savings (AARP, 2004). There are also gender and ethnic differences in expressed satisfaction with retirement funds among workers. While men were more likely than women to feel as if they would have plenty of money in retirement, the rate who felt "very positive" about postretirement earnings was low for both men and women (34 percent versus 21 percent). Many low-income ethnic groups expressed at least some level of satisfaction with their retirement savings (AARP, 2004). Sixty five percent of African Americans and 58 percent of Hispanics have at least a modest level of satisfaction with savings. These statistics can be misleading, however, because there is often a mismatch between the amount of money set aside and the amount of money needed for retirement. Many individuals have an unrealistic dependence on Social Security as well as pensions, and therefore may be satisfied with low levels of savings (Center for Retirement Research at Boston College, 2004).

Low-income respondents to an AARP survey of baby boomers showed perhaps an overly optimistic dependence on the Social Security system for retirement funds. Seventy one-percent of low-income individuals expressed that they would depend on this system for income, while only 51 percent of higher income respondents expected to depend on Social Security (AARP, 2004). Not surprisingly, the "have-nots" also expressed significantly less confidence in their ability to supplement their retirement income with home equity, pensions, and other investments (AARP, 2004). A disproportionate number of middle- and low-income Americans are saving too little at a time when employers and the Social Security System are shifting responsibilities for retirement income to workers (Tyson, 2005). Thus, these unrealistic expectations regarding the amount and source of funding needed to meet financial needs may be viewed as an impediment to planning behavior.

A second reason why people may not engage in planning is a simple lack of information on how to plan. A Workforce Report on Retirement Planning conducted by Prudential Financial in 2004 summarized the responses of over 1000 full-time employees ages 55 to 65 regarding their financial planning behavior. While more than 4 out of 5 respondents indicated that it was important to generate retirement income, only 1 out of 5 indicated that they felt informed enough to make specific plans. When asked how accurate their estimates of their retirement income would be, 55 percent indicated that they either had only a "ballpark" idea of their needed income or no idea at all.

There is a realization on the part of many low-income individuals and minorities that they may need assistance or more data in order to plan effectively. In a recent survey, 72 percent of upper-income individuals were confident in their ability to prepare for retirement, only 49 percent of low-income individuals felt the same degree of confidence (AARP, 2004). More ethnic minorities than Whites express a need for more information in order to plan. Forty five percent of Hispanics and 37 percent of African Americans believe they need more information on retirement; only 21 percent of Whites express this need (AARP, 2004).

A third reason why we do not see more planning from low-income workers is that they simply lack the money to invest in retirement planning. An Annual Retirement Conference Survey conducted by AARP and other cosponsors in 2004 indicated that only 6 out of 10 workers are able to save for retirement. This problem may stem from simple financial realities: low-income workers have a problem finding the money required to meet basic needs that many of us take for granted. More than 40 percent of all respondents, regardless of gender or ethnicity, said that it was difficult to save for retirement (AARP, 2004). An astounding 50 percent of respondents at midlife or older indicated that they are concerned about their ability to meet basic needs such as food and utilities. This rate is 68 percent for African Americans, 60 percent for Hispanics, and 66 percent for American Indians. When basic needs are unmet, retirement savings are irrelevant.

A fourth reason why planning does not occur for low-income workers is that it is often harder for them to access formal planning programs. Few low-income workers are in a job where planning seminars are offered on a routine basis. Thus, outreach programs and informal planning (e.g., that available from Web sites) may be critical for reaching these groups. Simply recruiting and retaining low-income individuals into financial planning programs may pose practical difficulties, particularly when there are few tangible incentives for participation (Anderson, Zhan, & Scott, 2004).

SUMMARY: UNDERSTANDING THE PLANNING PROBLEM

Why is it the case that low-income workers fail to plan, and why is this problem exacerbated for women? The answer to this question is a critical step in designing more effective financial planning interventions. Based on the findings reviewed thus far, there are several possible reasons for this problem:

1. A real or perceived inability to set aside funds for retirement
2. Lack of access to formal financial planning resources that may be available to more high-income workers

3. An overly optimistic view of the supportive role of Social Security or pension plans as a source of income in retirement

4. A lack of information regarding how to financially plan for retirement, including

    a. lack of understanding of investment options

    b. an inability to calculate the needed funds for retirement

    c. an inability to compare different investment options

5. Lack of knowledge of the available planning resources that are low-cost or free

6. Psychological variables, including a lowered sense of control over the process, which may lead to avoidance of planning, a fatalistic view of one's own economic wellbeing, and a sense that the financial aspects of retirement planning are simply beyond one's understanding.

Thus, effective planning must address all of these issues; it must provide low-income workers with a way to realistically assess the funds they need for retirement; it must provide education about the limitations of Social Security without distressing the planner; and it must provide knowledge of the investment options and the steps involved in saving for retirement, and this knowledge must be accessible to low-income workers. Finally, the information should be presented in a way that makes the low-income worker feel as if they can master the task, to foster a greater sense of control and a greater sense of self-efficacy over the process.

Planning cannot solve all the problems endemic in the low-income population. It does not relieve the financial burdens of poor health or the income disadvantages associated with a physical disability (Lum & Lightfoot, 2003; Osawa & Hong, 2003). It does not compensate for the lack of a pension due to an interrupted work history and it does not ease the financial cost imposed by dependents who still rely on the low-income worker for financial support. It cannot remove the effects of low levels of education on wage depression. Thus, it would be very unrealistic to think that planning alone is a solution to the problems faced by this population. Similarly, it is unrealistic to think that older workers will have easy access to the formal planning that is often available to high-income workers.

This does not mean that we should give up on providing assistance and guidance. Despite its limitations, planning can serve two important practical and psychological goals: it can help the individual make the most of the income that they have, and it may lead to a greater sense of control over one's financial wellbeing. In order to be effective in maximizing the financial wellbeing of low-income workers, remedies should focus on the more controllable aspects of the failure to plan noted above. All of these revolve around increasing knowledge regarding the criticality of personal savings for retirement, the options for retirement savings, and encouraging people to set clear financial goals. Increasing accessibility to and knowledge of retirement planning assistance is also important. In addition, presenting the information in a way that is not intimidating or off-putting to older workers will help them develop the confidence needed to delve into their financial situation.

IMPLICATIONS FOR PRACTICE: IMPROVING FINANCIAL PLANNING FOR LOW-INCOME WORKERS

Accessibility of Programs

It is clear that seeking out retirement help is more likely among those with higher incomes who are in better financial shape than those with lower incomes (Joo & Grable, 2001), probably because it is more accessible in high-income jobs, and less intimidating when one has adequate funds. Realistically, older low-income workers could best be served if organizations designed to assist older workers and community centers provided free planning advice and aggressively marketed this advice to low-income workers.

An alternative to increase the planning knowledge of low-income workers is from reputable sources on the Internet that provide free planning assistance. Increasing accessibility of Internet resources should be one way to help low-income workers gain access to retirement planning, if they have computer access at home or in a public facility, such as work, a library, or a community center. An excellent example is on the AARP website, www.aarp.org. This Web site has an area specifically for financial planning in retirement. It contains clear and user-friendly advice on the steps to take to plan for retirement and provides links to other helpful sites. It is important to note that these are free of charge. Sherman (1997) provides a long list of resources for financial planning that includes books, Internet resources, and lists of financial firms. Again, given financial constraints and situational constraints of low-income workers, these low-cost alternatives are most likely to be accessible than more formal plans.

Other options might include free group level counseling offered by firms. Making counseling free, convenient, and emphasizing the benefits of planning and the need for planning might increase participation rates in these programs. The more sources that provide free structured counseling, whether it is in an employment setting, a community center, or on the Internet, the better. Accessibility is an issue that should not be ignored.

Content of Programs

The content of effective retirement planning seminars targeted toward low-income older workers should emphasize the decreasing role of Social Security as a source of potential income, while providing information on how to save for retirement. Given the research reviewed earlier, part of the failure to plan may stem from overconfidence in the Social Security system or from a lack of understanding of the amount of money needed for retirement.

Other decision-making errors that should be addressed in retirement planning include a bias toward overly conservative investment options. Studies of retirement planning behavior suggest that perhaps planners would be best served if a variety of savings options at different risk levels were available to planners, and the pros and cons of the plans were made clear to them (Dulebohn, Murray, & Sun, 2000).

Last, planning seminars should be tailored based on gender and ethnicity. Women may have very different career paths than men and may have unique concerns relevant to planning (Quick & Moen, 1998; Szinovacz, DeViney, & Davey, 2001). Similarly, financial planning programs should be tailored to the needs of specific minority groups, since savings and credit management behavior may differ as a function of ethnicity (Bradford, 2003).

Active Versus Passive Involvement In Planning

There is limited available research on how the presentation of planning material impacts behavior. In a rare study in this area, Hershey, Mowen, and Jacobs-Lawson (2003) compared three different types of planning programs. They contrasted a purely informational planning seminar with one that focused only on setting financial goals. The third type of seminar combined both information and goals, and had the strongest impact on participants. As the authors note, this suggests that goal setting can be a critical element in inducing financial planning behavior, and can improve the effectiveness of information-only seminars or training modules. Similar research by Taylor-Carter and Cook (1995) found that an information-based seminar with a question-and-answer session increased knowledge of retirement issues but had a minimal impact on retirement self-efficacy, or the belief that one could effectively manage the changes in retirement.

Personal goal setting and active involvement in the process of retirement planning may be one way to enhance feelings of control over personal finances. As noted earlier, this is particularly important for low-income women and ethnic minorities who have not been engaged in managing their financial resources. The long-term effects of setting concrete goals may be quite beneficial, and may produce more ongoing, informed, and persistent behavior that improves one's financial standing.

A second positive outcome of such active involvement is that it provides corrective feedback for participants. Research on the effectiveness of information-only seminars designed to enhance financial planning suggests that you can increase subjects' knowledge of financial domains without necessarily increasing the accuracy of their financial decision-making (Hershey, Walsh, Brougham, Carter, & Farrell, 1998). These authors found that many individuals were naïve about estimating the financial resources needed across the years of retirement and made mistakes in planning that were equivalent to losses of 5 to 8 years of retirement income.

One might question whether individuals who are unfamiliar with financial planning are able to make sound financial decisions after training. While research in this area is limited, it is quite encouraging. Hershey and Walsh (2000/2001) found that they could significantly improve the financial planning decisions of novices after a guided 6-hour intervention.

Planning is a central means of trying to enhance the financial future of low-income workers. Another major source of income is employment. In the next segment, we examine the obstacles faced by low-income workers who seek to improve or maintain their financial status through continued employment, and we make suggestions for improving the success of low-income job seekers.

Low-Income Workers and Continued Employment

A number of different issues impact the ability of low-income workers to find jobs. Some of these stem from the educational and training deficits of low-income groups, and others come from limitations in the broader societal and employment system. In this segment, we explore the personal, occupational, and societal factors that constrain the ability of these workers to gain employment and, even more importantly, to gain employment in jobs with higher incomes. We end this segment with suggestions to remedy some of the issues identified.

Clearly there is a desire on the part of older employees to remain in the workforce. A recent survey of 800 workers found that seven out of ten older workers expect to work full- or part-time past the *normal* retirement ages of 62 and 65. Income has a significant impact on being able to retire when one wants to leave the workforce, with those in low-income categories being less likely to retire when they want (Reynolds, Ridley, & Van Horn, 2005). Related research suggests that this interest in employment extends to part-time work, and seeking part-time employment is also higher among those with lower incomes (Adams & Rau, 2004). Thus, low-income workers expect to work longer and may be highly motivated to seek out employment as well.

There are similarities in the underlying motivation for finding new work across older workers, as noted by Feldman in his chapter later in this book. The desire to find a new job or career stems from a broad range of individual-level, job-level, and occupational-level motivations, and mobility out of *dead end* jobs can be a critical means for older employees to obtain more satisfying work.

While these same rules apply to low-income workers, there are a large number of barriers that restrict employment mobility and opportunities for this group. O'Rand's (1999) hypothesis of relative advantage, discussed earlier, is relevant here. The lack of training and education that is inherent in low-income work serves to restrict access to higher paying jobs. Similarly, less availability of formal job networks, coupled with negative stereotypes regarding low-income older workers, may have a potent debilitating effect on the ultimate success of low-income job seekers.

Perhaps the most severe impediment to the career opportunities of low-income workers is a lack of skills training and education. Lack of formal training is a fundamental impediment in regards to the ability of any worker, regardless of age, to find a job. This is exacerbated in the case of the older employee. Older workers are viewed as less likely to have the technological skills needed for a job and less likely to be able to gain these skills (Cohen, 2003) and may be less likely to be targeted for training, as discussed by Maurer in his chapter later in this book. In addition, the older employee may self-select out of training. As a worker ages, he or she may have weaker incentives to invest in learning for the sake of employment and may become susceptible to technological obstacles that make future employment difficult (Katz, 1974).

This lack of skills may keep older employees in jobs that do not offer career paths or training that would lead to higher income work. Most low-income work is concentrated in retail trade, service, and manufacturing jobs where training is often unavailable (Bernstein & Gittleman, 2003). Not surprisingly, there is a fairly clear link between low wage jobs and low levels of occupational skills, decreasing the competitiveness of the typical low-income worker in the labor market (Bernstein & Gittleman, 2003).

The occupational opportunities in the United States have shifted to favor those who have technological skills and training. There is an increase in outsourcing unskilled jobs to countries where labor rates for such work is low. The combined effect of this shift in the nature of work itself and the limited skills of the low-income worker create what researchers have termed a *working-poverty trap* (Ferguson, 2005). The low-income older worker literally cannot afford to leave the job they have, and the job they have does not provide the skills training that would allow them to gain access to better work.

In a related domain, low education, more prevalent among low-income workers, is a clear barrier to occupational attainment and the ability to find and keep a job. Those with lower incomes tend to be more disadvantaged in terms of both health and education; both of these variables are related to the ability to find and keep employment, with those with low health and low education being less likely to find and keep work (McNamara & Williamson, 2004).

Among older workers, education is particularly important for the career opportunities and post retirement satisfaction of White, Hispanic, and African American women (Munnell & Jivan, 2005; Zhan & Pandey, 2004). The relatively lower education levels of women, particularly African American and Latino women, limits them to jobs that in turn, limit their income and increase their dependency on work (Taniguchi & Rosenfeld, 2002). Post retirement satisfaction among women is more strongly related to employment in jobs that require higher levels of skill and education than to simply being employed (Choi, 2001). Given that educational attainment is lower among women and minorities in these groups, it is clear that they face many challenges when attempting to enter the labor market or to change jobs (Butrica & Iams, 2003; Davies & Denton, 2002).

In summary, this lack of education and training and its association with entrenchment in a low-paying job, severely restricts the mobility of low-income workers, thus making job changes challenging. Feldman's discussion of the importance of older workers moving out of undesirable employment seems critical here. The ability to change employers is crucial for low-income workers, since many low-income jobs are dead end jobs with no career path, and outcomes are more positive for those low-income workers who can change employers (Holzer, Lane, & Vilhuber, 2004). This leads into the second challenge, effectively matching low-income workers with better jobs.

As Holzer et al. (2004) note, our ability to match low-income workers with more promising employment paths is a critical step in improving their success in the labor market and their long-term career success. However, a second impediment to the job seeking success of low-income workers is related to their access to formal employment networks. Low-income workers may be less tied into formal networks that provide needed contacts for employment. Research suggests, for example, that many low-income women find work through informal social contacts (Rankin, 2003). Unfortunately, these informal sources of information are more likely to lead to low-income jobs than to jobs of higher promise. Women's occupational outcomes are better when they use more formal job search techniques. This suggests that job search training may be an important contributor to the success of low-income job applicants, particularly for minorities and women (McNamara & Williamson, 2004).

A third limitation in the ability of lower-income older workers to find employment is social in nature; stereotypes with respect to age and poverty have implications for the way low-income older workers are viewed. While some employers view older workers as more reliable and having more experience than younger ones, surveys of human resource professionals reveal that they are also seen as having fewer technological skills and being less flexible (Cohen, 2003). Academic investigations of stereotypes yield similarly negative results, with older individuals being viewed as less competent that younger ones (Cuddy, Norton, & Fiske, 2005).

These stereotypes have significant implications for the success of low-income older applicants. While stereotypes of older workers may be more positive than in the past, negative assessments of their ability to change persist

(Weiss & Maurer, 2004). These effects may be exacerbated when older individuals apply for *age-incongruent* jobs (Perry, Kulik, & Bourhis, 1996).

This is exacerbated by negative stereotypes regarding those who live in poverty. Overall, Americans believe that internal, dispositional causes such as laziness and low intelligence are more plausible explanations for poverty than societal discrimination (Cozzarelli, Wilkinson, & Tagler, 2001). Related research by Hunt (2004) also showed that individuals were more likely to make these internal attributions for those living in poverty than external ones. We blame the victims of poverty for their state.

There are ways to decrease the role of these stereotypes. A recent meta-analysis suggests that these stereotypes are most powerful when judgments are based on limited information and when the evaluations focus on stereotypic traits rather than on behaviors (Kite, Stockdale, Whitley, & Johnson, 2005). When positive information regarding the competence of older workers is increased, the role of negative stereotypes is more limited.

Legal, institutional, and organizational barriers to work impact the opportunities of all older workers, including low-income employees (Penner, Perun, & Steuerle, 2002). The Organization for Economic Co-operation and Development (OECD; 2006) emphasizes the need for rewarding positions with attractive organizational environments. Some of the top job ideas for older workers require respected job skills and would seem to be set in comfortable environments: teacher assistant, consultant, bank teller, floral assistant, customer greeter, tour guide, security screener, English instructor, home care assistant, and mystery shopper (AARP, 2002). However, when one considers the fact that many of these *older worker jobs* would exceed the skills of low-income older applicants, the opportunities available to low-income workers are more limited.

Legal and bureaucratic limitations of the system impact all older workers, including low-income workers, and deserve mention as well. OECD suggests replacing outdated employee compensation programs (originally designed to replace long-term workers with cheaper, younger workers) with programs focused on the hiring and retention of older workers as a way to maintain job stability. Organizations that offer competitive financial incentives to prolong working and prevent early retirement would have strong benefits for low-income older workers looking for a sense of job stability. Regulatory barriers that discourage phased retirement should also be lifted to encourage workers to return to part-time work after the traditional retirement age (Butrica, Johnson, Smith, & Steuerle, 2004)

Social policies, organizational practices, and executive attitudes have historically discouraged working at an older age, and are being confronted by workers who are prolonging retirement for economic or personal reasons. Denying low-income older workers access to available jobs is a costly problem for the workers, industry, and society. Steps must be taken to promote better employment opportunities for low-income workers in this group of employees.

IMPLICATIONS FOR PRACTICE: SUGGESTIONS FOR LOW-INCOME WORKERS AND JOB SEEKERS

Regardless of whether an older person is seeking to sustain, gain, or change employment, certain suggestions can be gleaned from the research and applied literature.

1.   Programs encouraging adult and older worker education, including job-training services, should be made more available to low-income workers. We need to evaluate the relative success of different educational programs and to find ways to make them more accessible to low-income workers.
2.   Reducing older worker bias through training and through assignment of older workers to high-visibility, high-prestige jobs is a viable way for firms to reduce negative beliefs about their value to the organization.
3.   Low-income older workers could also profit from resume-writing programs at career counseling centers. The resume should communicate the ability to achieve high performance, a sense of purpose, competence, and enthusiasm for continued work. Older workers also need to make sure that their resume highlights the variety of skills and experience gained over the years as a unique trait. This approach capitalizes on the positive aspects of stereotypes regarding older workers and consciously challenges the negative aspects of the stereotype.
4.   Low-income workers can benefit from more extensive job networking. This could take place through contacts with job placement agencies, community programs, job support groups, fellow job seekers, and online job boards for jobs that may be available in their area. This is a continuing challenge for older employees who live in low-income areas, since they are likely to have less access to or be aware of resources that support these efforts.
5.   Legislative changes governing penalties for part-time and full-time employment during the receipt of Social Security benefits and the raised age for receipt of benefits may have a positive net effect for those low-income workers who are able to continue employment.

DIRECTIONS FOR FUTURE RESEARCH ON LOW-INCOME OLDER WORKERS

Throughout this chapter we have attempted to emphasize the need for assisting low-income older workers and have made suggestions for improving financial planning and the job search efforts of this group. Many of these are as relevant to researchers as to practitioners. However, there are specific gaps in the academic literature that should be addressed:

1. We need more complex models of the relationship between finances and wellbeing. These models need to be based on a careful consideration of the nature of the variables used (affective versus objective financial predictors; subjective versus objective dependent measures). We should not presume that objective and subjective measures are interchangeable.
2. We also need to consider environmental and personal moderators of the relationship between measures of financial wellbeing and adjustment.
3. There is not enough research modeling the financial planning behavior of low-income workers. Many of our models are based on middle- or high-income groups and these models may not apply to those who are living on the edge of poverty. We may need to develop qualitatively different models of work behavior tailored to the needs and constraints faced by this population.
4. Research exploring the effectiveness of different job search methods and training on job search techniques would help us understand the specific challenges facing low-income job seekers, and would provide valuable information for seniors interested in changing or acquiring new employment positions.
5. There is a pressing need to understand the employment behavior of low-income minority groups and women. Available research suggests that models based on White males, particularly upper-income White males, may not be generalizable to these subgroups.
6. There is a need for research on different types of low-income workers. The etiology of low-income can stem from sources as varied as long-term poverty and the restrictions associated with this status, unexpected job loss or loss of health, death of a wage-earning spouse, and expenses and income loss from divorce. The temporal nature of low-income varies as well; it can be a long-term state of affairs from entrenchment in poverty, or it can happen from a sudden shift in financial status. It is unlikely that the challenges faced by these different groups are the same, yet low-income workers are often treated as a homogeneous group.

SUMMARY

It is clear that low-income workers face a number of disadvantages. They live daily under stressors foreign to those of us fortunate enough to have the means not only to meet, but also to exceed, our needs. Researchers and practitioners in this arena clearly have the motivation to raise awareness of the problems facing this vulnerable group of employees. However, solutions to the problems will require more research, more intensive applied interventions, and investment in social programs designed to benefit the long-term wellbeing of this group.

REFERENCES

AARP. (2004). *Baby Boomers Envision Retirement II: Survey of Baby Boomers' Expectations for Retirement.* Washington, DC: Author.

Adams, G., & Rau, B. (2004). Job seeking among retirees seeking bridge employment. *Personnel Psychology, 57,* 719–745.

Anderson, S. G., Zhan, M., & Scott, J. (2004). Targeting financial management training at low-income audiences. *The Journal of Consumer Affairs, 38,* 167–177.

Armstrong, P. S., & Schulman, M. D. (1990). Financial strain and depression among farm operators: The role of perceived economic hardship and personal control. *Rural Sociology, 55,* 475–493.

Austrom, G., Perkins, A. J., Damush, T. M., & Hendrie, H. C. (2003). Predictors of life satisfaction in retired physicians and spouses. *Social Psychiatry and Psychiatric Epidemiology, 38,* 134–142.

Beedon, L., & Wu, K. B. (2003). *Social security and Hispanics: Some facts.* AARP Public Policy Institute. http://www.aarp.org

Beedon, L., & Wu, K. B. (2004). *African Americans age 65 and older: Their sources of income.* AARP Public Policy Institute. www.aarp.org

Beedon, L., & Wu, K. (2005). Women age 65 and older: Their sources of income. AARP Public Poverty Institute, October 2005. http://www.aarp.org

Bernstein, J., & Gittleman, M. (2003). Exploring low-wage labor with the National Compensation Survey. *Monthly Labor Review,* Nov/Dec.

Bond-Huie, S. A., Krueger, P. M., Rogers, R. G., & Hummer, R. A. (2003). Wealth, race, and mortality. *Social Science Quarterly, 84,* 667–684.

Bradford, W. D. (2003). The savings and credit management of low-income, low-wealth Black and White families. *Economic Development Quarterly, 17,* 53–74.

Butrica, B. A., & Iams, H. M. (2003). The impact of minority group status on the projected retirement income of divorced women in the Baby Boom cohort. *Journal of Women and Aging, 15,* 67–88.

Butrica, B. A., Johnson, R. W., Smith, K. E., & Steuerle, E. (2004). *Does work pay at older ages?* CRR WP 2004–30. Boston, MA: Center for Retirement Research, Boston College.

Center for Retirement Research at Boston College (2004). *Findings from the 2004 Retirement Confidence Survey: People think they have more pension coverage than they do.* Author.

Choi, N. G. (2001). Relationship between life satisfaction and postretirement employment among older women. *International Journal of Aging and Human Development, 52,* 45–74.

Chou, K. L., & Chi, I. (2001). Stressful life events and depressive symptoms: Social support and sense of control as mediators. *International Journal of Aging and Human Development, 52,* 155–172.

Cohen, D. J. (2003). Older workers. Statement before the Senate Special Committee on Aging Forum on the Older Workforce, Sept. 3. http://aging.senate.gov/public/_files/fr108dc.pdf

Committee for Economic Development. (1999). *New opportunities for older workers. A statement by the Research and Policy Committee of the Committee for Economic Development.* Author.

Cozzarelli, C., Wilkinson, A. V., & Tagler, M. J. (2001). Attitudes toward the poor and attributions for poverty. *Journal of Social Issues, 57,* 207–227.

Cuddy, A. J. C., Norton, M. I., & Fiske, S. T. (2005). This old stereotype: The pervasiveness and persistence of the elderly stereotype. *Journal of Social Issues, 61,* 267–285.

Danigelis, N. L., & McIntosh, B. R. (2001). Gender's effect on the relationships linking older Americans' resources and financial satisfaction. *Research on Aging, 2,* 410–428

Davies, S., & Denton, M. (2002). The economic wellbeing of older women who become divorced or separated in mid or later life. *Canadian Journal on Aging, 21,* 477–493.

Dittman, M. (2004). A new face to retirement. *American Psychologist, 35,* 78–79.

Dulebohn, J. H., Murray, B., & Sun, M. (2000). Selection among employer-sponsored pension plans: The role of individual differences. *Personnel Psychology, 53,* 405–432.

Dunn, A. "Southeast Asians Highly Dependent on Welfare in US," *New York Times,* May 19, 1994, A1. "Asian-Americans' success story a myth; report," Agence France Presse, May 17, 1994.

Elman, C., & O'Rand, A. M. (2004). The race is to the swift: Socioeconomic origins, adult education, and wage attainment. *American Journal of Sociology, 110,* 123–160.

Ertner, S. L., & Grzywacz, J. (2003). Socioeconomic status and health among Californians: An examination of multiple pathways. *American Journal of Public Health, 93,* 441–444.

Ferguson, R. F. (2005). The working poverty trap. *The Public Interest,* Winter, 71–82.

Gall, T. L., & Evans, D. R. (2000). Preretirement expectations and the quality of life of male retirees in later retirement. *Canadian Journal of Behavioral Science, 32,* 187–197.

Glass, J. C., & Kilpatrick, B. B. (1998). Gender comparisons of baby boomers and financial preparation for retirement. *Educational Gerontology, 24,* 719–745.

Goodman, J. C. (January 27, 2004). *America's private retirement system: The need for reform.* Statement before the U.S. Senate Special Committee on Aging. http://www.aging .senate.gov

Greenspan, A. (March 15, 2005). *Exploring the Economics of Retirement.* Statement before the Senate Special Committee on Aging. http://www.aging.senate.gov

Guerriero-Austrom, M., Perkins, A. J. Damush, T. M., & Hendrie, H. C. (2003). Predictors of life satisfaction in retired physicians and spouses. *Social Psychiatry and Psychiatric Epidemiology, 38,* 134–142.

Hershey, D. A., Jacobs-Lawson, J. M., & Neukam, K. A. (2002). Influences of age and gender on workers' goals for retirement. *International Journal of Aging and Human Development, 55,* 163–179.

Hershey, D. A., Mowen, J. C., & Jacobs-Lawson, J. M. (2003). An experimental comparison of retirement planning intervention seminars. *Educational Gerontology, 29,* 339–359.

Hershey, D. A., & Walsh, D. A. (2000/2001). Knowledge versus experience in financial problem solving performance. *Current Psychology: Developmental, Learning, Personality, Social, 19,* 261–291.

Hershey, D. A., Walsh, D. A., Brougham, R., Carter, S., & Farrell, A. (1998). Challenges of training pre-retirees to make sound financial planning decisions. *Educational Gerontology, 25,* 447–470.

Holzer, H. J., Lane, J. I., & Vilhuber, L. (2004). Escaping low earnings: The role of employer characteristics and changes. *Industrial and Labor Relations Review, 57,* 560–578.

Hunt, M. O. (2004). Race/ethnicity and beliefs about wealth and poverty. *Social Science Quarterly, 85*, 827–853.

Johnson, R. L. (2005). Gender differences in health promoting lifestyles of African Americans. *Public Health Nursing,* Mar–Apr, *22*, 130–137.

Joo, S., & Grable, J. E. (2001). Factors associated with seeking and using professional retirement-planning help. *Family and Consumer Sciences Research Journal, 30*, 37–63.

Katz, A. (1974). Schooling, age, and length of unemployment. *Industrial and Labor Relations Review, 27*, 597–605.

Kim, J. E., & Moen, P. (2002). Retirement transitions, gender, and psychological wellbeing: A life-course, ecological model. *Journal of Gerontology: Psychological Sciences, 57b,* 212–222.

Kite, M. E., Stockdale, G. D., Whitley, B. E., & Johnson, B. (2005). Attitudes toward younger and older adults: An updated meta-analytic review. *Journal of Social Issues, 61,* 241–266.

Krause, N. (1987). Chronic financial strain, social support, and depressive symptoms among older adults. *Psychology and Aging, 2,* 185–192.

Leavitt, J., & Lingafelter, T. (2005). Low wage workers and high housing costs. *Labor Studies Journal, 30,* 41–60.

Lichtenwalter, S. (2005). Gender poverty disparity in US cities: Evidence exonerating female-header families. *Journal of Sociology and Social Welfare, 32,* 75–96.

Loewentheil, N., & Weller, C. E. (2005). The renter squeeze: Minority and low-income renters feel pressures from housing boom and weak labor market. *Review of Policy Research, 22,* 755–769.

Lum, Y. S., & Lightfoot, E. (2003). The effect of health on retirement savings among older workers. *Social Work Research, 27,* 31–44.

MacEwen, K. E., Barling, J., Kelloway, E. K., & Higginbottom, S. F. (2001). Predicting retirement anxiety: The roles of parental socialization and personal planning. *The Journal of Social Psychology, 135,* 203–213.

McNally, J., Voon, C. P., & Park, K. S. (2004). *Poverty among elderly Asian Americans in the 21st century.* Paper presented at the annual meeting of the American Sociological Association, San Francisco, CA.

McNamara, T. K., & Williamson, J. B. (2004). Race, gender, and the retirement decisions of people ages 60 to 80: Prospects for age integration in employment. *International Journal of Aging and Human Development, 59,* 255–286.

Munnell, A. H., & Jivan, N. (2005). What makes older women work? Center for Retirement Research at Boston College, Series 1. http://www.bc.edu/centers/crr/issues/wob_1.pdf

O'Rand, A. (1999). *Age and inequality: Diverse pathways through later life.* Colorado: Westview Press.

Organization for Economic Co-operation and Development. (2006). Aging and Employment Policies- Live Longer, Work Longer. http://www.oecd.org

Osawa, M. N., & Hong, B. E. (2003). Disability and economic wellbeing in old age. *Journal of Disability Policy Studies, 13,* 231–243.

Panel on Poverty and Family Assistance, Committee on National Statistics, Commission on Behavioral and Social Sciences and Education, & National Research Council (1995). *Measuring Poverty: A New Approach.* C. F. Citro and R. T. Michael (Eds.), Washington: National Academy Press.

Penner, R. G., Perun, P., & Steuerle, E. (2002). Legal and institutional impediments to partial retirement and part time work by older workers. http://www.urban.org?url.cfm?id = 410587

Perkins, K. (1992). Psychosocial implications of women and retirement. *Social Work, 37,* 526–532.

Perry, E. L., Kulik, C. T., & Bourhis, A. C. (1996). Moderating effects of personal and contextual factors in age discrimination. *Journal of Applied Psychology, 81,* 628–647.

Quick, H., & Moen, P. (1998). Gender, employment, and retirement quality: A life course approach to the differential experiences of men and women. *Journal of Occupational Health Psychology, 3,* 1–21.

Rankin, B. (2003). How low-income women find jobs and its effects on earnings. *Work and Occupations, 30,* 281–301.

Reitzes, D. C., & Mutran, E. J. (2004). The transition to retirement: Stages and factors that influence retirement adjustment. *International Journal of Aging and Human Development, 59,* 63–84.

Reynolds, S., Ridley, N., & Van Horn, C. E. (2005). *A work-filled retirement: Workers' changing views on employment and leisure.* John J. Heldrich Center for Workforce Development and Center for Survey Research and Analysis. Development/www.heldrich.rutgers.edu/Resources/Publication/191/WT16.pdf

Rix, S., & Beedon, L. (2003). *Social security of women. Some Facts.* AARP Public Policy Institute. http://www.aarp.org

Rosenkoetter, M. M., & Garris, J. M. (2001). Retirement planning, use of time, and psychosocial adjustment. *Issues in Mental Health Nursing, 22,* 703–722.

Sherman, R. H. (1997). Sources of help in financial preparation for retirement. *Generations, 21,* 55–61.

Stoller, M. A., & Stoller, E. P. (2003). Perceived income adequacy among elderly retirees. *The Journal of Applied Gerontology, 22,* 230–251.

Smith, D. B., & Moen, P. (2004). Retirement satisfaction for retirees and their spouses: Do gender and the retirement decision making process matter? *Journal of Family Issues, 25,* 262–285.

Spiegel, P. E., & Shultz, K. S. (2003). The influence of preretirement planning and transferability of skills on Naval Officers' retirement satisfaction and adjustment. *Military Psychology, 15,* 285–307.

Stoller, M. A., & Stoller, E. P. (2003). Perceived income adequacy among elderly retirees. *The Journal of Applied Gerontology, 22,* 230–251.

Szinovacz, M. E., DeViney, S., & Davey, A. (2001). Influences of family obligations and relationships on retirement: Variations by gender, race, and marital status. *Journal of Gerontology: Social Sciences, 56B,* 20–27.

Taniguchi, H., & Rosenfeld, R. A. (2002). Women's employment exit and reentry: Differences among Whites, Blacks, and Hispanics. *Social Science Research, 31,* 432–471.

Taylor, M. A., & Doverspike, D. (2003). *Retirement Planning and Preparation.* In G. A. Adams & T. A. Beehr's *Retirement: Reasons, Processes and Results* (pp. 53–82). New York: Springer.

Taylor-Carter, M. A., & Cook, K. (1995). Adaptation to retirement: Role changes and psychological resources. *The Career Development Quarterly, 44,* 67–82.

Tower, R. B., & Kasl, S. V. (1995). Depressive symptoms across older spouses and the moderating effect of marital closeness. *Psychology and Aging, 10,* 625–638.

Turner, M. J., Bailey, W. C., & Scott, J. P. (1994). Factors influencing attitudes toward retirement and retirement planning among midlife university employees. *Journal of Applied Gerontology, 13*, 143–156.

Tyson, L. D. (2005, June 6). Retirement savings: A boost for the needy. *Business Week,* 30.

U.S. Census Bureau (2004). *Income, poverty, and health insurance in the U.S.* Report P60, 229, p. 45. http://pubdb3.census.gov/macro/032005/pov/toc.htm

Weiss, E. M., & Maurer, T. J. (2004). Age discrimination in personnel decisions: A reexamination. *Journal of Applied Social Psychology, 34,* 1551–1562.

Wrosch, C., Heckhausen, J., & Lachman, M. E. (2000). Primary and secondary control strategies for managing health and financial stress across adulthood. *Psychology and Aging, 15,* 387–399.

Wu, K. (2001). Older persons find it hardest to exit poverty. AARP Public Policy Institute Report, May. http://www.aarp.org

Wu, K. (2003). In brief: Poverty experience of older persons: A poverty study from a long term perspective. AARP Public Policy Institute, March 2003. http://www.aarp.org

Wu, K. (2004). African Americans age 65 and older: Their sources of income. AARP Public Policy Institute Report, Sept. http://www.aarp.org

Wu, K., & Beedon, L. (2004). Hispanics 65 and older: Sources of Retirement Income. AARP Public Policy Institute Report, September. http://www.aarp.org

Zhan, M., & Pandey, S. (2004). Postsecondary education and the wellbeing of women in retirement. *Journal of Marriage and Family, 66,* 661–673.

4

Diversity Issues for an Aging Workforce

Caren Goldberg

This chapter summarizes the literature on the work outcomes experienced by aging women and minorities. The chapter begins with an overview, followed by a summary of the simple effects of age, gender, and race on organizational entry, job performance, training, mobility, and compensation. Next, the available evidence for combined age and gender, as well as age and race effects on these work outcomes is reviewed. Two theoretical explanations for the findings (additive effects and interactive effects) are discussed. At the end of the chapter I propose a model that bridges these two perspectives. The model identifies opportunities for organizations and society to improve the work experiences of older women and minorities.

The general trend towards an aging population has been well documented (Kausler & Kausler, 2001), as have the projected increases in the proportions of women and minorities in the work place. Fullerton and Toossi (2001), for example, note that the Bureau of Labor Statistics estimates that the percentage increase in women's labor force participation between 2000 and 2010 will be 15 percent, compared to only a 9 percent increase in men's participation. Likewise, whereas the change in Whites' labor force participation between 2000 and 2010 is estimated at 6 percent, Asians', African Americans' and Hispanics' participation rates are expected to change by 37 percent, 17 percent, and 36 percent, respectively, during the same period. However, while numerous prior studies have examined the effects of age, race, or gender on work-related outcomes, very few researchers have explored the effects of more than one demographic characteristic simultaneously. This is somewhat disconcerting, in light of the gender and race differences in the aging worker population. In particular, as women live an average of seven years longer than men

(Kolb, 2002), the Bureau of Labor Statistics (Fullerton & Toosi, 2001) projects an increase in the workforce participation rate for women over 55 of 6 percent, compared to a projected increase of only 3.8 percent for their aging male counterparts. Likewise, while the workforce, as a whole, is getting older, the most recent Current Population Survey indicates that the percentage of the civilian labor force in the 55 and older category varies markedly by race, with a low of 6.5 percent for African Americans and a high of 14.5 percent for Whites (Fullerton & Toosi, 2001).

Despite these statistics, very few studies have examined the joint impact of gender and age on work-related criteria, and virtually no empirical studies have examined whether the effects of aging on employment consequences differ across racial categories. This chapter examines gender and race differences in the effects of aging on work outcomes. The few studies that have explored "gendered aging" effects (Barnum, Liden, & DiTomaso, 1995; Goldberg, Finkelstein, Perry, & Konrad, 2004) found that aging tends to result in more adverse employment consequences for women than for men. Although no empirical studies of work outcomes of aging minorities have been published, conceptual work seems to indicate that the processes that affect older women's work outcomes also operate for older minority employees (Kolb, 2002).

Studies of gender differences in aging effects have focused on two explanations for the finding that older women fare worse than older men do. One explanation is that older women are at "double jeopardy" for discrimination (Barnum et al., 1995). That is, the employment discrimination that women face at the early stages of their careers is cumulative over their work lives. Thus, the longer a woman is in the workforce, the more discrimination she encounters. Similarly, the work place discrimination faced by minorities (Hosoda, Stone, & Stone-Romero, 2003) is likely more pronounced for older non-White employees than for younger non-White employees.

An alternative explanation suggests that rather than additive effects, the unfavorable situations faced by older female or minority employees is attributable to interactive processes. That is, women and minorities who are older are less able to fulfill the prototypic ideal for their respective gender or race. Thus, whereas older men are often as able (or more so) as younger men to fulfill the success-object ideal of the masculine stereotype, older women are not as able as younger women to fulfill the sex-object ideal of the feminine stereotype (Konrad & Cannings, 1997). Consequently, the job rewards (e.g., selection, promotion, pay) afforded to younger men and women and older men for matching prototypical expectations are not available to older women. Likewise, African Americans are perceived as being better suited to work that is more physically demanding and less cognitively demanding than their White counterparts (Folsom & Cook, 1991; Hosoda et al., 2003). As physical abilities decline with age (Borgatta, 1991; Salthouse, 1987), older minorities are less able to fit the prototype ideal of strong, able-bodied workers. Moreover, the physical demands of these jobs may lead to an inability to continue work, forcing them into earlier retirement.

In this chapter we review the scant empirical research linking gender and age to work-related criteria and propose incorporating both the cumulative discrimination and sex role stereotype views of older men's and women's work outcomes (organizational entry, job performance, training, mobility, and compensation). Further, it is proposed that similar phenomena operate to impede the career progress of aging minorities. Drawing upon the two explanations for aging women's and aging minorities' unfavorable work outcomes, a model that incorporates both gender and race and the effects of aging on work outcomes is proposed. The chapter concludes with some directions for future research and some prescriptive avenues for managers.

SIMPLE EFFECTS OF AGE, GENDER, AND RACE ON WORK OUTCOMES

Research on employment decisions suggests that older workers, women, and non-Whites generally fare less well than their younger, male, and White counterparts. In this section, the findings of studies examining the simple effects of age, gender, and race are summarized. The subsequent section discusses the joint effects of age and gender, as well as age and race.

Organizational entry. U.S. Bureau of Labor Statistics (2004) data indicate that workers age 55 and over take 7 to 9 weeks longer, on average, to find a job than do their counterparts who are younger than 55. Studies of applicant selection provide somewhat mixed results. Although field studies have reported inconsistent findings (Arvey, Miller, Gould, & Burch, 1987; Goldberg & Shore, 2003; Raza & Carpenter, 1987), these studies have suffered from restricted age ranges. In contrast, Finkelstein, Burke, and Raju's (1995) meta-analysis of laboratory studies of selection showed that when raters evaluated both young and old applicants, young applicants were rated as significantly more qualified than old applicants. This suggests that the ages of other applicants may play an important role in understanding how target age impacts selection.

Women's unemployment ($M = 18.8$ weeks) tends to be of a shorter duration than men's ($M = 20.3$ weeks) on average; however, selection studies have generally found that women fare worse than men do in the context of selection (see Tosi & Einbender, 1985 for a meta-analytic review). Moreover, as jobs that are *male-typed* tend to be higher status and command higher pay than do *female-typed* jobs, women typically end up in less desirable jobs than their male counterparts (Cotter, DeFiore, Hermsen, Kowalewski, & Vanneman, 1997).

White job seekers spend considerably less time in unemployment (M = 18.5 weeks) than do their African American counterparts (M = 23 weeks; U.S. Bureau of Labor Statistics, 2004). Huffcutt and Roth's (1998) meta-analysis of race and interview outcomes showed that African Americans' and Hispanics' interview assessments were one quarter of a standard deviation lower than Whites' interview assessments. Other studies suggest that interviewee race effects are attributable to rater-ratee similarity preferences (Lin, Dobbins, & Farh, 1992; Prewett-Livingston, Field, Veres, & Lewis, 1996). However, given that most interviewers are White, similarity effects tend to favor White applicants. Further, evidence that many other employment tests adversely affect African Americans and Hispanics (Schmidt & Hunter, 1998) suggests that individuals from these groups are apt to encounter difficulties in organizational entry.

Job performance.   Although meta-analytic studies concerning the effects of employee age on job performance ratings have shown weak support (Avolio, Waldman, & McDaniel, 1990; McEvoy & Cascio, 1989; Waldman & Avolio, 1986) for adverse effects on older workers, few of the primary studies examining the age-performance relationships included workers older than 60 years of age. Further, the relationship between age and performance is influenced by occupation (Waldman & Avolio, 1986). Jobs have become more technology oriented in the time since these meta-analyses were conducted, a shift which carries negative implications for the relationship between age and performance in the 21st century: Although older workers are capable of becoming as proficient with new technology as their younger counterparts (Elias, Elias, & Robbins,& George, 1987), Martocchio (1993) found that they were less interested in enrolling in technology training to improve their work skills and were less likely to be offered training. Moreover, as discussed later in this chapter, advanced age may be perceived as a poor person-job fit in a high-tech job that is apt to result in negative assessments.

Meta-analytic findings (Bowen, Swim, & Jacobs, 2000; Eagly, Makhijani, & Klonsky, 1992) linking gender with performance suggest that gender differences in performance appraisals are negligible. However, consistent with Powell and Butterfield's (1989, 2000) finding that stereotypes of the typical manager are highly consistent with their stereotypes of the typical male, but less consistent with the stereotypes of the typical female, Bowen et al.'s meta-analysis showed significant differences in performance ratings favoring men in higher status, male-typed jobs.

Stauffer and Buckley (2005) recently concluded that a significant proportion of variance in performance ratings can be explained by ratee race. This effect was particularly pronounced when supervisors were White, suggesting a similarity bias. As disproportionately more Whites than non-Whites occupy supervisory positions (Kaufman, 2001), race differences in performance ratings are likely quite pervasive.

Training.   As Maurer and Rafuse (2001) note, 55 to 60 year olds are much less likely to receive training than 35 to 44 year olds. Further, several studies suggest that organizations and managers are less willing to invest in training opportunities for older workers (Cleveland & Shore, 1992; Heywood, Ho, & Wei, 1999; Shore, Cleveland, & Goldberg, 2003). Likewise, Finkelstein, Allen, and Rhoton (2003) found that younger protégés reported receiving more frequent career-related mentoring, and that mentors reported spending fewer hours per week with their older protégés than with younger protégés.

In addition, research findings indicate that women are afforded fewer training opportunities than men (Knoke & Ishio, 1998). In addition, women face a number of obstacles with regard to mentoring opportunities. Although protégés of female mentors receive fewer promotions and annual salaries that are nearly $20,000 less than their colleagues with male mentors (Ragins & Cotton, 1999), male mentors typically prefer male protégés (Noe, 1988). Consequently, female managers report having had fewer mentorship experiences in their careers than men do (Lyness & Thompson, 2000).

That African Americans receive fewer opportunities for on-the-job training than Whites do has been documented for decades (c.f., Flanagan, 1973). Indeed, many authors have cited decreased training access as one of the primary barriers to minority advancement within organizations (Watane & Gibson, 2001). Studies linking race to mentoring outcomes provide an even more disconcerting picture. In particular, African Americans and Hispanics are less likely than Whites to establish relationships with White mentors, resulting in a compensation difference of nearly $17,000 per year (Dreher & Cox, 1996). Moreover, cross-race mentoring relationships provide significantly less psychosocial support than do same-race mentorships (Thomas, 1990).

Mobility and compensation.   Several studies have shown a negative relationship between age and managers' assessments of promotability (Cox & Nkomo, 1992; Lawrence, 1988; Shore et al., 2003), as well as the actual number of promotions received (Goldberg et al., 2004). Cox and Nkomo propose that this may result from perceptions that younger workers afford more time for the organization to recoup its investment. Given the high correlation between age and work experience, it is not surprising that older workers generally receive higher salaries than their younger counterparts do (Goldberg et al., 2004); however, as one ages, wage growth tends to slow, resulting in lower real wages for older workers (Hirsch, Macpherson, & Hardy, 2000).

Research on race has consistently shown that non-Whites are seen as less promotable by their supervisors (Landau, 1995). Likewise, compared to their

White counterparts, the length of time between promotions is longer (James, 2000) and the total number of promotions is lower (Maume, 1999) for African Americans, even when human and social capital factors are controlled. Moreover, an African American-White wage gap of over 24 percent exists for all workers, but the highest differential is among individuals with Master's degrees (Lawrence, 2004). Grodsky and Pager's (2001) recent multilevel analysis indicates that the race wage gap is attributable both to individual differences and to occupational segregation.

Studies linking gender with mobility and compensation outcomes show fairly consistent effects favoring men. For example, Spurr (1990) found that women are less likely to be promoted than men are. Consistent with this, Edwards, Robinson, Welchman, and Woodall's (1999) study indicated that men reach higher organizational levels than do their female counterparts. The evidence regarding the gender gap in earnings is well documented (Roos & Gatta, 1999). Even when factors such as job type, industry, willingness to relocate, family responsibilities, and work centrality were controlled for, researchers have found that women are paid less than men (Goldberg et al., 2004; Stroh, Brett, & Reilly, 1992), with the current gender gap in earnings at 76.5 percent (Institute for Women's Policy Research, 2005).

EMPLOYMENT CONSEQUENCES FOR OLDER WOMEN AND MINORITIES

Given the disadvantages faced by older workers, women, and minorities, individuals belonging to more than one of these categories are likely to experience particularly negative work-related outcomes. Although empirical research examining the joint effects of age and gender, as well as age and race is scant, the few empirical studies that have examined such effects appear to support the notion that aging results in particularly unfavorable consequences for women and minorities. For example, Goldberg et al. (2004) found a marked difference between older and younger men's salaries, but a relatively flat slope for younger versus older women's salaries. Moreover, the results of their study suggest that age-context matching (rewarding those whose age matches the age context, for example a young person in an industry that is age-typed as *young*, and punishing those whose age does not match the age context) appears to be more important to women's career advancement than to men's. Likewise, Barnum et al. (1995) found that the disparity between pay rates of African American and Hispanic managers compared with White managers increased with age, as did the disparity between aging men's and women's pay rates.

Two theoretical perspectives have been advanced to explain the unfavorable treatment experienced by individuals who belong to at least two disadvantaged groups (e.g., African American female). I refer to these perspectives as the double jeopardy (also called, *additive effects*) and interactive process models (Barnum et al., 1995; Hosoda et al., 2003). Both of these theoretical perspectives are discussed next.

THE DOUBLE JEOPARDY
(ADDITIVE PROCESS) EXPLANATION

Developmental theorists have suggested that the effects of discrimination are cumulative over one's lifetime or career. For example, Stoller and Gibson (2000, p. 19) note that "membership in a specific birth cohort (i.e., being born in a particular time period) shapes the aging experience. Within cohorts, however, the experience of aging differs depending on one's position in systems of inequality based on gender, race or ethnicity, or class." Likewise Kolb (2002, p. 313) argues that "discrimination throughout the life span results in an accumulation of disadvantage in old age."

The additive model suggests that the adverse consequences that stem from belonging to the category of *older worker* are separate and distinct from the adverse consequences that stem from belonging to the category *female worker* or *minority worker*. The additive effects proposed by this model may result from belonging to two or more disadvantaged groups at a single point in time (e.g., an older Hispanic employee being laid off before an older White employee or a younger Hispanic employee) or they may be cumulative, over the course of one's career (e.g., an older male employee being promoted over an older female employee, after the female had been repeatedly denied access to training). In the former case, the target individual experiences the adverse effects of belonging to two disadvantaged categories at the same time. That is, an organizational decision maker sees individuals in the older female worker or older minority worker categories as possessing all of the negative traits associated with the target belonging to the older worker category *plus* all of the negative traits associated with the target belonging to the female worker or minority worker category. Hosoda et al. (2003) suggest that the sum of the effects of double disadvantage status puts these individuals at a marked disadvantage relative to others who belong to either one of the disadvantaged groups (or to neither disadvantaged group).

In the latter case, the adverse effects of belonging to one disadvantaged category (race or gender) is additive over time. Consequently, women or people of color are apt to be at a particular disadvantage when they become older, as a result of the sum of negative consequences they experienced during their careers up to that point in time. Barnum et al. (1995, p. 866) state that

> accumulation of biased decisions in such areas as training, promotion, job assignments, and salary allocation may be reflected in increased disparity in pay between White men on the one hand and minorities and women on the other as

people grow older. These circumstances, which we termed, "double jeopardy," result from both (1) an individual's being a member of an affected group and (2) the aggregate effects of discrimination reflected in disparity increasing with age.

While the research presented here provides evidence for the additive model, a number of researchers have suggested that age and other demographic characteristics interact, such that the process of aging occurs differently for men versus women or Whites versus non-Whites. The next section highlights the research on the interactive model explanation.

THE INTERACTIVE MODEL EXPLANATION

The interactive model suggests that aging connotes separate things for men versus women and for Whites versus non-Whites. Havighurst and Albrecht (1953) note that older people must come to terms with loss of physical attractiveness and vigor, characteristics associated with feminine and masculine ideals, respectively. However, these changes mean different things to men and women, because, in our society, men and women are valued for different things. The feminine ideal is that of sex object, whereas the masculine ideal is that of a success object. Older men are often as able as younger men to fulfill the success-object ideal of the masculine stereotype, whereas older women are not as able as younger women to fulfill the sex-object ideal of the feminine stereotype (Konrad & Cannings, 1997). Similarly, as jobs that are stereotypically African American or Hispanic are more physically demanding, whereas jobs that are stereotypically White are more cognitively demanding (Hosoda et al., 2003), the declines in physical skills that typically accompany aging (Borgatta, 1991) are apt to have a more deleterious effect on non-Whites than on Whites. Indeed, AARP data (2003) indicate that African Americans are disproportionately more likely than the rest of the population to receive disability benefits.

Empirical examinations of the effects of aging on men versus women have been relatively recent; however, lifespan scholars have discussed such differences for decades. Although many early developmental theorists focused on men (c.f., Levinson, Darrow, Klein, Levinson, & McKee, 1978; Peck, 1968), Cumming and Henry's (1961) disengagement theory suggests that aging ought to affect men and women differently. In particular, they note that "Because the central role of men in American society is instrumental and the central role of women is socio-emotional, the process of disengagement will differ between men and women" and "because the abandonment of life's central roles—work for men, marriage and family for women—results in dramatically reduced social life space, it will result in crisis and loss of morale unless different roles appropriate to the disengaged state, are available" (Cumming & Henry, 1961,

p. 211). More recent studies on gender differences in disengagement from work support this view (Becker & Moen, 1999; Smith & Moen, 2004). Although no empirical research, to date, has examined whether aging results in different employment consequences for individuals of different races, the stereotypic ideal of what constitutes employability for White and non-White individuals suggests that aging non-Whites would face particular disadvantages relative to aging Whites.

BRIDGING THE TWO EXPLANATIONS

Person stereotypes. It is likely that stereotypes play a role in the negative outcomes experienced by older women and minorities. A good deal of research suggests that stereotypes held of older workers, women, and minorities are considerably less favorable than are those of younger workers, men, and Whites. For example, research suggests that although older workers are perceived as possessing the desirable trait of reliability, the more pervasive stereotypes portray older workers as being untrainable, less physically capable, inflexible, and less interpersonally adept (Cleveland & Landy, 1983; Crew, 1983; Goldberg & Shore, 2003; Perry & Bourhis, 1998; Rosen & Jerdee, 1976a, 1976b). Research on gender stereotypes (Bem, 1974; O'Neill & Blake-Beard, 2002; Powell & Butterfield, 1989, 2000) indicates that women are also seen as possessing less of the traits that most employers would deem desirable. For example, they are seen as less ambitious, assertive, analytical, and effective at leading others than their male counterparts. Stereotypes associated with African Americans (intellectually incompetent, lacking in ambition and drive, immature, and untrustworthy; Dovidio & Gaertner, 1996; Hosoda et al., 2003; Smith & Stewart, 1983), Hispanics (lazy, criminal, and lacking in ambition; Chang & Kleiner, 2003; Feagin & Feagin, 1996), and Native Americans (alcoholic, lazy, and dependent; Chang & Kleiner, 2003; Tan, Fujioka, & Lucht, 1997) also tend to paint a picture of someone whom most employers would not want in their work place.[1]

Motowidlo (1986) notes that stereotypes of individuals based on multiple group memberships cause greater bias than single stereotypes do. Consistent with this notion, Brewer, Dull, and Lui (1981) found that subjects' prototypes of elderly men generally comprised attributes that are valued in the work place (e.g., competitive, intelligent, dignified), whereas the prototype of an elderly woman generally comprised traits that are less relevant and/or less desirable in

---

[1]Although there are a few negative stereotypes regarding Asians (i.e., that they are spies; Chang & Kleiner, 2003), generally, the content of stereotypes regarding Asians tends to be positive (i.e., that they are good in math and driven to succeed). Therefore, I did not include them in the discussion of negative racial stereotypes.

the work place (e.g., old-fashioned, kindly, emotional). Likewise, Kite, Deaux, and Miele (1991) found that whereas subjects listed intelligence as an attribute associated with 35-year-old male and female targets, when presented with 65-year-old targets, the same subjects listed intelligence for the male, but not the female target. In short, given the unfavorability of the stereotypes associated with older workers, women, and minorities noted in the preceding paragraph, if being old is bad, then being an old woman or old minority is worse.

Job stereotypes. While person stereotypes may help explain the negative work experiences of older women and minorities, these categorical perceptions do not occur in a vacuum. Rather, individuals are evaluated vis-à-vis decision makers' preconceived notions about what characteristics a job incumbent should possess. Consequently, a good deal of research over the last several decades has focused on examining the content of job stereotypes and the role it plays in employment-related decisions.

Much of the early research on job stereotypes focused on the types of jobs that individuals considered old- versus young-typed, male- versus female-typed, and to a lesser extent, African American- versus White-typed jobs. For example, gender researchers (Shinar, 1975) have noted that jobs also vary as to the extent to which they are perceived as being male-typed and female-typed. Likewise, research by Cleveland and her colleagues (Cleveland & Berman, 1987; Cleveland & Landy, 1987) and Gordon and Arvey (1986) suggest that students and managers share similar perceptions about the age-types of jobs. Although research on race-typing of jobs has been less systematic, Hosoda et al. (2003) note that raters might view African Americans as more suitable than Whites for physical jobs and/or jobs requiring low levels of cognitive ability because of negative stereotypes about African Americans. Other authors have provided anecdotal accounts, suggesting that even among white-collar jobs, race-typing occurs. For example, Steinberg (1995, p. 198) notes that the Civil Rights era created a host of decent paying jobs that are "pegged for blacks," particularly in government (Collins, 1997).

Research by Gordon and Arvey (1986) and Krefting, Berger, and Wallace (1978) indicates that job age- and gender-types emerge largely as a result of the characteristics of the actual job holders. This suggests a cyclical process in which breaking into a stereotype-inconsistent field is difficult. That is, the Attraction-Selection-Attrition model (Schneider, 1987) suggests that individuals are attracted to organizations to which they are similar. Indeed, the recruitment literature indicates that women and minorities are more attracted to organizations that have higher proportions of female and minority incumbents (Avery, 2003; Rynes, Bretz, & Gerhart, 1991; Sorensen, 2004; Thomas & Wise, 1999). However, because individuals from disadvantaged groups are dissuaded from entering certain occupations, their proportional representation remains low, thus deterring subsequent job seekers from applying.

Unfortunately, the barriers to stereotype-inconsistent jobs do not end with deterrence from applying. Ample evidence suggests that even when individuals overcome their reluctance to apply to a job for which they do not match the job stereotype, organizational decision-makers perceive the individuals to be a mismatch, and evaluate them accordingly. For example, several researchers (Atwater & VanFleet, 1997; Glick, Zion, & Nelson, 1988; Perry, 1994, 1997; Perry & Bourhis, 1998) have provided an abundance of evidence that an applicant's age and job age-type, as well as gender and job gender-type interact such that better matches result in more favorable selection outcomes and poorer matches result in less favorable selection outcomes. These researchers suggest that a cognitive matching process occurs, whereby those who possess characteristics that are consistent with the prototypical job incumbent are evaluated more favorably than are those who lack such prototypical attributes. This, in turn, contributes to persistence of stereotypes regarding the fit of African Americans and women with jobs, since the stereotype is not often challenged. Findings from a recent study by Hosoda et al. (2003) suggest that a similar prototype matching process operates in determining the suitability of Whites and African Americans to stereotypically White and African American jobs.

However, the adverse effects of prototype matching on employees from disadvantaged groups do not end with selection. Field studies suggest that older workers in young-typed jobs are seen as less promotable and are afforded fewer developmental opportunities than are their stereotype-consistent counterparts (Cleveland & Shore, 1992). Likewise, results from Goldberg and Konrad's (2002) meta-analysis indicate that women receive significantly lower performance ratings and rewards when they are in male-dominated contexts. Similarly, Hosoda et al. (2003, p. 149) note that the findings of other studies of ratings of African American and White managers may reflect the fact that "the stereotypes associated with Whites are more consistent with the stereotypical views of the requirements of managerial jobs."

Unfortunately, researchers have rarely examined the effects of person stereotype x job stereotype matching on multiple characteristics simultaneously. Although Goldberg et al. (2004) found that target-job mismatches resulted in less favorable outcomes for older women than for older men, they did not examine the four-way effects of age, job age-type, gender, and job gender-type. Likewise, no studies to date have examined the four-way effects of age, job age-type, race, and job race-type.

SUMMARY MODEL AND IMPLICATIONS FOR PRACTICE

The foregoing suggests that unfavorable treatment of female and minority older workers results from the interplay of target demographics, labor market realities, person and job stereotypes, cognitive matching, and organizational decision-making, within the broader societal context. Figure 4–1 depicts these relationships discussed above, and adds some additional relationships that suggest opportunities to improve the current situation. The solid lines indicate the relationships that currently exist; the dashed lines indicate opportunities to positively impact the treatment of older women and minorities. Although the

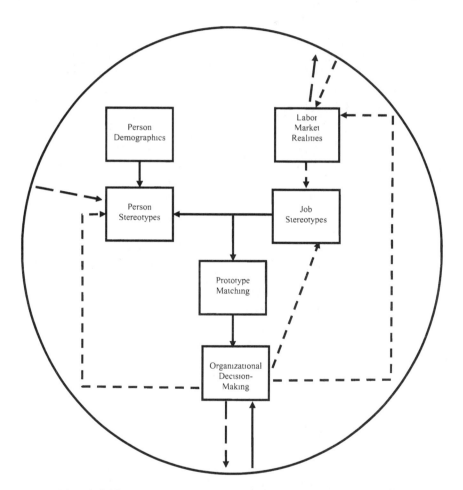

Note. Solid lines represent current relationships; dashed lines represent opportunities for organizations to positively influence the treatment of older women and minorities.

FIGURE 4–1.   The relationship between labor market realities, target demographics, and employment decisions about older female and minority employees, within the broader social context.

relationships depicted as dashed lines may currently exist, they generally result in negative treatment of older women and minorities. For example, there is unquestionably a relationship between the broader social context and labor market realities. However, this is indicated as a dashed line to suggest that societal changes have the potential to favorably impact labor market segmentation.

The top portion of this figure describes how stereotypes are activated or made salient. As Anderson (1991) notes, stereotypes are rooted in some truth. For example, it is the case that on average, age is negatively related to physical strength, stamina, reaction time, and one's ability to recover from strain and stress (Borgatta, 1991; Salthouse, 1987). Thus, the top left portion of the figure shows target demographics influencing person stereotypes. Although individuals may possess stereotype-inconsistent characteristics, Kanter (1977) suggests that these traits do not fit into the perceiver's existing cognitive schema. To resolve the inconsistency, rather than recognizing that the target is not representative of their category, the perceiver will typically look for other category-consistent characteristics, so that the target person may be more easily assimilated into the perceiver's schema. Alternatively, the individual may be viewed as an "exception to the rule" so that the stereotype is maintained even after exposure to those who violate it.

The center of Figure 4–1 represents the prototype matching process, whereby stereotypes of individuals are matched with stereotypes of jobs to make assessments about the degree of match (c.f., Perry, 1994, 1997). As shown in the figure, the interaction of person stereotypes and job stereotypes leads to an assessment of match. This match assessment, in turn, results in organizational decisions that favor or disfavor the target individual, as shown by the relationship between prototype matching and organizational decision-making.

Several developmental theorists have suggested that our society can play a proactive role in the outcomes associated with aging. For example, Havighurst, Neugarten, and Tobin (1996) note that aging people desire the same social interaction as middle-aged people, but have decreased social interaction because society withdraws from older people. Likewise, Rowe and Kahn (1998, p. 18) note that "what people can do for themselves depends to some extent on opportunities and constraints in the form of attitudes and expectations regarding older adults, as well as on social policies." Consistent with this, Busse and Maddox (1985) found that individuals who actively decided to stop working did not show any change in life satisfaction, whereas those who retired involuntarily showed a decrease in life satisfaction. Consequently, the model in Figure 4–1 suggests a number of potential ways in which the broader social context (and organizations, more specifically) may address some of these problems.

The model suggests that the broader social context impacts labor market realities, but also that labor market realities have the potential to impact the broader social context. As an example, low-quality inner city schools are certainly one factor resulting in the disproportionate representation of minorities in low-status jobs. However, as social policy aimed at more evenly distributing resources to schools has the potential to change the occupational segregation observed across racial groups, the line between the social context and labor market realities is drawn as a dashed line. Likewise, the economy is shifting towards technology jobs, which are generally *young* typed. Increased government spending on programs aimed at training older workers in technology would be a viable means of reducing age-based occupational segregation.

Along with the general economic shift toward jobs that have been traditionally young typed, baby boomers are aging and competition for scarce human resources will likely become fierce. As a result of such labor market conditions, it is likely that older workers will retire later and begin occupying more traditionally young jobs, thus influencing labor market segmentation. These changes are likely to result in policy changes to our health-care system and social security program. Likewise, they are also likely to reiterate the call for increased government spending on technology training for the aging workforce. Thus, a dashed line is drawn from labor market realities to the broader societal context.

The top right portion of the figure depicts the emergence of job stereotypes. As noted earlier in this chapter, several authors have noted that labor market realities, such as the distribution of older, female, or minority workers in a particular field, set expectations of what a typical incumbent *should* look like (Gordon & Arvey, 1986; Shinar, 1975). Thus, there is a clear link between labor market realities and job stereotypes. To quote Gerald Weinberg, "things are the way they are, because they got that way." That is to say, young (male/White) jobs are considered young (male/White) because they've historically been held by younger (male/White) people. Thus, as shortages in labor supply increase and older workers, women, and minorities are hired into young-typed jobs, it is likely that perceptions of what a typical incumbent should look like will also change. Therefore, the relationship between labor market realities and job stereotypes is depicted as a dashed line. It should be noted, however, that this change is likely to be very slow.

The changes in the labor market and the ensuing need to hire older people into young jobs are inextricably intertwined with organizational decisions to hire and retain older women and minorities. That is, ultimately the changes in labor market segmentation rest on the shoulders of employers, who will undoubtedly need to fill positions. Thus, the dashed lines between organizational decision-making and labor market realities, as well as between organizational decision-making and the broader social context indicate that organizations are a key variable in breaking down the barriers to the advancement of older women and minorities, as a result of their power as a lobbying force for government reform and their direct influence on the realities of the labor market.

Likewise, as organizations begin to hire individuals into more stereotype-inconsistent jobs, perceptions of the typical job incumbent will begin to change in the long term. As an example, the job of pharmacist was historically viewed as a male-typed job. Over time, however, more female pharmacists were hired, such that the occupation is now considered female-typed (Tanner, Cockerill, Barnsley, & Williams, 1999). Thus, a dashed line is drawn between organizational decision-making and job stereotypes.

Finally, there are two dashed lines leading to person stereotypes. The first comes from the broader social context; the second comes from organizational decision-making. Although stereotypes change slowly, they are not completely immutable. For example, despite evidence that barriers exist for older workers, women, and minorities, a good deal of research suggests that these barriers have been declining since the passage of civil rights legislation in the 1960s (see Kaufman, 1994). Other social reform legislation, such as training programs subsidization, is also likely to slowly erode negative stereotypes held about older workers' trainability (Goldberg & Shore, 2003) and about the lower cognitive abilities of women and minorities (Hosoda et al., 2003).

DIRECTIONS FOR FUTURE RESEARCH

Much of this chapter has focused on the centrality of person and job stereotypes to the work experiences of older women and minorities. However, while there is evidence for a person by job matching process for age, gender, and race, separately (Goldberg et al., 2004; Hosoda et al., 2003; Perry, 1994, 1997), as noted earlier, research to date, has not expressly examined the stereotype matching process for multiple characteristics simultaneously. Future research examining the four-way effects of age, job age-type, gender, and job gender-type, as well as age, job age-type, race, and job race-type may shed some much needed light on the impact of belonging to two disadvantaged groups on individuals' work outcomes.

The proposed model also suggests that organizations can play an important role in reducing the barriers that exist to the employment and advancement of older women and minorities. However, very little research has examined the impact of organizational policies and practices on the outcomes of older women and minorities. Thus, research is needed to determine the effectiveness of such policies at increasing the selection and advancement of older female and minority employees.

Finally, as labor market realities are proposed to impact the suitability of older individuals to young-typed jobs, a longitudinal examination of the impact of stereotypes would further our understanding of how stereotypes might be abated. In particular, as labor market shortages are predicted in a number of fields in the coming years (Kindelan, 1998), a longitudinal examination may shed some light on the impact of such shortages on organizations' (and ultimately, society's) acceptance of older women and minorities in jobs traditionally held by young men and/or young Whites.

In conclusion, while older women and minorities have clearly faced obstacles in their access to and advancement in organizations, there is cause for optimism. As a society, it is unlikely that we can rely on the munificence of organizations to remedy inequality. However, labor market realities are likely to be an invisible hand that guides employers and society, at large, to reduce the barriers faced by older women and minorities.

REFERENCES

AARP (2003). Social Security and African Americans: Some Facts. Retrieved February 15, 2006 from http://www.aarp.org/research/socialsecurity/benefits/aresearch-import-366-FS94.html#SEVENTH

Anderson, N. H. (1991). Stereotype theory. In N. Anderson (Ed.), *Contributions to Information Integration Theory*. Hillsdale, NJ: Lawrence Erlbaum Associates.

Atwater, L. E., & VanFleet, D. D. (1997). Another ceiling? Can males compete for traditionally female jobs? *Journal of Management, 23*, 603–626.

Arvey, R. D., Miller, H. E., Gould, R., & Burch, P. (1987). Interview validity for selecting sales clerks. *Personnel Psychology, 40*, 1–12.

Avery, D. (2003). Reactions to diversity in recruitment advertising—Are differences Black and White? *Journal of Applied Psychology, 88*, 672–679.

Avolio, B. J., Waldman, D. A., & McDaniel, M. A. (1990). Age and work performance in nonmanagerial jobs: The effects of experience and occupation type. *Academy of Management Journal, 32*, 407–422.

Barnum, P., Liden, R. C., & DiTomaso, N. (1995). Double jeopardy for women and minorities: Pay differences with age. *Academy of Management Journal, 38*, 863–880.

Becker, P. E., & Moen, P. (1999). Scaling back: Dual-earner couples' work/family strategies. *Journal of Marriage and the Family, 61*, 995–1008.

Bem, S. L. (1974). The Measurement of Psychological Androgyny. *Journal of Consulting and Clinical Psychology, 42*, 155–62.

Borgatta, E. F. (1991). Age discrimination issues. *Research on Aging, 13*, 476–484.

Bowen, C., Swim, J. K., & Jacobs, R. R. (2000). Evaluating gender biases on actual job performance of real people: A meta-analysis. *Journal of Applied Social Psychology, 30*, 2194–2209.

Brewer, M., Dull, V., & Lui, L. (1981). Perceptions of the elderly: Stereotypes as prototypes. *Journal of Personality and Social Psychology, 41*, 656–670.

Busse, E., & Maddox, G. (1985). *The Duke longitudinal Studies of normal aging, 1955–1980: Overview of history, design, and findings*. New York: Springer.

Chang, S., & Kleiner, B. H. (2003). Common racial stereotypes. *Equal Opportunities International, 22*, 1–9.

Cleveland, J. N., & Berman, A. H. (1987). Age perceptions of jobs: Agreement between samples of students and managers. *Psychological Reports, 61*, 565–566.

Cleveland, J. N., & Landy, F. J. (1983). The effects of person and job stereotypes on two personnel decisions. *Journal of Applied Psychology*, 68, 609–619.

Cleveland, J. N., & Landy, F. J. (1987). Age perceptions of jobs: Convergence of two questionnaires. *Psychological Reports*, 60, 1075–1081.

Cleveland, J. N., & Shore, L. M. (1992). Self- and supervisory perspectives on age and work attitudes and performance. *Journal of Applied Psychology*, 77, 469–484.

Collins, S. M. (1997). *Black corporate executives: The making and breaking of the Black middle class*. Philadelphia: Temple University Press.

Cotter, D. A., DeFiore, J., Hermsen, J. M., Kowalewski, B., & Vanneman, R. (1997). All women benefit: The macro level effect of occupational integration on gender earnings equality. *American Sociological Review*, 62, 714–734.

Cox, T., & Nkomo, S. M. (1992). Candidate age as a factor in promotability ratings. *Public Personnel Management*, 21, 197–210.

Crew, J. C. (1983). Age stereotypes as a function of race. *Academy of Management Journal*, 27, 431–435.

Cumming, E., & Henry, W. (1961). *Growing old: The process of disengagement*. New York: Basic.

Dovidio, H. F., & Gaertner, S. L. (1996). Affirmative action, unintentional racial biases, and intergroup relations. *Journal of Social Issues*, 52, 41–75.

Dreher, G. F., & Cox, T. H. (1996). Race, gender, and opportunity: A study of compensation attainment and the establishment of mentoring relationships. *Journal of Applied Psychology*, 81, 297–309.

Eagly, A. H., Makhijani, M. G., & Klonsky, B. G. (1992). Gender and the evaluation of leaders: A meta-analysis. *Psychological Bulletin*, 111, 3–22.

Edwards, C., Robinson, O., Welchman, R., & Woodall, J. (1999). Lost opportunities? Organizational restructuring and women managers. *Human Resource Management Journal*, 9, 55–64.

Elias, P. K., Elias, M. F., Robbins, M. A., & George P. (1987). Acquisition of word-processing skills by younger, middle age, and older adults. *Psychology and Aging*, 2, 340–348.

Feagin, J. R., & Feagin, C. B. (1996). *Racial and Ethnic Relations*. Englewood Cliffs, NJ: Prentice Hall.

Finkelstein, L. M., Allen, T. D., & Rhoton, L. (2003). An examination of the effects of age diversity in mentoring relationships. *Group and Organization Management*, 28, 249–262.

Finkelstein, L. M., Burke, M. J., & Raju, N. S. (1995). Age discrimination in simulated employment contexts: An integrative analysis. *Journal of Applied Psychology*, 80, 40–45.

Flanagan, R. J. (1973). Segmented market theories and racial discrimination. *Industrial Relations*, 73, 253–258.

Folsom, A. R., & Cook, T. C. (1991). Differences in leisure-time physical activity levels between Blacks and Whites in population based samples: The Minnesota heart survey. *Journal of Behavioral Medicine*, 14, 1–9.

Fullerton, H. N., Jr., & Toosi, M. (2001). Labor force projections to 2010: Steady growth and changing composition. *Monthly Labor Review*, 124(11), 21–38.

Glick, P., Zion, C., & Nelson, C. (1988). What mediates sex discrimination in hiring decisions? *Journal of Personality and Social Psychology*, 55, 178–186.

Goldberg, C., Finkelstein, L., Perry, E., & Konrad, A. (2004). Job and industry fit: The effects of age and gender matches on career progress outcomes. *Journal of Organizational Behavior*, 25, 807–829.

Goldberg, C., & Konrad, A. (2002). The effects of gender context: A meta-analysis. Presented at the Academy of Management Conference. Denver, CO.

Goldberg, C., & Shore, L. M. (2003). The impact of age of applicants and of referent others on recruiters' assessments: A study of young and middle-aged job seekers. *Representative Research in Social Psychology, 27*, 11–22.

Gordon, R. A., & Arvey, R. D. (1986). Perceived and actual ages of workers. *Journal of Vocational Behavior, 28*, 21–28.

Grodsky, E., & Pager, D. (2001). The structure of disadvantage: Individual and occupational determinants of the black-white wage gap. *American Sociological Review, 66*, 542–608.

Havighurst, R. J., & Albrecht, R. A. (1953). *Older People.* New York: Longmans, Green Publishers.

Havighurst, R., Neugarten, B., & Tobin, S. (1996). Disengagement, personality, and life satisfaction in the later years. In D. Neugarter (Ed.), *The Meanings of age: Selected papers of Bernice L. Neugarten* (pp. 281–287). Chicago: University of Chicago Press.

Heywood, J. S., Ho, L., & Wei, X. (1999). The determinants of hiring older workers: Evidence from Hong Kong. *Industrial and Labor Relations Review, 52*, 444–459.

Hirsch, B. T., Macpherson, D. A., & Hardy, M. A. (2000). Occupational age structure and access for older workers. *Industrial & Labor Relations Review, 53*, 401–418.

Hosoda, M., Stone, D. L., & Stone-Romero, E. F. (2003). The interactive effects of race, gender, and job type on job suitability ratings and selection decisions. *Journal of Applied Social Psychology, 33*, 145–178.

Huffcutt, A., & Roth, P. (1998). Racial group differences in employment interview evaluations. *Journal of Applied Psychology, 83*, 179–190.

Institute for Women's Policy Research. (2005). *Persistent Inequalities: Poverty, Lack of Health Coverage, Wage Gaps Plague Economic Recovery, Says Institute for Women's Policy Research.* Retrieved September 1, 2005 from http://releases.usnewswire.com/GetRelease.asp?id = 52292

James, E. H. (2000). Race-related differences in promotions and support: Underlying effects of human and social capital. *Organization Science, 11*, 493–512.

Kanter, R. M. (1977). Some effects of proportions on group life: Skewed sex ratios and responses to token women. *American Journal of Sociology, 82*, 965–990.

Kaufman, B. E. (1994). *The Economics of Labor Markets* (4th ed.). Fort Worth, TX: The Dryden Press.

Kaufman, R. (2001). Race and labor market segmentation. In I. Berg & A. Kalleberg (Eds.), *Sourcebook of labor markets* (pp. 645–668). New York: Kluwer Academic Publishing.

Kausler, D. H., & Kausler, B. C. (2001). *The Graying of America: An encyclopedia of aging, health, mind, and behavior.* Urbana, IL: University of Illinois Press.

Kindelan, A. (1998). Older workers can alleviate labor shortages, *HRMagazine, 43*, 200.

Kite, M., Deaux, K., & Miele, M. (1991). Stereotypes of young and old: Does age outweigh gender? *Psychology and Aging, 6*, 19–27.

Kolb, P. J. (2002). Developmental theories of aging. In S. G. Austrian (Ed.), *Developmental theories through the life cycle* (pp. 264–324). New York, NY: Columbia University Press.

Konrad, A. M., & Cannings, K. (1997). The effects of gender role congruence and statistical discrimination on managerial advancement. *Human Relations, 50*, 1305–1328.

Knoke, D., & Ishio, Y. (1998). The gender gap in company training. *Work and Occupations, 25*, 141–168.

Krefting, L. A., Berger, P. K., & Wallace, M. J. (1978). The contribution of sex distribution, job content, and occupational classification to job sextyping: Two studies. *Journal of Vocational Behavior, 13*, 181–191.

Landau, J. (1995). The relationship of race and gender to managers' ratings of promotion potential. *Journal of Organizational Behavior, 16*, 391–400.

Lawrence, B. S. (1988). New wrinkles in the theory of age: Demography, norms, and performance ratings. *Academy of Management Journal, 31*, 309–337.

Lawrence, C. (2004, January 4). Race pay gap persists at all grad levels. *Chicago Sun-Times*, 3A.

Levinson, D., Darrow, C., Klein, E., Levinson, M., & McKee, B. (1978). *The seasons of a man's life*. New York: Knopf.

Lin, T. R., Dobbins, G. H., & Farh, J. L. (1992). A field study of race and age similarity effects on interview ratings in conventional and situational interviews. *Journal of Applied Psychology, 77*, 363–371.

Lyness, K., & Thompson, D. E. (2000). Climbing the corporate ladder: Do female and male executives follow the same route? *Journal of Applied Psychology, 85*, 86–99.

Maume, D. J. (1999). Glass ceilings and glass escalators: Occupational segregation and race and sex differences in managerial promotions. *Work & Occupations, 26*, 483–509.

Maurer, T. J., & Rafuse, N. E. (2001). Learning, not litigating: Managing employee development and avoiding claims of age discrimination. *Academy of Management Executive, 15*, 110–121.

McEvoy, G. M., & Cascio, W. F. (1989). Cumulative evidence of the relationship between employee age and job performance. *Journal of Applied Psychology, 74*, 11–17.

Motowidlo, S. (1986). Information processing in personnel decisions. In K. M. Rowland & G. R. Ferris (Eds.), *Research in Personnel and Human Resources Management: Vol. 4* (pp. 1–44). Greenwich, CT: JAI Press.

Noe, R. (1988). Women and mentoring: A review and research agenda. *Academy of Management Review, 13*, 65–79.

O'Neill, R., & Blake-Beard, S. (2002). Gender barriers to the female mentor–male protégé relationship. *Journal of Business Ethics, 37*, 51–64.

Peck, R. (1968). Psychological developments in the second half of life. In B. Neugarten (Ed.), *Middle Age and Aging: A Reader in Social Psychology* (pp. 88–92), Chicago: University of Chicago Press.

Perry, E. L. (1994). A prototype matching approach to understanding the role of applicant gender and age in the evaluation of job applicants. *Journal of Applied Social Psychology, 24*, 1433–1473.

Perry, E. L. (1997). A cognitive approach to understanding discrimination: A closer look at applicant gender and age. In G. R. Ferris (Ed.), *Research in Personnel and Human Resources Management: Vol. 15* (175–240). Greenwich, CT: JAI Press.

Perry, E. L., & Bourhis, A. C. (1998). A closer look at the role of applicant age in selection decisions. *Journal of Applied Social Psychology, 28*, 16–30.

Powell, G. N., & Butterfield, D. A. (1989). The "good manager": Did androgyny fare better in the 1980s? *Group & Organization Studies, 14*, 216–233.

Powell, G. N., & Butterfield, D. A. (2000). Gender and managerial stereotypes: Have the times changed? *Journal of Management, 28*, 177–193.

Prewett-Livingston, A., Field, H., Veres, J., & Lewis, P. (1996). Effects of race on interview ratings in a situational panel interview. *Journal of Applied Psychology, 81*, 178–186.

Ragins, B. R., & Cotton, J. L. (1999). Mentor functions and outcomes: A comparison of men and women in formal and informal mentoring relationships. *Journal of Applied Psychology, 84*, 529–541.

Raza, S. M., & Carpenter, B. (1987). A model of hiring decisions in real employment interviews. *Journal of Applied Psychology, 72*, 596–603.

Roos, P. A., & Gatta, M. L. (1999). The gender gap in earnings: Trends, explanations, and prospects. In G. Powell (Ed.), *Handbook of gender & work* (pp. 263–280). Thousand Oaks, CA: Sage Publications.

Rosen, B., & Jerdee, T. H. (1976a). The influence of age stereotypes on managerial decisions. *Journal of Applied Psychology, 62*, 428–432.

Rosen, B., & Jerdee, T. H. (1976b). The nature of job-related age stereotypes. *Journal of Applied Psychology, 62*, 180–183.

Rowe, J., & Kahn, R. (1998). *Successful aging.* New York: Pantheon.

Rynes, S. L., Bretz, R. D., & Gerhart, B. (1991). The importance of recruitment in job choice: A different way of looking. *Personnel Psychology, 44*, 487–521.

Salthouse, T. A. (1987). Age, experience, and compensation. In C. Schooler & K. Schaie (Eds.), *Cognitive functioning and social structure over the life course.* New York: Ablex.

Schmidt, F. L., & Hunter, J. E. (1998). The validity and utility of selection methods in personnel selection: Practical and theoretical implications of 85 years of research findings. *Psychological Bulletin, 124*, 262–274.

Schneider, B. (1987). The people make the place. *Personnel Psychology, 40*, 437–453.

Shinar, E. H. (1975). Sexual stereotypes of occupations. *Journal of Vocational Behavior, 7*, 99–111.

Shore, L. M., Cleveland, J. N., & Goldberg, C. (2003). Work attitudes and decisions as a function of manager age and employee age. *Journal of Applied Psychology, 88*, 529–537.

Smith, A., & Stewart, A. J. (1983). Approaches to studying racism and sexism in Black women's lives. *Journal of Social Issues. 39*, 1–15.

Smith, D. B., & Moen, P. (2004). Retirement satisfaction for retirees and their spouses: Do gender and retirement decision making process matter? *Journal of Family Issues, 25*, 262–290.

Sorensen, J. B. (2004). The Organizational Demography of Racial Employment Segregation. *American Journal of Sociology, 110*, 626–671.

Spurr, S. J. (1990). Sex discrimination in the legal profession: A study of promotion. *Industrial & Labor Relations Review, 43*, 406–418.

Stauffer, J. M., & Buckley, R. M. (2005). The existence and nature of racial bias in supervisory ratings, *Journal of Applied Psychology, 90*, 586–591.

Steinberg, S. (1995). *Turning back: The retreat from racial justice in American thought and policy.* Boston, MA: Beacon Press.

Stoller, E., & Gibson, R. (2000). *Worlds of difference: Inequality in the aging experience.* Thousand Oaks, CA: Pine Forge Press.

Stroh, L. K., Brett, M. J., & Reilly, A. H. (1992). All the right stuff: A comparison of female and male managers' career progression. *Journal of Applied Psychology, 77*, 251–260.

Tan, A., Fujioka, Y., & Lucht, N. (1997). Native American stereotypes, TV portrayals, and personal contact. *Journalism and Mass Communication Quarterly, 73*, 265–284.

Tanner, J., Cockerill, R., Barnsley, J., & Williams, A. P. (1999). Gender and income in pharmacy: Human capital and gender stratification theories revisited. *The British Journal of Sociology, 50*, 97–109.

Thomas, D. A. (1990). The impact of race on managers' experiences of developmental relationships (mentoring and sponsorship): An intra-organizational study. *Journal of Organizational Behavior, 11*, 479–493.

Thomas, K. M., & Wise, P. G. (1999). Organizational attractiveness and individual differences: Are diverse applicants attracted by different factors? *Journal of Business and Psychology, 13*, 375–390

Tosi, H., & Einbender, S. (1985). The effects of the type and amount of information in sex discrimination research: A meta-analysis. *Academy of Management Journal, 28*, 712–723.

U.S. Bureau of Labor Statistics (2004). Unemployed persons by age, sex, race, Hispanic or Latino ethnicity, marital status, and duration of unemployment. Retrieved September 1, 2005 from ftp://ftp.bls.gov/pub/special.requests/lf/aat31.txt

Waldman, D., & Avolio, B. (1986). A meta-analysis of age differences in job performance. *Journal of Applied Psychology, 71*, 33–38.

Watane, C., & Gibson, J. (2001). Barriers to employment-related training in New Zealand: Differences across ethnic groups. *New Zealand Journal of Industrial Relations, 26*, 227–235.

5

An Expanded View of Age Bias in the Workplace

Lisa M. Finkelstein and Sara K. Farrell

This chapter addresses the topic of age bias at work from a broad perspective, providing new insights to the field by taking into account research on age bias and bias in general. The tripartite model of attitudes and Fiske's (2004) social bias framework (subtle vs. blatant bias, core motives of bias) are both used to structure the discussion of age bias research. Motives, mediators (e.g., stereotyping, attribution, communication accommodation), and moderators (e.g., context at varying levels, ratee/rater characteristics) of age bias are each considered and research in each of these areas is reviewed. Practical suggestions for reducing age bias at work are considered from the perspective of the bias holder, the target, the organization, and the larger culture. The chapter concludes with suggestions for future research on the measurement of workplace bias, on considering social-psychological theories of bias, and on collecting evidence for potential solutions to age bias at work.

A TALE

Amy knocked on her supervisor's door. "Joan, I'm sorry but I really don't think that I am going to get through all of these reports by our 5:00 deadline." Joan sighed and thought for a minute. "Okay, let's look at our options. I think either Margaret or Jessica should be able to spare a few hours." "Thanks, Joan." Amy turned to leave and pondered which cubicle to approach. Tight deadline, reviewing, and editing reports via computer . . . better ask Jessica. Margaret must be 55 or so; that might be a bit much for her. She knocked on the wall at the entrance of Jessica's cubicle. "Hey, Jessica! I really need your help. Can you work on reports with me so we can get them out by 5? Joan says it's okay."

Two hours later . . .

"Well, that should do it. Sure feels good to have the last report out of our hands." Jessica leaned on the desk. *"Hey, do you think we should ask Margaret to come along?"* Amy turned to look at Jessica. *"Are you kidding? I'm sure the last thing she would want to do is hang out at a place like Lenny's after work . . . rock music, big crowd . . . I'm sure she just wants to get home and have dinner."*

Our question to you, the reader: Is this a tale of age bias in the workplace?

OUR PURPOSE

Our purpose for this chapter is to tackle the issue of age bias against older individuals in the workplace from a broad perspective, acknowledging the very complex nature of bias. Age bias at work is not a new research focus, although it arguably has received considerably less attention than other social biases (Nelson, 2005). A small but steady stream of empirical studies began in the 1970s and has continued to flow over the years. Laments by reviewers of the literature of methodological drawbacks, a scattered focus of issues, and lack of attention to theory (e.g., Finkelstein, Burke, & Raju, 1995) continue to be addressed more and more. Reviews have begun to appear with more frequency, updating where the research stands on major issues and providing more helpful conceptual frameworks for understanding age discrimination (e.g., Gordon & Arvey, 2004; Perry & Parlamis, 2005; Shore & Goldberg, 2004). This is encouraging and emphasizes an appreciation of this issue to the world of work. However, it left us pondering, what can we add?

We realized that the workplace age bias literature could benefit from a step back—a wider lens—that takes a broader look at advances in the literature on age bias in general (outside the workplace), and an even more panoramic lens taking into account newer approaches to studying bias in general (not just age). In addition, while access discrimination has been a common focus of the age bias literature, the everyday treatment of older workers with regard to issues such as communication and social networks (as demonstrated in the tale above) are deserving of attention as well. Our goal, then, was to borrow from the developments in these broader literatures to see if they could (a) provide some new insight to the work already done in age bias at work, and (b) point to new avenues for future work that would be solidly grounded in developed theory. We will begin by providing a taste of this general literature, and then review the existing age bias at work literature with this broader perspective in mind. We organize our review around what we anticipate to be key questions in the mind of the reader (Why? How? When/Where? Who? What can we do?) regarding the problem of age bias at work.

AGE BIAS AT WORK: WHAT ARE WE TALKING ABOUT?

We thought it might be informative to let the reader in on a behind-the-scenes conversation that ensued between the two authors of this chapter, and later between the first author and one of the editors. After accepting the honor of writing a chapter for this book, the two authors sat down and (as we imagine many coauthors do) looked at each other, took a deep breath, and said, "Okay, how do we start?" We reviewed the chapter specs provided from our editors, and saw once again that we were to write about age bias in the workplace. We realized that although we were quite sure we knew what a workplace was, we weren't absolutely sure we knew what we should cover under this umbrella of age bias. What *is* age bias, anyway?

Embarrassing as it was, the first author arranged for a phone meeting with one of our fine editors, and laid our concerns on the line. Are we talking about age stereotypes? Discrimination? Prejudice? Ageist attitudes? It turns out he hadn't quite thought about that either at this stage, and agreed that these were important questions. The ultimate approach was left up to us.

These conversations were eye-openers in that they brought to light the fact that the age bias in employment literature has not been explicitly clear about what is meant by age bias and the myriad forms it can take in the workplace. This solidified our resolve that a broader social-psychological perspective on bias could do us all some good.

THE TRIPARTITE VIEW

Looking at the broader literature, one can see that the tripartite view of attitudes can provide a basic framework for tackling the complexity of the term bias (e.g., Fiske, 2004; Kite & Smith Wagner, 2002). This view holds that there are three distinct components to an attitude, or an evaluation of a social object. There is a cognitive component, comprised of beliefs and expectancies about a social object due to membership in a particular group—this is where our stereotypes come into play. Age stereotypes have been a central focus of the workplace age bias research. Reported in this body of research are stereotypes such as absent-minded (Kogan & Shelton, 1960), resistant to change, lacking in creativity, slow in judgment, lower physical capacity, disinterest in technology, untrainability (Rosen & Jerdee, 1976b, 1977; Taylor & Walker, 1998), making fewer contributions (Perry & Varney, 1978), less ambitious, more opinionated (Craft, Doctors, Shkop, & Benecki, 1979), lower potential for development (Crew, 1984; Gibson, Zerbe, & Franken, 1993; Rosen & Jerdee, 1976a), low energy (Levin, 1988), less flexible (Vrugt & Schabracq,

1996), not working well in teams (Lyon & Pollard, 1997), and being less economically beneficial (Finkelstein, Higgins, & Clancy, 2000). Conversely, some studies have either found a lack of endorsement of negative stereotypes (e.g., Connor, Walsh, Litzelman, & Alvarez, 1978; Drehmer, Carlucci, Bordieri, & Pincus, 1992; Hassell & Perrewe, 1995; Weiss & Maurer, 2004) or endorsement of other positive stereotypes, such as wise (Kogan & Shelton, 1960) and experienced (Finkelstein et al., 2000). Avolio and Barrett (1987) suggested that differences in judgments regarding older and younger workers might be due to a positive stereotype about younger workers, not necessarily a negative one about older workers.

There is also a behavioral component to an attitude, relating to our tendency to treat others in a particular manner due to their social category membership. The actual behavior toward individuals due solely to group membership and not relevant individuating characteristics is unfair discrimination. Age discrimination at work has also been a key focus of workplace age bias research (cf. Gordon & Arvey, 2004), largely focusing on major decisions in a workplace context (e.g., selection, promotion, training opportunities). It should be noted that age stereotypes are quite often assumed (and occasionally shown) to be a precursor to age discrimination, but we see from bias work in general that the cognitive and behavioral components are often only modestly related (e.g., $r =$ .16; Dovidio, Brigham, Johnson, & Gaertner, 1996, as reported in Fiske, 2004). Limiting the explanation of discrimination to stereotyping alone could obscure our understanding of what we can actually do to reduce discrimination. Further, lack of actual discrimination in employment-related decisions about people of different ages does not necessarily imply that stereotypes are not present and insidiously operating in other ways.

Third, there is an affective component of a biased attitude. This appears to be the least consistently conceptualized and measured in the bias literature. To some, this affective component is the actual evaluative component. In other words, is the social object good or bad along a general or specific dimension? (cf. Kite, Stockdale, Whitley, & Johnson, 2005). To others, the affective component is more indicative of actual feelings—or negative "hot" emotions on the part of the bias holder. Do we dislike, feel uncomfortable around, or even hate the social object? When we speak of prejudice, we may be talking of an overall evaluation encompassing our thoughts, feelings and behavioral tendencies, or we may be homing in on affect (Fiske, 2004). This lack of consistency in how this third component is interpreted has made it difficult to determine if the literature is truly tackling this affective piece of the puzzle. However, we feel comfortable asserting that this is the least examined form of age bias in the workplace literature, and may be one place we could do better in attempting to really understand what's happening.

So, what is age bias at work? It can be some or all of these things—our thoughts and beliefs about older workers, our feelings and evaluations of older workers, as well as our treatment of older workers in big decisions and in everyday interactions. We try to clarify which components of bias are being considered as we move through our literature review, and in Table 5.1 we provide an overview of this attempt. We stress that this is our attempt at categorizing these articles using our definitions of these three facets as described previously. Others could see it differently. We were encouraged to see that some very recent work by Rupp and colleagues (Rupp, Vodanovich, & Credé, 2005; in press) has begun applying the tripartite view to age bias at work; specifics of this work will be discussed in more detail later in this chapter. First, we continue to consider more specific theoretical perspectives on bias that may inform our overview and outlook.

SETTING THE STAGE

In addition to emphasizing the importance of the tripartite view of social biases, Fiske (2004) provided a meta-framework for classifying myriad views of bias into two main conceptual categories: subtle and blatant. She argues that historical and current theories of bias can be considered from this perspective, and that these types of bias are driven by different core human motives. To set the stage for the application of various bias theories to age bias at work, we created Table 5.2, borrowing from Fiske's framework to categorize and briefly describe several social-psychological theories of bias. Many of these were suggested in her chapter, and others we have found in other works on bias. Our treatment of each is admittedly cursory; the purpose is only to introduce the main ideas so that we can begin to apply them to the age bias at work literature, and encourage other researchers in the area to consider them in their work.

Fiske (2004) describes four core motives that underlie social bias. The first motive, *understanding*, reflects the idea that without malicious intention, individuals strive to make sense of the world and do this largely through the use of schemas, expectancies, and categories. The second motive, *belonging*, refers to the idea that as humans we are driven to feel a sense of being a part of a group, connected to others. Biases that favor one's own group can enhance this sense. *Controlling* is a third core motive that refers to our desire to have a sense of control in our lives and to avoid threat. Finally, the fourth core motive is *enhancing self* and refers to people's need to have a positive view of the self. The various motives can lead one to either a subtle, more insidious type of bias, or a more blatant and recognized type of bias. Subtle forms of bias are unlikely to be acknowledged by the bias holder, not merely out of social desirability concerns but out of true lack of awareness that the social bias is occurring.

TABLE 5.1.

Categorization of Age Bias at Work Articles According to the Tripartite View of Bias

Source	Stereotyping	Prejudice	Discrimination
Avolio & Barrett (1987)	X		X
Bird & Fisher (1986)	X	X	
Chiu, Chan Snape, & Redman (2001)	X	X	X
Cleveland & Landy (1983)	X		X
Cleveland & Landy (1987)	X		
Cleveland, Festa, & Montgomery (1988)	X		X
Connor, Walsh, Litzelman, & Alvarez (1978)	X	X	X
Craft, Doctors, Shkop, & Benecki (1979)	X		X
Crew (1984)	X		
Dedrick & Dobbins (1991)	X		X
Finkelstein & Burke (1998)	X		X
Finkelstein, Burke, & Raju (1995)	X		X
Finkelstein, Higgins, & Clancy (2000)	X		X
Fusilier & Hitt (1983)	X		X
Gordon & Arvey (1986)	X		
Gordon & Arvey (2004)	X		X
Gordon, Rozelle, & Baxter (1988)	X	X	X
Gordon, Rozelle, & Baxter (1989)	X		X
Haefner (1977)			X
Hassell & Perrewe (1995)	X		
Kalavar (2001)	X	X	X
Kogan & Shelton (1960)	X		
Lawrence (1988)	X		X
Lee & Clemons (1985)	X		X
Levin (1988)	X		
Liden, Stilwell, & Ferris (1996)	X		X
Lin, Dobbins, & Farh (1992)			X
Locke-Connnor & Walsh (1980)	X		X
Loretto, Duncan & White (2000)	X	X	X
Lyon & Pollard (1997)	X		
Perry & Varney (1978)	X		
Perry (1994)	X		X
Perry & Bouhris (1998)	X		X
Perry, Kulik, & Bourhis (1996)	X		X
Remery, Henkens, Schippers, & Ekamper (2003)	X	X	X
Rosen & Jerdee (1976b)	X		X
Rosen & Jerdee (1977)	X		X
Rupp, Vodanovich, & Credé (in press)	X	X	X
Shore, Cleveland, & Goldberg (2003)			X
Singer & Sewell (1989)	X		X
Singer (1987)	X		

(continued)

TABLE 5.1. (*Continued*)

Source	Stereotyping	Prejudice	Discrimination
Triandis (1963)			X
Vrugt & Schabraq (1996)	X		
Weiss & Maurer (2004)	X		X

Note. We attempted a comprehensive search of published articles on age bias in the workplace at the time this chapter was written, yet cannot guarantee that every relevant study is represented in this table. Additionally, our categorization is based on our understanding of three components of bias and our interpretation of whether these articles do (or do not) address these components. We realize that other researchers may have different interpretations.

*a*We chose the term "prejudice" to capture the affective and evaluative category. Articles here may differ to the degree that they are capturing pure affect and not a more cognitively laden evaluation, as described further in the text.

WHY MIGHT WE HOLD AGE BIASES AT WORK?
(THE MOTIVATORS)

Considering the multitude of theoretical perspectives on bias, what might motivate age bias at work? Fiske's (2004) approach is advantageous as it addresses what drives bias, and acknowledges that bias can be prompted from different needs in individuals. This type of consideration has been quite limited thus far in the age bias in employment literature, although Snyder and Miene (1994), in the general age bias literature, argued for an examination of the functions of age-biased attitudes. Several of Snyder and Miene's attitude functions map onto the core motives: a cognitive economy function (understanding), an ego-protective function (self-enhancement), and a social function (belonging). If we acknowledge that age bias at work can be driven internally by different forces in different people, or combinations of forces in any one person, we may be in a better position to tackle the problem from the source.

The core motive of understanding (Fiske, 2004) is certainly likely to operate in many circumstances in the workplace. Given complex environments encouraging multitasking, individuals are likely to seek shortcuts to understanding people at work. Cognitive underpinnings for age bias at work have been acknowledged in the literature. Certain situations or contexts may prompt a heightened need in an individual for understanding; we will discuss such contextual moderators throughout this chapter. Social role theory (cf. Kite & Smith Wagner, 2002) describes why the shortcuts we take under certain circumstances might result in age bias. As the portrayals of productive individuals in our society are not often old, we may not associate older people

TABLE 5.2.
A Selected Overview of Bias Research Applicable to Age Bias at Work

Theory	Example citation	General premise
Theories Reflecting Subtle Bias (*Core motives: understanding, enhancing self*)[a]		
Continuum Model of Stereotyping	Fiske & Neuberg (1990)	Stereotyping occurs unless individuating information is available, leading to more complex processing
Stereotype Content Model	Cuddy, Norton, & Fiske (2005)	All social groups can be categorized on two dimensions: competence and warmth.
Social Role Theory	Kite & Wagner-Smith (2002)	We come to associate characteristics of a particular social role with groups who tend fill that role, resulting in stereotypes
Illusory Correlation	Hamilton & Sherman (1994)	When a rare person and rare event co-occur, witnesses may perceive that they are related
Communication Adaptation Theory; Communication Enhancement Theory	Nussbaum, Pitts, Huber, Raup Krieger, & Ohs (2005)	People adjust their speech depending on their communication partner to increase efficiency, gain approval, or remain distinctive
Prototype Matching Theory	Perry (1994)	Raters compare worker information to job information to make decisions

Complexity-Extremity Effect	Linville (1982)	People have less complex schemas regarding outgroups leading them to evaluate outgroup members more extremely
Shifting Standards Model	Biernet, Mannis, & Nelson (1991)	The same absolute evaluation has a different meaning for members of different groups (e.g., smart when referring to a child versus an adult)
Implicit Ageism	Levy & Banaji (2002)	Some ageism is reflective of an implicit attitude, distinct from explicit, conscious ageism
Theories Reflecting Blatant Bias (*Core motives: control, belonging, enhancing self*)		
Social Identity Theory; Self Categorization Theory	Turner (1985)	People categorize themselves into groups that allow them to maintain a positive social identity
Career Timetables Perspective	Lawrence (1988)	Normative expectations of where a person should be in the organizational hierarchy at a given age
Social Judgability Theory	Leyens, Yzerbyt, & Schandron (1992)	People make judgments about others only when they feel entitled to do so
Terror Management Theory	Martens, Goldenberg, & Greenberg (2005)	When mortality is salient, the self is threatened leading people to respond negatively to outgroups
Realistic Conflict Theory	Bobo (1983)	Prejudice develops over actual competition over scarce and valued resources

*Categorization framework based on Fiske (2004).

with the role of effective worker. Moreover, research using the stereotype content model has found evidence that we may tend to automatically categorize older individuals as warm but not competent (Cuddy & Fiske, 2002), thus likely not considering an older person a match for many work environments. This also emphasizes that there is often ambivalence involved in our perceptions of older workers that might lead us to believe that we are truly not biased.

Research that looks at how this motive can be satisfied *without* ultimately resulting in age bias is needed. We should dig further into what might prevent us from realizing that we are making biased judgments in our quest for true understanding. As one example, the shifting standards model (Biernat, Manis, & Nelson, 1991) suggests that we may believe we are judging a person in a positive way (an older person as quick), but due to our different group standards (quick "for her age"), our biases may ultimately impact a choice among individuals.

The drive for belonging could be aroused in a workplace in many circumstances. An organizational culture that induces a strong sense of identity to the organization may satisfy the drive for belonging along a dimension other than age (or any other particularly salient social group). If age, however, is homogenous among a particular work group, it may be a salient feature upon which others are distinguished. A lack of a sense of strong social belonging in other areas of life could prompt a stronger tie to a work-related group. Social identity theory and self categorization theory (cf. Turner, 1985) have been applied to the age bias at work literature to explain preferences of one's own age group in ratings; we shall see that this finding has not been consistent in the literature, and this could be because (a) age is not a salient or important source of identity for everyone, and (b) other groups may be satisfying belonging motives.

The need for control may become aroused in the workplace if a situation arose that was seen as somehow threatening. Perhaps a major change in job responsibilities or impending restructuring could lead to an increased need for control, putting one on the road to age bias if somehow age became tied into the perceived threat. Realistic conflict theory (e.g., Bobo, 1983), for example, suggests that if there is seen to be a shortage of resources in a situation, biases can result from an effort to gain control.

A need for self-enhancement differs from the others in that it is personal in nature—it is not a tie to a group that is important but a need for a feeling of worth as an individual. Fiske (2004) notes that an immediate threat to one's self, as opposed to one's group, could increase derogation of different others. In terms of age bias at work, propping oneself up one might involve emphasizing the benefits of youth or the derogation of an older individual. A compatible view likely relevant to age bias in the workplace is terror management theory (TMT; Martens, Goldenberg, & Greenberg, 2005). This perspective suggests that when mortality is made salient, people may be driven to view themselves as less like older individuals *and* to view older individuals more negatively. Further, the strong fear component involved in TMT could motivate an age bias manifested more in affect—dislike, disgust, and desired avoidance. TMT implicates the core motive of self-enhancement because mortality salience awakens a threat to the "continuity of the self" (Fiske, 2004, p. 443). Could it also be that older workers awaken a threat to the "continuity of the *work* self," (e.g., retirement, obsolescence in productive society) eventually leading to bias?

In sum, we believe motives matter, and they may differ by individual and circumstance. Little attention in the age bias in employment literature has been given to motives, and we see that as a place for needed empirical work. We will continue to refer to potential motives that might drive bias in various circumstances and in different ways for different people throughout the chapter.

WHAT IS THE PROCESS THAT IT TAKES?
(THE MEDIATORS)

Now that we have considered various motives that may *initiate* bias, we can address the *process* that it takes in the workplace. Few studies have explicitly (statistically) tested mediators in this literature. Only with an understanding of the potential underlying causal mechanisms involved in producing age bias events at work will we be fully prepared to reduce their likelihood. In this section we have compiled the existing work on mediating mechanisms, or factors that provide reasons for the occurrence of incidents at work involving age bias.

The use of stereotypes to explain discrimination. As noted earlier, commonly held stereotypes about older workers are often used to explain why there is age discrimination in the workplace. Various theoretical approaches used to explain discrimination include stereotypes as a key link in the process (e.g., Shore & Goldberg, 2004). Surprisingly, little of the research on age discrimination in the workplace has made a direct, empirical link connecting an endorsement of general stereotypes about older workers to behaviors or decisions toward a specific older worker. One of the most commonly cited studies in the literature is Rosen and Jerdee's 1976b study (replicated in 1977), where discrimination was found against older workers described in scenarios based *around* assumed stereotypes regarding older workers' resistance to change, lack of creativity, slowness of judgment, lower physical capacity, disinterest in technology, and untrainability. These studies, however, did not measure participants' endorsement of those beliefs and, as such, do not provide direct evidence of stereotype elicitation as a mediator explaining discrimination, though they do imply that the reason one would differentiate a young and old person while other variables are held constant involves differing beliefs about the older or younger people along those dimensions. Notably, Weiss, and Maurer (2004) recently did an exact replication of that classic study and only found discrimination evidence in the resistance to change scenario.

Avolio and Barrett (1987) reasoned that if age stereotypes were being used in interview rating decisions, this could be detected by examining whether certain types of personality traits embedded in candidate information would be more salient if they corresponded with expected age stereotypes. Their study failed to yield this result. Cleveland and Landy (1983) found that a pattern of behavior stereotypical of an older person was predictive of negative personnel decisions whereas age per se was not. Age alone may not lead to stereotyping, but when a clear pattern of age-stereotypical behavior is present, discrimination may be more likely.

Perry (1994) elaborated on the stereotyping explanation for age-biased decisions by fleshing out the idea of person-in-job prototypes, emphasizing that a decision about a person in a job may elicit a prototype that includes both central and peripheral features, and that the importance of age in our ultimate decision is impacted by whether age is typically associated with the more central features of our person-in-job prototype. She did find supporting evidence for this process (Perry, 1994; Perry & Bourhis, 1998). As different jobs are associated with different person-in-job prototypes, this mediating mechanism must be considered in conjunction with job type, a moderator discussed in the next section. Perry, Kulik, and Bourhis (1996) directly addressed the link between age stereotypes (using semantic differentials) and discrimination in a simulated hiring context and did not find a simple relationship, but found it to be moderated by other contextual factors, discussed in the following section. Thus, Perry's program of research points to a complex interplay between cognition and context.

Finkelstein et al. (2000) content analyzed open-ended responses to see if raters would justify their decisions about an older applicant in a way that would be reflective of stereotypical beliefs. They found that age was more likely to be mentioned as a justification for decisions when a participant had made a decision about an older versus younger person. More specifically, justifications were often related to the cost of an older worker, suggesting an economic-based stereotype. Experience came up more often as a justification for those who viewed an older applicant than for those viewing the younger applicant, though experience was held constant. An early study by Craft et al. (1979) found less willingness to hire the older workers, and the explanation given was often a straightforward mention of their age. Those willing to hire the older individual often cited experienced as the reason, supporting this positive belief about older people (as there was no particular evidence that that person was particularly experienced).

Chiu, Chan, Snape, and Redman (2001) directly measured the relationship between endorsement of adaptability/work effectiveness stereotypes and behavioral intentions regarding decisions on training, promotion, retention, coworking, and a preference for choosing an older over younger worker. They did find adaptability stereotypes to predict these attitudes. Rupp, Vodanovich, and Credé (in press) found a connection between ageist stereotypes and endorsing harsher consequences in the face of poor performance for an older worker. Note that Rupp et al. discussed ageism as a moderator, in that those managers with ageist attitudes were more likely to be harsher toward an older person than those who were not. We review this here as a mediating mechanism as we view it to be theoretically related to the why of age-biased decisions.

The connection from affect to discrimination. The distinction between this section and the former is that here we look for work that has explained age-biased behavior at work through negative affect, rather than cognitions. As we've been emphasizing, the line here is blurry as many stereotypes carry with them a negative connotation. For example, being thought of as resistant to change implies a negative evaluation, particularly in a situation that calls for change. Thus, we believe it is important to distinguish this component of the tripartite view by looking specifically at work that has focused on affect or feelings about older people, or at a minimum has looked at evaluation (e.g., good/bad) in general, distinct from a specific cognition.

Most of what we found relevant to this question has been outside the area of workplace research. Rothbaum (1983), for example, expressed concern that measures of age bias needed to distinguish between beliefs about characteristics older people are likely to possess (stereotypes) and how people feel about those characteristics (affect/attitude). Other scale developers have alluded to the multidimensional nature of bias (e.g., Intrieri, von Eye, & Kelly, 1995; Kogan, 1961) but a clear distinction between affective and cognitive components is not often made. Recently Rupp et al. (2005) factor analyzed the Fraboni Scale of Ageism (FSA), which appears to be the first to measure ageism with consideration of the tripartite model. Rupp and colleagues (in press) showed that individuals higher on the affective subscale of ageism were likely to assign more negative recommendations for an older person following poor performance. Thus, they found evidence of a connection between affect and behavior *and* between stereotypes and behavior.

A recent nonwork study (Chasteen, Schwarz, & Park, 2002) demonstrated the distinction between affect and stereotypes and acknowledged the potential of implicit bias. In this study, a priming and reaction time measure was used to assess these cognitive and affective biases independently. They found that individuals responded faster to stereotypically old traits following an old prime (stereotyping), but did *not* find faster responses when negative (vs. positive) traits followed an old prime. In fact, both older and younger participants seemed to show more positive affect toward elderly than young people.

They tied this into the stereotype content model, indicating that this is commensurate with reactions to older people viewed as warm (such that we would like them) but not competent. They did not directly connect either affect or cognition to behaviors, however. Also, a line of work on subtypes of older people (e.g., Hummert 1990; Hummert, Garstka, & Shaner, 1997) has indicated that some subtypes are seen positively (e.g., grandmother), and others negatively (e.g., shrew/curmudgeon). Thus it is not clear if primed with a more negative subtype that implicit affect would remain positive. An explicit consideration of subtyping in consideration of older workers appears in order. Is older worker itself a subtype that has not been acknowledged in the subtyping literature, or is this still too broad—are there many older worker subtypes that elicit different feelings, beliefs, and behaviors?

The role of attributions.   Some researchers have considered whether differential decisions made between older and younger workers are due to different attributions made about these workers. For example, Connor and colleagues (Connor et al., 1978; Locke-Connor & Walsh, 1980) suggested that individuals might differentially attribute information about a success or failure at an interview depending on the age of the applicant. Although not supported in the first study, their second study demonstrated that more stable and external attributions were made after witnessing an unsuccessful older interviewee. Gordon, Rozelle, and Baxter (1989) found that an older applicant's interview performance was attributed more to dispositional causes, but only in a condition where raters thought they would be accountable to explain their ratings. Accountability as a moderator is discussed further in the section on moderators.

Dedrick and Dobbins (1991) directly examined attributions as a mediator and found that internal attributions explained the finding that older workers were less likely to be recommended to training after an episode of poor performance than were younger workers. Rupp et al. (in press) also found mediation effects such that internal, stable, and global attributions explained the relationship between age and the choice of a composite of the three harshest options they examined in light of poor performance (termination, requested resignation, and demotion).

Other mediating possibilities.   As mentioned, we've been surprised at the lack of measurement of mediators in the age bias at work literature, and have a few suggestions that tie into the theoretical work in bias we have been acknowledging. For example, the work on illusory correlation may be applicable to age. For example, Hamilton and Sherman (1994) found that infrequent exposure to both minorities and crime leads to a perceived link between the two. Might a similar process be occurring when we judge older workers if they are a minority in a group and we are making judgments about a negative or unusual workplace event?

A second idea is based on theoretical work by McCann and Giles (2002) and others who have stressed the importance of examining our communication patterns at work with and about older workers. It has been argued that the accommodations that we are likely to use in speaking to older people can lead to a self-fulfilling prophesy where they either will adapt to an expected role in that type of interaction, or will be unable to respond appropriately in a given work situation due to the way that they are being talked to. This could reinforce an idea of lack of competence and even further need for accommodation (Nussbaum, Pitts, Huber, Krieger, & Ohs, 2005).

WHEN IS IT MORE LIKELY TO OCCUR? (THE MODERATORS)

An investigation of moderators has been an important focus for some time. Researchers have been interested not as much in the question of *if* age bias occurs at work, but *when* it is likely to occur. Just as the *whys* of age bias are important in order to understand to ultimately reduce it, so too are the *whens*. This can be of practical value to help us narrow our effort to reduce age bias to where they are needed most. We have organized the moderators into three broad categories: the context, the rater, and the target.

The Context

Here, the context refers to the situation in which an instance of age bias may occur at work. We take a look at context from very narrow factors (i.e., the decision context) to very broad factors (i.e., the national or cultural context).

The decision context

Individuating information. The amount of information available to a decision maker regarding an older worker has received a considerable amount of research attention (e.g., Avolio & Barrett, 1987; Finkelstein et al., 1995; Finkelstein & Burke, 1998; Gordon & Arvey, 2004; Kite et al., 2005; Lee & Clemmons, 1985; Singer & Sewell, 1989; Vrugt & Schabracq, 1996). A cognitive approach has typically been taken, suggesting that when individuating information is provided about an older person, the perceiver may be less likely to rely on category-based processing and stereotypes and more likely to individuate the particular older person in question, reducing the likelihood of bias (Fiske & Neuberg, 1990). The typical approach in these studies is to compare decisions/ratings about an older person to that of a younger person under conditions where there is individuating information provided and where there is not.

Findings have been moderate and mixed. Kite et al.'s (2005) meta-analysis using work and nonwork studies concluded that bias is reduced (but does not disappear) when more information is provided about a target. Finkelstein et al.'s (1995) meta-analysis found support only given particular types of decisions. Gordon and Arvey's (2004) more recent meta-analysis revisited this question with additional studies and found that having a lot of information weakened age effects, but that having a little was worse than none at all. They speculate that having only information about age available could alert individuals to the possibility of basing their ratings on limited, and thus perhaps stereotypical, information, tempering negative effects.

Another point highlighted in Gordon and Arvey's (2004) work is that investigations in the field rather than in the lab tend to yield weaker age effects. One might logically assume that the lab setting artificially inflates effects, and that most decision contexts in the real world have the appropriate amount of information available to raters, and thus while the manipulation of information is an interesting academic issue, it is not of real relevance. However, this perspective assumes that relevant information is indeed always present and attended to, above and beyond any expectations the rater arrives with. Further, it doesn't consider any other motives other than an understanding motive, presumably underlying the desire to make the best decision. For example, researchers have found support for social judgeability theory, which states that if people think they have some information for making a decision against a particular target, *and* they feel they are entitled to judge, they become even more biased (e.g., Leyens, Yzerbyt, & Schadron, 1992). Fiske (2004) notes that this feeling of entitlement can be driven by individual differences with regard to need for control. Thus, to truly understand if information about a target is likely to reduce bias, we must look more carefully into what is driving the decision maker.

An additional point worth noting is that the age bias at work literature has looked mostly at the impact of individuating information on personnel decisions (e.g., hiring) or ratings presumably related to making such decisions (e.g., qualification). We don't yet know much about how individuating information will impact behavioral manifestations of bias in a more everyday treatment context. For example, will knowing more about an individual older worker one encounters lead that person to speak with the worker differently?

Absolute versus relative decisions. Sometimes decision contexts call for a comparative decision among people, where an older individual is being considered in some way relative to younger people. Other times the older person is the sole focus of consideration. This has been addressed in the literature directly within primary studies (Lee & Clemmons, 1985), or by meta-analysts who compared studies that used a comparative design (within-subjects; participants rate both old and young individuals) to an absolute design (between-subjects; participants rate either an old or young individual) (Finkelstein et. al, 1995; Gordon & Arvey, 2004; Kite et al., 2005).

For example, Lee and Clemmons (1985) found that an older worker was provided higher ratings for attending a conference when that worker was the only focus of consideration; when participants decided between a younger and older worker for a training program, the younger was favored. There are theoretical reasons to expect that studies using comparison methodology would find more bias against older people than those that don't. In considering this question, Finkelstein et al. (1995) suggested that age would be more salient in a comparison decision, and that salience could turn a rater's attention to age as a social category. In their meta-analysis, they did find some evidence for this age-salience hypothesis when considering job qualification ratings in the literature. However, there is also a compelling reason to expect the opposite effect. The salience of age produced by a comparison decision could alert individuals to the purpose of a study, and thus prompt socially desirable, less biased responding. This argument was put forth and supported by Gordon and Arvey (2004) in their more recent meta-analysis. From a methodological standpoint, this emphasizes the large role that research design can play in determining conclusions about the prevalence of an issue such as age bias at work.

This idea of absolute versus comparison decisions should continue to be considered from a practical standpoint. How often are decisions/impressions made in the workplace, or anywhere else for that matter, truly absolute? Even if a decision is not called for about another target, do we have images or exemplars to which we are comparing the target individual?

Accountability. Gordon and his colleagues (Gordon, Rozelle, & Baxter, 1988; 1989) looked at the accountability of the rater in a decision context. They proposed and supported a somewhat counterintuitive effect of accountability. One might surmise that a situation where raters are accountable for their decision would lead them to carefully consider an individual and thus rely on biases less. To the contrary, they explain, accountability pressures can have the effect of making one more motivated toward a very clear and organized impression, producing an over-reliance on stereotypes. Taken in combination, their studies provided evidence of raters finding younger interviewees as more attractive, having more positive traits, and being more hirable than older applicants when these raters believed they would have to justify their decision to a group of personnel managers following the task (i.e., accountable condition).

One might assume that accountability is a fact of organizational life and thus not actually a variable at work. However, some decision makers may not always be accountable to others for all personnel decisions. Further, it would be interesting to see what would happen if we defined accountability slightly differently. What if one was accountable not for explaining the reasoning behind one's decisions, but rather accountable for avoiding biases specifically?

Cognitive busyness. Perry et al. (1996) were the only researchers to directly manipulate this decision-context factor that should be important if indeed the cognitive motives for bias are operating. They found that cognitive busyness moderated effects of age bias on discrimination. Busy and biased (age stereotype endorsing) raters were not less positive about older workers when they were busy, but were more positive about younger workers under that condition. Busy and nonbiased raters tended to prefer the older applicant. The authors suggest that raters under high cognitive demand were relying on their positive stereotypes in making applicant ratings.

The job context

An earnest interest in the role of the job appeared in the 1980s (e.g., Cleveland & Landy 1983, 1987; Gordon & Arvey, 1986). These researchers successfully demonstrated that jobs could be age-typed. Perry and her colleagues (e.g., Perry & Finkelstein, 1999) have elaborated on the underpinnings of this process, noting that a direct match could occur between an individual's age and the age type of a job, or an indirect match could occur whereby age would be associated with specific characteristics of a person, and these features would be matched to the features needed for the job. Tying in other work on similarity-attraction theory (cf. Shore & Goldberg, 2004), it is possible that a rater may not doubt the skills/traits of an older individual, but might question an older individual's fit with the younger people in a job context.

What leads a job to develop an age type? Lawrence (1988) has suggested that we develop age norms for the appropriate time in which we will transition through an organization, and these shared norms (developed in part through actual distributions of people in an organization, a notable tie-in with social role theory, discussed earlier) can contribute to our age associations with particular jobs. Shore and Goldberg (2004) also note that our perceptions of whether one is "behind schedule" can be derived from others relative to our position. Shore, Cleveland, and Goldberg (2003), for example, found evidence that employees older than their manager were seen as less promotable than those who were not. In addition, Cleveland, Festa, and Montgomery (1988) found that the age composition of the applicant pool had an impact on the age type of a particular position, such that a job was seen as *older* when there were more older people applying for it. Age type could in some cases be associated with experience or status. If the word *Senior* is in the title of a position, a link could be made to a person with significant experience; the word *Assistant*, conversely, is likely to bring to mind the start of a career, which is often (misguidedly?) associated with youth. Also, jobs with technology language in their title might associate quickly with a younger person (Perry & Finkelstein, 1999).

Although several studies have jobs that could be clearly categorized, this has not been consistent, and the evidence for more prominent age bias in younger jobs has been mixed. Finkelstein et al. (1995) were limited in their ability to clearly test this hypothesis meta-analytically as they didn't find that all jobs used in studies to look at different decisions could be clearly categorized. Perry and Bourhis (1998) suggested that job typing be considered more of a continuum than a dichotomy; consistent with job-prototype matching theory, some jobs appear to have age as more or less of a central feature, rather than an all-or-no feature. Perry and Parlamis (2005), also suggest that other contextual factors, such as rater characteristics, might obscure job type effects. We concur and also suggest that this factor may only be a consideration when one assumes that age bias is driven by an understanding (cognitive) motive. Driven by other motives, people could ignore context, or perhaps even distort their perception of the context, to satisfy their desire to avoid older workers.

The organizational context

Perry (1994, 1997) has argued for the need for consideration of more macro-level, organizational factors and their impact on age bias, perhaps through their impact on more proximal contextual and cognitive factors. Perry and Finkelstein (1999) put forth a model of the role of three organizational factors—structure, values, and technology—and how they could impact age typing of jobs, activation of age stereotypes of people and jobs, and ability for these matches to be used in decision-making. To date, their model has not been tested empirically.

Lawrence (1988) has provided evidence that norms can develop in organizations about what ages are appropriate for different positions and can impact performance ratings. It is likely that the content of the norms in any organization is determined in multiple ways. For example, a high technology company that is permeated with messages of speed and change may harbor expectations that young people will quickly rise to the top (if they have not started there to begin with), and find any association with older age to be incompatible with their approach.

McCann and Giles' (2002) communication approach to understanding age bias, which they have recently suggested is important in a workplace context, stresses how conversations and language we use at work can have a substantial impact on the culture that develops around age. For example, if expressions like "young blood" and "old timers" are part of acceptable discourse, these can become a normative aspect of work life and impact our age norms. Further, drives for belonging may prompt ingroup communication patterns that heighten distinctions among in and outgroups, so to the degree that age bias in a particular context is driven by these motives, this might enhance the likelihood that these communication patterns abound.

Remery, Henkens, Schippers, and Ekamper (2003) report on a 1,000-company survey where organizational features were considered in the interpretation of beliefs and policies toward older workers. Considering the impact on four factors (beliefs about resistance to change, increase in experience, costs, and need for organizational adjustments), these researchers found that the average age of the workforce, the education level, and the size of the organization all impacted beliefs about older workers. Notably those in organizations with more older workers actually had more negative opinions about them; the meaning behind this is something that warrants additional exploration.

Chiu et al. (2001) considered several organizational factors, including sector (service vs. manufacturing/production), organizational size, and organizational ageism policy. Surprisingly they found very little impact of the organization, with the exception of the presence of an ageism policy being positively related to beliefs that older people were adaptable.

Perry and Parlamis (2005) point out that organizational factors may be relatively ignored in the literature due to a theoretical emphasis on cognitive and social identity theory to explain age bias. Although we have suggested previously how these macro factors may be integrated with cognitive processes and social identity concerns, this may be a fertile place for an expansion of theoretical perspective to account for when and how the larger organizational context will matter.

Country/Culture

The most macro of the contextual factors has indeed received the least attention in the literature. Forteza and Prieto (1994) highlighted aging demographic trends around the world, and to our knowledge the recent review by Perry and Parlamis (2005) was the first to comprehensively consider the potential impact of country/culture on ageism at work. Due to space considerations, we highlight just the main issues related to this factor here and refer the reader to Perry and Parlamis for a more complete treatment.

One reason for potential differences in ageism at work in different countries is legal. In some countries it is legal to use age as a consideration in hiring, and to mention age preferences in job ads, although government has encouraged voluntary age fairness policies. Clearly, the Age Discrimination in Employment Act (ADEA) in the U.S. has made blatant ageism such as this more difficult, but as we know ageism comes in many forms—some subtle—and our laws may just impact the form ageism takes. As of October 1, 2006, the UK has instituted an age discrimination law forbidding unfair discrimination of members of any age group based on their age. This could be a valuable opportunity to study longitudinally the impact of forbidding blatant bias on other forms of bias.

As culture of organizations are starting to be addressed, so too must the larger culture. The status of older people in various cultures may have an impact on whether bias occurs against older workers, and if so what role that bias might take. Chinese cultures, for example, have been known to be more respectful of older people (e.g., Levy & Langer, 1994). However, it is interesting to note that Cuddy, Norton, and Fiske (2005) recently found that the stereotype content model (older people warm and incompetent) held up in such places as Hong Kong, South Korea, and Japan. Chiu et al. (2001) found similar levels of bias in the U.K. and Hong Kong.

We echo Perry and Parlamis' (2005) call for more theory and research devoted to issues of national culture, particularly as our workforce becomes more global and cultures have more exposure to one another. For example, how might the norms toward aging in one culture permeate another, and thus change the amount and/or form of age bias in that culture?

The Rater

Age of rater.   Research has been mixed as to how rater age impacts whether age bias will occur. Raters may prefer targets from their own age group (i.e., ingroup bias), raters from a particular age group may provide higher or lower ratings generally (regardless of target age), or raters from one age group may prefer targets from another age group (e.g., age favorability bias).

The overall picture regarding ingroup age bias is mixed. In their meta-analysis, Finkelstein (1995) found an ingroup bias for young respondents only; old respondents showed no preference for younger or older workers. In a later study, Finkelstein and Burke (1998) proposed that an ingroup age bias would occur only when the rater identifies with his or her age group and when age is perceived as a salient category. Against their prediction, however, they found that among raters who highly identified with their age group, older raters viewed an older applicant as being *less* economically beneficial than a younger applicant. Shore et al. (2003) found older employees receiving lower performance ratings from older managers than younger ones. A later meta-analysis covering studies on age bias in general (Kite et al., 2005) found that older individuals stereotype younger individuals as slightly more competent than older individuals. Additionally, they found that it was middle-aged respondents who were most likely to favor younger over older targets. Terror management theory (TMT) may provide one potential explanation for this finding. Middle-aged respondents on the verge of becoming *old* may experience greater perceived threat, resulting in lower ratings for the older targets. Older people may have a different device to accommodate to aging. In a study on age bias in general, Rothbaum (1983) showed that while older people ascribe more elderly stereotypes to older adults, they view these stereotypes as more positive. The authors explain that older people may be accommodating to aging by devaluing youthful characteristics they no longer have.

Research looking at age bias in general has shown an age favorability bias for young respondents in which they provide more positive ratings to older targets than to younger targets (e.g., Jackson & Sullivan, 1988; Linville, 1982). In Linville's study, older targets were preferred to younger targets by young individuals when positive information was provided. This seems to support a complexity-extremity theoretical framework, whereby more extreme (and favorable) ratings are given to outgroup members when positive information is provided.

In some studies, older raters have been shown to be generally more positive in their ratings regardless of target age. For example, older raters in the Jackson and Sullivan (1988) study held more positive stereotypes about targets overall. Chasteen and colleagues (2002) found some evidence that young adults are more negative than older adults on an explicit measure of attitudes toward older people, but found no rater age differences on the implicit measures discussed in an earlier section. Bird and Fisher (1986) and Hassell and Perrewe (1995) both showed that older employees had more positive stereotypes regarding older workers than did younger employees. However, with the exception of those in the Jackson and Sullivan study, raters did not provide ratings of younger workers. Thus, it is unclear whether these results are a demonstration of ingroup bias or of older workers being more positive overall. Additionally, Locke-Connor and Walsh (1980) found that overall, middle-aged (ages 25–64) male raters had more negative expectations of applicants, suggesting that the relationship between rater age and overall favorability ratings may not be linear.

Status of rater. Earlier research found that hourly employees held more positive stereotypes about older workers than did supervisors (Kirchner & Dunnette, 1954; Bird & Fisher, 1986). Other research findings have shown that this effect depends on rater age. Hassell and Perrewe (1995) found that for hourly employees, but not for supervisors, older raters held more positive stereotypes about older workers than did younger raters. Chiu and colleagues (2001) similarly found that the positive relationship between respondent age and work effectiveness ratings were stronger for nonsupervisors than for supervisors. Bird and Fisher found that as rater age increased, the difference in the favorability of stereotypes held by hourly employees and supervisory employees became larger.

Researchers have also looked at the difference between student respondents and managerial respondents. In their meta-analysis, Gordon and Arvey (2004) found that student participants were more negative than supervisors in their evaluations of older workers. In one study, MBA students reported having more negative beliefs with regard to older workers than did personnel managers (Lyon & Pollard, 1997). However, Triandis' (1963) early study showed that personnel directors considered age more than did students in their hiring recommendations of hypothetical job applicants. Singer and Sewell (1989) compared a managerial sample with a student sample, finding that students preferred an older person for a high status job and managers preferred a younger person for a low status job. When exposed to positive information about older workers, however, the pattern was reversed.

Other rater characteristics.   A few studies have looked at variables other than age or status. These have demonstrated, for example, that female respondents may have more positive beliefs about older workers (Chiu et al., 2001; Connor et al., 1978; Kalavar, 2001; Rosen & Jerdee, 1976a) and that African American students may hold more extreme age stereotypes (i.e., some larger differences in ratings between older and younger workers) than do White students (Crew, 1984). The author suggests that differences in educational achievement in his sample may have contributed to these differences. We are unaware of any studies that have specifically investigated education level of raters as a predictor of age bias. While the findings described in this section demonstrate that characteristics of the rater influence age bias, characteristics of the target have also been found to impact whether bias will occur.

The Target

Age of target.   As discussed by Kite and Smith Wagner (2002), an important question to ask is, "how old is old?" Research on age bias has been far from consistent in its operationalization of old. Typically, research on age bias in general and in the workplace describes older workers as being between 55 and 65 (Kite, & Smith Wagner, 2002) and over 65 (Rupp et al., 2005), respectively. In terms of illegal age discrimination in the U. S., the old are considered to be 40 or older (Age Discrimination in Employment Act, 1967). Researchers should consider how their operationalization of old affects both research results (Bytheway, 2005) and applications (Rupp et al., 2005). We return to this issue in the Future Research section.

Competence of target.   In the section on individuating information, we discussed the effect of providing job relevant information versus no job relevant information. In this section, we consider the impact of the content of such job relevant information. In their meta-analysis, Kite and colleagues (2005) looked at the effect of the valence of information provided and found the greatest difference in ratings between younger and older targets, with lower ratings for older targets, when negative information was provided.

Triandis (1963) had personnel directors rate their likelihood of hiring job candidates and found an interaction of age and competence. Overall the 30-year-old competent White male was most likely to be hired, yet the 55-year-old competent African American female was on the verge of being rejected (i.e., average rating just above the rejection cutoff). Competence does matter, however: Even the 30-year-old barely competent White applicant was rejected.

Haefner (1977) showed an interaction of age and competence such that age mattered less for a barely competent job applicant than for a highly competent applicant. For highly competent job candidates, the younger applicant was preferred to the older applicant. In contrast, Lee and Clemons (1985) found that more favorable decisions were made about an older worker than a younger worker when they were both presented as moderately competent. The younger worker was rated higher when no information had been provided.

Fusilier and Hitt (1983) had undergraduate participants rate job applicants that varied on age and experience for an entry-level professional position. They found that the older applicant with no experience was rated worst. If experience is considered a proxy for competence, this suggests that providing negative competence information is more detrimental for older than for younger applicants. This ties in with findings described earlier indicating that experience appears to be a positive stereotype of age. Others, however, have found no evidence that competence affects the degree to which age stereotyping occurs in the workplace (Locke-Connor & Walsh, 1980; Perry & Varney, 1978). We should mention that while we have focused on the age and competence of the target, some studies have found that gender (Fusilier & Hitt, 1983; Hummert, 1999; Kite et al., 2005) and race also interact with age to impact the level of bias that occurs.

WHAT CAN BE DONE ABOUT IT? (THE SOLUTIONS)

We admit that this subheading is quite optimistic and don't claim to have definitive solutions. Rather, in the following section we outline potential paths toward solutions. Given the multifaceted nature of this problem, we believe all stakeholders at multiple levels can and must play a role.

What Can the Bias Holder Do?

As we've seen, we need to distinguish unintentional biases from those that are more purposeful. Making oneself aware that some forms of bias are very automatic and insidious is a first step toward bias reduction (Hummert, 1999; Levy & Banaji, 2002). Recognizing that bias driven from a motive to understand one's complex environment and comes from very natural cognitive processes may ease people's resistance to even acknowledge the bias.

Upon realization that automatic processes may be operating and perhaps impeding fair treatment, bias holders could refocus their efforts to make decisions on more careful analysis of individual information (Cuddy & Fiske, 2002). Even in one's everyday interactions with older people at work, and not just in the role of decision maker, people should take note of whether they are, for example, accommodating their conversation inappropriately (Nussbaum et al., 2005). Nussbaum and colleagues discuss the Communication Enhancement Model of Ageing (CEM) as a possible way for communication to serve as an upward spiral in age interrelations. CEM suggests that when an older person is individuated such that the appropriate communication strategy/level (or not) of accommodation is utilized, an empowered older individual will be able to respond most appropriately, potentially breaking down negative stereotypes over time. Hagestad and Uhlenberg (2005) suggest all people practice mindfulness in their interactions at work.

However, bias sometimes is driven by more complex motives and even fears within individuals that could be difficult to acknowledge, but may be key toward reducing bias based more in negative affect. Fear of death, obsolescence, or fading power/looks might result in an aversion to older individuals who serve as a reminder of this fear. Research pointing to a stronger age bias in middle-aged individuals (Kite et al., 2005) points to the likelihood that this affect-laden, fear based bias may operate insidiously at work as well. If people tried to work through these issues and took action to develop sources of esteem throughout their life that are not in areas more vulnerable to age (Martens et al., 2005), this type of bias may be reduced.

What Can the Older Worker Do?

Giles and Reid (2005) noted that we know relatively little about how older individuals react to the bias they encounter, and Levy and Banaji (2002) state that older people are often not strong enough advocates against age bias. As we've seen throughout this review, they have been sometimes shown to hold negative attitudes about aging. An awareness of how older people foster bonds *within* their ingroups (satisfying belongingness needs) in regard to age may be telling. Could using terms like *senior moments* with colleagues, for example, perpetuate and reinforce stereotypes (Giles & Reid, 2005)?

Awareness that some bias that others have toward them may be automatic and resultant of cognitive shortcuts should encourage older workers to do their best to discourage easy categorization. For example, Perry (1994) suggested that older workers intentionally play up their characteristics that match the central features that are prototypic to a typical jobholder. Findings such as Finkelstein et al.'s (2000) that experience stands out as a plus leads us to suggest that playing up experiences relevant to those needed at a particular job would be beneficial. Focusing on the type and *relevance* of experience, rather than *years* of experience, may be more effective as years could call more attention to age and other associations thereof.

What Can An Organization Do?

Cuddy and Fiske (2002), among others, have noted that individuals are motivated tacticians, and are likely to individuate when judging others when we have the means and reasons to do so. The organization has a hand in this, as it has the power to create situations where bias is formally discouraged and good, nonrushed, well-informed decision making is encouraged (Perry, 1994). Although we see accountability for decisions is a tricky thing (cf. Gordon et al., 1988; 1989) as it might actually backfire and lead to more simplified processing, perhaps accountability specifically to avoid bias could work to reduce reliance on stereotyping. We need to really study this in a situation that mimics the quick-paced demands of organizational life—can we strike a balance between those needs and effortful processing?

A promising avenue for reducing bias—and likely that steeped in affect as well as cognition—is increased contact between people of all age groups at and outside of work. Several researchers have begun to note that more exposure to older workers tends to be associated with more positive beliefs about them and desire to work with them (cf., Chiu et al., 2001; Hassell & Perrewe, 1995). Hagestad and Uhlenberg (2005) note, from a sociological standpoint, just how little inter-age contact we tend to have in our society, and how this segregation could be an important root of bias. However, just as mere contact with other types of groups (e.g., interracial) only tends to be successful under specific circumstances and indeed could backfire under others, so too with age (cf. Remery et al., 2003). It is crucial that sustained contact is consistently fostered in an organizational setting in ways that allow individuals to really have the opportunity to forge friendships and positive affect, and allow for recategorization of individual members of other age groups out of *age* as an important differentiating category to others, such as interest or skill groups. Giles and Reid (2005) note that forcing mixed age contact may not be easy or welcome, as people (of all ages) do enjoy spending time with other members of their generation. Chiu et al.'s (2001) study seemed to find better results for moderate than frequent contact. A good mix of both perhaps is the key.

There have been a couple of interesting lab interventions to age bias that may hold some promise as something that perhaps an organization could attempt in the process of training or socialization. For example, Snyder and Meine (1994) found some evidence that exposure to a story of an individual who realized ways that that they were biased and how they planned to change actually was helpful in some circumstances, given particular motives for the bias. Dasgupta and Greenwald (2001) found support for an intervention that appeared to reduce implicitly but not explicitly measured age bias. They exposed participants to photos of well-liked famous older people and commonly disliked famous younger people and found a reduction in implicit bias against the aged. Although this wasn't a work-related study, perhaps some kind of similar intervention in a training program at work could have similar effects. Of course, there could be questions of the promotion of unfair bias toward the young in such a scenario.

At a broader level, organizations wanting to reduce bias may need to be more cognizant of the norms developing within their culture regarding what is *on time* or *behind schedule* and attempt to address the distributions directly. Lawrence (1988) has found that perceptions of age norms may lag behind changes in actual distributions, and so perhaps a proactive approach on the part of an organization to directly affect perceptions may be needed (Perry, 1994). Further, age bias policies within organizations that acknowledge the problem and have procedures in place for dealing with it have shown some promise (Chiu et al., 2001).

What Can A Country/Culture Do?

At a more macro level, age discrimination laws are important. Although the ADEA has certainly not rid our country of age bias (particularly the more affective/cognitive type), blatant discrimination is more difficult and discouraged. Other countries that do not have these laws face direct discrimination as an accepted part of the culture. Not only is this a problem because a company is allowed not to hire, for example, someone due to age, but seeing ads looking just for younger people, for example, is likely to be planting seeds very early on in a society that one's role as one ages is no longer that of productive worker (Kite et al., 2005; Lyon & Pollard, 1997). Many cultures, even those with laws, are sending insidious messages about the worth of older people every day. For example, the lack of strong, effective older people in television has been noted (Donlon, Ashman, & Levy, 2005) and Hagestad and Uhlenberg (2005) point out the very accepted tradition of sarcastic birthday cards and gags that have institutionalized ageism in our cultural humor. Having a sense of humor about age and all the issues it may or may not bring may serve a valuable function on some levels, but it also could be leading us to not question much of the age bias around us. More public awareness of the myths versus realities of aging is imperative.

A Caveat: Will This Take Care of Itself?

We would be remiss not to return to a point made in various places throughout this chapter that some work on this topic has pointed to evidence that perhaps age bias is no longer the problem it once was (cf. Hassell & Perrewe, 1995), and may continue to right itself as the baby boomers continue to age and diversity in general is more of a concern at work (cf. Weiss & Maurer, 2004). Further, some evidence for age discrimination found in the past could have been at least in part driven by methodological artifacts (Gordon & Arvey, 2004). These are all valid observations and we hope that they are true, but just as racism has seemed to shift to a more modern, ambivalent, implicit type, perhaps we must focus our efforts on the possibility of a *modern ageism*. More focus on the tripartite view of bias, underlying motives for bias, implicit styles of bias, and bias in everyday interactions may help us to do so.

WHAT NEXT? (FUTURE RESEARCH)

We began this chapter encouraged that there has been more sophisticated research attention to age bias at work and have noted throughout that we think we can expand the focus by applying theory on bias specifically to the workplace. In the following section we note a few specific areas we believe are most in need of attention, and encourage the reader to make additional connections between broader theory and age bias at work. We spend a bit more attention on measurement issues, as they jumped out at us often in our reading of the literature.

Sticky Wickets in Measurement

What is old?   It is difficult to really understand older worker bias if we do not know what we are talking about when we use the word *old*, as we mentioned previously in our discussion of target age. According to the ADEA, an older worker is over 40. We're betting many of our readers in their 40s (and possibly 50s, 60s . . .) do not think of themselves as older workers. Others might. Age identity as a measurement issue needs continued refinement (cf. Finkelstein & Burke, 1998; Martens et al., 2005). Further, even grouping individuals 55 and older, as many do on surveys as the *old* category, may be obfuscating huge differences among people (Bytheway et al., 2005). The work specific age bias literature needs to start looking at this systematically.

Older people, older workers, or a specific older worker?   Asking a research participant to respond to questions in regard to age in general or older people in general may be calling to mind a different referent than directing their mind toward an older worker. Older workers could conjure far different images, and perhaps be getting the attitude measurement closer to the object toward which we are likely also measuring behaviors. It has been noted by some that while we may find evidence that people feel a particular way about an age group in general, they may not necessarily carry that over into how they feel about a specific older person (e.g., Braithwaite, Gibson, & Holman, 1986). Furthermore, we have cited literature finding quite a few popular subtypes of older people (cf. Hummert, 1999)—we encourage work to discover whether older worker itself is a subtype, and/or whether older worker comprises many distinct subtypes that operate differently in various contexts. We also encourage comparisons between views of older people and those of younger, as only looking at people's views of older workers without knowing their views of other age groups only paints part of the picture (Goebel, 1984).

Explicit versus implicit?   The vast majority of the literature on age at work thus far has used more explicit measurement of age attitudes or ageist behavior. Some research (e.g., Levy & Banaji, 2002; Perdue & Gurtman, 1990) has started to consider implicit measurement and we encourage more work in that direction. We would like to see more work on developing implicit measures of ageism that focus specifically in the realm of work-related ageism.

What type of bias?   The fuzziness of what is meant by bias has been emphasized throughout the chapter and it is a measurement issue as well as a conceptual issue. Efforts to piece apart affect, cognition, and behavior have just begun to come forth (cf. Rupp et al., 2005, in press), and we agree with Rupp and associates that we need more work in this area, particularly with the focus on a workplace context, as at this point the multidimensional measures are still more general rather than workplace specific. We call special attention to a need for focus in the area of affective biases as we found this tackled least often and least clearly in the aging at work literature. As affect at work seems to be growing in popularity in the Industrial/Organizational (I/O) psychology field (Brief & Weiss, 2002), we hope this may be a natural byproduct of that movement. A cognitive approach to understanding age bias at work has been the norm, and although that is valuable and important, it will not complete the picture. Changing stereotypes and/or reducing the likelihood of their use, no easy feats in and of themselves, will not necessarily make people enjoy, seek out, and genuinely like older workers.

> ### TAKEAWAY POINTS
>
> - Age bias can have a lot of meanings—attitudes, affect, stereo-typing, and discrimination. The literature on age bias at work has not always made this clear.
> - Age bias at work is not solely a matter of access discrimination, but can include bias in everyday interactions as well.
> - There may be many motives for being biased against older workers, many of which have been empirically under tested.
> - A complete understanding of age bias at work requires consideration of many potential mediators and moderators to clarify the process and context.
> - There are many subtypes of *old person*—*older worker* itself may be a subtype, or there may be further subtypes of older workers to be more fully understood.
> - Solutions to age bias will need to come from multiple levels, including the bias holder, the target, the organization, and the larger culture. The suggested solutions invite empirical scrutiny.

Everyday Interactions

The work literature's focus on personnel decisions (e.g., hiring, promotion, training, and selection) as criteria is obviously necessary and important, but we would like to see more work looking beyond access discrimination to subtle, and even not-so-subtle, everyday treatment of older workers. An increased focus on communication (Finkelstein, 2005; McCann & Giles, 2002) and social networks will be a welcome expansion.

A Focus on Solutions

While we came up with some solutions in the previous section, and did so based on what we've learned in this literature, we do not feel we have enough hard evidence to be confident they would work, and maybe there are others that would work better. Further research needs to be cognizant of the motives, the process, and the context (Fiske, 2004; Snyder & Meine, 1994), as we've stressed throughout this chapter, but also needs to take this a step further and give good empirical attention to the ultimate solutions to the problem of age bias at work.

A Return to the Tale

We return now to the story that opened this chapter and our accompanying question to you: Is this a tale of age bias? In light of what we've reviewed, it is evident that age bias is a complex issue and is not always easy to detect. We leave you with some specific questions to guide an exploration of what is happening in the story. It may be useful to focus first on what type or types of bias may be occurring. Is there evidence of stereotyping? Prejudice? Unfair discrimination? If age bias is occurring, is it blatant or subtle? What core motives may be at work for Jessica and Amy? What interventions might the individuals or organization try in an attempt to remedy such age bias?

REFERENCES

Age Discrimination in Employment Act of 1967, 42 U.S.C. § 6101 et seq.

Avolio, B. J., & Barrett, G. V. (1987). Effects of age stereotyping in a simulated interview. *Psychology and Aging, 2*, 56–63.

Biernat, M., Manis, M., & Nelson, T. E. (1991). Stereotypes and standards of judgment. *Journal of Personality and Social Psychology, 60*, 485–499.

Bird, C. P., & Fisher, T. D. (1986). Thirty years later: Attitudes toward the employment of older workers. *Journal of Applied Psychology, 71*, 515–517.

Bobo, L. (1983). Whites' opposition to busing: Symbolic racism or realistic group conflict? *Journal of Personality and Social Psychology, 45*, 1196–1210.

Braithwaite, V., Gibson, D., & Holman, J. (1986). Age stereotyping: Are we oversimplifying the phenomenon? *International Journal of Aging and Human Development, 22*, 315–325.

Brief, A. P., & Weiss, H. M. (2002). Organizational behavior: Affect in the workplace. *Annual Review of Psychology, 53*, 279–307.

Bytheway, B. (2005). Ageism and age categorization. *Journal of Social Issues, 61*, 361–374.

Chasteen, A. L., Schwarz, N., & Park, D. (2002). The activation of aging stereotypes in younger and older adults. *Journal of Gerontology: Series B: Psychological Sciences, 57B*, 540–547.

Chiu, W. C. K., Chan, A. W., Snape, E., & Redman, T. (2001). Age stereotypes and discriminatory attitudes toward older workers: An East-West comparison. *Human Relations, 54*, 629–661.

Cleveland, J. N., Festa, R. M., & Montgomery, L. (1988). Applicant pool composition and job perceptions: Impact on decisions regarding an older applicant. *Journal of Vocational Behavior, 32*, 112–125.

Cleveland, J. N., & Landy, F. J. (1983). The effects of person and job stereotypes on two personnel decisions. *Journal of Applied Psychology, 68*, 609–619.

Cleveland, J. N., & Landy, F. J. (1987). Age perceptions of jobs: Convergence of two questionnaires. *Psychological Reports, 60*, 1075–1081.

Connor, C. L., Walsh, P., Litzelman, D. K., & Alvarez, M. G. (1978). Evaluation of job applicants: The effects of age vs. success. *Journal of Gerontology, 33*, 246–252.

Craft, J. A., Doctors, S. I., Shkop, Y. M., & Benecki, T. J. (1979). Simulated management perceptions, hiring decisions and age. *Aging and Work, 2*, 95–102.

Crew, J. C. (1984). Age stereotypes as a function of race. *Academy of Management Journal, 27*, 431–435.

Cuddy, A. J. C., & Fiske, S. T. (2002). Doddering but dear: Process, content, and function in stereotyping of older persons. In T. D. Nelson (Ed.), *Ageism* (pp. 4–26). Cambridge, MA: MIT Press.

Cuddy, A. J. C., Norton, M. I., & Fiske, S. T. (2005). This old stereotype: The pervasiveness and persistence of the elderly stereotype. *Journal of Social Issues, 61*, 267–286.

Dasgupta, N., & Greenwald, A. G. (2001). On the malleability of automatic attitudes: Combating automatic prejudice with images of admired and disliked individuals. *Journal of Personality and Social Psychology, 81*, 800–814.

Dedrick, E. J., & Dobbins, G. H. (1991). The influence of subordinate age on managerial actions: An attributional analysis. *Journal of Organizational Behavior, 12*, 367–377.

Donlon, M. M., Ashman, O., & Levy, B. R. (2005). Re-vision of older television characters: A stereotype-awareness intervention. *Journal of Social Issues, 61*, 307–320.

Dovidio, J. F., Brigham, J. C., Johnson, B. T., & Gaertner, S. L. (1996). Stereotyping, prejudice, and discrimination: Another look. In C. N. Macrae, C. Stangor, & M. Hewstone (Eds.), *Stereotypes and Stereotyping*. New York: Guilford.

Drehmer, D. E., Carlucci, C. A., Bordieri, J. E., & Pincus, L. B. (1992). Effects of age on ranking for reduction in workforce. *Psychological Reports, 70*, 1203–1209.

Finkelstein, L. M. (2005). Intergenerational issues inside the organization. In P. Beatty & R. Visser (Eds.), *Thriving on an aging workforce*. Melbourne, FL: Krieger.

Finkelstein, L. M., & Burke, M. J. (1998). Age stereotyping at work: The role of rater and contextual factors on evaluations of job applicants. *The Journal of General Psychology, 125*, 317–345.

Finkelstein, L. M., Burke, M. J., & Raju, N. S. (1995). Age discrimination in simulated employment contexts: An integrative analysis. *Journal of Applied Psychology, 80*, 652–663.

Finkelstein, L. M., Higgins, K. D., & Clancy, M. (2000). Justifications for ratings of older and young job applicants: An exploratory content analysis. *Experimental Aging Research, 26*, 263–283.

Fiske, S. T. (2004). Stereotyping, prejudice, and discrimination: Social biases. In *Social beings: A core motives approach to social psychology* (pp. 397–457). New Jersey: Wiley.

Fiske, S. T., & Neuberg, S. L. (1990). A continuum of impression formation, from category based to individuating processes: Influences of information and motivation on attention and interpretation. In M. P. Zanna (Ed.), *Advances in experimental social psychology* (Vol. 23, pp. 1–74). London: Academic Press.

Forteza, J. A., & Prieto, J. M. (1994). Aging and work behavior. In M. Dunnette, L. Hough, & H. Triandis (Eds.), *Handbook of industrial organizational psychology* (Vol. 4, pp. 447–483). Palo Alto, CA: Consulting Psychologists Press.

Fusilier, M. R., & Hitt, M. A. (1983). Effects of age, race, sex, and employment experience on students' perceptions of job applications. *Perceptual and Motor Skills, 57*, 1127–1134.

Gibson, K. J., Zerbe, W. J., & Franken, R. E. (1993). The influence of rater and rate age on judgments of work-related attributes. *The Journal of Psychology, 127*, 271–280.

Giles, H., & Reid, S. A. (2005). Ageism across the lifespan: Towards a self-categorization model of aging. *Journal of Social Issues, 61*, 389–404.

Goebel, B. L. (1984). Age stereotypes held by student nurses. *The Journal of Psychology, 116*, 249–254.

Gordon, R. A., & Arvey, R. D. (1986). Perceived and actual ages of workers. *Journal of Vocational Behavior, 28*, 21–28.

Gordon, R. A., & Arvey, R. D. (2004). Age bias in laboratory and field settings: A meta-analytic investigation. *Journal of Applied Social Psychology, 34*, 468–492.

Gordon, R. A., Rozelle, R. M., & Baxter, J. C. (1988). The effect of applicant age, job level, and accountability on the evaluation of job applicants. *Organizational Behavior and Human Decision Processes, 41*, 20–33.

Gordon, R. A., Rozelle, R. M., & Baxter, J. C. (1989). The effect of applicant age, job level, and accountability on perceptions of female job applicants. *The Journal of Psychology, 123*, 59–68.

Haefner, J. E. (1977). Race, age, sex, and competence as factors in employer selection of the disadvantaged. *Journal of Applied Psychology, 62*, 199–202.

Hagestad, G. O., & Uhlenberg, P. (2005). The social separation of old and young: A root of ageism. *Journal of Social Issues, 61*, 343–360.

Hamilton, D. L., & Sherman, S. J. (1994). Illusory correlations: Implications for stereotype theory and research. In D. Bar-Tal, C. F. Grauman, A. W. Kruglanski, & W. Shroebe (Eds.), *Stereotyping and prejudice: Changing conceptions* (pp. 59–84). New York: Springer.

Hassell, B. L., & Perrewe, P. L. (1995). An examination of beliefs about older workers: Do stereotypes still exist? *Journal of Organizational Behavior, 16*, 457–468.

Hummert, M. L. (1990). Multiple stereotypes of elderly and young adults: A comparison of structure and evaluations. *Psychology and Aging, 5*, 182–193.

Hummert, M. L. (1999). A social cognitive perspective on age stereotypes. In T. M. Hess & F. Blanchard-Fields (Eds.), *Social Cognition and Aging* (pp. 175–196). San Diego: Academic Press.

Hummert, M. L., Garstka, T. A., & Shaner, J. L. (1997). Stereotyping of older adults: The role of target facial cues and perceiver characteristics. *Psychology and Aging, 12*, 107–114.

Intrieri, R. C., von Eye, A., & Kelly, J. A. (1995). The aging semantic differential: A confirmatory factor analysis. *The Gerontologist, 35*, 616–621.

Jackson, L. A., & Sullivan, L. A. (1988). Age stereotype disconfirming information and evaluations of old people. *The Journal of Social Psychology, 128*, 721–729.

Kalavar, J. M. (2001). Examining ageism: Do male and female college students differ? *Educational Gerontology, 27*, 507–513.

Kirchner, W. K., & Dunnette, M. D. (1954). Attitudes toward older workers. *Personnel Psychology, 7*, 257–265.

Kite, M. E., & Smith Wagner, L. (2002). Attitudes toward older adults. In T. D. Nelson (Ed.), *Ageism: Stereotyping and prejudice against older persons* (pp. 129–161). Cambridge, MA: MIT Press.

Kite, M. E., Stockdale, G. D., Whitley Jr., B. E., & Johnson, B. T. (2005). Attitudes toward younger and older adults: An updated meta-analytic review. *Journal of Social Issues, 61*, 241–266.

Kogan, N. (1961). Attitudes toward old people: The development of a scale and an examination of correlates. *Journal of Abnormal and Social Psychology, 62*, 44–54.

Kogan, N., & Shelton, F. C. (1960). Differential cue value of age and occupation in impression formation. *Psychological Reports, 7,* 203–216.

Lawrence, B. S. (1988). New wrinkles in the theory of age: Demography, norms, and performance ratings. *Academy of Management Journal, 31,* 309–337.

Lee, J. A., & Clemons, T. (1985). Factors affecting employment decisions about older workers. *Journal of Applied Psychology, 70,* 785–788.

Levin, W. C. (1988). Age stereotyping: College student evaluations. *Research on Aging, 10,* 134–148.

Levy, B. R., & Banaji, R. B. (2002). Implicit ageism. In T. D. Nelson (Ed.), *Ageism: Stereotyping and prejudice against older persons* (pp. 49–75). Cambridge, MA US: MIT Press.

Levy, B., & Langer, E. (1994). Aging free from negative stereotypes: Successful memory in China among the American deaf. *Journal of Personality and Social Psychology, 66,* 989–997.

Leyens, J. P., Yzerbyt, V. Y., & Schadron, G. (1992). The social judgeability approach to stereotypes. In W. Stroebe & M. Hewstone (Eds.), *European review of social psychology* (pp. 92–120). Chichester, England: Wiley.

Liden, R. C., Stilwell, D., & Ferris, G. R. (1996). The effects of supervisor and subordinate age on objective performance and subjective performance ratings. *Human Relations, 49,* 327–347.

Lin, T. R., Dobbins, G. H., & Farh, J. L. (1992). A field study of race and age similarity effects on interview ratings in conventional and situational interviews. *Journal of Applied Psychology, 77,* 363–371.

Linville, P. W. (1982). The complexity-extremity effect and age-based stereotyping. *Journal of Personality and Social Psychology, 42,* 193–211.

Locke-Connor, C., & Walsh, R. P. (1980). Attitudes toward the older job applicant: Just as competent but more likely to fail. *Journal of Gerontology, 35,* 920–927.

Loretto, W., Duncan, C., & White, P. J. (2000). Ageism and employment: Controversies, ambiguities, and younger people's perceptions. *Ageing and Society, 20,* 279–302.

Lyon, P., & Pollard, D. (1997). Perceptions of the older employee: is anything really changing? *Personnel Review, 26,* 245–257.

Martens, A., Goldenberg, J. L., & Greenberg, J. (2005). A terror management perspective on ageism. *Journal of Social Issues, 61,* 223–240.

McCann, R., & Giles, H. (2002). Ageism in the workplace: A communication perspective. In Nelson, T. D. (Ed.), *Ageism: Stereotyping and prejudice against older persons* (pp. 163–199). Cambridge, MA: MIT Press.

Nelson, T. D. (2005). Ageism: Prejudice against our feared future self. *Journal of Social Issues, 61,* 207–222.

Nussbaum, J. F., Pitts, M. J., Huber, F. N., Krieger, J. L., & Ohs, J. E. (2005). Ageism and ageist language across the life span: Intimate relationships and non-intimate interactions. *Journal of Social Issues, 61,* 287–306.

Perdue, C. W., & Gurtman, M. B. (1990). Evidence for the automaticity of ageism. *Journal of Experimental Social Psychology, 26,* 199–216.

Perry, E. L. (1994). A prototype matching approach to understanding the role of applicant gender and age in the evaluation of job applicants. *Journal of Applied Social Psychology, 24,* 1433–1473.

Perry, E. L. (1997). A cognitive approach to understanding discrimination: A closer look at applicant gender and age. In G. R. Ferris (Ed.), *Research in personnel and human resources management* (vol. 15, pp. 175–240). Greenwich, CT: JAI Pess

Perry, E. L., & Bourhis, A. C. (1998). A closer look at the role of applicant age in selection decisions. *Journal of Applied Social Psychology, 28*, 1670–1697.

Perry, E. L., & Finkelstein, L. M. (1999). Toward a broader view of age discrimination in employment-related decisions: A joint consideration of organizational factors and cognitive processes. *Human Resource Management Review, 9*, 21–49.

Perry, E. L., Kulik, C. T., & Bourhis, A. C. (1996). Moderating effects of personal and contextual factors in age discrimination. *Journal of Applied Psychology, 81*, 628–647.

Perry, E. L., & Parlamis, J. D. (2005). Age and ageism in organizations: A review and consideration of national culture. In A. M. Konrad, P. Prasad, & J. K. Pringle, (Eds.), *Handbook of Workplace Diversity*. London: Sage.

Perry, J. S., & Varney, T. L. (1978). College students' attitudes toward workers' competence and age. *Psychological Reports, 42*, 1319–1322.

Remery, C., Henkens, K., Schippers, J., & Ekamper, P. (2003). Managing an ageing workforce and a tight labor market: Views held by Dutch employers. *Population Research and Policy Review, 22*, 21–40.

Rosen, B., & Jerdee, T. H. (1976a). The nature of job-related age stereotypes. *Journal of Applied Psychology, 61*, 180–183.

Rosen, B., & Jerdee, T. H. (1976b). The influence of age stereotypes on managerial decisions. *Journal of Applied Psychology, 61*, 428–432.

Rosen, B., & Jerdee, T. H. (1977). Too old or not too old? *Harvard Business Review, 55*, 97–106.

Rothbaum, F. (1983). Aging and age stereotypes. *Social Cognition, 2*, 171–184.

Rupp, D. E., Vodanovich, S. J., & Credé, M. (2005). The multidimensional nature of ageism: Construct validity and group differences. *Journal of Social Psychology, 145*, 335–364.

Rupp, D. E., Vodanovich, S. J., & Credé, M. (in press). Age bias in the workplace: The impact of ageism and causal attributions. *Journal of Applied Social Psychology*.

Shore, L. M., Cleveland, J. N., & Goldberg, C. B. (2003). Work attitudes and decisions as a function of manager age and employee age. *Journal of Applied Psychology, 88*, 529–537.

Shore, L. M., & Goldberg, C. B. (2004). Age discrimination in the workplace. In R. L. Dipboye & A. Colella (Eds.), *Discrimination at Work* (pp. 203–226). Mahwah, NJ: Lawrence Erlbaum Associates.

Singer, M. S. (1987). Age stereotypes as a function of profession. *The Journal of Social Psychology, 126*, 697–692.

Singer, M. S., & Sewell, C. (1989). Applicant age and selection interview decisions: Effect of information exposure on age discrimination in personnel selection. *Personnel Psychology, 42*, 135–154.

Snyder, M., & Miene, P. K. (1994). Stereotyping of the elderly: A functional approach. *British Journal of Social Psychology, 33*, 63–82.

Taylor, P., & Walker, A. (1998). Employers and older workers: Attitudes and employment practices. *Aging and Society, 18*, 641–658.

Triandis, H. C. (1963). Factors affecting employee selection in two cultures. *Journal of Applied Psychology, 47,* 89–96.

Turner, J. C. (1985). Social categorization and the self-concept: A social cognitive theory of group behavior. In E. J. Lawler (Ed.), *Advances in group processes* (Vol. 2, pp. 77–122). Greenwich, CT: JAI Press.

Vrugt, A., & Schabracq, M. (1996). Stereotypes with respect to elderly employees: The contribution of attribute information and representativeness. *Journal of Community and Applied Social Psychology, 6,* 287–292.

Weiss, E. M., & Maurer, T. J. (2004). Age discrimination in personnel decisions: A re-examination. *Journal of Applied Social Psychology, 34,* 1551–1562.

6

Employee Age and Performance in Organizations

Jeanette N. Cleveland and Audrey S. Lim

Aging is a multidimensional process. Further, conceptualizations and measurement of performance have evolved over the last two decades. To understand the complex linkages between age and performance, it is necessary to identify how age is defined and what facets of performance we are investigating. Historically, age effects have been assessed using chronological age. In addition, the construct of performance has been viewed as unidimensional. In the present chapter, we present a number of methods of age assessment, followed by a discussion of the evolving multifaceted domain of job performance, including task performance, contextual performance, counterproductive work behaviors, and adaptive performance. Each of these facets is discussed in relation to research on age. Potential context factors and moderators are described, as well as a brief discussion of 360-degree feedback and team performance systems. Importantly, implications for both future research and practice within organizations are proposed.

An organization's success depends upon the attraction, selection, evaluation, and retention of the best and the brightest employees. This is an especially important organizational issue given shrinkage in labor market entrants and concomitant growth in the proportion of retirement age baby boomer workers (Pitt-Catsouphes & Smyer, 2005). Few organizational challenges are of greater importance than assessing the contribution of employee performance to organizational success. Organizations that capitalize on effective evaluation and retention of the best employees regardless of their age, gender, or racial demographics will be optimally positioned to address current and future workforce challenges within the global economy. As implied throughout this edited book, and explicitly addressed within this chapter, few outcome variables are as critical in the field of psychology as those that tap the construct of performance (Campbell, McCloy, Oppler, & Sager, 1993).

In the present chapter, we review the research findings on the relationship between age and work performance. Considerable research in both lab and field settings indicates that job performance does not decline significantly with age (Salthouse & Maurer, 1996). However, there are a number of issues to consider in this research. First, what do we mean by age; specifically, how is age operationalized or measured? Second, how is the domain of performance construct defined? Performance measures reflect a variety of assessments including supervisory ratings, productivity indices, other objective measures (e.g., sales volume, turnover, and absenteeism), and reflect a variety of content (e.g., task performance, contextual performance, and so forth). There is evidence that the age-performance relationship varies with the content and the type of performance measure utilized (Cleveland & Shore, 1992). Finally, the age and performance relationship is influenced by a number of critical contextual and personal variables that serve to either enhance or limit the association of one's age to performance (Salthouse & Maurer, 1996). In this chapter, we begin by describing the typical as well as alternative ways of measuring age. Next, we review research during the last 20 years on performance evaluation in industrial and organizational psychology that has expanded our understanding of the construct of performance.

Given the variety of age measures and the expanding domain of job performance, one would expect a somewhat complex answer to the question, "Is age related to performance?" Our review suggests that the age-performance relationship is both complex and poorly understood. The majority of the chapter describes the evolving facets of performance and reviews pertinent age-performance research associated within the performance domain. The research literature on age and performance is reviewed. This is followed by a discussion of possible moderators of these relationships, future research and practical implications in order to identify what applied work psychologists know about age-performance relationships, what we do not know, and where to focus our energies to investigate and intervene.

CONCEPTIONS OF AGE

The study of aging and work, specifically industrial gerontology, examines issues concerning the employment and retirement of middle-aged and older workers. Aging is viewed as a multidimensional process that is difficult to capture in a single definition or measure. Therefore, not surprisingly, a continuing problem in research on older workers is the lack of consensus regarding the definition of a mature or older worker (Barak, 1987; Lawrence, 1988; Sterns & Alexander, 1987; Sterns & Doverspike, 1989). There are a number of approaches to define an older worker's age that can be categorized into two general groups: person-based age measures and context-based age measures. Person-based measures focus chiefly on the age characteristics of the individual, whereas context-based measures incorporate aspects of the work situation and often reflect comparisons among persons in the situation.

Person-based measures of age. Chronological or legal age is the most widely used person-based measure in research on older workers. The Age Discrimination in Employment Act (ADEA) of 1967 (amended in 1978 and 1986) protects workers age 40 and older. The ADEA reflects the fact that personnel or human resources practices and decisions may disproportionately have adverse effects on applicants and employees who are 40 years and older. The Job Training Partnership Act and Older American Act is another legal reference that recognizes individuals over 55 years as older workers (Sterns & Doverspike, 1989). Although legally and scientifically convenient, chronological age may provide a narrow view of the role of age and aging at work. Chronological age is often used as a proxy for the meaning that an individual attributes or ascribes to age or for functional or biological age (Barak, 1987; Baum & Boxley, 1983; Kastenbaum, Derbin, Sabatini, & Artt, 1972; Steitz & McClary, 1988).

Subjective, personal, or perceived age refers to how old or young individuals perceive themselves to be (Steitz & McClary, 1988). Often it is measured using questions similar to, "Would you say you feel young, middle-aged, old or very old?" (Barak & Stern, 1986) or "Do you feel older, the same, or younger than your real age?" (Baum & Boxley, 1983). It reflects the age group with which the individual feels closest, either directly (i.e., on the basis of chronological age) or indirectly (i.e., on the basis of shared characteristics). An individual's interpretation of his or her age may reflect perceptions of health, appearance, and/or energy. As a result, two individuals with the same chronological age may vary dramatically in terms of the subjective meaning that age has for them. These differences, in turn, may be reflected in their attitudes and behavior.

A third largely person-based age measure is functional or biological age (Salthouse, 1986; Sterns & Doverspike, 1989). As chronological age increases, individuals change both biologically and psychologically, reflecting declines in some attributes such as eyesight, reaction time, and hearing, as well as increases in other areas including experience and judgment. In fact, there is evidence that there is greater variability among older employees than among younger employees (cf. Barak, 1987; Sterns & Alexander, 1987). Within the gerontology as well as the industrial and organizational psychology literature, the concept of functional age has been criticized on a number of bases. The major limitation is the use of a single index and the assumption of decline with increasing chronological years. More appropriate assessment strategies and measures need to be developed that assess attributes directly related to job performance. Even when there are measurable age-related functional changes, such changes may not translate to performance decrements in any particular job.

Context-based age measures. Both psychosocial and organizational definitions of older workers reflect examples of context-based age measures. Psychosocial definitions are based on the social perceptions of the individual, including stereotypical perceptions of older workers age. Social age has important applications to the work setting. Social or interpersonal age refers to the age status or perceived age of an individual as evaluated by others (Kastenbaum et al., 1972). Social age can be assessed from the perspective of one or several observers and evaluated either at one time or over a more extended period of time. These perceptions may depend, in part, on features of the situation or specific context referent.

Rather than the individual as the unit of analysis, the organizational approach to age uses the group (Cleveland & Shore, 1992), peers or cohort group (Lawrence, 1988) or the organization (Lawrence, 1988) as the unit of focus. When the average age of employees in an organization is high, the organization itself may be perceived as older. Perceived relative age (Cleveland & Shore, 1992; Lawrence, 1984; Pfeffer, 1983) refers to the perceived age of an individual in comparison with some normative group, often consisting of other individuals in the immediate or proximal environment (Cleveland, Festa, & Montgomery, 1988). For example, these assessments include employee perceptions of age compared to work group members, perceptions of one's own and others' age compared to one's supervisor, and perceptions of self and others in relation to the typical age within a given occupation or career path. Each of these is an example of perceived relative age although the comparison referent (e.g., workgroup or supervisor) varies (Cleveland & Shore, 1992).

In order to fully explore the relationship between age and performance, it is important to keep in mind how each construct constructs is conceptualized and measured. Much of the research presented in the next section reviews the relationship between chronological age and task performance. Less is known about the links between alternative measures of age and performance. In addition, research historically has narrowly defined the construct of performance. In the next section, we discuss the more recent developments in the conceptualization and measurement of work performance and age-performance research exemplars.

WHAT IS PERFORMANCE?: AGE LINKAGES WITH THE DOMAIN OF PERFORMANCE

Construct explication and domain of work performance. Campbell et al. (1993) state that performance is one of the most important outcome variables within psychology. Like the construct of age, there are a number of measures of performance. Yet, until recently, little attention has been given to the explication of the content or domain of performance. Although there are theories of abilities and personality, research using the dependent variable of performance has assumed that this construct is unidimensional, despite empirical evidence to the contrary (Campbell et al., 1993). One reason for this is the Classic Model of performance that has dominated thinking in applied research. The Classic Model states that performance is one general factor and will account for most of the variations among different measures. Therefore, the objective with our performance measures is to develop the best possible measure of the general factor. However, Campbell and others (Borman & Motowidlo, 1993; Cleveland, 2005; Johnson, 2003) indicate that the notion of an ultimate criterion or single general performance factor has no meaning and is not the best representation of the performance construct.

Task Performance

Campbell et al. (1993) present a model of performance that provides a multidimensional alternative to the one-factor model. Relevant to this chapter, individual performance is defined as the set of behaviors that are relevant to the organization's goals. It is what people actually do and is observable. Further, performance involves goal-directed actions that are under the control of the individual and that can be measured in terms of the level of the individual's contribution to those goals (Johnson, 2003).

The model that Campbell et al. (1993) propose is an eight-factor model of performance with no general factor. The eight factors (job-task proficiency, non job specific task proficiency, written and oral communication proficiency, demonstrating effort, maintaining personal discipline, facilitating peer and team performance, supervision/leadership and management/administration) are assumed to be the highest-order factors that are sufficient to describe the latent hierarchy among all jobs. That is, the construct of performance cannot be meaningfully understood by combining these factors into a smaller subset or one general factor. Although the content of the factors may vary slightly across jobs, the focus of each is in terms of the observable and behavioral things that people do which are under their control. The eight-factor model is presented along with a brief description of the factors in Table 6.1.

Age and objective task performance. Studies have looked at age and the evaluation of task performance, the latter variable being measured using objective indices. For example, Sharit and Czaja (1999) examined age differences pertaining to the performance of a computer task by employees in the banking industry. Of the three age groups in this study (younger, middle-aged, and older participants), Sharit and Czaja found that younger participants were

TABLE 6.1.
Emerging Domain of Performance

Task Performance	Contextual Performance	Counterproductive Performance	Adaptive Performance
job-task proficiency	demonstrating effort,	Property deviance	Uncertain/
non job specific task	maintaining personal	Production deviance	unpredict-
proficiency	discipline, facilitating	Personal aggression	able
written and oral	peer and team	Political deviance	situations
communication	performance		Planning/
proficiency	(Campbell et al., 1993)		adjusting to
supervision/leadership	personal support		change
and management/	organizational support		
administration	conscientious initiative		
(Campbell et al.,			
1993)			

able to balance a larger number of transactions than both the other age groups. In addition, they found that middle-aged participants fared better than the older participants. Measures of task performance included work output, work time, use of the reset function and sending memos to the customer. Sharit and Czaja (1999) highlighted several points concerning age and computer-based task performance; specifically, computer experience predicted older participants' performance (cf. Sharit & Czaja, 1994 for an overview of the issues associated with the relationships between aging, computer-based task performance and stress). Sharit et al. (2004) also investigated the performance of older individuals on a simulated telecommuting task (performance measures included the number of e-mails responded to correctly), finding that both groups of older participants demonstrated better performance across sessions.

The greater average experience of older individuals in a variety of domains often results in positive relationships between age and knowledge (Warr, 2001). Knowledge has been operationalized as both declarative and procedural knowledge, and a positive relationship has been found between age and both forms of knowledge. However, according to Warr (2001), the individual's experience must be relevant to the knowledge domain being assessed, as there are significant individual differences in amounts of individual knowledge across domains and younger and older individuals may vary in the amounts of experience they have in various knowledge domains (Ackerman, 2000). Further, there is little research information about job-relevant knowledge at different ages (Warr, 2001). However, the hypothesis that older workers will, on average, have more knowledge than younger workers seems a reasonable one.

Meta-analyses have shown a trend that job knowledge on average is positively related with job performance (e.g., Dye, Reck, & McDaniel, 1993) despite limited research on job-relevant knowledge. Further, the greater knowledge that an older employee possesses may compensate for age-related declines in information processing (Warr, 2001). Overall, however, research indicates that the age of the employee does not consistently predict objective task performance (Borman, 1993; Farr & Ringseis, 2002; McEvoy & Cascio, 1989; Park, 1994; Waldman & Avolio, 1986; Warr, 2001). That is, older workers may know more than younger workers (although there is little definitive research on this), and they may use this knowledge to offset age-related declines (although evidence of these declines is equivocal), but on the whole, older workers do not perform their core tasks better or worse than younger workers.

Other objective measures used in the research on aging and job performance have included health indicators such as illness, accidents, absenteeism, and turnover as key indicators. Below, we discuss research on age, illness, and accidents. We discuss both absenteeism and turnover under the heading of counterproductive work behaviors.

Health-related performance indicators. Health indicators have been used as measures of task performance, especially within the human factors literature. Harma (1996), for example, notes that older shift workers, compared to workers who perform their job during the day exclusively, have greater illness-related absenteeism. However, even though older workers experience greater difficulty adapting to the physical adjustments required of shift work, such adjustment can be facilitated through diet and exercise. Further, health indicators include blood pressure, musculoskeletal problems, and hypertension (Fischer et al., 2002). Griffiths (1997) notes that high work-related stress accelerates aging, which may lead to various diseases (Goedhart, 1992).

Accidents. Another objective indicator of task performance is the number of accidents and age-related injuries. Sterns, Barrett, and Alexander (1985) note that older adults usually experience more serious accident consequences and disabilities. Further, recovery from accidents for older workers is much slower. This is reinforced by Warr (1994) who concludes that although the incidence of injuries is actually lower for older workers (Sterns et al., 1985), older employees once injured take longer to recover and return to work. More frequent and minor work injuries may also be age-related. Choi, Levitsky, Lloyd, and Stones (1996) found that beyond age 30 minor age injuries affecting short-term work capacity occur more often. Older workers may lose more work time as a result of accidents than their younger counterparts, even though the frequency of some types of accidents declines with age.

Hansson, DeKoekkoek, Neece, and Patterson (1997) emphasize that instead of using the results discussed herein to justify stereotypical perceptions of older workers as lower performers in hazardous settings, individual differences must be noted. For example, Landy (1996) found that individuals over 50 years old in certain occupations, such as firefighting and policing, were less likely to die from catastrophic illness than workers in other stressful jobs. This is further supported by Kay et al. (1994) who found that pilot accident rates declined with age and leveled off at the mid-40s. Warr (1994) further points out that cross-sectional data regarding age-related differences in physical condition may be subject to cohort effects. This means that younger cohorts are in better physical condition than older cohorts when they were at the same age. Finally, Warr (1994) notes that longitudinal research concerning worker physical performance is limited and recommends that instead of focusing on chronological age, functional capacity in terms of relevant abilities and competencies should be the target of investigation.

Age and subjective ratings of task performance. Although there has been fairly extensive research on the effects of employee chronological age on subjective ratings of task performance, any conclusions drawn from this research should be viewed with caution (Shore & Goldberg, 2005). Meta-analytic studies have shown weak support for age-task performance rating relationships (Avolio, Waldman, & McDaniel, 1990; McEvoy & Cascio, 1989; Waldman & Avolio, 1986). Methodological limitations of research linking age with performance ratings have been identified by a number of reviews including: (a) most studies have failed to include workers older than 60 years of age; (b) small sample sizes which may limit the power of the design to detect performance differences that may exist; (c) much of the research is cross-sectional; (d) longitudinal research suggests nonlinear relationships, and (e) age-performance relationships may vary as a function of several third variables including occupation (Salthouse & Maurer, 1996; Waldman & Avolio, 1993). Further, as this review highlights, most research on age and performance has operationalized age as chronological age and performance as task performance. Much less research has included alternative measures of age or non-task performance.

Czaja's (1994) review of the relationship between aging and subjective ratings of task performance notes the overall lack of empirical evidence supporting the popular idea that age is associated with a decline in performance. She specifically notes that information in this area is lacking, particularly for work involving technology. Both meta-analyses by Waldman and Avolio (1986) and later by McEvoy and Cascio (1989) also failed to find practically significant (and negative) relationships between subjective ratings of task performance and age. However, the authors warn against methodological limitations in the studies conducted as noted earlier in this chapter. Finally, a review by Sterns and McDaniel (1994) of several meta-analyses indicated, at best, a weak positive relationship between age and performance. Czaja (1994) appropriately notes that the relationship between age and performance is neither simple nor easily understood.

Part of the explanation for the lack of relationship between age and subjective ratings of task performance may lie in the need to consider several moderating factors (cf. Griffiths, 1997). For example, differences in performance measurement and occupational groups make a difference when studying aging and job performance (Waldman & Avolio, 1986). While more objective measures do not indicate a negative association between age and job performance, some research using subjective supervisory ratings does. It should be noted that even when job and occupational types are taken into account, mixed relationships have surfaced (cf. Czaja, 1994, for a review of findings). Finally, Hansson et al. (1997) note that it is also important to differentiate between different areas of task performance that may be pertinent to age. For example, Gilbert, Collins, and Valenzi (1993) found differences between age groups in the four performance domains of overall performance, technical competence, job commitment, and positive work relations, but no linear relationships between age and performance.

Age and predictors of task performance. A related issue is the relationship between cognitive ability and job performance. In terms of cognitive task performance (cognitive abilities), when age differences are found, most of the research has consisted of laboratory investigations (Warr, 2001). Many of these age performance differences are observed in cross-sectional data (Warr, 2001), whereas longitudinal data often do not show much decline until individuals are in their 60s and beyond (Schaie, 1994). However, both general and specific measures of intelligence reveal age-related declines in performance that can emerge as young as age 40 years (Park, 1994). On average, older individuals show lower performance on measures that require complex forms of information processing, including selective and divided attention, memory for previously experienced material, use of working memory, dual task performance, and speeded responses to presented information (Warr, 2001). However, there are large individual differences in the performance of such tasks among older individuals. Further, a variety of interventions, such as retraining older individuals in the use of cognitive resources, buffering their task self-efficacy, and providing memory aids reduces the magnitude of the decrements.

Park (1994) examined several hypotheses pertaining to why there may not be a consistent association between age and work performance. The nature of such hypotheses involved the types of jobs older adults occupy, the role of experience, the development of knowledge job structures, and stronger environmental support. Relatedly, Salthouse and Maurer (1996) also offer potential explanations of why declines in cognitive abilities that are age related do not necessarily lead to a negative association between age and job performance. This is especially pertinent as Hunter and Hunter (1984) report cognitive ability as being one of the best predictors of job performance. Griffiths (1997) notes that population- or laboratory-based studies indicate a decline in some cognitive abilities over age, at the same time questioning the ecological validity of such studies to job performance. Murphy (1989b) further argues that cognitive ability differences predict work performance best when learning is required. Thus, older employees who perform primarily maintenance tasks should display limited performance dips. Colonia-Willner (1998) further suggests practical intelligence may work to compensate for abilities that have dipped in old age. Avolio and Waldman (1994) further note that when experience, education, and occupational type are controlled, age and sex tend to account for only a limited amount of variance in ability test scores.

Subjective age and task performance.   Studies of aging and job performance have also used employee subjective assessments of age, although these studies are fewer in number. For example, Iskra-Golec (2002) notes that nurses who feel older than their chronological age considered themselves exerting greater effort in order to perform their jobs, were more tired, and possessed poor work abilities. Kaliterna, Larsen, and Brkljacic (2002) also note that employees who felt younger were more competent in meeting various work demands. Workers who thought themselves younger than their counterparts did not try as hard physically, while workers who wanted to be younger than they were, felt more tired after the workday. Finally, Barnes-Farrell, Rumery, and Swody (2002) report a positive relationship between job-related strain and feeling old relative to the employee's chronological age across different countries.

Summary.   Hence, research looking at the specific relationship between aging and task performance has not produced consistent relationships. Not only has there been examination of plausible hypotheses of why this might be so, there has also been research in subjective self-assessments of age and an understanding of methodological limitations of research in this area. One reason that there may be inconsistent age-performance findings is that the construct of performance has been treated as unidimensional. However, as discussed earlier in this chapter, the construct of performance is multidimensional in nature (Borman & Motowidlo, 1993; Campbell et al., 1993). It may be that older workers perform some components of job performance better than younger workers, while they perform other components less well than younger workers.

Contextual Performance
(Organizational Citizenship Behavior)

Several researchers have asserted that job performance involves more than task performance (Borman & Motowidlo, 1993; Organ, 1988). Borman and Motowidlo (1993), for example, proposed a model of performance with two components at the highest level: task performance as we have already discussed and contextual performance. Smith, Organ, and Near (1983) labeled a similar construct *organizational citizenship behavior* (OCB). While task performance consists of required behaviors for a given job that either directly produces goods and services by the organization or maintains the technical core or required tasks, contextual performance consists of behaviors that support the broader environment in which the required tasks or technical core must operate (Borman & Motowidlo, 1993).

Contextual performance or OCBs include behaviors such as volunteering for tasks not formally part of the job, demonstrating effort, helping and cooperating with others, following organizational rules and supporting organizational objectives (Borman & Motowidlo, 1993). A number of these behaviors would fall under a subset of components identified by Campbell et al. (1993). Although there is little consensus on the dimensionality of OCBs, Borman, Penner, Allen, and Motowidlo (2001) found that the structure of citizenship behaviors could be described using three categories. Personal support includes behaviors benefiting individuals in the organization including helping, motivating, cooperating with, and showing consideration. Organizational support includes behaviors benefiting the organization including representing the organization favorably, showing loyalty, and complying with organizational rules and procedures. Conscientious initiative includes behaviors benefiting the job or task including persisting with extra effort to complete tasks, taking initiative, and engaging in self development activities (Borman et al., 2001; Johnson, 2003).

Age and predictors of OCBs/contextual performance.   There is some evidence that age may be related to predictors or correlates of OCBs. For example, Wagner and Rush (2000) found evidence that the antecedents of altruistic behavior (a facet of OCB) may differ by employee age. Consistent with theoretical explanations of OCB, contextual factors such as job satisfaction, organizational commitment and management trust predicted the extent to which younger employees showed altruistic behaviors. On the other hand, such contextual factors did not predict altruism among older employees. Rather, the dispositional variable of moral judgment was a predictor of OCB among older employees. In addition, mean personality trait differences have been found for younger and older individuals on both the Big Five traits and on more specific traits (Farr & Ringseis, 2002; Warr, 2001). According to Farr and Ringseis (2002), older individuals have higher average scores on measures of conscientiousness and agreeableness, but lower scores on openness to experience and change orientation. Conscientiousness is a key correlate of OCBs.

Although previous research (Organ & Konovsky, 1989) has not found age main effects using OCB, age may serve as a moderator of the relationship between antecedents and OCBs. That is, even though there may be few differences between younger and older employees in terms of the frequency of OCBs, the reasons that older and younger employees engage in such behavior may vary. However, the work performance implications of these findings are not clear. More research needs to be conducted to assess the consistency of these findings and whether or not they translate to age-performance relationships, or whether personality-performance relationships moderate the age-performance relationship (Farr & Ringseis, 2002). In sum, according to Farr and Ringseis (2002), demographic variables have not been strong predictors of OCB. Although tenure (which is highly correlated with employee age) was found not to be predictive of OCBs, chronological age or age diversity and OCBs has rarely been investigated empirically (Organ & Lingl, 1995; Organ & Ryan, 1995).

Adaptive Performance

Hesketh and Neal (1999) have suggested that there is a third major component of job performance, adaptive performance, which is distinct from both task and contextual performance. Adaptive performance is the proficiency with which a person alters his or her behavior to the demands of the environment, an event or a new situation (Pulakos, Arad, Donovan, & Plamondon, 2000). Pulakos et al. found support for eight dimensions that comprised adaptive performance. However, six of these dimensions have subsequently been classified as either task or citizenship performance (Johnson, 2003). Although two dimensions are most similar to Hesketh and Neal's (1999) as well as London and Mone's (1999) concept of adaptive performance, one of these dimensions, learning work tasks, technologies and procedures in response to changing conditions, contains aspects of both task and contextual performance. However, the dimension of dealing with uncertain and unpredictable work situations may be distinct from task and citizenship performance (Johnson, 2003.

Related to the construct of adaptive performance, Abraham and Hansson (1995; Hansson et al., 1997) note that recent conceptualization of successful aging refers to the construct as successfully adjusting to change that is developmental (Baltes & Baltes, 1990) or as competently adapting or adjusting (Featherman, 1992). Hansson et al. (1997) highlight four themes of successful aging within the literature (Dixon & Backman, 1995; Schulz & Heck-hausen, 1996): planning to adjust psychologically to the loss of competency or standing at work, planning to prevent decline of functioning, planning to re-cover lost skills, and developing alternative compensations for inevitable losses due to age. Using Baltes and Baltes's (1990) model of successful aging at work, Abraham and Hansson (1995) developed measures of the model's key con-structions of strategies of selection, optimization, and compensation (with spe-cific reference to impression management) specific to the work environment. Selection refers to reducing the breadth of activities, optimization includes the maximization of resources, and compensation is the deliberate effort to make up for losses over the developmental lifespan. Abraham and Hansson (1995) found that the measures developed were reliable and indicative of tap-ping different factors. Future research on age-adaptive performance links is likely to be the most productive and also the most challenging for both theo-retical development and application within organizational settings.

A related construct within the career success literature involves career timetables (Shore & Goldberg, 2005). Career timetables reflect organizational norms pertaining to the age by which an employee should achieve a certain ca-reer stage within an organization. The emphasis is on the extent to which the age characteristic of a target employee matches the age composition of work-ers typical for a given career stage. For example, research on managers who are *behind schedule* indicate that such managers tend to experience poorer work satisfaction and work orientation; at the same time, they also tend to receive the lowest performance ratings (Lawrence, 1984; 1988). Further, approaches treating age mismatches have been adopted and these look at the proportion of older workers in a work group and the impact on older applicant ratings (Cleveland, Festa, & Montgomery, 1988) or decisions about older workers (Cleveland, Montgomery, & Festa, 1984). Finally, Shore, Cleveland, and Gold-berg (2003) noted that older employees may be viewed as being behind sched-ule when there is a younger supervisor.

A related age and adaptive performance (and career success) issue, espe-cially from a life span perspective, is that of professional competence. Sterns and Dorsett (1994) noted that the relationship between age and obsolescence is thus far inconclusive. They argue that findings linking age to obsolescence may be occupation-specific (Willis & Tosti-Vasey, 1986; Shearer & Steger, 1975) and that the risk of obsolescence is not necessarily dependent on age. However, Sterns and Dorsett (1994) caution that it is possible that factors such as the availability of challenging work and organizational support may differ-entially affect the participation of older and younger workers in competency training activities that develop competencies at different points in the lifespan. Salthouse and Maurer (1996) discuss individual level and systemic level fac-tors that may affect older worker participation in development activities. Finally, Kanfer and Ackerman (2004) present a model outlining how individual age-related changes affect motivation and work outcomes. This model looks at work motivation across the lifespan and examines four intraindividual trajectories of change: gain (growth of crystallized intelligence over age), loss (a gradual decline in cognitive ability), reorganization (some form of developmental discontinuity resulting in different patterns of action motivation), and exchange (changes in the importance and strength of motives).

The current literature on adaptive performance and successful aging both emphasize an ongoing, developmental and sociopsychological perspective. With the rapidly changing nature of work, it appears that employees who can scan a work situation and adapt their behavior appropriately to address the changing needs within that context will be the most successful. Below we discuss a set of work behaviors than often do not have positive organizational outcomes yet are considered as part of the performance domain. These behaviors are known as organizational deviant behaviors.

Organizational Deviant Behaviors

Organizational deviant behaviors have negative value for organizational effectiveness and have been proposed as a fourth distinct component of job performance (Sackett & Wanek, 1996; Viswesvaran & Ones, 2000) as shown in Table 6.1. This component is known as counterproductive behavior. Robinson and Bennett (1995) define organizationally deviant behavior as voluntary behaviors that violate organizational norms and also threaten the viability and wellbeing of the organization and/or its members. They found that deviant behavior can vary along two factors: (1) organizational/interpersonal and (2) serious/minor. Crossing these two factors yields four categories of deviant behaviors including property deviance (serious deviance directed towards the organization), production deviance (minor deviance directed toward the organization), personal aggression (serious deviance directed toward an individual), and political deviance (minor deviance directed toward individuals). However, there is little consensus regarding the dimensionality of counterproductivity. For example, other researchers have identified property damage, substance abuse, and violence on the jobs as facets (Sackett & Wanek, 1996) and withdrawal behaviors such as tardiness, absenteeism and turnover or even social loafing or withholding effort (Kidwell & Bennett, 1993). Absenteeism and turnover have been extensively examined in relation to age. Both measures can be viewed as examples of CWB (define CWB), specifically production deviance.

Absenteeism. Warr (1994) cites meta-analytic research (e.g., Hackett, 1990; Martocchio, 1989) indicating that voluntary absenteeism is negatively associated with male employee age; interestingly, the meta-analytic research did not find any relationship for female employees. Importantly, Warr (1994) emphasizes the need to consider organizational culture and absenteeism rates. Nicholson and Johns (1985), for example, note that there is an absence culture within organizations that informally sanctions what is acceptable. Thus, it appears that even objective performance indicators must be interpreted within larger organizational systems. Finally, while there appears to be a negative correlation between age and avoidable absences (those under the employee's control; Thompson, Griffiths, & Davison, 2000), for unavoidable absences, the correlation with age is positive. In addition, as discussed in the previous section, older workers may be more likely than younger workers to have health problems that result in longer absences.

Turnover.   Research suggests there is a negative correlation between age and turnover in the range of −.20 to −.25 (Beehr & Bowling, 2002). A number of explanations have been offered for this relationship (Arkes & Blumer, 1985; Warr, 1994). First, older workers stay in their jobs because they do not believe they have alternative employment options. Second, older workers tend to be more satisfied and tend not to seek employment elsewhere (Warr, 1994). One reason for this is they often occupy relatively good paying jobs. Another explanation for lower turnover among older employees is due to sunk cost; that is, the worker's notion that is he or she has already expended much time and effort on this job so it is not worth seeking employment elsewhere. Shore and Goldberg (2005) note in their review on age discrimination in the workplace that the research on organizational exit and voluntary turnover is not predicted by age, with the population correlation a mere −0.08 (Healy, Lehman, & McDaniel, 1995). However, Warr (1994) states that employee age may affect turnover through work team composition. For example, McCain, O'Reilly, and Pfeffer (1983) suggest that organizations employing cohorts who are age discontinuous may encounter more turnover due to enhanced conflict and communication difficulties. Therefore, multiple perspectives exist as to why an inverse relationship may exist between age and turnover.

Theft, overt destruction, and white-collar crime.   In addition, age is correlated with other CWBs including theft. According to Lau, Au, and Ho (2003) the estimated population value of the correlation between age and theft is −.21, suggesting that there is a moderate age effect with younger employees engaging in more theft. Further, employees with a shorter tenure were more likely to engage in thefts (estimated population correlation of −.12) and to come to work late (estimated population correlation of −.13).

Age appears to be the most powerful demographic predictor of counterproductive behaviors. As employees get older, they engage in less theft, production deviance, lateness, and absenteeism (Lau et al., 2003). Research in crime causation has found that older nonwhite-collar employees engage in less organizational misbehavior.

Although most scholars conceptualize white-collar and nonwhite-collar crime as discrete entities (Walters & Geyer, 2004), Gottfredson and Hirschi (1990) posit that there are few real differences between the two and that all crime is a result of low self control. Weisburd, Chayet, and Waring (1990) tested this theory of white-collar crime using federal offenders of white-collar crime including antitrust offenses, securities and exchange fraud, postal and wire fraud, false claims and statements, credit and lending institution fraud, bank embezzlement, IRS fraud, and bribery. They found that there was an older age of onset and lower frequency of offending than observed among nonwhite-collar offenders. Further, Walters and Geyer (2004) found that white-collar offenders without a history of nonwhite-collar crime were significantly older, more highly educated than the nonwhite-collar control group.

Finally, in a survey of restaurant and fast food employees, a number of differences were found between managers and entry-level employees in work related behaviors (McGraw-Hill/London House and National Food Service Security Council, 1995). For example, managers (older employees) were more likely to leave work early without permission than entry-level employees. Entry-level employees used drugs and alcohol at work, intentionally overcharged or short-changed customers, and abused sick days more often than managers. Employees who were male or younger than 30 years of age, had less than two years with the company, or worked the night shift tended to steal cash, merchandise, and property of greater value and with greater frequency than others. Employees who admitted using or coming to work hungover from drugs or alcohol tended to be men who were younger than 35 years old.

Summary. Why is it important to understand and explicate the construct of performance when studying the relationship between age and job performance? Past research focuses on age and task performance with some attention to counterproductive objective measures such as turnover or absence. However, there is little aging research on more recently conceptualized facets of performance. Theoretically there has been little systematic structuring of age-performance research by such performance taxonomies as Campbell et al. (1993) or Borman and Motowidlo (1993) that incorporates OCBs, or adaptive performance. Although progress has been made in systematically explicating a critical dependent variable in applied psychology, there are other components that are yet to be recognized as part of this construct. Employee health and wellbeing, stress, marital quality, and parental performance are all potentially aspects of an emerging performance domain within the larger context of our lives and are inextricably linked with work organizations (Cleveland, 2005). Behavior at work affects behavior away from work and vice versa, and a truly comprehensive definition of job performance and effectiveness is likely to include factors (e.g., health and wellbeing) that have traditionally not been part of the performance domain.

Finally, research on aging and job performance components should be located within a systemic view of organizations (cf. Sterns & Miklos, 1995). Specifically, understanding how organizational systems of selection, job design, and training and performance evaluation affect specific job performance components is integral in enriching our knowledge of aging and job performance. Such systems themselves are affected by the legal and economic environment. While these are the formal systems that structure our understanding of job performance, it is emphasized that job performance components and their attendant processes and indices of performance evaluation operate ultimately within a sociopsychological context (cf. Levy & Williams, 2004; Murphy & Cleveland, 1995, for a sociopsychological perspective of performance evaluation).

Multi-Source and Team-Based Measures of Performance

Subjective evaluations of job performance may be implemented in several ways. Supervisory ratings of the employee on relevant dimensions of work performance are the most frequent basis of subjective measures (Murphy & Cleveland, 1995). In this case, performance ratings are only from one source. There are also multisource feedback ratings where performance ratings are obtained from the supervisor, peers, subordinates, and even customers. This is known as 360-degree feedback (London & Beatty, 1993). London and Smither (1995) note that the purpose of multisource feedback is to enhance the employee's self-development in areas relevant to the organization by giving employees a sense of how others view their performance (cf. Mount & Scullen, 2001 for a review of multisource feedback ratings and its implications for research and practice).

According to Warr and Hoare (2002), age research on multisource ratings typically uses averaged judgments or ratings about employees. Such research has revealed inconsistent findings (Atwater & Yammarino, 1997). In some studies, average self-ratings and subordinate-ratings of managers were unrelated to age (Wohlers, Hall, & London, 1993), whereas in other research, average ratings were significantly more positive at older ages (Church, 1997). No significant relationships were found between focal manager's age and self-ratings or supervisory ratings using averaged ratings (Warr & Bourne, 1999). However, when ratings of separate behaviors were examined, a differentiated pattern was found. For example, no differences were found between younger and older managers in their self-ratings of flexibility at work. However, older managers were rated less positively on flexibility by their supervisors. Further, supervisory ratings of strategic thinking did not differ by age, although older managers rated themselves higher than did younger managers.

In follow-up research that examined specific behaviors rather than averaged judgments, Warr and Hoare (2002) found age differences in six self-rated behaviors. Specifically, older employees rated themselves more positively than younger employees in terms of problem solving, business awareness, quality orientation, organization, resilience, and using initiative. Using supervisory ratings, age differences were found for problem solving, specialist knowledge, business awareness, and using initiative. Older employees were significantly more likely to rate themselves higher relative to their supervisor's ratings on five of the 16 behaviors including problem solving, quality orientation, organization, resilience, and using initiative. Although supervisors rated older employees more positively than younger employees on almost all these behaviors, employees' own rating were more strongly associated with age (i.e., differences in source of ratings occurred from the more positive self-ratings by older employees). Warr and colleagues have led the research on age comparisons in multisource ratings; however, additional empirical research needs to be conducted.

Proximal context factors and age (Moderators).   Subjective performance evaluation has been studied by Vecchio (1993) who notes that employees older than their supervisors received ratings that were just as positive as other employees. At the same time, older employees evaluated their working relationship with their supervisor as being more positive and also viewed their supervisors in a better light. These findings should, however, be tempered against the meta-analytic research suggesting that attitudes towards older adults are more negative than attitudes towards younger adults across several dimensions, including evaluation (Kite, Stockdale, Whitley, & Johnson, 2005).

Findings reviewed thus far suggest that a consideration of the social context of performance evaluation is necessary. The social context of performance evaluation was illustrated by Cleveland and Shore (1992). In a study on age perceptions, they found that subjectively younger and relatively younger employees received lower promotability ratings than subjectively younger but relatively older employees. Ferris, Judge, Chachere, and Liden (1991) found evidence showing an interactive effect between work group age composition and supervisor age on supervisor ratings on employee performance. Specifically, older supervisors were more likely to give higher ratings to subordinates in groups made up mainly of younger workers than in older groups. On the other hand, younger supervisors were more likely to give higher ratings to employees in older workgroups than in younger groups. Henkens (2000) also found that most supervisors were not supportive of having large numbers of older employees continue with their jobs until the official retirement age; this was, however, tempered when supervisors felt that older employee retirement would lead to a loss of expertise. Supervisors also tended to indicate difficulties with different aspects of older employee work performance.

In sum, we know less about the age-subjective rating links by source of rating (e.g., supervisor, coworker, subordinate). Although there is evidence that older employees rate themselves higher than their supervisors, this rating pattern is also found among younger employees. It is not clear whether older employees show greater or less agreement than younger workers in ratings with coworkers and/or direct reports. An understanding of subjective performance of aging employees should therefore include sociopsychological aspects of job performance. Most research in aging and job performance has tended not to look at multisource feedback pertaining to older workers.

Team performance. In a study comparing the team performance of 15 teams comprised of three different age groups (young, middle-aged and old), Streufert, Pogash, Piasecki, and Post (1990) found that older teams were not as responsive as other teams to incoming information, were less strategic, and did not have as broad a task overview. Older teams could still exploit opportunities and manage a simulated emergency as well as the younger teams. Multiple measures were used in this study including activity and speed, information orientation, approach diversity, strategy, and planning and emergency management.

Research on aging and teams suggests that work attitudes play an important role. For example, Hayslip, Methany, Miller, Yeatts, Beyerlein, and Johnson (1996) found that older employees viewed passivity of a supervisor more negatively in self-managed work teams where employees have discretion over and responsibility for decisions that affect group outcomes. Hayslip et al. suggest that older employees may benefit more from self-managing work environments where autonomy is high. The finding further supports this suggestion that older employees in self-managed work teams tended to report more positive views of informational access critical to their work performance. Earlier research by Wright and Hamilton (1978) supported these results and found that older workers particularly value a supportive social work environment, including freedom and authority.

IMPLICATIONS FOR FUTURE RESEARCH

Since the landmark book and *Psychological Bulletin* article in 1983 by Rhodes and colleagues (Doering, Rhodes, & Schuster, 1983; Rhodes, 1983) there have been important advances in our understanding of age and performance in multiple areas including (1) our conceptualization of performance as a critical construct and outcome in psychological research, and (2) our theorizing of the role of age in relation to important organizational behaviors and performance.

Applied work psychologists have made a tremendous contribution during the last 20 years in enhancing our understanding of the nature of work performance through careful construct explication, articulation, and documentation (Campbell et al, 1993; Borman & Motowidlo, 1992; Pulakos et al., 2000; Sackett & DeVore, 2001). Historically, performance has been viewed as largely unidimensional and as reflecting task performance or required core job behaviors. Within this tradition, the influence of age on performance was assessed using largely generic assessments of task-loaded performance measures. However, the expansion in the criterion domain involves the identification and explication of contextual performance or organizational citizenship behaviors. There is a recognition and general acceptance that previous assessments of employee performance have been deficient in capturing the overall contribution or value of an individual's behavior to the organization (Borman & Motowidlo, 1993; Johnson, 2003).

In addition, Sackett and colleagues Viswesvaran and Ones have developed greater theoretical and empirical rationale for a broader consideration of counterproductive work behaviors as part of the expanding work performance domain. While withdrawal behaviors such as absenteeism, tardiness, and turnover have long been used as passive, negative (yet objective) performance indicators, applied psychology is increasingly recognizing the importance of understanding and managing overtly negative work behaviors including work property destruction, as well as passive and malicious behaviors such as gossiping. Finally, within the global context of an ever-changing work place and continuous learning by organizations with the increasing need for individuals to initiate career enhancing activities, the notion of adaptive performance is one that we predict will receive increasing research and organizational attention. As the theoretical bases for counterproductive work behaviors, adaptive performance and contextual performance continue to develop; it is critically important to incorporate theories of aging within the performance theory development process.

Recent research on age and performance has not only examined age as a moderator between antecedents and important performance outcomes, but also indicated that predictors or antecedents of performance may in fact *differ* for older and younger employees. Certainly this is not a new development. However, what the recent research highlights is not only the importance of assessing the main effect of age-performance relationships, but also the need to reexamine our performance and discrimination theories to include alternative roles that age may play in relation to important work outcomes. For example, currently there is little research on the extent to which age bias is present (or degree of age changes) in contextual performance evaluations and adaptive performance. Given the expanding domain of the performance construct and the dynamics associated with the aging workforce, we need to ex-amine the presence and influence of age stereotypes upon all our measures of performance in organizations. There is little empirical evidence available con-cerning age links with these emerging performance constructs. Further, we need to understand whether age biases are enhanced or inhibited with the use of specific assessment methods, especially 360-degree evaluation or feed-back systems and team performance appraisal systems.

IMPLICATIONS FOR PRACTICE

Performance evaluation is one area within industrial and organizational psy-chology where scientists or academics and practitioners inform each other on problems rather than one perspective taking a dominant role. Performance appraisal systems for older employees are really no different than those for younger workers (Hedge, Borman, & Lammlein, 2006). Valid and legally de-fensible systems should represent job related constructs as shown in a job analysis, be aligned with organizational objectives, have clear rating procedures such that judgments and ratings can be reasonably accurate reflections of per-formance, and raters must be qualified to make accurate performance assess-ments. Yet age bias in ratings is a measurable characteristic that places older employees in a more negative light and reflects negative age stereotypes and norms. Therefore, it is important to ensure that performance evaluations are based on the unique performance of each individual employee rather than on group membership or group stereotypes (Hansson et al., 1997).

Performance is a reflection of employee ability and motivation. Yet re-search on performance and older workers has focused more on the relation-ships between age-ability related characteristics (and declines) and task per-formance. Although older workers show some age decrements in abilities, these appear not to translate into significant work performance declines. More important, fewer researchers have framed issues surrounding the performance of older employees in terms of the motivation of workers as they age. We be-lieve that this is especially critical given the aging demographics of our soci-ety generally and our workforce more specifically. From the research on task performance, it is clear that older workers *can* (are capable of doing) perform well on the job over the lifespan. The key issue for organizations given the shrinking availability of skilled employees is how to design or construct the workplace to attract, retain, and motivate older employees so the best em-ployees want or are motivated to continue to perform well. For example, some research suggests that older employees consider a smaller quantity of infor-mation before making a decision or taking an action (e.g., Sharit & Czaja,

1999). It may be that older workers are more strategic in the information used (information has higher quality) than the larger amount of information used by younger employees. Yet when an organization implements a 360 degree feedback system to provide employees with supervisory, peer, subordinate, and customer evaluative information (multiple sources and large quantities), older employees may react differently than younger employees to this multisource performance feedback in terms of processing, acting upon, and affective reactions to the information. Understanding such situations would provide greater theoretical and practical understanding about the behavior of younger and older organizational members.

SUMMARY

In conclusion, recent research continues to provide evidence of few age-related differences in task performance. Much less is known about the age influences on contextual performance, counterproductive work behaviors, and adaptive performance. We believe that both the contribution and value of older employees in organizations will be more accurately and fully assessed as we approach our research on workplace aging with well-articulated performance theories and empirical support.

PEDAGOGICAL TOOL

In Good Company

Dan Foreman, a 50-something head of advertising sales, is demoted when the company he works for is acquired in a corporate takeover. His new boss, a business school prodigy, Carter Duryea, is half Dan's age. Dan developed his client base through handshake deals and nurturing long-term relationships putting decency, loyalty, and integrity first. Carter promotes the magazine with the cell phone division. He is brought in to shake things up, cut costs and so forth; never mind that he has no experience in the field. He begins to improvise his job, is forced to fire workers, and decides to keep Dan around—wisely so—as an "awesome wingman." After the magazine is purchased again, Carter, the young hotshot boss, is fired and Dan is restored to his rightful position.

REFERENCES

Abraham, J. D., & Hansson, R. O. (1995). Successful aging at work: An applied study of selection, optimization, and compensation through impression management. *Journal of Gerontology, 50,* 94–103.

Ackerman, P. L. (2000). Domain-specific knowledge as the "dark matter" of adult intelligence: Gf/Gc, personality and interest correlates. *Journals of Gerontology: Series B: Psychological Sciences and Social Sciences, 55B,* 69–84.

Arkes, H., & Blumer, C. (1985). The psychology of sunk cost. *Organizational Behavior and Human Decision Processes, 35,* 124–140.

Atwater, L. E., & Yammarino, F. J. (1997). Self-other rating agreement: A review and model. *Personnel and Human Resources Management, 15,* 121–174.

Avolio, B. J., & Waldman, D. A. (1994). Variations in cognitive, perceptual, and psychomotor abilities across the working life span: Examining the effects of race, sex, experience, education, and occupational type. *Psychology and Aging, 9,* 430–442.

Avolio, B. J., Waldman, D. A., & McDaniel, M. A. (1990). Age and work performance in nonmanagerial jobs: The effects of experience and occupation type. *Academy of Management Journal, 32,* 407–422.

Bailey, L. L., & Hansson, R. O. (1995). Psychological obstacles to job or career change in late life. *Journal of Gerontology: Psychological Sciences, 50B,* 280–288.

Baltes, P. B., & Baltes, M. M. (1990). Psychological perspectives on successful aging: The model of selective optimization with compensation. In P. B. Baltes & M. M. Baltes (Eds.), *Successful aging: Perspectives from the behavioral sciences* (pp. 1–33). Cambridge, UK: Cambridge University Press.

Barak, B. (1987). Cognitive age: A new multidimensional approach to measuring age identity. *International Journal of Aging and Human Development, 25,* 109–128.

Barak, B., & Stern, B. (1986). Subjective age correlates: A research note. *Gerontologist, 26,* 571–578.

Barnes-Farrell, J. L., Rumery, S. M., & Swody, C. A. (2002). How do concepts of age relate to work and off-the-job stress and strains? A field study of health care workers in five nations. *Experimental Aging Research, 28,* 87–98.

Baum, S. K., & Boxley, R. L. (1983). Age identification in the elderly. *Gerontologist, 23,* 532–537.

Beehr, T. A., & Bowling, N. A. (2002). Career issues facing older workers. In D. Feldman (Ed.), *Work careers: A developmental perspective* (pp. 214–241). San Francisco: Jossey-Bass.

Borman, W. C. (1993). Job behavior, performance, and effectiveness. In M. D. Dunnette & L. M. Hough (Eds.), *Handbook of Industrial and Organizational Psychology* (Vol. 2, pp. 271–326). Palo Alto, CA: Consulting Psychologists Press.

Borman, W., & Motowidlo, S. (1993). Expanding the criterion domain to include elements of contextual performance. In N. Schmitt, & W. C. Borman (Eds.), *Personnel selection in organizations* (pp. 71–98). San Francisco: Jossey-Bass.

Borman, W. C., Penner, L. A., Allen, T. D., & Motowidlo, S. (2001). Personality predators of citizenship performance. *International Journal of Selection and Assessment, 9,* 52–69.

Campbell, J. P., McCloy, R. A., Oppler, S. H., & Sager, C. E. (1993). A theory of performance. In N. Schmitt & W. C. Borman Associates (Eds.), *Personnel selection in organizations* (pp. 35–70). San Francisco: Jossey-Bass.

Choi, B. C. K., Levitsky, M., Lloyd, R. D., & Stones, I. M. (1996). Patterns and risk factors for sprains in Ontario Canada 1990: An analysis of the Workplace Health and Safety Agency database. *Journal of Environmental and Occupational Medicine, 38,* 379–389.

Church, A. H. (1997). Managerial self-awareness in high-performing individuals in organizations. *Journal of Applied Psychology, 82,* 281–292.

Cleveland, J. N. (2005). What is success? Who defines it? Perspectives on the criterion problem as it relates to work and family. In E. E. Kossek & S. J. Lambert (Eds.), *Work and life integration: Organizational cultural and individual perspectives* (pp. 319–345). Mahwah, N.J.: Lawrence Erlbaum Associates.

Cleveland, J. N., Festa, R. M., & Montgomery, L. (1988). Applicant pool composition and job perceptions: Impact on decisions regarding an older applicant. *Journal of Vocational Behavior, 32,* 112–125.

Cleveland, J. N., Montgomery, L., & Festa, R. M. (1984). *Group composition and job perceptions: Impact on decisions about suitability of applicants for group membership.* Unpublished manuscript, Department of Psychology, Baruch College, City University of New York.

Cleveland, J. N., & Shore, L. M. (1992). Self- and supervisory perspectives in age and work attitudes and performance. *Journal of Applied Psychology, 77,* 469–484.

Colonia-Willner, R. (1998). Practical intelligence at work: Relationship between aging and cognitive efficiency among managers in a bank environment. *Psychology and Aging, 13,* 45–57.

Czaja, S. J. (1994). Employment opportunities for older adults: Engineering design and research issues. *Experimental Aging Research, 20,* 265–273.

Dixon, R. A., & Backman, L. (Eds.). (1995). *Compensating for psychological deficits and declines: Managing losses and promoting gains.* Hillsdale, NJ: Lawrence Erlbaum Associates.

Doering, M., Rhodes, S. R., & Schuster, M. (1983). *The aging worker: Research and recommendations.* Beverly Hills, CA: Sage Publications.

Dye, D. A., Reck, M., & McDaniel, M. A. (1993). Moderators of the validity of written job knowledge measures. *International Journal of Selection and Assessment, 1,* 153–157.

Farr, J. L., & Ringseis, E. L. (2002). The older worker in organizational context: Beyond the individual. In C. L. Cooper & I. T. Robertson (Eds.), *International Review of Industrial and Organizational Psychology,* (Vol. 17, pp. 31–76). Chichester, England: John Wiley.

Featherman, D. L. (1992). Development of reserves for adaptation to old age: Personal and societal agendas. In E. Cutler, D. W. Gregg, & M. P. Lawton (Eds.), *Aging, money, and life satisfaction: Aspects of financial gerontology* (pp. 135–168). New York: Springer.

Ferris, G. R., Judge, T. A., Chachere, J. G., & Liden, R. C. (1991). The age context of performance evaluation decisions. *Psychology and Aging, 6,* 616–622.

Fischer, F. M., Bellusci, S. M., Teixeira, L. R., Borges, F. N., Ferreira, R. M., Goncalves, M. B. L., Martins, S. E., & Christoffolete, M. A. (2002). Unveiling factors that contribute to functional aging among health care shift workers in Sao Paulo, Brazil. *Experimental Aging Research, 28,* 73–86.

Gilbert, G. R., Collins, R. W., & Valenzi, E. (1993). Relationship of age and job performance: From the eye of the supervisor. *Journal of Employee Assistance Research, 2,* 36–46.

Gottfredson, M., & Hirschi, T. (1990). *A general theory of crime.* Stanford, CA: Stanford University Press.

Goedhart, W. J. A. (1992). *Aging and the work environment.* Aging at Work: Proceedings of a European Colloquium (pp. 57–66), Paris, June 1991. Dublin: European Foundation for the Improvement of Living and Working Conditions.

Griffiths, A. (1997). Aging, health and productivity: A challenge for the new millennium. *Work & Stress, 11,* 197–214.

Hackett, R. D. (1990). Age, tenure, and employee absenteeism. *Human Relations, 43,* 601–619.

Hansson, R. O., DeKoekkoek, P. D., Neece, W. M., & Patterson, D. W. (1997). Successful aging at work: Annual Review, 1992–1996: The older worker and transitions to retirement. *Journal of Vocational Behavior, 51,* 202–233.

Harma, M. (1996). Aging, physical fitness and shift work tolerance. *Applied Ergonomics, 27,* 25–29.

Hayslip, Jr., B., Methany, W., Miller, C., Yeatts, D., Beyerlein, M. B., & Johnson, D. (1996). Employee age and perceptions of work in self-managing and traditional work groups. *International Journal of Aging and Human Development, 42,* 291–312.

Healy, M. C., Lehman, M., & McDaniel, M. A. (1995). Age and voluntary turnover: A quantitative review. *Personnel Psychology, 48,* 335–345.

Hedge, J. W., Borman, W. C., & Lammlein, S. E. (2006). *The aging workforce: Realities, myths, and implications for organizations.* Washington, DC: American Psychological Association.

Henkens, K. (2000). Supervisors' attitudes about the early retirement of subordinates. *Journal of Applied Social Psychology, 30,* 833–582.

Hesketh, B., & Neal, A. (1999). Technology and performance. In D. R. Ilgen & E. D. Pulakos (Eds.), *The changing nature of performance: Implications for staffing, motivation, and development* (pp. 21–55). San Francisco: Jossey-Bass.

Hunter, J. E., & Hunter, R. F. (1984). Validity and utility of alternative predictors of job performance. *Psychological Bulletin, 96,* 72–98.

Johnson, J. W. (2003). Toward a better understanding of the relationship between personality and individual job performance (pp. 83–120). In M. R. Barrick and A. M. Ryan (Eds.), *Personality and work: Reconsidering the role of personality in organizations.* San Francisco: Jossey-Bass.

Iskra-Golec, I. (2002). Personal age and assessment of work stress in Polish nurses. *Experimental Aging Research, 28,* 51–58.

Add Johnson, 2003

Kaliterna, L., Larsen, Z. P., & Brkljacic, T. (2002). Chronological and subjective age in relation to work demands: Survey of Croatian workers. *Experimental Aging Research, 28,* 39–49.

Kanfer, R., & Ackerman, P. L. (2004). Aging, adult development and work motivation. *Academy of Management Review, 29,* 440–458.

Kastenbaum, R., Derbin, V., Sabatini, P., & Artt, S. (1972). The ages of me: Toward personal and interpersonal definitions of functional age. *International Journal of Aging and Human Development, 3,* 197–212.

Kay, E. J., Harris, R. M., Voros, R. S., Hillman, D. J., Hyland, D. T., & Deimler, J. D. (1994). *Age 60 study, part III: Consolidated database experiments final report.* Washington, DC: Federal Aviation Administration (NTIS No. DOT/FAA/AM-94-22).

Kidwell, R. E., & Bennett, N. (1993). Employee propensity to withhold effort: A conceptual model to intersect three avenues of research. *Academy of Management Review, 18,* 429–456.

Kite, M. E., Stockdale, G. D., Whitley, Jr., B. E., & Johnson, B. T. (2005). Attitudes toward younger and older adults: An updated meta-analytic review. *Journal of Social Issues*, *61*, 241–266.

Landy, F. J. (1996). *Mandatory retirement and chronological age in public safety workers*. Testimony before the United States Senate Committee on Labor and Human Resources (March 8, 1996). Washington, DC: American Psychological Association.

Lau, V. C., Au, W. T., & Ho, J. M. C. (2003). A qualitative and quantitative review of antecedents of counter productive behavior in organizations. *Journal of Business and Psychology*, *18*, 73–99.

Lawrence, B. S. (1984). Age grading: The implicit organizational timetable. *Journal of Occupational Behavior*, *13*, 181–191.

Lawrence, B. S. (1988). New wrinkles in the theory of age: Demography, norms, and performance ratings. *Academy of Management Journal*, *31*, 309–337.

Levy, P. E., & Williams, J. R. (2004). The social context of performance appraisal: A review and framework for the future. *Journal of Management*, *30*, 881–905.

London, M., & Beatty, R. W. (1993). 360-degree feedback as a competitive advantage. *Human Resource Management*, *32*, 353–372.

London, M., & Mone, E. M. (1999). Continuous learning. In D. R. Ilgen & E. D. Pulakos (Eds.), *The changing nature of performance: Implications for staffing, motivation, and development* (pp. 119–153). San Francisco: Jossey-Bass.

London, M., & Smither, J. W. (1995). Can multi-source feedback change perceptions of goal accomplishment, self-evaluations, and performance-related outcomes? Theory-based applications and directions for research. *Personnel Psychology*, *48*, 803–839.

Martocchio, J. J. (1989). Age-related differences in employee absenteeism: A meta-analysis. *Psychology and Aging*, *4*, 409–414.

McCain, B. E., O'Reilly, C., & Pfeffer, J. (1983). The effects of departmental demography on turnover: The case of a university. *Academy of Management Journal*, *26*, 626–641.

McEvoy, G. M., & Cascio, W. F. (1989). Cumulative evidence of the relationship between employee age and job performance. *Journal of Applied Psychology*, *74*, 11–17.

McGraw-Hill/London House & National Food Service Security Council, 1995.

Mount, M. K., & Scullen, S. E. (2001). Multisource feedback ratings: What do they really measure? In M. London (Ed.), *How people evaluate others in organizations* (pp. 155–176). Mahwah, NJ: Lawrence Erlbaum Associates.

Murphy, K. R. (1989b). Is the relationship between cognitive ability and performance stable over time? *Human Performance*, *2*, 183–200.

Murphy, K. R., & Cleveland, J. N. (1995). *Understanding performance appraisal: Social, organizational, and goal-based perspectives*. Thousand Oaks, CA: Sage.

Nicholson, N., & Johns, G. (1985). The absence culture and the psychological contract — who's in control of absence? *Academy of Management Review*, *10*, 397–407.

Organ, D. W. (1988). *Organizational citizenship behavior*. Lexington, MA: D.C. Health.

Organ, D. W., & Konovsky, M. (1989). Cognitive versus affective determinants of organizational citizenship behavior. *Journal of Applied Psychology*, *74*, 157–164.

Organ, D. W., & Lingl, A. (1995). Personality, satisfaction, and organizational citizenship behavior. *Journal of Social Psychology*, *135*, 339–350.

Organ, D. W., & Ryan, K. (1995). A meta-analytic review of attitudinal and dispositional predictors of organizational citizenship behavior. *Personnel Psychology*, *48*, 775–802.

Park, D. C. (1994). Aging cognition and work. *Human Performance, 7,* 181–205.

Pfeffer, J. (1983). Organizational demography. *Research in Organizational Behavior, 5,* 299–357.

Pitt-Catsouphes, M., & Smyer, M. A. (July 18, 2005). *Perspectives: Aligning business needs with older workers' preferences and priorities.* Boston College: The Sloan Center for Flexible Work Options and Older Workers. Paper resulting from meeting convened by the Sloan Work & Family Research Network and Workplace Flexibility 2010, "Flexible work options: A pathway to healthy and productive aging."

Pulakos, E. D., Arad, S., Donovan, M. A., & Plamondon, K. E. (2000). Adaptability in the workplace: Development of a taxonomy of adaptive performance. *Journal of Applied Psychology, 85,* 612–624.

Rhodes, S. R. (1983). Age-related differences in work attitudes and behavior: A review and conceptual analysis. *Psychological Bulletin, 93,* 328–367.

Robinson, S. L., & Bennett, R. J. (1995). A typology of deviant workplace behaviors: A multidimensional scaling study. *Academy of Management Journal, 38,* 555–572.

Sackett, P. R., & DeVore, C. J. (2001). Counterproductive behaviors at work. In N. Anderson, D. S. Ones, H. K. Sinangil, & C., Viswesvaran (Eds.), *Handbook of industrial, work and organizational psychology* (Vol. 1, pp. 145–164). Beverly Hills, CA: Sage.

Sackett, P. R., & Wanek, J. E. (1996). New development in the use of measures of honesty, integrity, conscientiousness, dependability, trustworthiness, and reliability for personnel selection. *Personnel Psychology, 49,* 787–830.

Salthouse, T. A. (1986). Functional age. In J. E., Birren, P. K., Robinson, & S. E. Livingston (Eds.), *Age, health, and employment* (pp. 78–92). Englewood Cliffs, NJ: Prentice-Hall.

Salthouse, T. A., & Maurer, T. J. (1996). Aging, job performance, and career development. In J. E. Birren & K. W. Schaie (Eds.), *Handbook of the Psychology of Aging* (4th ed., pp. 353–364). New York: Academic Press.

Schaie, K. W. (1994). The course of adult intellectual development. *American Psychologist, 49,* 304–313.

Schulz, R., & Heckhausen, J. (1996). A life span model of successful aging. *American Psychologist, 51,* 702–714.

Sharit, J., & Czaja, S. A. (1994). Aging, computer-based task performance, and stress: Issues and challenges. *Ergonomics, 37,* 559–577.

Sharit, J., & Czaja, S. A. (1999). Performance of a computer-based troubleshooting task in the banking industry: Examining the effects of age, task experience, and cognitive abilities. *International Journal of Cognitive Ergonomics, 3,* 1–22.

Sharit, J., Czaja, S. J., Hernandez, M., Yang, Y., Perdomo, D., Lewis, J. E., Lee, C. C., & Fair, S. (2004). An evaluation of performance by older persons on a simulated telecommuting task. *Journal of Gerontology, 59B,* 305–316.

Shearer, R. L., & Steger, J. (1975). Manpower obsolescence: A new definition and empirical investigation of personal variables. *Academy of Management Journal, 18,* 263–275.

Shore, L. M., Cleveland, J. N., & Goldberg, C. B. (2003). Work attitudes and decisions as a function of manager age and employee age. *Journal of Applied Psychology, 88,* 529–537.

Shore, L. M., & Goldberg, C. B. (2005). Age discrimination in the workplace. In R. L. Dipboye & A. Colella (Eds.), *Discrimination at work: The psychological and organizational bases* (pp. 203–225). Mahwah, NJ: Lawrence Erlbaum Associates.

Smith, C. A., Organ, D. W., & Near, J. P. (1983). Organizational citizenship behavior: Its nature and antecedents. *Journal of Applied Psychology, 68,* 655–663.

Steitz, J. S., & McClary, A. M. (1988). Subjective age, age identity and middle-age adults. *Experimental Aging Research, 14,* 83–88.

Sterns, H. L., & Alexander, R. A. (1987). Industrial gerontology: The aging individual and work. *Annual Review of Gerontology and Geriatrics, 7,* 243–264.

Sterns, H. L., Barrett, G. V., & Alexander, R. A. (1985). Accidents and the aging individual. In J. E. Birren & K. W. Schaie (Eds.), *Handbook of the Psychology of Aging* (2nd ed., pp. 703–724). New York: Van Nostrand Rinehold.

Sterns, H. L., & Dorsett, J. G. (1994). Career development: A life span issue. *Experimental Aging Research, 20,* 257–264.

Sterns, H. L., & Doverspike, D. (1989). Aging and the training and learning process. In I. L. Goldstein (Ed). *Training and Development in Organizations* (pp. 299–332). San Francisco, CA: Jossey Bass.

Sterns, H. L., & McDaniel, M. A. (1994). Job performance and the older worker. In S. Rix (Ed.), *Older workers: How do they measure up? An overview of age differences in costs and performances* (pp. 27–51). Washington, DC: Public Policy Institute. American Association of Retired Persons.

Sterns, H. L., & Miklos, S. M. (1995). The aging worker in a changing environment: Organizational and individual issues. *Journal of Vocational Behavior, 47,* 248–268.

Streufert, S., Pogash, R., Piasecki, M., & Post, G. M. (1990). Age and management team performance. *Psychology and Aging, 5,* 551–559.

Thompson, L., Griffiths, A., & Davison, S. (2000). Employee absence, age and tenure: A study of nonlinear effects and trivariate models. *Work & Stress, 14,* 16–34.

Vecchio, R. P. (1993). The impact of differences in subordinate and supervisor age on attitude and performance. *Psychology and Aging, 1,* 112–119.

Viswesvaran, C., & Ones, D. S. (2000). Perspectives on models of job performance. *International Journal of Selection and Assessment, 8,* 216–226.

Wagner, S. L., & Rush, M. C. (2000). Altruistic organizational citizenship behavior: Context, disposition, and age. *Journal of Social Psychology, 14,* 379–391.

Waldman, D. A., & Avolio, B. J. (1986). Meta-analysis of age differences in job performance. *Journal of Applied Psychology, 71,* 33–38.

Waldman, D. A., & Avolio, B. J. (1993). Aging and work performance in perspective: Contextual and development considerations. *Research in Personnel and Human Resource Management, 11,* 133–162.

Walters, G. D., & Geyer, M. D. (2004). Criminal thinking and identity in male white-collar offenders. *Criminal Justice and Behavior, 31,* 263–281.

Warr, P. B. (1994). Age and employment. In H. Triandis, M. Dunnette, & L. Hough (Eds.), *Handbook of Industrial and Organizational Psychology* (Vol. 4, 2nd ed., pp. 485–550). Palo Alto, CA: Consulting Psychologists Press.

Warr, P. B. (2001). Age and work behaviour: Physical attributes, cognitive abilities, knowledge, personality traits, and motives. *International Review of Industrial and Organizational Psychology, 16,* 1–36.

Warr, P. B., & Bourne, A. (1999). Factors influencing two types of congruence in multi-rater judgments. *Human Performance, 12,* 183–210.

Warr, P. B., & Hoare, S. (2002). Personality, gender, age and logical overlap in multi-source ratings. *International Journal of Selection and Assessment, 10*, 279–291.

Weisburd, D., Chayet, E. F., & Waring, E. J. (1990). White-collar crime and criminal careers: Some preliminary findings. *Crime & Delinquency, 36*, 342–355.

Willis, S. L., & Tosti-Vasey, J. L. (1986, April). *Professional obsolescence among mid-career college faculty.* Paper presented at the annual meeting of the American Educational Research Association, San Francisco.

Wohlers, A. J., Hall, M. J., & London, M. (1993). Subordinates rating managers: Organizational and demographic correlates of self/subordinate agreement. *Journal of Occupational and Organizational Psychology, 66*, 263–275.

Wright, J. D., & Hamilton, R. F. (1978). Work satisfaction and age: Some evidence for the 'job change' hypothesis. *Social Forces, 56*, 1141–1158.

7

Age and Work Attitudes

Janet L. Barnes-Farrell and Russell A. Matthews

It has been observed that older workers report more favorable attitudes toward their jobs than those reported by younger workers. However, this is an oversimplified view of the roles of age and aging in the development of positive work attitudes and engagement in work. Therefore, in this chapter we summarize published evidence regarding the nature of relationships between worker age and significant work attitudes, work motives, and work motivation. We also consider individual, developmental, organizational and "outside the workplace" explanations for these relationships. This is followed by a discussion of research questions and methodological considerations that should be addressed for a fuller understanding of how our aging workforce responds to their work situations, and identification of practical recommendations that emerge from what we do know about these issues.

How people feel about the work they do, the jobs they hold, the people they work with, and the organizations that employ them represent important phenomena in any consideration of how employees respond to their work situations. Such issues have been the topic of literally thousands of studies in the fields of industrial and organizational psychology, organizational behavior, and related behavioral science fields. It is also well understood that individual characteristics of workers as well as features of their jobs, working conditions, and the larger sphere in which their work lives operate all contribute to such feelings.

A worker's age represents a key individual characteristic that has the potential to impact the work experiences and conditions to which an individual will be exposed (e.g., the nature of work assignments, opportunities for advancement, and rewards available to a worker). Affective reactions to work and features of the work environment may likewise be linked to age. The consistent growth of the older segments of our workforce and the development of new organizational structures and career/retirement patterns place increased emphasis on the importance of understanding when and how age and age-related processes are related to work attitudes. In particular, a clearer understanding of the attitudes and motives of older workers can help to guide management practices and organizational policy aimed at meeting the needs of an aging workforce and encouraging older workers to remain engaged and active members of the workforce. In this chapter, we summarize published evidence regarding the relationship of worker age with the work attitudes employees espouse and their motivation to invest themselves in their jobs, careers, and organizations. This is accompanied by a consideration of several functional and theoretical explanations for age differences in worker affective reactions toward their work situations. We will also provide an overview of research questions and methodological considerations that should be addressed for a fuller understanding of how our aging workforce responds to their work situations, and some practical recommendations that flow from what we do know about these issues.

WORK ATTITUDES

Our first goal is to examine how worker age is related to beliefs and attitudes that workers develop regarding their jobs, their work organizations, and their careers. These include attitudes such as job satisfaction, job involvement, and organizational commitment, as well as attitudes toward work processes such as skill development and technological change.

Age and Job Satisfaction

One of the most consistently reported findings regarding age and work attitudes is a positive relationship between worker age and overall job satisfaction (Bourne, 1982; Rhodes, 1983). The first major review of work attitudes as they relate to worker age, published by Rhodes in 1983, summarized the results of 60 studies conducted between 1957 and 1982 that included bivariate or multivariate analyses of this relationship. Rhodes concluded that, in general, older workers report more positive attitudes toward their jobs than younger workers do, citing that ". . . there is overwhelming evidence that overall job satisfaction is positively associated with age" (Rhodes, 1983, p. 331).

Since the publication of that review, a number of studies have provided additional evidence consistent with this broad-brush statement about the relationship between worker age and overall job satisfaction (cf. Barnes-Farrell, Lewis & Matthews, 2006; Bedeian, Ferris, & Kacmar, 1992; Cunningham & MacGregor, 2000; Ekerdt & DeViney, 1993; Kacmar & Ferris, 1989; Kirkman & Shapiro, 2001; McFarlin & Sweeney, 1992; Robie, Ryan, Schmieder, Parra, & Smith, 1998; Schwoerer & May, 1996; White & Spector, 1987). Furthermore, although most of the research addressing this issue has been conducted in the United States and western European countries, the positive age-job satisfaction relationship has been observed in a variety of cultural settings. Specifically, similar findings have been reported in studies conducted in China (Siu, Spector, Cooper, & Donald, 2001), Japan (Kalleberg & Loscocco, 1983), and Turkey (Nichols, Sugur, & Tasiran, 2003). However, it should be pointed out that this finding, while typical, is by no means uniform. For example, Rhodes indicated that several individual studies in her review reported no significant relationship between age and overall job satisfaction, or they reported age-job satisfaction relationships that were limited to particular sub-samples in the study. Likewise, a number of more recent investigations have reported that they did not observe a reliable relationship between worker age and job satisfaction. These have included studies based on samples of full-time white-collar workers (Cleveland & Shore, 1992; Glisson & Durick, 1988; Spreitzer, Kizilos, & Nason, 1997), blue-collar workers (Pond & Geyer, 1991), and part-time workers (Feldman, Doerpinghaus, & Turnley, 1995; Kaye, Alexander, & Kauffman, 1999). Other studies only find the positive relationship with age for those in relatively attractive work situations (cf. Riordan, Griffith, & Weatherly, 2003). Riordan et al. (2003) reported the expected positive correlation between age and measures of job satisfaction and commitment for nurses with high pay status. However, the relationship of age with job satisfaction and commitment was negative for those with low pay status.

Taken together, findings pertinent to aging and job satisfaction suggest that although the *general* relationship between worker age and overall job satisfaction may be positive, there is much more to the story. In the following sections we will examine some of what is known and speculated about the nature of that story. Then we will turn to a consideration of what is known about other relevant work attitudes.

Facet Satisfaction

A number of studies that directly or indirectly studied the relationship between age and job satisfaction have moved beyond assessments of global satisfaction to examine satisfaction with various aspects of work. From the perspective of age relationships, the most frequent distinction has been between those aspects of job satisfaction that are concerned with intrinsic satisfactions (e.g., the meaningfulness of work) and those that are primarily concerned with extrinsic satisfactions (e.g., pay and promotions). A reliable positive relationship between age and intrinsic work satisfaction (the meaningfulness of work) has been demonstrated across a variety of samples and occupational groups (Rhodes, 1983). Satisfaction with this aspect of work seems to increase with age up until the period immediately preceding retirement (Bourne, 1982). However, satisfaction with extrinsic facets of work, such as pay and promotions, does not show the same consistent pattern of results (Rhodes, 1983; Kacmar & Ferris, 1989). As such, it has been argued that the frequently reported positive associations between age and job satisfaction are largely driven by reactions to intrinsically satisfying aspects of work.

WHAT IS THE FORM OF THE RELATIONSHIP BETWEEN AGE AND JOB SATISFACTION?

Although it has typically been assessed and reported as a positive linear relationship, some researchers have argued that the age-satisfaction relationship may be nonlinear in form. Herzberg and colleagues proposed many years ago that the relationship between age and job satisfaction was U-shaped (Herzberg, Mausner, Peterson, & Capwell, 1957). In the intervening period, that idea was largely discarded because it was rarely replicated. However, part of the reason that it may not have been reproduced is that the sample sizes and age ranges included in many studies were insufficient to detect such a relationship. More recently, two studies have provided data suggesting that the age-satisfaction relationship may indeed be nonlinear.

The first was a study conducted by Kacmar and Ferris (1989), which argued that the relationship between age and satisfaction with intrinsic and extrinsic aspects of one's job takes different forms. Consistent with their theorizing, they found a U-shaped relationship between age and extrinsic job satisfaction, and the usual positive linear relationship between age and intrinsic satisfaction. More recently, a large-scale study of British workers carefully examined the U-shaped hypothesis. Clark, Oswald, and Warr (1996) analyzed data from a sample of over 5,000 employed individuals who participated in the 1991 wave of the British Household Panel Study. They found robust evidence consistent with a U-shaped relationship between worker age and job satisfaction. When they examined the pattern of overall job satisfaction, extrinsic job satisfaction and intrinsic job satisfaction across the age span, they found a clear pattern of satisfaction that initially declined, bottoming out at about age 31, then increased in a fairly linear fashion until one's early 60s. They repeated the analyses, controlling for a total of 80 potential covariates and controlling for general wellbeing ("context free mental health"). After the set of age-correlates was introduced into the analysis, the U-shaped relationship remained, although the age at which job satisfaction was at a minimum shifted to age 36.

Other researchers have proposed that age functions as a moderator of relationships between job satisfaction and features of the work environment, such as perceived work alternatives (Pond & Geyer, 1987, 1991). Pond and Geyer conducted a pair of studies that examined the interactive relationship between age and perceived work alternatives with job satisfaction. They argued that the perceived availability of work alternatives would be of less interest to older workers, so there should be only a weak relationship between perceived work alternatives and job satisfaction for this group. On the other hand, younger workers should report lower job satisfaction when they are aware that there are work alternatives available to them. In a pair of studies conducted with a white collar sample and a blue collar sample, respectively, they found that age was unrelated to job satisfaction, but it did moderate the negative relationship between perceived work alternatives and job satisfaction as they hypothesized.

ARE OLDER WORKERS BETTER OFF, OR ARE THEY JUST EASIER TO PLEASE?

Some of the more interesting issues raised by the observation that age is associated with increasingly positive job satisfaction include questions about *why* and *when* age should be associated with positive work attitudes. As pointed out by Warr (1994), much of the published work on age-job satisfaction relationships has not taken into account or explored the complex nature of this relationship. However, a number of reasons for age-related increases in job satisfaction have been posited. They range from functional reasons that rely on the covariation of age with job circumstances that produce satisfaction to developmental explanations that emphasize systematic changes in the central life interests and emotional functioning of adults that unfold as workers age.

To begin with, any consideration of the relationship between age and worker feelings or behaviors must recognize several possible sources of covariation between the two. For example, a number of variables that are also associated with job satisfaction, such as work experience, organizational tenure, job level, and income, tend to be correlated with age. Older workers typically have longer tenure and more work experience, and have advanced to higher occupational levels, providing them with jobs that offer many of the outcomes that contribute to job satisfaction. Thus, the bivariate relationship that is observed between age and job satisfaction may be an artifact of other events that come along with spending time in the workforce—older workers may simply have had more time to reap the rewards embedded in occupational structures. Some investigations that report positive relationships between age and job satisfaction have statistically controlled for these relationships; others have not. In some studies, especially those based on data from a single organization, these variables are so closely intertwined as to make it almost impossible to tease apart their independent effects. Multivariate studies that control for such opportunity biases generally do account for some of the relationship between age and job satisfaction. However, large-scale population studies that have statistically controlled for relevant covariates typically report that opportunity variables do not completely account for the age-satisfaction relationship (cf. Rhodes, 1983; Clark, Oswald, & Warr, 1996).

It is worth mentioning that changes in organizational structures and career patterns that disrupt the normative association between worker age and work status variables likewise have the potential to affect the relationship between age and job satisfaction. For example, the classic career development model can be loosely characterized as an age-graded sequence of entry and development, maintenance, withdrawal and exit phases, followed by retirement from the workforce. Newer models of careers (cf. Hall & Mirvis, 1995; Sterns & Miklos, 1995) propose that workers may engage in multiple cycles of entry, development, and withdrawal that involve entry and exit from multiple organizations and several distinct *careers* over the course of a working life. Increasingly, workers in their 50s and 60s will choose (voluntarily or involuntarily) to enter new fields in which they have no more status or experience than workers in their 20s and 30s. To the extent that job tenure, occupational level, and similar variables are responsible for positive job attitudes, the assumption that older workers can be expected to report higher levels of job satisfaction than their younger coworkers may not be tenable in the future.

A second explanation for age differences in job satisfaction and other work attitudes is cohort based. Cohort explanations emphasize common sociocultural experiences that affect the perspectives and values of adults born during a particular period of time. For example, adults who grew up during the Depression developed ideas about job security and the meaning of work in a very different economic and political climate than members of the Baby Boom generation. Age differences in job satisfaction reported in any particular study are likely to confound worker age with worker cohort. Thus, for example, age differences in work attitudes observed in a cross-sectional study that includes workers from multiple generations are likely to mask the fact that adults born during the Baby Boom generation may react differently to work conditions than Generation X adults will react when they reach the same age. It is methodologically difficult to disentangle cohort effects from age differences that emanate from other sources, and very few studies have tackled this problem. An exception is a recent study (described later) that examined evidence for generational and developmental explanations for age differences in work values and concluded that generational differences accounted for much of the relationship between age and work values (Smola & Sutton, 2002).

Another *external* explanation for age differences in job satisfaction is the so-called *job change* hypothesis, which argues that, over time, workers gravitate to jobs that are a closer fit with their needs and expectations. Because job satisfaction is often conceptualized as a response to the congruence between worker desires/needs/values and job characteristics, this logic leads to the expectation that older workers, on average, will report more positive reactions to their job situations. Support for this explanation was provided in a study that examined the job satisfaction of government managers (White & Spector, 1987). These researchers found that locus of control and job congruence explained the bulk of the relationship between age and job satisfaction in their sample.

Developmental processes (i.e., aging) refer to patterns of feelings and behaviors that unfold in largely the same way for all people as time passes. Thus older workers may report more satisfaction with their jobs, for example, because they have mellowed with time. For example, one alternative theoretical explanation suggests that aging is associated with a gradual lowering of expectations and aspirations. According to this line of thought, as workers age, they adjust their standards from overly idealistic standards to more realistic (and lower) ones. This allows older workers to be well satisfied with situations that would not have been satisfying at an earlier point in their lives. Thus we would expect gradually increasing levels of job satisfaction, even for individuals whose work circumstances have not improved in any objective way.

Other possible explanations for the age-satisfaction relationship draw on the idea that workers experience developmental shifts in role concerns from those of "getting by and getting ahead" that characterize the early years of adulthood to concerns with attaching meaning to one's life that have been posited by lifespan theorists to characterize later stages of adulthood. This corresponds with a tendency to reflect on positive experiences and the ability to savor them. Research on emotional regulation throughout the life course provides evidence consistent with this position. A longitudinal study that examined age-related differences and changes in positive and negative affect found that positive levels of positive affect remain fairly stable until late in life, but negative affect decreases with age (Charles, Reynolds, & Gatz, 2001). Similarly, a study of daily emotional experiences reported that the frequency with which adults experience positive affect remains constant, but the frequency with which negative affect is experienced declines until about age 60. Furthermore, among older adults, highly positive emotional experiences tend to endure and highly negative emotional experiences tend to dissipate (Carstensen, Pasupathi, Mayr, & Nesselroade, 2000). In other words, older workers are better able to recognize the good and let go of the bad.

IMPLICATIONS OF RETIREMENT AS A PSYCHOLOGICAL OPTION FOR OLDER WORKERS

The shift to thinking about retirement as an alternative role also represents a unique feature of the work-lives of older workers that has implications for how they evaluate their jobs. As workers approach the window of time when retirement becomes a socially acceptable and economically viable alternative, their evaluation of the work role is carried out in the context of concomitant evaluations of the desirability of the retirement role (Barnes-Farrell, 2003). Satisfaction with the work role may be partly a function of whether it serves to hinder movement to a more desired role (the *pull* of an attractive retirement role) or allows one to avoid a less desirable role (the *push* force associated with negative attitudes toward retirement). Retirement researchers report that a sense of personal control over the decision to work or retire is of primary importance to the wellbeing of older adults; this seems to be more important than whether they are working or retired (Heckhausen & Schulz, 1995; Isaksson & Johansson, 2000; Shultz, Morton, & Weckerle, 1998). As such, job satisfaction for employed older workers may be partly a function of the voluntariness of their employment status.

Another interesting proposal regarding the relationship between age and job satisfaction that recognizes the importance of retirement as a relevant feature of the terrain is one forwarded by Ekerdt and DeViney (1993). They propose that attitudes toward work may indeed become more positive with age, in part due to gravitation to more satisfying positions and in part due to developmental processes that allow older workers to reevaluate what they expect from their work situations. However, they argue that a second ongoing process for older workers is the gradual increase in salience of "time remaining" at work. In particular, as workers approach planned retirement dates, they begin the process of disengaging from the workplace, and this includes increasingly harsh assessments of their work conditions. For example, they proposed that, independent of a worker's age, workers who were approaching a planned retirement date would begin to see work as increasingly burdensome. Based on data from a large sample of male workers ages 50–69 (drawn from the U.S. Veteran's Administration Normative Aging Study) who were not yet retired but were approaching a fixed retirement, their analyses demonstrated that as participants got older (ignoring planned retirement age), job attitudes became more positive, but as they got closer to retirement age (ignoring age), job attitudes became more negative. Because retirement age has become a more fluid concept, this suggests that the interplay between age and job attitudes is likely to be further complicated by the attention that workers give to their plans to shift from the work role to the retirement role.

JOB INVOLVEMENT AND ORGANIZATIONAL COMMITMENT

Of course, job satisfaction is but one of an array of important attitudes that workers develop regarding aspects of work. Two work-related attitudes that have received significant attention in recent years as important contributors to valued work behaviors are job involvement and organizational commitment. In her review, Rhodes (1983) concluded that the evidence generally supported the existence of a positive relationship between age and job involvement and a somewhat less consistent relationship between age and organizational commitment.

As is true with much of the research that provides the basis for the well-known relationship between age and job satisfaction, many studies concerned with attitudes like job involvement and organizational commitment measure age and include it as a statistical control in analyses; however, only a handful of studies are designed to examine the interplay between age and these attitudes. Examples of the former are a recent study concerned with emotional exhaustion and work attitudes that reported a positive relationship between age and organizational commitment in two samples of workers drawn from a variety of organizations and industries (Cropanzano, Rupp, & Byrne, 2003) and studies of career commitment among pharmacists and workers in financial services organizations, respectively, that found worker age to be unrelated to a host of work-related attitudes, including organizational commitment, career commitment, and job involvement (Goulet & Singh, 2002; Kong, 1995). Likewise, a study of job and family involvement that examined data from the Job Insecurity and Wellbeing project in Finland (Mauno & Kinnunen, 2000), found no evidence of a systematic relationship between worker age and job involvement or family involvement.

Studies that include age as a focal variable are much less common, but they offer some insight into the ways that investment in one's job or one's organization might be associated with worker age. Finegold, Mohrman, and Spreitzer (2002) were concerned with the sources of organizational commitment for workers of different ages. In a large sample of technical workers spanning multiple organizations, they found that older workers exhibited higher levels of organizational commitment than younger workers. When they investigated the sources of commitment, they observed that commitment was driven more by job security issues than anything else for older workers; for younger workers, satisfaction with work-life balance was the primary predictor of levels of organizational commitment. In a related vein, Kacmar and her colleagues reasoned that age should be positively correlated with organizational commitment because older workers have fewer alternatives available to them and generally longer investments in their employing organizations. However, in the sample of hospitality managers that they studied, age was not a good predictor of any aspect of organizational commitment (Kacmar, Carlson, & Brymer, 1999).

Cleveland and Shore (1992) reported a complex relationship between age variables and several job attitudes, including job involvement and organizational commitment, in a sample of over 400 workers in a U.S.-based multinational firm. Although chronological age was unrelated to any of the work attitudes they measured, when they included consideration of alternative measures of age, such as perceived age and relative age, they found that older workers who were old relative to others in their work groups and also "felt" old reported the highest levels of job involvement and organizational commitment, while workers who were older than others in their work groups but "felt" like younger workers reported the most negative attitudes. Taking a similar position, Green and colleagues theorized that age dissimilarity, rather than age per se, should have a negative impact on the quality of leader-member relationships, with consequences for a variety of work attitudes, including organizational commitment. In their study of public library employees, they did not find any support for this position. Age dissimilarity was unrelated to organizational commitment, job satisfaction, or the quality of leader-member relationships (Green, Anderson, & Shivers, 1996). A recent study concerned with demographic dissimilarity as an antecedent of attitudes that mediate deviant behaviors likewise reported that age dissimilarity was unrelated to levels of organizational commitment (Liao, Joshi, & Chuang, 2004).

Finally, two studies based on large archival databases offer information about age differences in work involvement. Lorence (1987) examined data from panels of workers who participated in the Quality of Employment surveys conducted in the U.S. during 1972–73 and 1977. He made the distinction between labor force involvement in general and psychological involvement with a particular job. He concluded that labor force involvement is positively associated with age and is best accounted for by developmental explanations, while psychological involvement with a particular job seems to be driven more strongly by cohort differences and differences in the job characteristics for workers of different ages.

ATTITUDES TOWARD CHANGE AND DEVELOPMENT

A key characteristic of organizations today is regular upheaval. Positive attitudes toward change, whether it be organizational change, adapting to new technology, or acquiring new skills may be important to workers and organizations that want to succeed in this kind of environment. Although most of us are familiar with stereotypes about older workers' general unwillingness to engage in change, a few empirical studies have reported data relevant to workers' attitudes toward personal and organizational change.

Maurer (2001) has developed a model of career-relevant development that explicitly considers the role that age plays in attitudes toward development and motivation to engage in development activities. Briefly, he theorizes that age will be negatively associated with important antecedents to the development of self-efficacy beliefs for development—mastery experiences, vicarious experiences, persuasion, and physiological influences—resulting in reduced levels of self-efficacy for development. This in turn affects attitudes toward development and intention to engage in development activities. A recent empirical study testing this model supported the basic premises of the model (Maurer, Weiss, & Barbeite, 2003). The authors noted that age effects were reassuringly small, but the findings nonetheless point to the value of developing interventions aimed at older workers' access to the kinds of experiences that are likely to enhance their sense of self-efficacy for development.

As the structure of jobs changes, we need to be concerned about the extent to which age affects reactions to features of jobs that are modified. For example, a common modification of many jobs is the increasing integration of technology with a variety of job tasks. Is there any reason to expect that older workers will be less inclined to take up such jobs or that they will be less motivated to devote their energies to jobs that have large technology-based components? A recent study provides some evidence relevant to this issue. Morris and Venkatesh (2000) reported on a study of user reactions and technology usage behavior for 118 workers who were being introduced to new software. They found that age was negatively associated with attitudes toward technology adoption. However, they noted that younger workers' technology usage behaviors were actually more strongly influenced by their attitudes than were older workers' behaviors.

Another common change to work design that has the potential for differential reactions among younger and older workers is the introduction of self-managing team structures for accomplishing work that was formerly carried out with traditional management structures. A study of employee age and perceptions of work in self-managing and traditional work groups found that older workers reacted positively to self-managing work groups (Hayslip et al., 1996).

Do older workers respond differently to negative events than younger workers? In a study of Canadian workers' reactions to plant closures, Mazerolle and Gangaram (1999) examined evidence for the relative preponderance of three possible reactions to plant closings: the "discouraged worker effect" (i.e., feeling discouraged from seeking reemployment), the "poisoning effect" (development of negative attitudes toward all employers), and the "career growth effect" (feeling that the plant closing had a net positive effect for the worker). They reported that older workers (those older than 55 years of age) who had been laid off were less likely to report negative attitudes and more likely to report positive career outcomes than younger workers who were laid off. Another study that focused specifically on the reactions of older workers to downsizing examined a sample of employees at a Swedish insurance company that offered early retirement options to some of its workers during a downsizing effort. A comparison of workers who stayed or took early retirement during the downsizing showed that attitude toward the downsizing was primarily dependent on whether the worker's status (employed or retired) was voluntary (Isaksson & Johansson, 2000).

AGE-RELATED REACTIONS TO OTHER FORMS
OF ORGANIZATIONAL TREATMENT

It is reasonable to expect that worker age and the manner in which workers of different ages are treated may also be associated with the extent to which the work environment is experienced as a supportive and welcoming place by younger and older workers. For example, age discrimination, which is encountered by many older workers in a variety of intended and unintended ways, should have consequences for perceptions of fair treatment at work. Consistent with this expectation, there is some limited evidence that worker age is negatively associated with perceptions of procedural and interactional justice (VanYperen, Hagedoorn, Zweers, & Postma, 2000).

WORK MOTIVATION AND WORK MOTIVES

Age and Work Motivation

In its most general sense, work motivation refers to workers' willingness to direct their energies toward organizationally valued behaviors and outcomes. A whole host of questions arise when we begin considering the issue of motivating older workers. First, and perhaps most obvious, is this: Do older workers exhibit generally different overall levels of work motivation than younger workers? Consistent with this kind of evidence are reports that age is negatively associated with aspiration levels and overall levels of motivation (Sturman, 2003). However, other work provides evidence of positive relationships between age and motivation. For example, Bégat, Ellefsen, and Severinsson (2005) observed a positive correlation between age and measures of motivation and work engagement for a sample of Norwegian nurses. Likewise, age was positively correlated with internal work motivation in a sample of temporary workers (Feldman et al.,1995).

In light of the importance of continuous learning among workers of all ages, motivation to engage in training and career development activities has received particular attention. As noted earlier, Maurer and his colleagues (Maurer et al., 2003) have presented evidence that worker age is negatively associated with motivation to engage in development activities, mediated by opportunities to develop self-efficacy for development. Other perspectives on the relationship between age and training have taken somewhat different theoretical approaches. Based on human capital theory, Renaud, Lakhdari, and Morin (2004) argued that older workers should have lower motivation to voluntarily engage in training because of the shorter time that they have available to recoup their investments, making it an unwise investment of their time

and energies. They presented data from a large Canadian financial organization that was consistent with this hypothesis. Interestingly, Simpson, Greller,
and Stroh (2002) took a contrary position and questioned the usefulness of
human capital theory as an explanation for older workers' career and work
development motivation. Instead, they argued that a life-span career development model that proposes older workers can and do invest in their own careers provides a better description of workers on-the-job and off-the-job career
development activities. By recognizing workers' off-the-job career development activities as additional reflections of career and work motivation, they
suggested that data were consistent with the argument that older workers actually exhibit quite high levels of career and work development motivation.
Consistent with this argument, they presented data indicating that late-career
workers (ages 50–65) were actually *more* active in pursuing focused career development activities outside the workplace than were earlier-career workers.

Caldwell, Herold, and Fedor (2004) included consideration of worker age in
a study that examined the effectiveness of change management attempts in a
number of organizations. They found that older workers were less motivated to
participate in change and adapted less well to changes that were implemented.
They suggested that the kinds of change management practices required to
encourage change in older workers may be different from the kinds of traditional suggestions for motivating change that have been developed in the context of studies of younger workers—that is, extrinsic rewards and training. In particular, they identified perceived organizational support as a construct that may
appeal more directly to the kinds of motives that become salient as workers
age—that is, feeling secure and valued.

Work Motives and Values

Does worker age affect the kinds of outcomes that are valued? In fact, most of
what is known about work motivation and aging is concerned with motives
and values that may affect the kinds of outcomes and experiences workers of
different ages will find attractive. Empirical data and theory drawn from the
fields of lifespan psychology and career development provide some insight
into this question.

Lifespan theories of human development provide information about the
kinds of motives that adults of different ages will seek to satisfy at work. For
example, finding meaning in existing relationships is a central life task that
emerges in late life (Carstensen et al., 2000). This should increase the importance of opportunities to maintain social connections at work as a source of
satisfaction and as a motive for investing efforts in one's work. In this vein,
Greller and Stroh (1995) suggest a particularly important role for outcomes

that meet intrinsic needs and relationship needs for older workers. With respect to relationship needs, Greller and Simpson (1999) suggest further that the types of relationships people prefer may change as we age. As we move into our 50s and 60s, we tend to seek emotion from our relationships rather than instrumental value. For example, older workers may be more concerned with developing and maintaining work (and life) situations that provide them with warm, nurturing social relationships in preference to seeking to develop networks of people who can provide career assistance. This argues for the importance of providing opportunities for high-quality social interactions and social/emotional support for older workers.

In a slightly different manner, Mor-Barak (1995) has proposed a theoretical framework for understanding the meaning of work for older adults seeking employment. Building on Alderfer's ERG theory of work motivation, she proposed that four factors contribute to the meaning of work. The first three—Financial, Social and Personal—generally correspond to Alderfer's Existence, Relatedness, and Growth needs. The fourth factor is Generativity, which refers to opportunities to transfer knowledge and experience to younger generations, which she posited may be of particular value to older adults.

The studies reported by Rhodes (1983) in her review of the literature supported the expectation of increasing interest in meeting affiliation needs with increasing age, but they generally did not offer consistent evidence of reliable relationships between age and the desire to satisfy growth or self-actualization needs. However, a more recent study by Leviatan (1992) found support for the argument that older workers' motives are dominated by a desire to meet higher order needs. In a study of 235 kibbutz workers ages 45 and older, job characteristics that allowed workers to meet higher-order needs explained more variance in work satisfaction and motivation to contribute to the job than did features such as physical conditions that allowed them to meet lower-order needs. Likewise, a study that focused on the motivation of workers between the ages of 45 and 59 reported that, among these older workers, jobs that provided intrinsic motivators or a combination of intrinsic and extrinsic motivators were the most positively received (Valentine, Valentine, & Dick, 1998). Generally consistent with these findings were the results of a study of work values in Japan and the U.S., which concluded that older workers were more committed to work as a valued activity, they valued good relations with coworkers more highly, and they valued promotions less highly than younger workers did (Loscocco & Kalleberg, 1988). In contrast, Lacy, Bokemeier, and Shepard (1983) examined responses to the General Social Survey during the period 1973 to 1980 and found no evidence for age differences in job attribute preferences, including meaningfulness of work, promotions, income, security, and hours.

Several researchers have examined age differences in motives and values associated with money and similar extrinsic rewards. Tang and Gilbert (1995), for example, observed significant positive correlations between worker age and two aspects of money ethics. In particular, older workers were more likely to endorse money as something that is valued because it provides opportunities for freedom and power (a cognitive aspect of reactions to money), and they were more likely to indicate that they budget their money (a behavioral aspect of reactions to money). Fox, Geyer, and Donohue (1994) examined the valence of pay for a sample of women in a production setting. They found that pay had decreasing ability to meet worker needs as age increased, up to the age of 40, but pay valence was unrelated to age for workers older than age of 40. Another study that specifically examined work motives of women was a qualitative examination of the meaning of paid work among older women (Altschuler, 2004). Themes extracted from detailed interviews with 53 women ages 55–84 revealed that independence from men and the opportunity to pursue lost dreams were frequent reasons that paid work was important in later life.

Turning to motives that are particularly pertinent to task performance, Kanfer and Ackerman (2000) presented evidence regarding age differences in motivational traits indicating that age is negatively correlated with the strength of competitive excellence motives, such as mastery and competitiveness. More recently, Kanfer and Ackerman (2004) have also made the argument that current theories of work motivation do not accommodate the realities of changing motive structures. Salient motives may operate as positive incentives for work motivation when organizational conditions provide opportunities for motive satisfaction. As such, they point to age-related changes in the salience of motives as examples of why organizations and work motivation theorists should integrate age into their thinking about motivation processes and motivational interventions.

Finally, Smola and Sutton (2002) examined evidence for generational differences in work values (an *environmental* explanation for differences in work values) and evidence that work values change as we age (a *personological* explanation). By comparing the results of a survey they conducted with previous work value survey research conducted by Cherrington in the 1970s, they attempted to tease apart the influence of aging and generational differences in Cherrington's report of age differences in work values. They found evidence that Gen X (younger) workers put more emphasis on quick promotions than Boomers (older workers) did and put more value on the Moral Importance of work. Boomers, in contrast, place more importance on Work as Primary in One's Life. They also found evidence that workers' values change as they mature—unexpectedly, rather than becoming more responsible, workers develop a less idealized view of work as they age. Probably the most interesting finding in their analysis is that the stronger of the two effects found in their data (generational versus aging) was generational. That is, differences in work values between groups of workers of different ages were primarily a function of whether they were members of the Boomer Generation or the Gen–X generation, rather than their ages per se. This suggests that the cultural and societal conditions that a particular cohort experiences have an impact on the kinds of attitudes they are likely to form regarding the meaning of work; this is only moderately affected by the aging process.

Work Motives in Special Populations

With the exception of unwanted exits from the workforce, the typical work pattern for men is one of continued work until late life, at which point exit from the workforce is generally contemplated in terms of partial or complete retirement from the workforce. For women, working lives may exhibit a more complicated pattern, with one or more entries and exits, prompted by childbearing and changes in marital status, before retirement is contemplated. Doorewaard, Hendrick, and Verschuren (2004) studied a large sample of European *returners* to examine the relationship between age and work motives among women who have chosen to return to work after an absence from the workforce. Do older women return for different reasons? They found that older female workers who return to work have stronger job and people orientations to work than younger female workers who return; in contrast, younger women who return to work had significantly stronger money orientations.

Dendinger, Adams, and Jacobson (2005) conducted a study that focused specifically on an understudied, but growing, segment of the older workforce: bridge employees. As described in other chapters in this book, bridge employment is a form of employment that represents a stage in a worker's transition from the role of full-time career worker to the role of full retirement. They drew on Mor-Barak's (1995) theoretical argument that there are four primary reasons for work among older workers: social, personal, financial, and generative. In particular, they speculated that the reasons nonretired older workers continue to work and the reasons that bridge employee older workers engage in work may be different, and this may have implications for their work attitudes. Because generativity has been suggested as a motive that becomes central during late mid-life, it may be a particularly relevant motive for those engaging in bridge employment. They found that the strength of the generativity motive in bridge employment was systematically related to job satisfaction of bridge employees. Presumably, the jobs of the bridge employees they studied provided the opportunity to satisfy that motive. Findings of this kind point out that for older adults, employment serves a variety of functions beyond providing income, including social contact and social status, structure, and opportunities for developing self-esteem.

Work Motivation Processes

Although considerable theorizing and research has addressed the ways that worker age relates to the *what* and *why* of work motivation—that is, what do workers value and why do they work—surprisingly few studies have directly addressed the relationship between aging and motivational processes implied by popular work motivation frameworks such as expectancy-instrumentality theories. In two of the few studies to directly address aspects of the work motivation process, Heneman (1973) examined the relationship between age and motivation to perform on the job in the context of expectancy theory. He reported that older workers had lower expectancy beliefs, particularly when risk-taking was involved. A study by Arvey and Warren (1976) likewise reported lower expectancy beliefs on the part of older engineers who participated in a study of motivation and obsolescence. As noted previously, Kanfer and Ackerman (2004) have pointed out the theoretical shortcomings of extant process models of work motivation for accommodating the influence of worker age on work motivation processes, and they have begun to develop a framework for integrating individual differences like age into our thinking about motivational processes. They posit some intriguing motivational consequences for aging, built on the intersection between what is known about cognitive and other aspects of aging with mechanisms that are part of expectancy theories of work motivation.

SUGGESTIONS FOR RESEARCH AND PRACTICE

Future Research and Theorizing

What can we make of the findings from previous research? Probably the most consistent take-away point is that older workers are likely to value work and express generally positive attitudes toward work that satisfies motives and needs that are important to them. However, evaluation of the existing body of work in this field makes it clear that there is substantial room for rigorous research that contributes to our understanding of the role that worker age plays in the development and consequences of important work attitudes and the manner in which work motivation processes are affected by aging processes.

The review of existing theoretical and empirical work in this domain reveals three particular kinds of contributions that could make a real difference in our ability to make sense of the complex relationships between age and worker attitudes and motivations.

- First, and most basic, is a need for additional theoretically grounded empirical research that includes worker age as a *focal* issue. By virtue of its status as a demographic marker, worker chronological age is one of the most commonly included variables in most studies of work attitudes and work behavior. However, it is typically treated as a *noise* variable that is statistically controlled rather than treated as an important and interesting worker characteristic that forms the centerpiece of a study. As a result, we are often left trying to stitch together patterns of relationships involving age, often based on the observation of simple correlational associations extracted from studies and analyses that do not take into consideration the variety of contextual features that contribute to those relationships. Placing age front and center from the standpoint of theorizing and research design could do much to reduce the piece-meal nature of our knowledge.

- Second, from the standpoint of methodology, research designs that speak more directly to the kinds of questions being addressed in studies concerned with aging and work attitudes are needed. Much of the empirical research that forms the basis for our current understanding of the role of age and aging uses cross-sectional designs, which don't allow researchers to draw strong inferences about the relative viability of developmental, period, and cohort explanations for age differences when they are observed. Longitudinal designs and multiple cohort designs that include measures of the kinds of constructs relevant to questions in this field are challenging to carry out, but they provide substantial value in reducing ambiguity about the interpretation of findings.

- Third, common definitions and theoretically sound operational definitions of age constructs are needed. Undoubtedly, some of the conflicting findings that abound in the published research can be traced to differing, and often arbitrary, classifications of workers as older or younger. Thoughtful operationalizations of age variables that flow from extant information about the nature and meaning of age are needed.

- Finally, additional development of work-based theories that explicitly incorporate psychological and developmental aspects of age would enrich our thinking and provide frameworks for integrating worker age into our understanding of work attitudes and work motivation. In particular, empirical research concerned directly with work motivation processes as they might play out for workers of different ages or at different points in their work lives has been scant. Most work cited in discussions of age differences in work motivation focus on potential differences in the meaning of work or on the related topic of what kinds of outcomes workers of different ages value. They flow primarily from so-called *need theories* of work motivation, such as Maslow's Need Hierarchy theory, Herzberg's Motivator-Hygiene Theory, and Alderfer's Existence Relatedness Growth (ERG) Theory. Need theories of work motivation inform us about the kinds of outcomes that are likely to be salient and valued by workers—they provide information about the *content* of what workers are looking for at work, and thus are useful in identifying classes of incentives that managers and organizations should pay particular attention to as they develop incentive systems to enhance work motivation, increase job satisfaction, improve recruitment, and enhance retention. However, they do not inform us regarding the interplay between worker age and the processes that are called into play when workers choose to engage fully (or not) in efforts to meet work-related objectives, such as engaging in intense and persistent task performance or engaging in extra-role behaviors (e.g., organizational citizenship behaviors) that primarily meet the needs of the organization.

Practical Suggestions for Implementation and Policy

Managers who are interested in tailoring their practices to meet the needs of an aging workforce can take several messages away from the findings regarding aging and work attitudes. First, older workers are not a disgruntled lot, simply waiting out their time until retirement. However, in some respects the kinds of incentives that workers value may change over the course of a working life, consistent with developmental changes in central life interests. Based on what is known about these changes, there are three kinds of interventions that deserve particular attention:

- Opportunities to develop and maintain meaningful social relationships, regular access to sources of social support, and opportunities to mentor are likely to be valued outcomes for older workers that will enhance work motivation, work attitudes, and retention.
- In addition, regular exposure to mastery experiences through challenging assignments should be encouraged as ways of enhancing attitudes toward training and development.
- Finally, flexible working arrangements of various kinds are often reported as a particularly valued outcome for older workers (cf. Koopman-Boyden & McDonald, 2003) because such arrangements allow them to carry out other roles in their lives that take on increasing prominence as they move closer to exiting the workforce. For example, workers who value their work roles but wish to place more emphasis on family and leisure roles in their lives may find opportunities for reduced hours or intermittent work schedules very attractive because they allow them to maintain a valued work role rather than making a full transition to a retirement role.

How might the picture of age differences in work attitudes be different 25 years from now?

Work attitudes may indeed change across the life course in response to developmental shifts in interests, expectations and functioning. However, age differences in work attitudes also emanate from differential access or exposure to a variety of conditions that contribute to the formation of work attitudes. What happens when these conditions change? Twenty-five years from now, our understanding of age differences in work attitudes—and especially, the work attitudes of older workers—could be very different from the picture that we have today. Academics and practitioners alike should consider that 25 years from now:

- Our older workers will come from cohorts who were exposed to quite different conditions when they were preparing for workforce entry than those experienced by those who constitute the "older workers" in the extant published literature on work and aging. GenXers (and later, Millenials) who will comprise the bulk of older workers 25 years from now may expect, value, and desire different things from work than members of the Silent Generation and the Baby Boom generation who constitute the older workers in our current studies of work attitudes.
- Work organizations and jobs may be structured differently, in ways that may be either *more* or *less* compatible with the skills, needs, and desires of individuals who are in their 50's, 60's, and 70's. Furthermore, older workers of the future will have entered the workforce with different skill sets than those that characterize older workers in the year 2006. For example, they will have grown up in an environment where using sophisticated technology, culling the Internet for information, and working in teams have been a normal part of their lives and educational preparation, with implications for their attitudes toward technology, working in teams, and other aspects of work design.
- Older workers in the year 2030 may well have *more* total years of workforce tenure, but changes in organizational structure and changes in career patterns suggest that they are likely to have significantly *less* job and organizational tenure than the typical older worker in today's job market. This should have an impact on work attitudes that derive from the rewards that flow from seniority and occupational level, including job satisfaction and organizational commitment.
- What attracts older workers to certain organizations may be drastically different (e.g., increased concern with healthcare issues may drive some employees to seek jobs for lower pay but better healthcare coverage), with implications for job satisfaction and organizational commitment.
- Changes in the nature and timing of retirement transitions may affect our definitions of who is an "older worker" or a "late career worker," as well as what they are looking for in their jobs. Right now, most of what we know about the work attitudes of older workers represents the attitudes of workers in their 40's, 50's, and early 60's who are employed full-time. Studies of work attitudes conducted in 2030 are likely to include many workers in their 50's, 60's and 70's who are employed in "bridge employment" jobs. How will this affect what we learn about sources of job satisfaction, about job involvement, and about organizational commitment among organizational workers?
- * Emerging changes in family demands for older workers (e.g., increased eldercare responsibilities and more childcare responsibilities in terms of grandchildren) suggest that the work attitudes of tomorrow's older workers will be more heavily influenced by the manner in which they are able to manage their growing family demands and integrate them into their work lives.
- Optimistically, older workers twenty-five years from now will have benefited from *less* exposure to age discrimination emanating from stereotypes about the characteristics and capabilities of older workers. We might expect to see the indirect effects of this in the form of job satisfaction, more positive attitudes toward development (via increased self-efficacy for development) and the development of more positive attitudes regarding fair treatment.

REFERENCES

Altschuler, J. (2004). Beyond money and survival: The meaning of paid work among older women. *International Journal of Aging and Human Development, 58,* 223–239.

Arvey, R., & Warren, N. C. (1976). Motivation and obsolescence in engineers. *Industrial Gerontology, 3,* 113–120.

Barnes-Farrell, J. L. (2003). Beyond health and wealth: Attitudinal and other influences on retirement decision-making. In G. Adams & T. Beehr (Eds.), *Retirement: Reasons, processes, and results* (pp. 159–187). New York: Springer.

Barnes-Farrell, J., Lewis, W. R., & Matthews, R. (2006, March). Anticipating retirement: The roles of health, perceived control and optimism in important life domains. In G. Fisher, *Using archival data: Research examples studying issues among older workers.* Symposium presented at *Work, Stress, & Health 2006,* Miami, FL.

Bedeian, A., Ferris, G., & Kacmar, M. (1992). Age, tenure, and job satisfaction: A tale of two perspectives. *Journal of Vocational Behavior, 40,* 33–48.

Bégat, I., Ellefsen, B., & Severinsson, E. (2005). Nurses' satisfaction with their work environment and the outcomes of clinical nursing supervision on nurses' experiences of wellbeing—a Norwegian study. *Journal of Nursing Management, 13,* 221–230.

Bourne, B. (1982). Effects of aging on work satisfaction, performance, and motivation. *Research on Aging, 5,* 37–47.

Caldwell, S. D., Herold, D. M., & Fedor, D. B. (2004). Toward an understanding of the relationships among organizational change, individual differences, and changes in person–environment fit: A cross-level study. *Journal of Applied Psychology, 89,* 868–882.

Carstensen, L. L., Pasupathi, M., Mayr, U., & Nesselroade, J. R. (2000). Emotional experience in everyday life across the adult life span. *Journal of Personality and Social Psychology, 79,* 644–655.

Charles, S. T., Reynolds, C. A., & Gatz, M. (2001). Age-related differences and change in positive and negative affect over 23 years. *Journal of Personality and Social Psychology, 80,* 136–151.

Clark, A., Oswald, A., & Warr, P. (1996). Is job satisfaction U-shaped in age? *Journal of Occupational and Organizational Psychology, 68,* 57–81.

Cleveland, J. N., & Shore, L. M. (1992). Self- and supervisor perspective on age and work attitude and performance. *Journal of Applied Psychology, 77,* 469–484.

Cropanzano, R., Rupp, D. E., & Byrne, Z. (2003). The relationship of emotional exhaustion to work attitudes, job performance, and organizational citizenship behaviors. *Journal of Applied Psychology, 88,* 160–169.

Cunningham, J. B., & MacGregor, J. (2000). Trust and the design of work: Complementary constructs in satisfaction and performance. *Human Relations, 53,* 1575–1591.

Dendinger, V. M., Adams, G. A., & Jacobson, J. D. (2005). Reasons for working and their relationship to retirement attitudes, job satisfaction, and occupational self-efficacy of bridge employees. *International Journal of Aging and Human Development, 61,* 21–35.

Doorewaard, H., Hendrick, J., & Verschuren, P. (2004). Work orientation of female returners. *Work, Employment, and Society, 18,* 7–27.

Ekerdt, D., & DeViney, S. (1993). Evidence for a preretirement process among older male workers. *Journal of Gerontology: Social Sciences, 48*, S35–S43.

Feldman, D. C., Doerpinghaus, H. I., & Turnley, W. H. (1995). Employee reactions to temporary jobs. *Journal of Managerial Issues, 7*, 127–141.

Finegold, D., Mohrman, & Spreitzer, G. M. (2002). Age effects on the predictors of technical workers' commitment and willingness to turnover. *Journal of Organizational Behavior, 23*, 655–674.

Fox, J. B., Geyer, P. D., & Donohue, J. M. (1994). Age and, pay valence in a production field setting. *The Journal of Social Psychology, 134*, 79–88.

Glisson, C., & Durick, M. (1988). Predictors of job satisfaction and organizational commitment in human service organizations. *Administrative Science Quarterly, 33*, 61–81.

Goulet, L. R., & Singh, P. (2002). Career commitment: A reexamination and an extension. *Journal of Vocational Behavior, 61*, 73–91.

Green, S. G., Anderson, S. E., & Shivers, S. L. (1996). Demographic and organizational influences on leader-member exchange and related work attitudes. *Organizational Behavior and Human Decision Processes, 66*, 203–214.

Greller, M. M., & Simpson, P. (1999). In search of late career: A review of contemporary social science research applicable to the understanding of late career. *Human Resource Management Review, 9*, 309–347.

Greller, M. M., & Stroh, L. K. (1995). Careers in midlife and beyond: A fallow field in need of sustenance. *Journal of Vocational Behavior, 47*, 232–247.

Hall, D. T., & Mirvis, P. H. (1995). The new career contract: Developing the whole person at midlife and beyond. *Journal of Vocational Behavior, 47*, 269–289.

Hayslip, B. Jr., Metheny, W., Miller, C., Yeatts, D., Beyerlein, M., & Johnson, D. (1996). Employee age and perceptions of work in self-managing and traditional work groups. *International Journal of Aging and Human Development, 42*, 291–312.

Heckhausen, J., & Schulz, R. (1995). A life-span theory of control. *Psychological Review, 102*, 284–304.

Heneman, H. G. (1973). The relationship between age and motivation to perform on the job. *Industrial Gerontology, 16*, 30–36.

Herzberg, F. I., Mausner, B., Peterson, R. O., & Capwell, D. R. (1957). *Job attitudes: Review of research and opinion.* Pittsburgh: Psychological Service of Pittsburgh.

Isaksson, K., & Johansson, G. (2000). Adaptation to continued work and early retirement following downsizing: Long-term effects and gender differences. *Journal of Occupational and Organizational Psychology, 73*, 241–256.

Kacmar, K. M., Carlson, D. S., & Brymer, R. A. (1999). Antecedents and consequences of organizational commitment: A comparison of two scales. *Educational and Psychological Measurement, 59*, 976–994.

Kacmar, M., & Ferris, G. R. (1989). Theoretical and methodological considerations in the age-job satisfaction relationship. *Journal of Applied Psychology, 74*, 201–207.

Kalleberg, A. L., & Loscocco, K. A. (1983). Aging, values, and rewards: Explaining age differences in job satisfaction. *American Sociological Review, 48*, 78–90.

Kanfer, R., & Ackerman, P. L. (2004). Aging, adult development, and work motivation. *Academy of Management Review, 29*, 440–458.

Kanfer, R., & Ackerman, P. L. (2000). Individual differences in work motivation: Further explorations of a trait framework. *Applied Psychology: An International Review, 49*, 470–482.

Kaye, L. W., Alexander, L. B., & Kauffman, S. (1999). Factors contributing to job quality and satisfaction among ethnically diverse, lower income, elderly part-timers. *Journal of Gerontological Social Work, 31,* 143–167.

Kirkman, B. L., & Shapiro, D. L. (2001). The impact of cultural values on job satisfaction and organizational commitment in self-managing work teams: The mediating role of employee resistance. *Academy of Management Journal, 44,* 557–569.

Kong, S. X. (1995). Predictors of organizational and career commitment among Illinois pharmacists. *American Journal of Health-Systems Pharmacy, 52* (18), 2005–2011.

Koopman-Boyden, P .G., & MacDonald, L. (2003). Ageing, work performance and managing ageing academics. *Journal of Higher Education Policy and Management, 25,* 29–40.

Lacy, W. B., Bokemeier, J. L., & Shepard, J. M. (1983). Job attribute preferences and work commitment of men and women in the United States. *Personnel Psychology, 36,* 315–329.

Leviatan, U. (1992). Determinates of work motivation and work satisfaction among kibbutz workers. *Canadian Journal of Community Mental Health, 11,* 49–64.

Liao, H., Joshi, A., & Chuang, A. (2004). Sticking out like a sore thumb: Employee dissimilarity and deviance at work. *Personnel Psychology, 57,* 969–1000.

Lorence, J. (1987). Age differences in work involvement: Analyses of three explanations. *Work and Occupations, 14,* 533–557.

Loscocco, K. A., & Kalleberg, A. L. (1988). Aging and the meaning of work in the United States and Japan. *Social Forces, 67,* 337–356.

Mauno, S., & Kinnunen, U. (2000). The stability of job and family involvement: Applying the multi-wave, multi-variable technique to longitudinal data. *Work and Stress, 14,* 51–64.

Maurer, T. J. (2001). Career-relevant learning and development, worker age, and beliefs about self-efficacy for development. *Journal of Management, 27,* 123–140.

Maurer, T. J., Weiss, E. M., & Barbeite, F. G. (2003). A model of involvement in work-related learning and development activity: The effects of individual, situational, motivational, and age variables. *Journal of Applied Psychology, 88,* 707–724.

Mazerolle, M. J., & Gangaram, S. (1999). Older workers' adjustments to plant closures. *Relations Industrielles, 54,* 313–336.

McFarlin, D. B., & Sweeney, P. D. (1992). Distributive and procedural justice as predictors of satisfaction with personal and organizational outcomes. *Academy of Management Journal, 3,* 626–637.

Mor-Barak, M. (1995). The meaning of work for older adults seeking employment: The generativity factor. *International Journal of Aging and Human Development, 41,* 325–344.

Morris, M. G., & Venkatesh, V. (2000). Age differences in technology adoption decisions: Implications for a changing work force. *Personnel Psychology, 53,* 375–403.

Nichols, T., Sugur, N., & Tasiran, A. C. (2003). Signs of change in Turkey's working class: Workers' age-related perceptions in the modern manufacturing sector. *British Journal of Sociology, 54,* 527–545.

Pond, S. B., & Geyer, P. D. (1987). Employee age as a moderator of the relation between perceived work alternatives and job satisfaction. *Journal of Applied Psychology, 72,* 552–557.

Pond, S. B., & Geyer, P. D. (1991). Difference in the relation between job satisfaction and perceived work alternatives among older and younger blue-collar workers. *Journal of Vocational Behavior, 39,* 251–262.

Renaud, S., Lakhdari, M., & Morin, L. (2004). The determinants of participation in non-mandatory training. *Relations Industrielles, 59*, 724–743.

Rhodes, S. R. (1983). Age-related differences in work attitudes and behavior: A review and conceptual analysis. *Psychological Bulletin, 93*, 328–367.

Riordan, C. M., Griffith, R. W., & Weatherly, E. W. (2003). Age and work-related outcomes: The moderating effects of status characteristics. *Journal of Applied Social Psychology, 33*, 37–57.

Robie, C., Ryan, A. M., Schmieder, R., Parra, L., & Smith, P. (1998). The relation between job level and job satisfaction. *Group and Organization Management, 23*, 470–495.

Schwoerer, C. E., & May, D. R. (1996). Age and work outcomes: The moderating effects of self-efficacy and tool design effectiveness. *Journal of Organizational Behavior, 17*, 469–487.

Shultz, K. S., Morton, K. R., & Weckerle, J. R. (1998). The influence of push and pull factors on voluntary and involuntary early retirees' retirement decision and adjustment. *Journal of Vocational Behavior, 53*, 45–57.

Simpson, P. A., Greller, M. M., & Stroh, L. K. (2002). Variations in human capital investment activity by age. *Journal of Vocational Behavior, 61*, 109–138.

Siu, O., Spector, P. E., Cooper, C. L., & Donald, I. (2001). Age differences in coping and locus of control: A study of managerial stress in Hong Kong. *Journal of Applied Psychology, 16*, 707–710.

Smola, K. W., & Sutton, C. D. (2002). Generational differences: Revisiting generational work values for the new millennium. *Journal of Organizational Behavior, 23*, 363–382.

Spreitzer, G. M., Kizilos, M. A., & Nason, S. W. (1997). A dimensional analysis of the relationship between psychological empowerment and effectiveness, satisfaction, and strain. *Journal of Management, 23*, 679–704.

Sterns, H. L., & Miklos, S. (1995). The aging worker in a changing environment: Organizational and individual issues. *Journal of Vocational Behavior, 47*, 248–268.

Sturman, M. C. (2003). Searching for the inverted U-shaped relationship between time and performance: Meta-analyses of the experience/performance, tenure/performance, and age/performance relationships. *Journal of Management, 29*, 609–640.

Tang, T. L. P., & Gilbert, P. R. (1995). Attitudes toward money as related to intrinsic and extrinsic job satisfaction, stress, and work-related attitudes. *Personality and Individual Differences, 19*, 327–332.

Valentine, S., Valentine, W. R., & Dick, J. (1998). Intrinsic and extrinsic motivators and older employees' attitudes towards their current jobs. *Perceptual and Motor Skills, 87*, 407–410.

VanYperen, N. W., Hagedoorn, M., Zweers, M., & Postma, S. (2000). Injustice and employees' destructive responses: The mediating role of state negative affect. *Social Justice Research, 13*, 291–312.

Warr, P. (1994). Age and employment. In H. C. Triandis, M. D. Dunnette, & L. M. Hough (Eds.), *Handbook of industrial and organizational psychology* (2nd ed., Vol. 4, pp. 485–550). Palo Alto, CA: Consulting Psychologists Press.

White, A. T., & Spector, P. E. (1987). An investigation of age-related factors in the age-job-satisfaction relationship. *Psychology and Aging, 2*, 261–265.

8

Employee Development and Training Issues Related to the Aging Workforce

Todd J. Maurer

As training and development continue to be important in the workplace, and as the average age of workers continues to increase, it will be critical to manage the development and learning of aging workers. Therefore, literature on age-related differences in training and development behavior is reviewed, including differences in participation and performance in training and development. Individual and situational factors that may contribute to the age effects are highlighted. Implications for both research and practice are explored.

Workplace training and development remain very important to employee and organizational effectiveness. Literature in this area has even suggested that continuous learning and development have become core career competencies and that these are so critical that those employees who do not stay skilled may even end up having to cut short their careers (cf. Greller & Stroh, 1995; Hall & Mirvis, 1995). This suggests that being successfully involved in employee development and learning will remain an important endeavor for all employees, including older ones.

Age has been addressed in various ways in the literature on training and development, sometimes being included as an influence on various measures of training or development participation, performance, and/or motivation. For example, in a large-scale meta-analytic path analysis of predictors of training motivation, age was included along with other individual variables and some situational variables to predict various other constructs, including job, career, motivational, transfer, and learning variables (Colquitt, LePine, & Noe, 2000). This kind of study was not designed to primarily understand age-related effects, and so age as a variable was not explored in relation to all context and individual variables. In other research, individual and situational variables have been explicitly linked with age as potential underlying explanatory variables that can account for age-related effects (cf. Maurer, Weiss, & Barbeite, 2003). Consistent with the latter approach, the present review directly addresses age in relation to other individual and situational variables that may help explain relationships between age and outcomes such as training and development participation, motivation, and performance. Participation is the extent to which older workers actively engage in various types of training and development activities (e.g., take training, volunteer for special assignments in which something new must be learned), while the related concept of motivation for training and development is the degree to which the person desires to participate and pursue this type of behavior. Performance is the level of achievement within these activities. Age has been linked with these kinds of variables in the literature.

The present chapter will review literature in this area, not with the intent of providing an exhaustive review, but rather to highlight possible situational and individual factors that may contribute to age effects, as well as differences in participation and performance within developmental activities at work. In addition, some research ideas and general recommendations for practice will be identified.

SITUATIONAL INFLUENCES

There are several factors in work situations that might contribute to age-related effects on employee development and training behavior. These factors include stereotypes of older workers in relation to employee learning and development, possible discriminatory treatment, differences in access to job experiences and social support.

Stereotypes about older workers' learning and development behavior. In a recent meta-analysis of attitudes toward younger and older adults, Kite, Stockdale, Whitley, and Johnson (2005) found that across all categories of dependent variables, there was a bias against older adults. However, this bias was largest when stereotypic beliefs and perceptions of attractiveness were assessed, and the bias was smaller when behaviors or behavioral intentions or affective evaluations were measured. Competence ratings fell roughly between these two extremes. The authors assert that these results and other findings within their study confirm that perceptions of older adults are complex and multidimensional, not unitary stereotypes. This suggests that research should focus on the dimension of stereotype most relevant to the domain in question, which in the current discussion is training and development.

In a study by Forte and Hansvick (1999), 98 employers reported their attitudes toward older workers on various dimensions related to work. Older employees were rated lower on ability to learn quickly, energy and stamina, and flexibility. They received higher ratings than younger employees on academic skill levels, attendance, ability to get along with coworkers, work ethics, salary expectations, and supervisory skills. The findings partially support the idea that people believe older workers are less capable of development because the dimensions on which older workers were rated lower are those closely related to learning and development. In this vein, the American Association of Retired Persons (AARP; 1995) suggested that among the impediments to employers retaining older workers for employment were the perceptions that they resist technology and are not very willing to adapt to technological changes, and also that older workers lack flexibility and are unwilling to take on new tasks and adapt to changes. In the literature, it is not uncommon to find the perception that older employees are slower, not as interested in training, possess less flexibility, and they may be more prone to fatigue than their younger colleagues (Doering, Rhodes, & Schuster, 1983; Heron & Chown, 1961; Stagner, 1985; Warr, 1994a).

In Europe, results of a study documented a perception that older workers were less adaptable (i.e., less able to grasp new ideas, adapt to change, and learn quickly) than their younger colleagues (Warr & Pennington, 1993). Older workers may be perceived as less receptive to new ideas, less able to learn, less adaptable, and more rigid than younger workers (Rosen & Jerdee, 1976a, 1976b). Capowski (1994) discusses a finding that 59 percent of businesses state that older employees resist training. This research suggests that some people perceive older workers as being less interested in or motivated toward engaging in learning and development activities.

Finkelstein, Burke, and Raju (1995) conducted a meta-analysis of these kinds of studies and found lower ratings for older workers than younger ones on dimensions related to having potential for development. Maurer, Andrews, and Weiss (2003) addressed these kinds of stereotypes (beliefs about older workers' ability and motivation for development) along with a model of possible antecedents and consequences. They suggested that the stereotypes can be influenced by first-hand experience with older worker behavior (observing older workers failing in training or not being interested in developmental experiences), perceived external inhibitors (such as situational impediments in which older workers are not given learning opportunities or are not supported for training) and also perceived internal inhibitors, such as beliefs about changes that occur with age including declines in overall capabilities that may influence learning.

A stereotype about development capability and motivation might have a basis or origin in more general stereotypical beliefs or ideas about older people. Research has suggested that people believe there are a larger proportion of expected losses and fewer expected gains associated with older ages. Heckhausen and Baltes (1991) found that undesirable attributes were expected to increase in older adulthood and that these aging-related increases in undesirable attributes may be uncontrollable. As an example, other research shows a relation of age and a perception of decline in memory abilities (cf. Ryan & See, 1993; Dixon, 1989). Older people are thought of as being forgetful, absent-minded, or slower (Heckhausen, Dixon, & Baltes, 1989; MacNeil, Ramos, & Magafas, 1996), as possessing less creativity (Rosen & Jerdee, 1976b), and being less physically capable (Netz & Ben-Sira, 1993; Rosen & Jerdee, 1976b; Slotterback & Saarnio, 1996).

Directly addressing this issue, Wrenn and Maurer (2004) investigated the relationship between beliefs about the decline of various specific abilities that could contribute to learning and beliefs about older workers' ability to develop and beliefs about their inclination to develop. Those authors found that beliefs about the decline of learning relevant abilities predicted beliefs about older workers' lack of ability to successfully develop. That is, to the extent that participants believed that various abilities declined after age 50, they also tended to hold negative beliefs about older workers' ability to learn and develop. This suggests that an important determinant of people's negative perceptions of older workers' development capability is their belief about the decline of abilities with age in general. Beliefs about the decline of scholastic aptitude and resistance to stress best predicted beliefs about older workers' ability to develop. The finding involving scholastic aptitude is interesting because cross-sectional and longitudinal research has focused extensively on age differences and changes in mental ability, showing varying degrees of actual decline.

In this same research by Wrenn and Maurer (2004), beliefs about the decline of abilities also predicted beliefs about older workers' general inclination to develop. To the extent that participants believed that learning-relevant abilities decline after age 50, they also held negative beliefs concerning older workers' inclination to participate in development activities. Beliefs about the decline of development orientation and self-objectivity were most related to beliefs about older workers' inclination.

Another interesting outcome of the study by Wrenn and Maurer (2004) is that beliefs about older workers' inclination to develop were significantly more negative than were beliefs about older workers' ability to develop. Other research also suggests that older workers are seen as unmotivated to develop (cf. Rosen & Jerdee, 1976a), but the fact that beliefs about older workers' inclination are more negative than beliefs about their ability suggests that this type of belief is of primary importance when examining age stereotypes in relation to learning and development.

Possible discriminatory treatment. Literature has suggested a link between these types of stereotypes and adverse decisions and treatment of older workers in relation to training and development resources for older workers (Maurer, Andrews, & Weiss, 2003). Rosen and Jerdee (1976b) studied simulated managerial decisions. Participants in the research read a scenario that depicted an older or a younger employee. Participants in the research perceived older employees to be less desirable for retraining opportunities (preferring termination and replacement to retraining), more difficult to persuade to change, and less motivated to keep up to date. Rosen and Jerdee (1977) replicated this study using individuals who subscribed to Harvard Business Review and obtained similar results. Stagner (1985) also reviewed research that suggests people are aware of discriminatory treatment and obstacles that older workers may face when it comes to training, and Mercer (1981) reported that 61 percent of executives agreed that older employees are discriminated against, but the same executives denied that this kind of discrimination took place in their firms. This literature suggests that older workers may face discriminatory obstacles in pursuing developmental experiences.

However, Rosen and Jerdee's (1976a) classic study on age discrimination, conducted over 25 years ago, was recently replicated by Weiss and Maurer (2004). While in the original study participants rated older targets as being less desirable and suitable in a variety of work-related scenarios, in the more recent study by Weiss and Maurer older and younger targets were rated as similarly qualified and suitable for training, promotion, and hiring. Far fewer significant effects were found in the recent study than were originally reported in the Rosen and Jerdee (1976a) study. Weiss and Maurer (2004) suggested that one possible explanation for the difference in results is that there simply is not as much age discrimination now as there was in the mid 1970s. Since the 1976 study was done, two amendments have been made to the Age Discrimination in Employment Act (1967, amended 1978 & 1986), and substantial precedence has been set in case law that makes overt, intentional age discrimination an undesirable practice. In addition, because the sizable baby boomer generation is entering the age group in question, older people are more prevalent in all walks of life, including the workforce. Thus, societal attitudes may have changed in relation to this national demographic shift.

Maurer and Rafuse (2001) addressed this question of how age-related differences might occur in training and development opportunities as a result of these kinds of stereotypes. They concluded that this could occur in two ways that differ in the degree to which it is obvious that discrimination may have occurred. First, an individual may be denied access to the training and development experiences. This is perhaps the most overt and obvious way. Second, an individual may not receive support and/or encouragement (and possibly is even discouraged) in the pursuit of these activities from an organizational or psychological perspective. This is perhaps a less overt or obvious way. Either way this kind of effect can be harmful to the development of older workers.

Differences in access to developmental job experiences, training and social support. Do older workers get access to developmental experiences to the same extent that younger workers do? Various sources of literature on this topic suggest that they sometimes do not. Maurer (2001) reviewed literature reflecting the idea that older workers in organizations may become suscepti- ble to "lost opportunities" for development just as minorities might (Ilgen & Youtz, 1986). In relation to developmental activities, one key example of a lost opportunity is not getting a challenging or complex job assignment. Diffi- cult job assignments can be a very valuable source of employee development (Davies & Easterby-Smith, 1984; McCall, Lombardo, & Morrison, 1988; McCauley, Ruderman, Ohlott, & Morrow, 1994). Further, challenging work can actually help facilitate participation in skill development activities (cf. Kozlowski & Farr, 1988). However, older workers are sometimes given more rou- tine (rather than complex and challenging) job assignments (Price, Thompson, & Dalton, 1975; Salthouse & Maurer, 1996; Stagner, 1985). Because supervisors may not believe that older workers have the ability to complete complex as- signments effectively, they may minimize the risks associated with assigning older workers to such assignments (Fossum, Arvey, Paradise, & Robbins, 1986).

Likewise, managers or executives who allocate developmental experiences may perceive older workers as not being comfortable with new technology (The DYG, Inc., 1989). Older workers may experience fewer transitions and be less likely to get assigned to a change in job content, status, or location (all of which offer valuable developmental opportunities). Some research suggests that older workers tend to be given familiar situations where they can rely on established routines (Ohlott & Eastman, 1994). Boerlijst (1994) found that older workers tended to have positions that provided fewer growth and devel- opment opportunities.

In addition, when it comes to formal training, Capowski (1994) discussed data that suggested that only 3 of 10 companies may include older adults in their training programs. In addition, Dutch researchers have shown that older workers were less likely to have taken training courses in their field of special- ization (Boerlijst, 1994). Simon (1996) asserts that 55 to 64 year olds are only a third as likely as 35 to 44 year olds to receive training in the workplace, ac- cording to a study by the U.S. Department of Labor. Simon suggests that many employers may discourage older workers from obtaining training. A study con- ducted by SHRM and AARP (1998) found that 47 percent of respondents' organizations provide training to upgrade skills of older workers. This all sug- gests that older workers may sometimes experience less formal training than younger ones.

Another area where developmental resources or opportunities may be experienced with lower frequency is in relation to social relationships that enhance development and learning. Tsui and O'Reilly (1989) studied comparative ages in supervisor-subordinate dyads and found that older workers were rated lower, liked less, and experienced more role ambiguity compared to younger workers. Zenger and Lawrence (1989) showed that the frequency of communication between an older worker and younger coworkers was likely to be lower than communication among the younger workers. Other research found that older workers were less likely than younger workers to receive career counseling from their supervisors (Cleveland & Shore, 1992).

In addition, older employees may lack opportunities to form special, intimate peer relationships at work that provide high psychosocial support (Kram & Isabella, 1985). Some research found that age was negatively related to career encouragement and educational encouragement (Tharenou, Latimer, & Conroy, 1994). Schabracq (1994) suggests that social networks decay with time, which may result in older employees being confronted with the loss of emotional support, and they may become more isolated. This literature suggests that older employees have fewer opportunities to receive support from coworkers, supervisors, and other people. This combined with stereotypes and changes in the older workers themselves might lead to decreased tendency to develop.

INFLUENCE OF INDIVIDUAL CHARACTERISTICS

Differences in individual characteristics of employees related to age may also contribute to differences in their training and development behavior. Maurer et al. (2003) asserted that differences in treatment and stereotypes about development capability and interest might indirectly influence behavior of older workers themselves through a kind of self-fulfilling prophecy. They may influence older workers' perceptions of what is appropriate or possible for individuals in their age group. Along these lines, Greller and Stroh (1995) suggest that workers' concepts of appropriate aging behavior might be influenced by stereotypes when they look for cues and role definitions provided by others regarding what is appropriate for people of their age (Aries, 1962). Maurer et al. (2003) suggested that these stereotypes might influence the development behavior by older worker themselves.

Maurer (2001) reviewed literature to illustrate how various social and organizational processes might together negatively influence the self-efficacy for development of older workers. Applying Bandura's (1997) self-efficacy framework, to the extent that older workers have fewer mastery experiences in learning and development activities, they have few vicarious experiences in which they observe older role models who successfully engage in development activities, they receive little or no persuasion from others who support and encourage them to participate, and to the extent that they experience physiological impediments such as anxiety during the experiences, this could negatively influence their self-efficacy for development. This construct (self-efficacy for development) has been found to consistently and significantly predict motivation and involvement in employee development activities (cf. Maurer, Weiss, & Barbeite, 2003).

In addition, other research has shown a decline in various cognitive reasoning capabilities with age (Verhaeghen & Salthouse, 1997), and these kinds of changes could contribute to performance in cognitively challenging learning situations. In relation to employee development behavior, Maurer et al. (2003) examined differences in relevant individual-level constructs in relation to worker age. They found that older workers felt less cognitively able and had lower perceptions of themselves as possessing learning qualities compared to younger workers. Workers who perceived their age relative to their coworkers to be higher perceived their own intelligence to be lower and perceived their own minds to have declined in recent years. Further, chronological age was positively related to this perception that their minds had declined and negatively related to perceptions that they possessed the qualities needed for learning. However, the differences on these variables mentioned here were quite small and they did not seem to handicap older workers in any way in overall involvement in development (i.e., there were no differences in participation in development activities).

DIFFERENCES IN PARTICIPATION RATES AND PERFORMANCE

Literature does suggest there can be age differences in participation rates in developmental activities and also in performance in learning experiences. With respect to differences in participation in training and development with age, some authors have suggested that younger adults are more likely to volunteer for training (Rosen, Williams, & Foltman, 1965) and that age is negatively related to developmental experiences (Cleveland & Shore, 1992). Tucker (1985) found that most workers had their last training experience less than one year ago, but the majority of workers who reported their last training was more than three years ago were in the 60 and over age group. Warr (1994b) reported that the proportion of older workers participating in job-related training and the hours of off-the-job training declined across age groups and that age predicted training incidence and duration negatively irrespective of tenure. Workers less than 40 years of age reported an average of 10 days of training while those over 60 years old reported half as many days training. This difference was due to activities during work time.

With respect to training performance differences by age, other literature has documented a finding that older employees may perform worse in training than younger employees (Gist, Rosen, & Schwoerer, 1988; Kubeck, Delp, Haslett, & McDaniel, 1996). Outside of the traditional job training setting, older individuals may also have fewer successful college classroom experiences (Rebok & Offerman, 1983). A meta-analysis by Kubeck et al. (1996) shows that older adults, relative to younger adults, showed less mastery of training material, completed the final training tasks more slowly, and took longer to complete the training program. However, these authors also reported relatively high variability in performance.

In the majority of the samples studied by Kubeck et al. (1996), the variance for older adults' performance was larger than for younger adults, indicating that there were greater individual differences among older adults than among younger adults. This aspect of the study by Kubeck et al. is in agreement with an analysis of results from several studies published in *Psychology and Aging* and the *Journal of Gerontology* by Morse (1993). Morse reported that older adults as a group are more variable than younger groups in basic and general abilities like memory, fluid intelligence, and reaction time. Therefore, the characteristics of *individuals* need to be considered independently from aggregate findings about a group of which he or she is a member (i.e., older workers).

In addition, Kubeck et al. (1996) found that although there was a negative relationship between age and training mastery performance, there was also a negative relationship between age and pretraining competence. This means that much if not all of the performance differences associated with age after training might be accounted for by existing competence differences before training. There was little data available to directly reflect actual amount learned in training, but available data showed only a very small negative relationship between age and amount learned in training. This suggests that existing cohort differences between age groups (e.g., education, experience/skill with technology) might be causing the pretraining differences. Therefore, if equally competent older and younger workers are selected for training, the negative effects on success might be smaller. These facts about variability suggest that group averages do not represent older individuals very well, and thus, stereotypes based on averages may not be very accurate in describing individual behavior. Also, if individual differences are considered in selecting people for training (e.g., pre-training competence and other training-relevant characteristics), the negative age effects suggested in prior research may be significantly smaller.

Maurer et al. (2003) and Maurer and Rafuse (2001) contrast the literature on aging, which reflects important differences in performance and personal characteristics between older and younger groups, with literature on race and sex. In literature on race and sex differences, there are also differences in job-relevant characteristics. However, in that literature there is the very clear idea that people should be treated as individuals because of wide variability within race and sex categories. Stereotypical ideas that broadly portray members of those categories in an unfavorable light are offensive. However, Maurer and Rafuse (2001) assert that although most employees are very sensitive to sexism and racism, somehow the idea that "you can't teach an old dog new tricks" does not seem to carry the same taboo status in society and the work place. Yet it is just as important in this area to be sensitive to the fact that one size does not fit all, and there can be older individuals who are both interested in and able when it comes to learning.

In this vein of exploring whether and how older trainees might be most successful in training, Callahan, Kiker, and Cross (2003) explored whether three different instructional methods in training (lecture, modeling, and active participation) and four different instructional factors (materials, feedback, pacing, and group size) made a difference on observed training performance among older trainees. The meta-analysis focused solely on older learners, emphasizing samples ages 60 and older and including only trainees over age 40. The results showed that all three instructional methods and two instructional factors, self-pacing and group size, explained unique variance in observed training performance. Self-pacing explained the greatest proportion of the observed variance. This latter finding is consistent with aging literature that finds physical and cognitive declines and illustrates that self-pacing provides older learners with a way to achieve results despite any age-related declines that may have occurred for them. The results finding unique effects for multiple methods suggest that training that integrates multiple tactics could be useful when training older learners. Callahan et al. (2003) suggest that the positive effects of lecture for older learners refute the assumption that because older adult learners have been out of traditional classroom settings for an extended period of time, the method will not be effective for older adults. The method seems to have value among older adults. In addition, the data suggested that modeling (i.e., observing another person perform the task being trained) generalizes to the special case of the older learner. Further, active participation (i.e., the trainee engaging in the learning process by actually performing the focal task) was effective for older adult trainees.

DIRECTIONS FOR FUTURE RESEARCH

There are several important research questions that emerge from a discussion of this literature. First, a continuing and important research question is the extent to which people stay involved in learning and development activities for the purposes of continually improving their career-relevant skills, and understanding the individual and situational constructs that contribute to that behavior. From the point of view of aging workers, it is important to continue to examine these variables as they relate to age and to training and development behavior. Just how much of a difference is there in participation and performance by age—and what variables account for these effects?

Another area is in relation to stereotypes, judgments, and decisions in relation to training and development activities for older workers. As suggested by Maurer et al. (2003), it is difficult to draw conclusions from simple differences in participation rates in training and development activities. It would be interesting to know whether access to opportunities is being blocked by actual discriminatory decisions. For example, are learning-rich jobs or training opportunities being given to older workers? When a job assignment must be made that will involve a high degree of learning, is an older worker nominated or chosen? Are older workers given attention when it comes to development at work in performance feedback processes, and do they get encouragement toward challenging, developmental situations? Are older workers kept "in the loop" when it comes to learning and development (Maurer et al., 2003)? Alternatively, do older workers themselves avoid these experiences?

One challenge in research on age differences in this and in other areas are confounds that exists with the age variables. Maurer et al. (2003) suggested that there are demographic variables that are naturally and usually confounded with age of workers that *could be* driving the effects for age. It might sometimes be necessary to control for factors such as the job experience of the older worker, job type, years from retirement, and other variables to rule out their influence in age relationships. This is one way to examine whether effects are truly a result of age, per se, or things correlated with age. In the study by Maurer et al. (2003), controlling for demographic variables significantly reduced or eliminated age relationships. Older workers may simply be more experienced on average, or their job assignments may be different (cf. Salthouse & Maurer, 1996). Thus, these variables, rather than age, could account for these effects.

For example, Maurer and Weiss (2003) explored whether several content dimensions of managerial work are associated with reported continuous learning skill demands in 50 different jobs. Manager experience was a unique predictor of continuous learning skill requirements when controlling for manager age and job, but age was not a unique predictor when controlling for manager experience and job. Uncontrolled for the effects of other variables, age alone significantly predicted continuous learning skill requirements, but these effects became nonsignificant once experience and job were controlled for. These studies highlight the possible importance of statistical control of other variables when examining age effects in this area.

Another research issue centers on the importance that training and development resources will have in careers and the extent to which they will become the focus of legal actions in which discrimination is alleged. Maurer and Rafuse (2001) point out that in previous time periods in the work place an environment or culture that discouraged workers from developmental experiences might have been viewed as not very significant, but as those experiences grow in value and tangible importance to workers, this may be viewed as increasingly important. To the extent that developmental experiences are important for survival in the world of work (i.e., closely associated with promotion, demotion, transfer, hiring, or reductions in force), then perhaps they will be viewed as key parts of employment. If this happens, age differences in learning/development opportunity may be increasingly involved as key evidence of discrimination. It will be interesting to monitor these trends from a legal perspective to see if training and development become increasingly intertwined with allegations of age discrimination at work.

IMPLICATIONS FOR PRACTICE

Some general practical recommendations also emerge from this discussion. Maurer and Rafuse (2001) offered several ideas for avoiding age discrimination in training and development opportunities that relate to better management of the learning and development process. The suggestions can be roughly categorized into four overlapping classes of concerns. First, with respect to "Culture and policies" it is important that the organization set a direction in the management of human resources in which development opportunities such as training classes, job assignments and rotations, or other developmental experiences or resources are allocated on an age-neutral basis. Second, "Decisions about training and development opportunities" should be made in such a way that developmental experiences are assigned on an individual-by-individual basis, and not based on assumptions associated with a person's age group membership. Related to this idea, Maurer (2001) asserted that one should be conscious of the potential for "lost opportunities" for older workers when it comes to training and developmental assignments. It is important to make an effort to ensure that, when they are qualified, older workers have access to challenging tasks and learning resources such as training, job assignments that offer learning and "stretch" opportunities, and other valuable experiences that promote development. Third, "Supervision and supportive developmental relationships" should be structured in such a way that managers are made accountable for development plans and support for all employees, not just younger ones. Fourth, "Training managers on ADEA and on the effects of stereotypes" is important so that it can be made clear that the organization has a zero-tolerance policy with respect to any discrimination including age. Maurer, Andrews, and Weiss (2003) pointed out the value of individuating information in relation to these issues. To the extent that workers are regarded on an individual-by-individual basis and relevant information is available for each of them, stereotypes have less of an influence on decisions and evaluations. Training younger workers to have greater awareness of the variability in older workers' capabilities can help in that regard, as can exposure to older workers on teams and projects.

CONCLUSION

As learning and development continue to be important in the workplace, and as the average age of workers continues to increase, it will be important to manage the development and learning of aging workers. A variety of issues have been addressed in this chapter which highlight the need for more research and also attention in practice to ensuring that we both understand age differences where they do exist and that human resources are utilized effectively regardless of worker age. It seems likely that more attention in both research and practice are needed.

REFERENCES

AARP. (1995). *American business and older workers: A road map to the 21st century.* Washington, DC: DYG, Inc.

Aries, P. (1962). *Centuries of childhood: A social history of family life.* New York: Vintage Press.

Bandura, A. (1997). *Self-efficacy: The exercise of control.* New York: Freeman.

Boerlijst, J. (1994). The neglect of growth and development of employees over 40 in organizations: A managerial and training problem. In J. Snel & R. Cremer (Eds.), *Work and aging: A European perspective* (pp. 251–271). London: Taylor & Francis, Ltd.

Callahan, J. S., Kiker, D. S., & Cross, T. (2003). Does method matter? A meta-analysis of the effects of training method on older learner training performance. *Journal of Management, 29,* 663–680.

Capowski, G. (1994). Ageism: The new diversity issue. *Management Review, 83,* 10–15.

Cleveland, J. N., & Shore, L. M. (1992). Self and supervisory perspectives on age and work attitudes and performance. *Journal of Applied Psychology, 77,* 469–484.

Colquitt, J. A., LePine, J. A., & Noe, R. A. (2000). Toward an integrative theory of training motivation: a meta-analytic path analysis of 20 years of research. *Journal of Applied Psychology, 85,* 678–707.

Davies, J., & Easterby-Smith, M. (1984). Learning and developing from managerial work experiences. *Journal of Management Studies, 21,* 169–183.

Doering, M., Rhodes, S. R., & Schuster, M. (1983). *The aging worker.* Beverly Hills, CA: Sage.

Dixon, R. (1989). Questionnaire research on metamemory and aging: Issues of structure and function. In L. Poon, D. Rubin, & B. Wilson (Eds.), *Everyday cognition in adulthood and late life* (pp. 395–415). Cambridge, NY: Cambridge University Press.

Finkelstein, L. M., Burke, M. J., & Raju, N. S. (1995). Age discrimination in simulated employment contexts: An integrative analysis. *Journal of Applied Psychology, 80,* 652–663.

Forte, C. S., & Hansvick, C. L. (1999). Applicant age as a subjective employability factor: A study of workers over and under age fifty. *Journal of Employment Counseling, 36,* 24–34.

Fossum, J., Arvey, R., Paradise, C., & Robbins, N. (1986). Modeling the skills obsolescence process: A psychological/economic integration. *Academy of Management Review, 11,* 362–374.

Greller, M. M., & Stroh, L. K. (1995). Careers in midlife and beyond: A fallow field in need of sustenance. *Journal of Vocational Behavior, 47,* 232–247.

Gist, M., Rosen, B., & Schwoerer, C. (1988). The influence of training method and trainee age on the acquisition of computer skills. *Personnel Psychology, 41,* 255–265.

Hall, D. T., & Mirvis, P. H. (1995). The new career contract: Developing the whole person at midlife and beyond. *Journal of Vocational Behavior, 47,* 269–289.

Heckhausen, J., & Baltes, P. B. (1991). Perceived controllability of expected psychological change across adulthood and old age. *Journal of Gerontology, 46,* 165–173.

Heckhausen, J., Dixon, R. A., & Baltes, P. B. (1989). Gains and losses in development throughout adulthood as perceived by different age groups. *Developmental Psychology, 25,* 109–121.

Heron, A., & Chown, S. M. (1961). *Aging and the semi-skilled: A survey in manufacturing industry on Merseyside.* London: Her Majesty's Stationery Office.

Ilgen, D., & Youtz, M. (1986). Factors affecting the evaluation and development of minorities in organizations. *Research in Personnel and Human Resource Management, 4,* 307–337.

Kite, M. E., Stockdale, G. D., Whitley, B. E. Jr., & Johnson, B. T. (2005). Attitudes toward younger and older adults: An updated meta-analytic review. *Journal of Social Issues, 61,* 241–266.

Kozlowski, S., & Farr, J. (1988). An integrative model of updating and performance. *Human Performance, 1,* 5–29.

Kram, K., & Isabella, L. (1985). Mentoring alternatives: The role of peer relationships in career development. *Academy of Management Journal, 28,* 110–132.

Kubeck, J., Delp, N., Haslett, T., & McDaniel, M. (1996). Does job-related training performance decline with age? *Psychology and Aging, 11,* 92–107.

MacNeil, R. D., Ramos, C. I., & Magafas, A. M. (1996). Age stereotyping among college students: A replication and expansion. *Educational Gerontology, 22,* 229–243.

Maurer, T. (2001). Career-relevant learning and development, worker age, and beliefs about self-efficacy for development. *Journal of Management, 27,* 123–140.

Maurer, T., Andrews, K., & Weiss, E. (2003). Toward understanding and managing stereotypical beliefs about older workers' ability and desire for learning and development. *Research in Personnel and Human Resources Management, 22,* 253–285.

Maurer, T., & Rafuse, N. E. (2001). Learning, not litigating: Managing employee development and avoiding age discrimination. *Academy of Management Executive, 15,* 110–121.

Maurer, T., Weiss, M., & Barbeite, F. (2003). A model of involvement in work-related learning and development activity: The effects of individual, situational, motivational and age variables. *Journal of Applied Psychology, 88*, 707–724.

McCall, M., Lombardo, M., & Morrison, A. (1988). *The lessons of experience: How successful executives develop on the job.* Lexington, MA: Lexington Books.

McCauley, C. D., Ruderman, M. N., Ohlott, P. J., & Morrow, J. E. (1994). Assessing the developmental components of managerial jobs. *Journal of Applied Psychology, 79*, 544–560.

Mercer, W. M. (1981). *Employer attitudes: Implications of an aging workforce.* New York: William M. Mercer, Inc.

Morse, C. K. (1993). Does variability increase with age? An archival study of cognitive measures. *Psychology and Aging, 8*, 156–164.

Netz, Y., & Ben-Sira, D. (1993). Attitudes of young people, adults, and older adults from three-generation families toward the concepts "ideal person," "youth," and "old person." *Educational Gerontology, 19*, 607–621.

Ohlott, P., & Eastman, L. (1994). *Age differences in developmental job experiences: Evidence of a gray ceiling?* Paper presented at the Annual Conference of the Academy of Management, Dallas.

Price, R., Thompson, P., & Dalton, G. (1975). A longitudinal study of technological obsolescence. *Research Management, November*, 22–28.

Rebok, G., & Offerman, L. (1983). Behavioral competencies of older college students: A self-efficacy approach. *The Gerontologist, 23*, 428–432.

Rosen, B., & Jerdee, T. H. (1976a). The influence of age stereotypes on managerial decisions. *Journal of Applied Psychology, 61*, 428–432.

Rosen, B., & Jerdee, T. (1976b). The nature of job-related age stereotypes. *Journal of Applied Psychology, 61*, 180–183.

Rosen, B., & Jerdee, T. H. (1977). Too old or not too old? *Harvard Business Review, 7*, 97–108.

Rosen, N., Williams, L., & Foltman, F. (1965). Motivational constraints in an industrial retraining program. *Personnel Psychology, 18*, 65–79.

Ryan, E., & See, S. (1993). Age-based beliefs about memory changes for self and others across adulthood. *Journal of Gerontology, 48*, 199–201.

Salthouse, T., & Maurer, T. (1996). Aging, job performance, and career development. In J. Birren & K. Schaie (Eds.), *Handbook of the psychology of aging* (4th ed., pp. 353–364). San Diego, CA: Academic Press.

Schabracq, M. (1994). Motivational and cultural factors underlying dysfunctioning of older employees. In J. Snel & R. Cremer (Eds.), *Work and aging: A European perspective* (pp. 235–249). London: Taylor & Francis, Ltd.

Simon, R. (1996). Too damn old. *Money, 25*, 118–126.

Slotterback, C. S., & Saarnio, D. A. (1996). Attitudes toward older adults reported by young adults: Variation based on attitudinal task and attribute categories. *Psychology and Aging, 11*, 563–571.

Society for Human Resource Management/AARP. (1998). *Older workers survey.* Alexandria, VA.

Stagner, R. (1985). Aging in Industry. In J. Birren & W. Schaie (Eds.), *Handbook of Psychology of Aging* (2nd ed., pp. 789–817). New York: Van Nostrand Reinhold Co.

Tharenou, P., Latimer, S., & Conroy, D. (1994). How do you make it to the top? An examination of influences on women's and men's managerial advancement. *Academy of Management Journal, 37*, 899–931.

The DYG, Inc. (1989). *Business and older workers: Current perspectives and new directions for the 1990s.* Washington, DC: American Association of Retired Persons.

Tsui, A., & O'Reilly, C. (1989). Beyond simple demographic effects: The importance of relational demography in superior-subordinate dyads. *Academy of Management Journal, 32,* 402–423.

Tucker, F. D. (1985). A study of the training needs of older workers: Implications for human resources development planning. *Public Personnel Management Journal, 14,* 85–95.

Verhaeghen, P., & Salthouse, T. A. (1997). Meta-analysis of age-cognitions relations in adulthood: Estimates of linear and nonlinear age effects and structural models. *Psychological Bulletin, 122,* 231–249.

Warr, P. B. (1994a). Age and employment. In H. C. Triandis & M. D. Dunnette (Eds.), *Handbook of industrial and organizational psychology* (pp. 485–550). Palo Alto, CA: Consulting Psychologists Press.

Warr, P. (1994b). Training for older managers. *Human Resource Management Journal, 4*(2), 22–38.

Warr, P., & Pennington, J. (1993). Views about age discrimination and older workers. In P. Taylor, A. Walker, B. Casey, H. Metcalf, J. Lakey, P. Warr, & J. Pennington (Eds.), *Age and employment: Policies, attitudes and practices* (pp. 75–106). London: Institute of Personnel Management.

Weiss, E., & Maurer, T. (2004). Age discrimination in personnel decisions: A reexamination. *Journal of Applied Social Psychology, 34,* 1555–1562.

Wrenn, K., & Maurer, T. (2004). Beliefs about older workers' learning and development behavior in relation to beliefs about malleability of skills, age-related decline and control. *Journal of Applied Social Psychology, 34,* 223–242.

Zenger, T., & Lawrence, B. (1989). Organizational demography: The differential effects of age and tenure distributions on technical communication. *Academy of Management Journal, 32,* 353–376.

9

Career Mobility and Career Stability Among Older Workers

Daniel C. Feldman

This chapter examines the individual-level, job-level, and occupational-level factors that influence whether older workers remain with or change career paths after age 50. We begin with a discussion of the construct of *career change* and how it can be distinguished from related constructs like job change and bridge employment. The chapter then turns to the construct of *career embeddedness*. Here, we suggest that career stability and mobility are a function of both motivation to change careers and ability to change careers. More specifically, we examine: (a) older workers' networks and links to the current career path; (b) their fit with current career paths; (c) sacrifices that would be associated with leaving that career path; and (d) barriers to gaining entry into alternative careers. The chapter concludes with implications for future theoretical work in this area and implications for management practice.

Over the past 10 years, there has been considerable attention paid to the idea of a boundaryless career (Arthur & Rousseau, 1996; Feldman, 2002a) and the fact that individuals are not staying with any one organization or career for their entire work lives. However, while the career mobility of young adults has been widely researched (Morrison, 2002; Scandura, 2002), the career mobility of older adults has been largely ignored. By and large, researchers have not studied the career mobility of workers over age 40 (namely, the last presumed burst of change associated with mid-career crises). Thereafter, older workers' career mobility has only been examined in a few contexts, most notably, CEO succession (Ward, Sonnenfeld, & Kimberly, 1995), retirement (Feldman, 1994), and bridge employment (Kim & Feldman, 1998, 2000). The unfortunate stereotype that "you can't teach old dogs new tricks" seems to have expanded to include the stereotype that "old dogs don't want to learn new tricks."

This chapter seeks to redress those misperceptions by exploring career mobility and career stability in late career. In trying to make sense of the lower career mobility of older workers, people have often made the "fundamental attribution error" (Kelly, 1973) and assumed that older workers don't change careers because they have no motivation to do so and that this lack of motivation to change is a relatively stable individual difference over time. Here, we argue that older workers' mobility is not only a function of their *motivation* to change careers, but also their *ability* to do so. Moreover, the forces for, and against, career change are both *internal* (within the person) and *external* (inherent in the situation) in nature.

Building on recent research on *job embeddedness* (Mitchell, Holtom, Lee, Sablynski, & Erez, 2001), we introduce the construct of career embeddedness and suggest that older workers' career mobility and stability are a function of: (a) older workers' networks and links to the current career path; (b) their fit with current career paths; (c) sacrifices that would be associated with leaving a career; and (d) barriers to gaining entry into new careers. We use this construct to understand the individual-level, job-level, and occupational-level factors that influence whether older workers are stable in their current career paths until retirement or change careers after age 50.

THE CONSTRUCT OF CAREER CHANGE

Here, we define *careers* as the series of jobs that a person holds over the course of a work life and *career change* as "entry into a new occupation which requires fundamentally different skills, daily routines, and work environments from the present one" (Feldman, 2002b, p. 76). Although career change may be conceptually similar to other types of job transitions, it can also be clearly distinguished from them.

For example, the term *job change* refers to taking a different position within an organization (e.g., moving from being an auditor in one department to being an auditor in another department). A job change is not, in and of itself, a career change; in the previous example, there are no major changes in important skills or daily routines. However, moving from being an internal auditor to being an accounting professor would be considered a career change because of the magnitude of difference in requisite skills, daily routines, and work environments. Using the same logic, then, the term *organization change* refers to taking a position with a different employer. If the organization change does not entail any fundamental changes in skills or work environments, such a transition would not be considered a career change (e.g., moving from being a customer service representative at Target to being one at Walmart). On the other hand, moving from being a customer service representative at Target to being a brand manager for Procter and Gamble would be considered a career change because of the degree of novelty in the new tasks and work routines (Feldman, 2002b).

In the context of older workers' careers, an additional clarification is warranted. Many older workers *retire* from a long-held job or career, but then continue to be employed for several years thereafter (Doeringer, 1990; Feldman, 1994). If that subsequent employment is part time or temporary in nature and is a low-involvement activity, we consider such work *bridge employment* (Feldman, 2002b, p. 77). For example, an archaeology professor who retires and then occasionally leads tours to historic sites would be considered to be engaging in such bridge employment. On the other hand, a physician who leaves medicine, gets an MBA, and starts a full-time consulting business would be considered to have changed careers. In this case, the older worker is sustaining the same level of psychological involvement in the new position as in the old position, and at the same time is experiencing fundamental changes in required skills, daily routines, and work contexts. As we will see next, there are both internal and external forces which influence older workers' motivation to change careers and their ability to do so in practice.

THE MOTIVATION TO CHANGE CAREERS AMONG OLDER WORKERS

As Feldman (2002b) notes, there is always some uncertainty and risk associated with a major career change. Moreover, the motivation to change careers varies across career stages. For example, number of children to support may be an important motivator for young adults to change careers so that they can increase their earnings and provide their families with greater financial stability; that motivation, though, is largely absent for older workers. At the same time, the physical demands of an occupation may be a greater motivator of career change for older adults than for younger adults. While we will not attempt to provide a comprehensive list of all the factors that may motivate older workers to change careers, we will highlight the individual-level, job-level, and occupational-level factors that are most likely to impel late-career employees to make this transition.

Individual-Level Factors

While recent research suggests that individuals' personalities are not fully formed by age 21 but continue to evolve in early adulthood, there appears to be much less fluidity of personality later in life (Eysenk, 1994; Mischel, 1973). Consequently, enduring personality attributes may play a significant role in individuals' motivation to change careers after age 50 (Alderfer & Guzzo, 1979).

Of the Big Five personality traits most frequently studied in organizational research (Digman, 1989), the two that seem most likely to influence career change are *openness to experience* and *neuroticism*. Because career change always entails some risk, older workers who are open to experience are more likely to perceive alternative careers positively and to not exaggerate the potential hazards of major transitions. Older workers who are in good mental health and who have realistic and positive self-regard are also more likely to estimate their chances of success in a new career to be higher as well. Some other personality variables which might be important here are extraversion and self-efficacy.

Two other individual-level factors are also likely to predispose older workers to change careers, namely, *health* and *wealth* (Kim & Feldman, 1998). As workers experience greater cognitive deficits and more physical problems, they are often pressured to find new careers as they get older. Thus, poor health appears to be a strong motivator to change careers (while, unfortunately, also making it harder for older workers to enter alternative careers).

In addition, in the case of many older workers, a change of career can mean a temporary loss in income and potentially a significantly lower stream of income well into the future. Changing careers can also entail investments in new training, new offices, and geographical relocation, all of which can require considerable resources. Thus, older workers with more financial resources may be more motivated (and better able) to undertake career changes despite the financial uncertainty associated with doing so (Doeringer, 1990; Feldman, 1994).

Job-Level Factors

The motivation to change careers later in life can be a function of both the attributes of the present occupation and the perceived attributes of alternative careers. In other words, the decision to change careers later in life is a function of both the *pushes* out of the present job and the *pulls* exerted by other occupations.

It appears that many of the push factors related to late-career change revolve around *job stress* (Kahn & Byosiere, 1992). Much of the research on late adult development, for example, suggests that people in their 50s and 60s prefer to increase the time they spend with families and friends; many older workers start shifting their priorities from accumulating professional accomplishments to developing and sustaining more intimate relationships (Baltes & Graf, 1996). Consequently, older workers, particularly those with financial means, may be more willing to leave highly stressful occupations and seek out those that they find more socially meaningful or personally fulfilling (Feldman, Leana, & Bolino, 2002).

Another set of factors that motivate older workers to change careers revolve around *boredom* and *lack of appreciation*. After 25–30 years in an occupation, some older workers feel like they are merely going through the motions on tasks they have performed hundreds (or thousands) of times previously (Shultz, Morton, & Weckerle, 1998). In addition, sometimes older workers feel like they are taken for granted. Enormous amounts of resources may go into attracting and rewarding younger workers while the salaries of older workers performing the same jobs remain flat (in real dollar terms) or grow much more slowly. In some cases, there is even serious salary inversion, where neophytes with little or no experience are being hired at more than competent veterans make (Carnazza, Korman, Ference, & Stoner, 1981). These factors, too, energize older workers to consider changing occupations in late career.

Of course, there are also numerous individual-level factors that might impel older workers to change careers, too. The loss of a spouse, through either death or divorce, might cause an older worker to want to start all over in a new occupation, a new community, or a new job. Along the same lines, a traumatic job event—such as downsizing or termination—might have similar effects.

Occupation-Level Factors

Probably the occupation-level factor that most motivates older workers to enter new careers is the *degree of change in skills and work context* over the course of a 20–30 year period (Hermans & Oles, 1999). This change can come from a variety of sources. In some cases, the skills that used to be critical in a career are no longer valued highly or the skills themselves are obsolescent. Thus, people who entered medicine in the 1970s with a motivation to provide patient care may now be spending much more time digitizing their medical records, justifying medical procedures requested to hospital utilization committees, and tracking down insurance reimbursements. In other cases, the motivation to change may stem from declines in the quality of work relationships or work climates in an occupation. For instance, young adults who became high school teachers in the 1970s with an enthusiasm for sharing their knowledge may now find themselves working in buildings with metal detectors, alarmed by the level of violence and drug use in their schools, and hamstrung by state and federal regulations on how and what they can teach. In short, the careers they originally entered no longer bear much resemblance to the careers they now hold (Kruger, 1994). As a result, some older workers are motivated to change careers despite their investments in their current occupations.

Another factor that may play a role in whether older workers are motivated to change careers is the *decline in the demand for labor* in their occupation (Albrecht, Edin, Sundstrom, & Vroman, 1999). Over time, the demand for labor in different occupations varies depending upon a series of environmental factors. For example, in the 1960s there was a shortage of aeronautical engineers as the space race heated up; today, there is an excess of aeronautical engineers in the wake of shuttle disasters and government funding cuts. Some older workers see the handwriting on the wall and are motivated to change careers because their future professional prospects look bleak. Using the same logic, older workers are motivated to change careers when there is *perceived age discrimination* in the occupation. This age discrimination can affect how older workers experience their careers on a day-to-day basis at work. Thus, older advertising executives often see themselves being shuttled to more peripheral activities and assignments, not because they are less competent than their younger peers, but because they are perceived as being less *edgy*. Over time, the corrosive effects of this perceived discrimination can motivate older workers to seek out new careers—a goal, as we shall see later, that is often easier set than achieved (Beehr & Bowling, 2002).

CAREER STABILITY AND CAREER EMBEDDEDNESS

Without question, we have seen dramatic changes in the context of career development over the past 20 years. There are new forms of employment that have emerged as important alternatives to *normal* 9-to-5 permanent jobs, including telecommuting, outsourcing, and off-shoring. In addition, there are forms of employment that once appealed to small segments of the labor market but are now held by much higher percentages of workers, including self-employment, part-time work, temporary work, subcontracting, leased workers, and loaned executives (Feldman, 2002a). Not surprisingly, the academic community and the popular press alike have paid considerable attention to these changes in the career landscape (Arthur & Rousseau, 1996).

Nonetheless, underneath the surface of these dramatic environmental changes, there is an impressive amount of stability within individuals' careers over time (Feldman, 2002a, p. 4). Individuals' first few jobs are pivotal in shaping their work skills and personal values for years to come (Habermas & Bluck, 2000). Moreover, as the research on career anchors suggests, work skills and personal values developed in one's 20s play a major role in anchoring lifelong career decisions (Feldman & Bolino, 1997; Schein, 1990). And, even in the literature that examines *lack of fit* as a predictor of occupational change, the findings have been at best mixed (Spokane, Meir, & Catalano, 2000; Tinsely, 2000). As Ostroff, Shin, and Feinberg (2002) suggest, it is often hard to untangle the disparate effects of poor person-job fit, person-group fit, and person-organization fit from those of poor person-occupation fit.

The lack of widespread career changes among older workers, though, has often been attributed primarily to the aging process itself rather than to systematic forces within the labor market that anchor the vast majority of people to their current career paths. Nonetheless, there is some research that suggests that older workers are somewhat more reluctant to change occupations voluntarily (Warr, 1994). Below, we consider why older workers may be more embedded in their occupations than their younger colleagues.

Job Embeddedness

In a seminal article, Mitchell and his colleagues (2001) introduced the construct of *job embeddedness*. Rather than focusing on the traditional turnover approach that looks at why people leave their jobs, Mitchell and his colleagues examine the reasons why people stay. They describe job embeddedness as "a net or a web in which an individual can get stuck" (2001, p. 1104). More specifically, they identify the three key elements of job embeddedness as: (1) the extent to which people have *links* to other people and activities, (2) the extent to which their jobs and communities *fit* other aspects of their lives, and (3) the *sacrifices* that would have to be made to break these links. While Mitchell et al. (2001) acknowledge that job attitudes (e.g., job satisfaction and organizational commitment) certainly contribute to decisions to stay or leave, they make an important observation about the role of embeddedness in explaining mobility patterns; that is, low embeddedness makes employees more susceptible to job dissatisfaction and increases their likelihood of looking for new jobs when they do become dissatisfied.

Career Embeddedness

We suggest that there is an analogous phenomenon here that we will call *career embeddedness*. People don't only get embedded in jobs; they get embedded in careers as well. Thus, we suggest that individuals will become embedded in their career paths (i.e., show greater occupational stability) when: (1) they have extensive links to other people in the profession and occupational activities; (2) their current career paths fit with other aspects of their lives; (3) they would have to make great sacrifices to break their occupational ties; and (4) there are significant constraints on their ease of entry into alternative careers. And, because individuals typically remain in careers longer than they remain in any given job or organization, we have good reason to expect that career embeddedness would be even higher for older workers than job embeddedness is.

Links. One link to the current career path is *amount of time spent within a career*. The longer people have been in an occupation, the more contacts they have, the more tacit knowledge they have about work responsibilities and professional politics, and the more enmeshed they become in professional associations and activities. For older workers with high occupational tenure, then, their roots in the current career path run deep. Moreover, since older workers, as a group, have greater occupational tenure than their younger colleagues, their career embeddedness is likely to be greater as well.

Along similar lines, the *amount of task interdependence* is also likely to increase career embeddedness (O'Reilly, Caldwell, & Barnett, 1989). For example, working closely with a wide variety of colleagues, customers, suppliers, and contractors can help enmesh employees in both job activities and social networks. In situations where there is high task interdependence, people can come to feel that others depend upon them, and this, too, creates greater attachment to the present occupation. Because older workers are more likely to have supervisory jobs, to have *boundary spanning* responsibilities, and to have leadership positions in professional activities, this greater task interdependence embeds them more deeply in their careers.

It is also important to note that Mitchell et al. (2001) suggest that links to the community as well as links to the job can embed an individual in his/her current position. Thus, in general, we would expect *length of time in a community* to enmesh older workers in their current career paths as well. However, in terms of career embeddedness, we also have to consider *the extent to which career alternatives are location specific*. For instance, if someone in the field of agribusiness decided he wanted to be an options trader, such a career change would almost certainly require a move out of a rural community. In this case, the probability of being able to simultaneously change careers and stay in the same community (or even the same type of community) would be very low— and career embeddedness would be correspondingly high. In contrast, it is fairly easy to become a nurse or a public school teacher in any location, so older workers who want to transition into these occupations should feel much less embedded in their current careers.

Fit.   There are a variety of ways fit can be conceptualized (Kristof, 1996). At its broadest level, fit refers to some sort of congruence between an individual's attributes and a specific position's requirements and work context. For instance, there can be fit in terms of matching individual skills with job demands (person-job [P-J] fit), matching an individual's personal style with the personal styles of workgroup members (person-group [P-G] fit), or matching an individual's needs and values with the culture of the organization as a whole (person-organization [P-O] fit).

The research evidence suggests that different types of poor fit motivate different kinds of career transitions (Ostroff et al., 2002, pp. 70–72). In particular, it appears that changes in occupation are most likely to occur *when both P-J fit and P-G fit are low*. In such cases, workers will not be enmeshed by either the work itself or by fulfilling social relationships with colleagues. Consequently, it will not take a powerful external force to pry them loose from their current career trajectory.

In contrast, when only person-organization fit is low, there is much less likelihood that individuals will look for new occupations. That is because context factors (organizational values and norms) play a much less significant role in driving occupational change than P-J fit and P-G fit do (Austin & Hanisch, 1990). When the source of dissatisfaction is the organization itself, the most likely reaction is to look for a new place to work rather than to reject the career itself. In colloquial terms, people are less likely to "throw the baby out with the bath water" just because they are unhappy with a particular employer.

Like the *links* construct, the *fit* construct can also be conceptualized in terms of both work and community (Mitchell et al., 2001). In terms of fit with the community, the biggest predictors of career stability are likely to be *value fit* and *lifestyle fit*. The values component refers to personal congruence with prevailing religious and social norms in the present community; for example, a person likes the liberal/conservative values that underlie the education and cultural opportunities in the community. The lifestyle-fit component refers to personal congruence with the kinds of leisure activities and daily routines available in a community, be they athletic pursuits like skiing or lifestyle issues like low cost of living and low crime rates. To the extent that career changes require leaving a particular community, career embeddedness would be much higher. Moreover, because older workers have typically lived in their communities a longer time than their younger colleagues and have adjusted to a particular way of life, we would expect community fit to embed older workers even more strongly.

Sacrifices. Changing careers is not a cost-free activity. As noted earlier, there can be expensive transaction costs associated with winding down a career, moving geographically, getting additional training, and even potentially earning less money in a new career. Emotionally, people can experience considerable stress as they are stripped of old routines and have to develop new ones (Kim & Feldman, 2000; Richardson & Kilty, 1991). Furthermore, the costs associated with a career change are not borne solely by the individual. Spouses, partners, extended family members, and children may bear some of those costs, too, since their careers and daily routines may be disrupted as well (Stroh, Brett, & Reilly, 1996).

Chief among the sacrifices that might embed people in their careers are *employee benefits*, particularly those that are *longevity based* (Kim & Feldman, 1998, 2000). For example, older workers may have to stay with their present employers for a given number of years (and thus, most likely, in their present careers) in order to be eligible for lifetime insurance coverage or to get maximum pension benefits. Some organizations also grant sick leave, annual leave, and vacation leave on the basis of longevity, and these, too, might be put at risk with a career change. Since older workers are those who have accrued the greatest rewards associated with longevity-based benefits, such benefits play a much larger role in embedding older workers in their careers (Shaw, Delery, Jenkins, & Gupta, 1998), particularly when those benefits are not portable.

Another sacrifice to be considered here is the level of initial financial investment in obtaining occupational training (either in terms of past outlays of funds or current indebtedness for past education). A neurosurgeon who has invested hundreds of thousands of dollars in an education and has accumulated substantial debt doing so would have to make an enormous sacrifice to change careers—a much greater sacrifice of income, for example, than a pre-school teacher would be making to enter the business world.

Other work factors that might embed older workers in their careers are *opportunities for promotion and advancement* (Mitchell et al., 2001; Shaw et al., 1998). In career paths where years of service are very highly correlated with promotions and rank (e.g., the military and civil service), older individuals may be especially reluctant to change careers before they accrue the full measure of rewards they expected at the start of their careers. In addition, when employees change careers later in life, their opportunities for reaching equally senior positions in the next career are also lower.

Family responsibilities also serve to embed older workers in their current careers (Eby, Allen, & Douthitt, 1999). These responsibilities can impact the career embeddedness of older workers in numerous ways. For example, people with *working spouses* might be more career embedded because any career changes on their part might cause disruptions for their partners. Moreover, because working spouses also have concerns about pensions and other employee benefits, the financial sacrifices associated with such transitions would have greater ripple effects. Also, the research on retirement suggests that spouses try to time their retirements together (Talaga & Beehr, 1995). Thus, some older workers may simply *hang on* to their current careers until their spouses are ready to retire, too. *Responsibilities for elderly parents* may also embed older workers in their communities, a factor of much less concern to younger workers.

Constraints on Entry into Alternative Careers

While the embeddedness literature focuses on the factors that enmesh older workers in their current career paths, another issue that needs to be considered here is barriers to entry into other occupations. Older workers may be highly motivated to change careers, but don't make the transition because they perceive there aren't suitable alternatives in the labor market.

TABLE 9.1.
When Will Older Workers Continue to Work After They Retire?

In a series of studies, Kim and Feldman (1998, 2000) examined the circumstances under which older professional employees will retire and then continue to work after they retire. Their study took place in the University of California system, where a series of three early retirement incentives had been offered to faculty over a period of several years. Nine hundred twenty-four (924) professors who accepted these early retirement incentives were also eligible for continued part-time employment at their universities, and Kim and Feldman surveyed those workers about their retirement plans and their plans for continued employment after retirement.

The individual factors that were most highly correlated with taking bridge employment at the university (continued part-time employment after full-time employment ends) were health and age. Older workers in good health were significantly more likely to accept bridge employment. Faculty members in their late 50's and early 60's were much more likely to accept bridge employment after retirement than faculty who were in their seventies.

The job factor that most highly predicted taking bridge employment was organizational tenure. The longer a faculty member had worked in the University of California system, the more likely he or she was to accept bridge employment. This finding supports the notion that long-time employees tend to be more career embedded.

There were no significant differences between males and females in terms of their decisions to work after retirement. However, retirees were more likely to accept bridge employment if their spouses were still working. Similarly, the number of children under 18 still living in the household also motivates workers to accept bridge employment opportunities in their current organizations. Thus, family circumstances—such as having a working spouse or minor children to support—also serve to embed older workers in their current occupations.

Finally, Kim and Feldman investigated the impact of engaging in bridge employment well-being on older workers' well-being. They found that bridge employment—either at their current university or at another job altogether—was positively related to both satisfaction with retirement and satisfaction with life in general.

Chief among these concerns is *age discrimination in employment*. Even assuming older workers exhibit minor decrements in cognitive skill or physical ability over time, there remains considerable age bias against older workers trying to get new jobs (Hassell & Perrewe, 1995). While there are fewer hard data available on this next issue (Cascio, 1995), there also seems to be some *age discrimination in access to training* (Beehr & Bowling, 2002). It is often hard for older workers who want to go back to school to get academic degrees to start new careers. Even in academia, which is reputably liberal in its attitudes, one rarely sees Ph.D. students in their 50s or new faculty in their 60s (Kim & Feldman, 1998). Moreover, older workers are somewhat less likely to want to get new training and they tend to take longer to train than younger workers do (Kubeck, Delp, Haslett, & McDaniel, 1996). Thus, to the extent that career changes require new training, older workers are somewhat more reluctant and somewhat less successful in obtaining it.

Another impediment to seeking new careers is the extent to which those occupations require *extensive exposure to new technology*. In a particularly relevant study, Czaja and Sharit (1993) found that age is associated with slower response times and more errors on computer-based tasks. Moreover, age has a negative impact on performance on computer-based tasks even when previous computer experience was held constant. Beehr and Bowling (2002, p. 218) interpret these findings as suggesting that it is the aging process itself, and not just the lack of computer experience, that is associated with poorer performance with technology. Not surprisingly, then, as more and more careers are becoming technologically complex, older workers may perceive there are fewer alternative careers for them to enter. Whether this phenomenon will change in the next generation, where children grow up with extensive exposure to computer technology before even entering school, remains to be seen.

DIRECTIONS FOR FUTURE RESEARCH

The career embeddedness perspective, then, can be usefully employed to understand the forces that keep older workers in their current positions or to energize them to seek alternative career paths. In this section, we consider some other directions for future research on this increasingly important topic.

Career Embeddedness of CEOs

The work of Sonnenfeld and his colleagues (Sonnenfeld, 1988; Ward et al., 1995) highlights the particular career challenges faced by senior executives forced out of their jobs. In many ways, the stripping away of these positions is as painful psychologically as it is financially. Because their work lives are so entwined with their personal lives and friendship networks, executives who lose top management positions feel like the fabric of virtually every aspect of life has been ripped.

How does this particular group of older workers face the thought of changing careers? To date, the evidence doesn't appear that they embrace such forced change well. As Sonnenfeld and his colleagues note, there is often a profound sense of loss associated with exits from senior management positions and more energy seems to go into trying to hang on to former power and glory than into moving on.

One avenue for future research that might prove fruitful here is considering the career embeddedness of CEOs more fully in the context of broader network theory. In network theory, Zukin and DiMaggio (1990) have identified four forms of embeddedness: structural, cognitive, political, and cultural. What all these forms of embeddedness have in common is the concept of a relationship tie (Granovetter, 1985) that keeps individuals tethered to their existing career paths. In the case of senior executives, the possession of a top management seat gives them entrée into the political and cultural elite, too. By virtue of their positions as senior executives, they are also often given seats on the boards of directors of interlocking businesses, major not-for-profit organizations, and even local and national policy-making positions (Useem, 1984). For this population in particular, then, embeddedness in broader corporate elites has to be considered along side career embeddedness.

Career Embeddedness, Retirement, and Bridge Employment

The construct of career embeddedness might also dovetail nicely with the research on retirement and bridge employment (Doeringer, 1990; Feldman, 1994; Kim & Feldman, 2000). In early and mid career, those who switch occupations typically continue to work full time at their new vocations. In late career, however, the career options are somewhat different. Many individuals have the financial luxury of not working at all (retirement), continuing to work but with less intensity (bridge employment), or shifting to an alternate career. The career embeddedness construct might help researchers get a better handle on retirement and bridge employment decisions, too.

For instance, the retirement research paradigm has typically examined individual-level factors and organizational-level factors that predict whether older workers will retire. At the individual level, for example, researchers have looked at employees' financial holdings, their physical and mental abilities, and their current job performance (what Kim and Feldman [1998] refer to as "healthy, wealthy, or wise"). Similarly, at the organizational level, researchers have examined the structure of early retirement packages, the amount of preretirement counseling, and age discrimination in the workplace (Beehr & Bowling, 2002).

What the career embeddedness construct suggests is that the retirement and bridge employment literature could be enriched by considering the social context in which exit decisions and career change decisions are made. To date, network ties within the present organization and the present occupation are rarely explored in retirement research, yet social and professional ties to coworkers may indeed keep older workers from retiring or retiring fully from their jobs. (Academe is just one of many professions where this employment pattern can be discerned.).

Alternatively, it can also happen that older workers' network ties to people in *other* occupations or in *other* organizations could be major enabling factors for career mobility. For example, employees might network extensively with major clients and, in so doing, form stronger bonds with clients than with those in the current firm or occupational group. Thus, the knowledge of alternative careers and the potential attractiveness of those careers may be driven by *receiving* networks as well as current occupational networks. (This has certainly been a common phenomenon in the military, where *retired* military officers become *Beltway bandits* working for companies bidding for defense contracts.) And, while *years in community* has often been used to study attachment in the retirement literature, *extent of involvement in community* has been largely ignored.

Career Embeddedness and Career Anchors

A third potential avenue for future research is examining the relationships between Schein's (1990) construct of career anchors and the present construct of career embeddedness. By the term *career anchor*, Schein means the set of self-defined interests, skills, and values that constrain individuals in making career choices. They typically develop between ages 30–35 and result in individuals making subsequent career choices within a narrowly circumscribed set of mobility options. For example, an individual with a *technical/functional* career anchor would try to find positions that capitalize on the use of specific technical skills and minimize managerial activity, while individuals with an *autonomy* career anchor would try to find positions that give maximum freedom around scheduling and work procedures and minimize close supervision.

While the career embeddedness construct gives us some insight into whether individuals are willing to change careers, the career anchors literature gives us some insight into how far away from their current careers individuals are willing to move and where they are likely to land (Feldman & Bolino, 1997). For example, Feldman and Bolino's octagonal model suggests that career anchors can be arrayed in terms of "degrees of difference"—and that these degrees of difference may be helpful in understanding where older career changers are likely to migrate. Thus, individuals with an autonomy career anchor might be willing to move into careers with an entrepreneurial orientation, but individuals with a *challenge* career anchor are much less likely to move into careers which have lifestyle or service orientations.

Over the course of a career, individuals are much more likely to change organizations than they are occupations (Ng, Eby, Sorensen, & Feldman, 2005). Individuals make investments in developing certain sets of skills and, over

time, the set of career paths that utilize those skills become somewhat circumscribed. In addition, what is often called *poor fit* with a job is often the result of dissatisfaction with coworkers, supervisors, and organizational values
rather than with the work per se (Ostroff et al., 2002). Consequently, there is
much more mobility across organizations than across occupations, particularly for older workers. Integrating career anchors research with future research
on career embeddedness would be helpful in understanding how far, and in
what direction, older workers are willing to stretch themselves in order to find
careers that are more satisfying and fulfilling.

IMPLICATIONS FOR PRACTICE

Changes in the environment over the past 25 years have resulted in the re-
questioning of many long-held assumptions about what a successful career
means (Arthur & Rousseau, 1996). Where once staying with one occupation
(and, indeed, with one organization) an entire career was the norm, widespread layoffs, corporate restructurings, globalization, and technological advances have made the likelihood of such career trajectories highly unlikely.
And, even if such career stability were possible, is it necessarily desirable? Is career stability a sign of personal stability, as was widely believed in the 1950s and
1960s, or simply a lack of ambition? Can any one occupation or organization
provide enough growth opportunities to keep individuals fully engaged over a
40-year period? Ultimately, then, is career embeddedness good or bad for
individuals and organizations?

For individuals, it can be argued that career embeddedness is beneficial if
it is a *conscious choice* rather than a default option. If individuals, as young
adults, have chosen careers wisely and after careful consideration, career embeddedness can actually create a self-reinforcing, positive cycle. That is, the
better an individual performs in a career path, the more likely s/he is to stay
in it, the more likely s/he is to make contributions, and the more likely s/he is
to get positive feedback.

On the other hand, if career embeddedness results from a series of bad
choices and lack of initiative, then this embeddedness can result instead in a
long period of plateaued performance and frustration. For instance, if middle-
aged individuals who have fallen out of step with their careers for whatever
reason—changes in job duties, work environments, or occupational values—
fail to change occupations, they might find themselves stranded in a painful
hanging-on process. The long-timer who is simply trying to get in 6, 8, or 10
more years so s/he can collect full retirement is a sad, and all too frequent,
career end for many older workers. And, given the current uncertainty about

Social Security benefits and increased concerns about pension fund security, there may well be more and more older workers in this situation.

For individuals themselves, then, probably the best advice would be: hope for the best, but prepare for the worst. That is, make the kinds of decisions that maximize the likelihood one could experience career longevity—doing research on the occupation before entering it, continuously upgrading skills, and building constructive relationships with others in the occupation. At the same time, there are no guarantees that careers will not change dramatically over time, and indeed the probabilities are high that such change will occur (Feldman, 2002a, 2002b). Older workers would be unwise to write off a decade (or more) of their lives to careers they don't like, particularly if alternatives— indeed, alternatives that might draw on the same skill set and value set—are readily available.

For organizations, the research on career embeddedness points to the need to move away from longevity-based incentives as the primary strategy for retaining employees. Particularly in organizations with defined benefit plans, many older workers are forced to remain in their current jobs (and occupations) way too long so they won't get penalized for retiring before age 65 or 30 years of service. Such compensation schemes force employees to stay well beyond their welcome—and age discrimination laws often make it difficult for companies to terminate older workers who are competent, if not stellar, in their jobs.

At the same time, the research on career embeddedness highlights another reason why bridge employment opportunities are a valuable tool for moving older workers gracefully out of the workforce and refreshing the talent pool. If there are, in fact, inertial forces that act against older workers' willingness to leave, then bridge employment represents a less painful and less dramatic way of weaning people away from long-held careers. Even in the worst-case scenario where people have hated their jobs for a long period of time, older workers still fear losing their positions and experiencing what life without work would be like—the career equivalent of the Stockholm syndrome. Thus, gradual disintegration of career ties might be more effective in lessening dysfunctional career embeddedness than the wrenching of those ties.

Robert Frost famously wrote that "before I built a wall, I'd ask what I was walling in and what I was walling out." Much the same can be said about career embeddedness. It can provide a long-term, nourishing environment, or it can entrap people in a perpetually frustrating, no-exit, career dead end. The seeds of dysfunctional late-career embeddedness, then, are often sown much earlier in life through poor initial job choices, lack of skill updating, and insufficient scanning of the environment. Being mindful and purposeful about managing one's own career, then, is as important at late career as it is at early career.

REFERENCES

Albrecht, J. W., Edin, P. A., Sundstrom, M., & Vroman, S. B. (1999). Career interruptions and subsequent earnings: A reexamination using Swedish data. *Journal of Human Resources, 24,* 294–311.

Alderfer, C. P., & Guzzo, R. A. (1979). Life experiences and adults' enduring strength of desires in organizations. *Administrative Science Quarterly, 24,* 347–361.

Arthur, M. B., & Rousseau, D. M. (1996). *The boundaryless career: A new employment principle for a new organizational era.* New York: Oxford University Press.

Austin, J. T., & Hanisch, K. A. (1990). Occupational attainment as a function of abilities and interests: A longitudinal analysis using Project TALENT data. *Journal of Applied Psychology, 75,* 77–86.

Baltes, P. B., & Graf, P. (1996). Psychological aspects of aging: Facts and frontiers. In D. Magnusson (Ed.), *The lifespan development of individuals: Behavioral, neurobiological, and psychosocial perspectives* (pp. 427–460). Cambridge, UK: Cambridge University Press.

Beehr, T. A., & Bowling, N. A. (2002). Career issues facing older workers. In D. C. Feldman (Ed.), *Work careers: A developmental perspective* (pp. 214–241). San Francisco: Jossey-Bass.

Carnazza, J., Korman, A., Ference, T. P., & Stoner, J. A. F. (1981). Plateaued and nonplateaued managers: Factors in job performance. *Journal of Management, 7,* 7–27.

Cascio, W. F. (1995). Whither industrial and organizational psychology in a changing world of work? *American Psychologist, 50,* 928–939.

Czaja, S. J., & Sharit, J. (1993). Age differences in the performance of computer-based work. *Psychology and Aging, 8,* 59–67.

Digman, J. M. (1989). Five robust trait dimensions: Development, stability, and utility. *Journal of Personality, 57,* 195–214.

Doeringer, P. B. (1990). *Bridges to retirement.* Ithaca, NY: Cornell University ILR Press.

Eby, L. T., Allen, T. D., & Douthitt, S. S. (1999). The role of nonperformance factors on job-related relocation opportunities: A field study and laboratory experiment. *Organizational Behavior and Human Decision Processes, 79,* 29–55.

Eysenk, M. W. (1994). *Individual differences.* Hillsdale, NJ: Lawrence Erlbaum Associates.

Feldman, D. C. (1994). The decision to retire: A review and reconceptualization. *Academy of Management Review, 19,* 285–311.

Feldman, D. C. (2002a). Stability in the midst of change: A developmental perspective on the study of careers. In D. C. Feldman (Ed.), *Work careers: A developmental perspective* (pp. 3–26). San Francisco: Jossey-Bass.

Feldman, D. C. (2002b). Second careers and multiple careers. In R. J. Burke & C. L. Cooper (Eds.), *The new world of work* (pp. 75–94). Oxford, UK: Blackwell.

Feldman, D. C., & Bolino, M. C. (1997). Careers within careers: Reconceptualizing the nature of career anchors and their consequences. *Human Resource Management Review, 6,* 145–163.

Feldman, D. C., Leana, C. R., & Bolino, M. C. (2002). Underemployment among downsized executives: Test of a mediated effects model. *Journal of Occupational and Organizational Psychology, 75,* 453–471.

Granovetter, M. (1985). Economic action and social structure: The problem of embeddedness. *American Journal of Sociology, 19,* 481–510.

Habermas, T., & Bluck S. (2000). Getting a life: The emergence of the life story in adolescence. *Psychological Bulletin, 126*, 748–769.

Hassell, B., & Perrewe, P. L. (1995). An examination of beliefs about older workers: Do stereotypes still exist? *Journal of Organizational Behavior, 16*, 457–468.

Hermans, H. J. M., & Oles, P. K. (1999). Midlife crisis in men: Affective organization of personal meanings. *Human Relations, 52*, 1403–1426.

Kahn, R. L., & Byosiere, P. (1992). Stress in organizations. In M. D. Dunnette & L. M. Hough (Eds.), *Handbook of industrial and organizational psychology* (2nd ed., Vol. 3, pp. 571–650). Palo Alto, CA: Consulting Psychologists Press.

Kelly, H. H. (1973). The processes of causal attribution. *American Psychologist, 28*, 107–128.

Kim, S., & Feldman, D. C. (1998). Healthy, wealthy, or wise: Predicting actual acceptances of early retirement incentives at three points in time. *Personnel Psychology, 51*, 623–642.

Kim, S., & Feldman, D. C. (2000). Working in retirement: The antecedents and consequences of bridge employment and its consequences for quality of life in retirement. *Academy of Management Journal, 39*, 367–380.

Kristof, A. L. (1996). Person-organization fit: An integrative review of its conceptualization, measurement, and implications. *Personnel Psychology, 49*, 1–49.

Kruger, A. (1994). The midlife transition: Crisis or chimera? *Psychological Reports, 75*, 1299–1305.

Kubeck, J. E., Delp, N. D., Haslett, T. K., & McDaniel, M. A. (1996). Does job-related training performance decline with age? *Psychology and Aging, 11*, 92–107.

Mischel, W. (1973). Toward a cognitive social learning reconceptualization of personality. *Psychological Review, 80*, 252–283.

Mitchell, T. R., Holtom, B. C., Lee, T. W., Sablynski, C. J., & Erez, M. (2001). Why people stay: Using job embeddedness to predict voluntary turnover. *Academy of Management Journal, 44*, 1102–1121.

Morrison, E. W. (2002). The school-to-work transition. In D. C. Feldman (Ed.), *Work careers: A developmental perspective* (pp. 126–158). San Francisco: Jossey-Bass.

Ng, T. W. H., Eby, L. T., Sorensen, K. L., & Feldman, D. C. (2005). Predictors of objective and subjective career success: A meta-analysis. *Personnel Psychology, 58*, 367–408.

O'Reilly, C. W., Caldwell, D. F., & Barnett, W. P. (1989). Work group demography, social integration, and turnover. *Administrative Science Quarterly, 34*, 21–37.

Ostroff, C., Shin, Y., & Feinberg, B. (2002). Skill acquisition and person-environment fit. In D. C. Feldman (Ed.), *Work careers: A developmental perspective* (pp. 63–90). San Francisco: Jossey-Bass.

Richardson, V., & Kilty, K. M. (1991). Adjustment to retirement: Continuity vs. discontinuity. *International Journal of Aging and Human Development, 33*, 151–169.

Scandura, T. A. (2002). The establishment years: A dependence perspective. In D. C. Feldman (Ed.), *Work careers: A developmental perspective* (pp. 159–185). San Francisco: Jossey-Bass.

Schein, E. A. (1990). *Career anchors: Discovering your real values.* San Diego, CA: Pfeiffer.

Shaw, J. D., Delery, J. E., Jenkins, G. D., & Gupta, N. (1998). An organization-level analysis of voluntary and involuntary turnover. *Academy of Management Journal, 41*, 511–525.

Shultz, K. S., Morton, K. R., & Weckerle, J. R. (1998). The influence of push and pull factors on voluntary and involuntary early retirees' retirement decision and adjustment. *Journal of Vocational Behavior, 53,* 45–57.

Sonnenfeld, J. A. (1988). *The hero's farewell: What happens when CEOs retire.* New York: Oxford University Press.

Spokane, A. R., Meir, E., & Catalano, M. (2000). Person-environment congruence and Holland's theory: A review and reconsideration. *Journal of Vocational Behavior, 57,* 137–187.

Stroh, L. K., Brett, J. M., & Reilly, A. H. (1996). Family structure, glass ceiling, and traditional explanations for the differential rate of turnover of female and male managers. *Journal of Vocational Behavior, 49,* 99–118.

Talaga, J. A., & Beehr, T. A. (1995). Are there gender differences in predicting retirement? *Journal of Applied Psychology, 80,* 16–28.

Tinsley, H. E. A. (2000). The congruence myth: An analysis of the efficacy of the person-environment fit model. *Journal of Vocational Behavior, 56,* 147–179.

Useem, M. (1984). *The inner circle: Large corporations and the rise of business political activity in the U.S. and U.K.* New York: Oxford University Press.

Ward, A. J., Sonnenfeld, J. A., & Kimberly, J. R. (1995). In search of a kingdom: Determinants of subsequent career outcomes for chief executives who are fired. *Human Resource Management, 34,* 117–139.

Warr, P. (1994). Age and employment. In H. C. Triandis, M. D. Dunnette, & L. M. Hough (Eds.), *Handbook of industrial and organizational psychology* (2nd ed., Vol. 4, pp. 485–550). Palo Alto, CA: Consulting Psychologists Press.

Zukin, S., & DiMaggio, P. (1990). *Structures of capital: The social organization of the economy.* New York: Cambridge University Press.

10

Aging and Occupational Health

Steve M. Jex, Mo Wang, and Anna Zarubin

This chapter examines the impact of aging on the health and safety of employees in organizational settings. The chapter begins with a brief discussion of the meaning of employee health. We then provide a general overview of the aging process—that is, changes that occur in people with increasing age regardless of the job they hold or the organization in which they work. The chapter then shifts to the impact of aging on the productivity, health, and safety of employees in work settings. We then discuss the interaction between characteristics of jobs and organizations with age, and, more specifically, which aspects of jobs and organizations will be experienced and responded to differently depending on one's age. The chapter concludes with a consideration of a number of interventions that may improve the health and wellbeing of older workers.

It has been well documented that the average age of the population is getting older (Moody, 2002), both in the United States and worldwide. While there are obviously great societal implications of the increased aging of the population, the implications of this for the workplace alone are staggering. Specifically, organizations must find ways to cope with large numbers of employees retiring, as well as find ways to integrate older employees into jobs that they hadn't performed in previous years.

Another potential implication of the increasing age of the workforce is in the area of employee health. Organizations have become much more concerned about employee health in recent years (Hofmann & Tetrick, 2003), due largely to astronomical increases in health insurance premiums. There has also emerged the new interdisciplinary field of Occupational Health Psychology which is concerned with using psychological theories and interventions to understand and enhance employee health and wellbeing. Given the importance of employee health, and the increased age of the working population, it would seem important to understand how the former affects the latter.

The major focus of this chapter therefore is to examine the relationship between aging and occupational health. This is no easy task, however, because little work has been done integrating these two areas despite the obvious need to do so. We believe, however, that these two areas should be integrated and attempt to do so in this chapter. The chapter begins by describing what precisely is meant by *employee health*. As will be shown, there are different perspectives on what exactly constitutes employee health, and these different perspectives are important to consider if we are to understand the relationship between aging and employee health.

We then shift to a discussion of the several perspectives on aging. There are obviously changes that occur as one ages that are independent of the work domain and these are important to understand when considering the impact of age on employee health. This will lead into a discussion of the interaction between age and organizational conditions in predicting employee health. This is the core portion of the chapter, given age most likely functions as a moderator variable that impacts employees' health-related reactions to job and organizational conditions. The chapter then shifts to a discussion of a number of interventions designed to enhance the health and wellbeing of older workers. We conclude with recommendations for research and practice.

WHAT IS EMPLOYEE HEALTH?

While age is the primary topic under consideration in this chapter, it is also true that *employee health* is of equal (if not of more) importance because it is the criterion that age impacts. Given this importance, it is necessary to provide some background to the reader on what we consider employee health to be. Thus, in this section we define this term, and explain the multiple ways in which it has been viewed in the medical, public health, and psychological literatures.

If viewed from a *traditional medical perspective*, health is equated with the *absence of physical pathology* (Boorse, 1975). For example, if a person is given a medical examination and everything assessed during this examination is *normal*, the individual is deemed healthy. The primary strength of this perspective is its simplicity: that is, a person is either healthy or not healthy. Unfortunately, the simplicity of the traditional medical model is also one of its primary weaknesses. This model fails to recognize that there are *degrees* of health, and that health is more than just a physical concept. In addition, the emphasis in the medical model on the existence of pathology fails to recognize the *potential* for future health problems. As an example, suppose a person was identified as healthy based on the traditional medical model. Further assume that this person had a very poor diet, engaged in little or no physical activity, and engaged in a number of risky behaviors. To say that such a person is healthy is misleading at best, yet according to the medical model there is no other classification into which such an individual could be placed.

A somewhat more contemporary way to view health is from a *wellness* perspective. According to Larson (1999), this perspective is based on the World Health Organization's (WHO) constitution that states that health is "a state of complete physical, mental, and social wellbeing." According to this view, health is much more than just the absence of physical pathology. Instead, a healthy person is not only someone who does not possess physical pathology, but is also a person who is mentally healthy and who is able to establish and maintain meaningful social relationships.

Another aspect of note in the wellness model is that its focus is on individuals' strength and ability to overcome illnesses. It also emphasizes an individual's continued striving to achieve better physical and psychological functioning. Given these emphases, this model is by nature a preventative model— that is, health is not just an issue to think about when one becomes ill. This model proposes that people should continually look at their lifestyles and examine whether or not they are as healthy as they could be. Recent organizational intervention programs that offer options such as fitness programs, nutritional counseling, and stress management training are all based on this wellness model of health.

A third way in which health may be viewed is from an *environmental perspective* (Parsons, 1972). This perspective looks at health in terms of the relationship between the employee and the environment. The primary difference between this and the wellness model is that the wellness model focuses primarily on the individual. The environmental perspective, in contrast, focuses on the *interaction* between the employee and his or her environment. As an example of how this perspective works, an employee would be deemed healthy if the demands of his or her job were compatible with his or her skills, abilities, and emotional temperament. Conversely, being unhealthy would involve being in a work environment that was not compatible. It should be noted that the environmental perspective is not only psychological, but also physical in nature. That is, an employee with a history of upper respiratory problems would not be healthy if he or she worked in an environment with a high level of smoke or other air pollutants.

In summary, employee health can be viewed in a number of different ways, three of which were discussed in this section. Based on these three perspectives, our view is that health is more than simply the absence of disease. We also reject the idea that health is strictly a physical phenomenon; rather, we view health as extending to psychological and social domains as well. Our view of health is that health is a state of physical, psychological, and social wellbeing.

PHYSICAL AND COGNITIVE CHANGES
RELATED TO AGING

Age in and of itself should be of little interest to researchers. Rather, the changes that occur as one ages are what researchers have attempted to study. Thus, any consideration of the impact of aging on occupational health must first consider the aging process independent of the work context. This is because certain aspects of the aging process, most notably those that are biological in nature, occur relatively independently of the work context. Thus, it is important to understand that age-related changes will occur in employees and will tend to occur regardless of what happens in the work context. It should also be noted that in describing these age-related changes, our intent will be to describe generalities, and thus recognize that the aging process may vary considerably from person to person.

Biological and gerontological perspectives on aging. The nature and causes of aging in individuals and populations are very complex. To date, no existing theory does a complete job of explaining all the normative changes. Here, we summarize some of the major biological and gerontological perspectives on aging.

Rate-of-living theory is one important biological perspective of aging. It postulates that people have only so much energy and resources to expend in a lifetime. For example, it has been found that the metabolic rate of various species is correlated with their life spans. The lower the metabolic rate, the longer the life span and the slower the aging process (Cristofalo, Tresini, Francis, & Volker, 1999). Evidence from laboratory experiments also suggests that reducing caloric intake slows down a wide range of normative age-related changes and results in longer life spans (Hayflick, 1996). Researchers have also found that the hormonal regulatory system's function plays a role in aging (Finch & Seeman, 1999). When an individual's stress level exceeds the adaptive range of the hormonal system, the aging process becomes faster and more significant.

Another important biological perspective emphasizes the phenomenon of *homeostasis* (Pedersen, Wan, & Mattson, 2001). It suggests that older adults may function at a normative level, but when a large stressor occurs, such as a disease, disorder, or injury, their ability to return to their prior health and functional status is impaired when compared to that of younger adults. This perspective is rooted in the notion that the number of times cells can divide is limited (Hayflick, 1996). The cells of older adults are capable of fewer divisions than those of younger adults. This makes the reestablishment of homeostasis more difficult for older adults.

Perspectives from gerontology usually consider aging as a set of age-related changes. In other words, gerontologists view aging as including a large set of partly malleable processes and functions that are not necessarily biologically predetermined (Arking, 1998). For example, the *life course perspective* on aging (Elder & Johnson, 2003) suggests that a vast set of biological, social, and environmental factors, which occur in adult development, play important roles in the nature and trajectory of aging. This theoretical framework acknowledges that the health, function, and survivorship of each older adult cohort will depend in part on life experience that occurred in the past, in addition to environmental exposures concurrent with aging. Given that there is great interindividual variation in early development and previous social exposures within a particular birth cohort, it is not surprising that there are important differences among individuals after 40 or 50 years.

Another important perspective in gerontology suggests that most general cognitive, physiological, and biological functions in older adults tend to have greater variation than in younger adults (Cavanaugh & Blanchard-Fields, 2002). This may be due to multiple reasons, such as the selective occurrence in subpopulations of specific medical conditions, varied availability of and access to optimal treatments, varied individual capacity to cope with and adapt to life changes, and the nature of the social and work environment. This perspective accounts for the observation that function and performance often do not correlate very well with chronological age (Mauo et al., 1998).

Cognitive ability changes.   When people grow older, even though their general knowledge remains stable or even increases, they tend to experience reduction in cognitive resources (Park, 2000). Specifically, older adults experience declines in processing speed, working memory, inhibition function, and sensations. These declines are the major reasons accounting for age-related differences in cognitive performance.

Salthouse (1991) pointed out that one of the factors accounting for age-related decline in cognitive performance was a general slowing of processing speed of mental operation with aging. For example, processing speed could account for age differences between young and older adults on a variety of verbal tasks (Salthouse, 1993). Based on considerable evidence, Salthouse (1996) further extended this *processing speed slowness* theory by indicating that such global processing speed decline could explain almost all age-related differences on most kinds of cognitive tasks, ranging from recall to reasoning. Processing speed slowness could result from earlier cognitive operations occupying extra time, which should be used to perform later operations (Park, 2000; Salthouse, 1996). Since older adults are slower than younger adults in executing mental operations, they may have less time to perform the later operation in a complex cognitive task.

Working memory is defined as the amount of on-line cognitive resources, which provides simultaneous storage and processing of information (Baddeley, 1992). When people grow older, their working memory capacity declines. Thus, older adults perform worse than young adults on those cognitive tasks requiring active engagement of working memory (e.g., Park, Smith, Morrell, Puglisi, & Dudley, 1990). Also, it was found that age differences between younger and older adults decreased significantly when the working memory load of the cognitive task was limited (Cherry, Park, Frieske, & Smith, 1996).

Hasher and Zacks (1988) proposed another factor that accounted for age-related variance in cognitive performance: *inhibition function.* They found that, with aging, people have more trouble inhibiting their attention to irrelevant information and concentrating on relevant information. For example, older adults are more likely to hold disconfirmed information in their memory than are younger adults, and in the subsequent cognitive processes the irrelevant information tends to affect the performance of older adults (Zacks, Radvansky, & Hasher, 1996).

Finally, Lindenberger and Baltes (1994; also see Baltes & Lindenberger, 1997) reported that nearly all of the age-related variance in cognitive ability was mediated by sensory functioning as measured by simple tests of visual and auditory acuity. Age-related changes in visual function are often due to a variety of diseases and conditions, such as hypertensive retinopathy, diabetic retinopathy, glaucoma, and cataracts. A substantial proportion of these visual decrements are correctable with appliances or surgical procedures. Age-related hearing loss is very common and can occur in 20–25 percent of people who are between 65 and 75 years old (Seidman, Ahmad, & Bai, 2002). Although the causes are still not well understood, some genetic and environmental factors have been suggested (Prince, 2002).

Physical and functional changes.   There is substantial data on physical and functional changes with age. Although the causal and contributing factors are still uncertain, they are likely to include environmental exposures, genetic factors, various health behaviors, and medical conditions. Here we provide a brief overview of age-related changes that are possibly related to occupational health.

With aging there is a gradual loss of muscle mass and muscle strength (McArdle, Vasilaki, & Jackson, 2002). Also, with increasing age, the time it takes to repair damaged tissue increases (Khalil & Merhi, 2000). Because of age-related loss of muscle strength, maximal exercise capacity declines with age as well (Fielding & Meydani, 1997). Men and women show no differences in the rate of muscle change (Spirduso & MacRae, 1990).

Normal aging is accompanied by the loss of bone tissue throughout the body. Bone loss begins in the late 30s, accelerates in the 50s, and slows by the 70s (Currey, Brear, & Zioupos, 1996). Once the process begins, women lose bone mass approximately twice as fast as men. Lower bone density may be a risk factor for degenerative arthritis (Sowers, 2001), which is the leading cause of disability among older adults within industrialized countries. It also leads to increased rates of traumatic fractures.

With aging, the rib cage and the air passageways become stiffer, making it harder to breathe. The maximum amount of air people can take into the lungs in a single breath begins to decline in the 20s, decreasing by 40 percent by age 85. In addition, the rate at which people can exchange oxygen for carbon dioxide drops significantly as the membranes of the air sacs in the lungs deteriorate (Whitbourne, 1999). However, how much of this is attributable to normal aging is uncertain because of varied exposure to environmental hazards, such as cigarette smoke, air pollution, various allergens, and occupational gases, fibers, and particulates.

In addition, metabolism generally drops as people grow older. For instance, with increasing age, mitochondria produce less adenosine tri-phosphate (ATP), the body's main metabolic source of energy. There is also an oxidative function reduction in aging livers, which may lead to age-related differences in responding to environmental chemical exposures (Jansen, 2002). This oxidative function reduction may also cause medication to stay in the body longer and to create the potential for toxicity if the medication schedule does not take this into account.

Research evidence suggests that the total number of lymphocytes in the body probably does not change with aging. Nevertheless, major changes occur in how well lymphocytes work (Aldwin & Gilmer, 1999). For example, older adults' immune systems take longer to build up defenses against specific diseases. As a result, older adults become more prone to serious consequences from illnesses that are easily defeated by young adults. Additionally, various forms of leukemia, which are cancers of the immune cells, increase with age.

Mental health changes.   Although older and younger adults may share similar mental health symptoms, the meaning of their symptoms may differ (Cavanaugh & Blanchard-Fields, 2002). Various chronic diseases, functional limitations, and other ailments can change behavior. Because health problems increase with age, it is important to be more cautious when interpreting older adults' mental health symptoms. In addition, significant changes in cognitive and physical functions with aging also warrant careful examination of older adults' mental health symptoms. In this section, we consider age differences in several of the most common mental health issues.

Contrary to popular belief, the rate of clinical depression actually declines across adulthood (Gatz, 2000). Young adults are at the most risk. However, if enlarging the research scope to include all people that report symptoms of depression, the highest rates occur in young adults and people over age 75. Middle-aged adults have a lower rate. Importantly, there is a cohort effect, with more recent-born cohorts showing higher rates of depression. Therefore, future groups of older adults may have higher rates of depression than current older adults (Gatz, Kasl-Godley, & Karal, 1996).

A substantial number of older persons report sleep problems, such as difficulty in initiating sleep, early awakening, and daytime sleepiness (Whitbourne, 1999). Poor sleep is likely to lead to moodiness, poorer performance on tasks involving sustained concentration, fatigue, and lack of motivation during the next day. To compensate for changes in the quality of sleep, older adults often take daytime naps. However, this may result in more disruptions of nighttime sleep (Vitiello, 1996). Among the most effective treatments of sleep disorders are increasing physical exercise, reducing caffeine intake, avoiding daytime naps, and making sure that the sleeping environment is as quiet and dark as possible. In addition, individuals who do not seek formal care for sleep problems tend to overmedicate their condition using over-the-counter (OTC) drugs, which may induce insomnia (Vitiello, 1996).

In recent years, chronic fatigue syndrome (CFS) has been recognized as a common clinical problem (Sharpe, Chalder, Palmer, & Wessely, 1997). Older adults with declining general health are more susceptible to developing CFS. The causes of CFS are still not certain, but variables including various lifestyle behaviors, personality traits, and work stress appear to lead individuals to develop CFS. Also, CFS may make individuals more susceptible to physical and mental diseases.

Many older adults have the problem of substance abuse. However, with the exception of alcohol, the substances most likely to be abused by younger and older adults are different. Younger adults tend to abuse illicit substances, whereas older adults are more likely to abuse prescription and OTC medications (Lisansky Gomberg & Zucker, 1999). According to Rigler (2000), one third of older alcoholic individuals developed problem drinking in later life, while the rest grew older sustaining the medical and psychosocial consequences of early-onset alcoholism. The consequences of alcohol abuse are generally known to be more serious among the elderly. Even with treatment, older adults take longer to withdraw from substances than young adults (Lisansky Gomberg & Zucker, 1999).

EFFECTS OF AGE ON WORK BEHAVIOR

Like general changes that occur with increased age, there have been changes in work behavior that have been associated with increased age. As was shown in the previous section, age-related changes may occur on many different levels. It is on these different levels that we examine the impact of age-related changes on work behavior.

Effect of experience and expertise. One thing that we know typically occurs as people age is that they gain experience and often have higher levels of task-related expertise. As one would probably imagine, experience is typically associated with higher levels of work performance. However, it has also been found that the relationship between experience and performance is nonlinear (McDaniel, Schmidt, & Hunter, 1988). Specifically, the greatest experience-related difference in performance is between an employee who has no experience and one that has one year of experience. Each subsequent year of experience tends to have less and less impact on performance.

A logical corollary to the finding of McDaniel et al. (1988) is that the experience and expertise that older employees bring to the workplace has little positive impact. While this may be true with respect to performance, there is some evidence that increased experience and expertise may increase safety. Hansen (1989), for example, found that age was negatively related to accident involvement in a large sample of petrochemical employees. We would hasten to add, however, that this finding probably does depend on the nature of the task. Increased experience may not necessarily lead to decreased accident involvement on tasks that require very quick reaction time or rapid cognitive processing.

Effects of cognitive aging at work. Given the age-related cognitive changes described earlier, it would appear that older workers would tend to have greater difficulty than younger employees performing tasks that require retention of large amounts of information or that require rapid cognitive processing. While it has been shown that older workers do have more difficulty on such tasks (Salthouse, 1993), there have also been studies showing no age-related differences in the performance of such tasks (Hartley & Little, 1999).

The reason that age-related differences in such tasks are inconsistent is two-fold. First, as was pointed out earlier, older employees typically have higher levels of task-related expertise. As a result, they may be able to develop strategies to compensate for their cognitive changes. Bunce and Sisa (2002), for example, found no age-related differences in the performance of a sustained attention or *vigilance* task. These authors stated that the reason no differences were found was that older subjects expended greater effort on the task than younger subjects. This implies that older employees may be able to compensate for cognitive changes in a manner that does not result in impaired task performance.

Effects of physical aging at work. Research has shown a general trend toward decreasing energy, and, as a result, reduced capacity for physically demanding tasks, with increasing age. The implication of this, obviously, is that age-related physical changes may make it more difficult for older employees to perform physically demanding tasks, and this has in fact been the case (e.g., Seitsamo & Martikainen, 1999). What types of jobs, then, would be most physically difficult for older employees? Those involving heavy lifting (e.g., baggage handling), or that require employees to perform physically demanding activity for long periods at a time (e.g., fire fighting) would appear to cause the most physical health problems for older employees. Another job condition that appears to be problematic is the requirement to work nonstandard shifts. Specifically, it has been shown that older employees have more difficulty adjusting physically to nonstandard work shifts than younger employees (Kawada, 2002).

Another general job condition that would appear to cause difficulty for older employees is tasks that must be performed very quickly. Many service-oriented jobs require employees to perform tasks very quickly in order to satisfy customers. For example, in retail establishments employees are required to complete sales transactions quickly and accurately. As people get older they can certainly perform such tasks, but may experience more difficulty performing them very rapidly than younger employees. Not only is this is due to physical changes associated with aging, but also to the previously mentioned cognitive changes.

Effects of mental state aging at work. As has previously been mentioned, there is evidence that increasing age is associated with a number of positive work-related psychological outcomes (Rhodes, 1983), yet is also associated with a higher prevalence of a number of psychiatric problems (Charatan, 1984). Given these differences, what implications might this have for the workplace? On the positive side, older employees are likely to be more satisfied, more involved in their jobs, and more committed to their organization than their younger counterparts. It has also been shown that older employees tend to be involved in fewer accidents, although the duration of disability from accidents tends to increase with age.

Another potential impact of aging is that because older employees have greater experience in a number of work-related situations, they may be able to handle certain stressors more effectively than younger employees. Mayes, Barton, and Ganster (1991), for example, found that older employees actually responded positively to responsibility for others, leader production emphasis, and role ambiguity in terms of both mental and physical health (measured by life satisfaction, health symptoms, and depression). The most likely reason for this finding is that through years of experience older employees have developed more effective coping skills than many younger employees. As a result, older employees may not only be able to handle stressors with minimal adverse effects, but may even be able to turn them into positives. Consider, for example, an older employee faced with ambiguous role requirements (e.g., role ambiguity). Based on past experience, such an employee may be able to use this ambiguity to change or mold the job in a way that is more satisfying or compatible with his or her preferences.

Despite these generally positive psychological outcomes associated with aging, there is a somewhat negative side as well. Given that older employees may be at a somewhat higher risk for depression, alcohol abuse, and organic brain conditions, it is certainly possible that older employees may utilize health care services at a much higher rate than younger employees. For organizations, this may lead to greater health insurance premiums, as older employees represent a greater percentage of the total employee population. It should be pointed out, however, that these effects are quite variable and may depend on the type of work people are performing.

EFFECT OF WORKPLACE EXPOSURES
ON OLDER WORKERS

In considering the impact of age on occupational health, we adopt the view that age has direct effects, but also functions as a *moderator* variable. The direct effects of age on occupational health are due to the health-related changes that occur over time which are independent of the workplace. In that sense, age is simply a proxy for those changes.

A moderator variable is any variable that changes the strength or form of the relationship between two or more other variables (Baron & Kenny, 1986). As applied to age and occupational health, what this means is that employees may react differently to certain organizational or job conditions depending upon their age. Stated differently, we believe that from a health point of view, older employees may react differently to certain job and organizational conditions compared to their younger counterparts. In this section we describe these conditions.

Job characteristics and stressors. Obviously jobs differ considerably on a number of dimensions. In addition, some jobs have higher levels of stressors than others. Therefore, what job characteristics and stressors seem to bother older employees the most? Given the physical changes that are typically associated with aging, jobs that place great physical and sensory demands on employees are likely to cause the most physical and mental health problems for older employees. Examples would be jobs that require high levels of sustained physical exertion (e.g., fire fighting), heavy lifting (e.g., baggage handling), or working in a harsh or inhospitable environment (e.g., work on oil rigs).

In terms of sensory demands of jobs, it is likely that older employees would have more difficulty performing jobs that require the ability to hear at very high or low frequencies, or that require very high visual acuity. As examples, this would probably rule out some jobs in law enforcement, as well as jobs involving long hours of driving or concentration. That is not to say that all older people are incapable of performing such jobs, but rather that on average older people would probably have more trouble than younger people.

Unfortunately, very little occupational stress research has examined age as either a main effect or moderator variable. In one of the few studies of this type conducted, Mayes et al. (1991) found in a sample consisting of police officers, fire fighters, electricians, and managers that in terms of mental and physical health, older employees responded more negatively to role conflict and underutilization of skills compared to younger employees. The fact that role conflict was more bothersome was possibly due to the fact that balancing these conflicts may have required higher levels of cognitive or physical resources than older employees possessed. With skill underutilization, older employees may be more bothered due to the fact that they are closer to the end of their careers than younger employees, and thus may fear being laid off.

Since very little research has examined age and occupational stress, few conclusions can be drawn as to whether age impacts reactions to other stressors. Based on recent reviews of the occupational stress literature (e.g., Jex, 1998), however, it is rather easy to speculate. One stressor that employees may react to differently depending on age is job insecurity (Sverke, Hellgren, & Naswall, 2002). Since older employees stand to lose much more financially if laid off, and may have limited prospects for reemployment as compared to younger employees, they may exhibit more negative psychological reactions to job insecurity.

Other than job insecurity, another stressor that may have a stronger effect on older employees is workload. While little evidence currently exists on age as a moderator of the effect of workload, given the physical effects of aging discussed earlier, it is certainly possible that older employees would have more physical health problems when performing jobs that require a heavy workload or that require long hours. This may be one reason why meta-analyses investigating the effects of work hours (see Sparks, Cooper, Fried, & Shirom, 1997) and perceived workload (see Spector & Jex, 1998) have shown relatively modest effects on physical health.

Effects of organizational climate.   Organizational climate has received a great deal of recent attention in organizational research, although the trend has been to examine climate with respect to specific organizational domains. For the purposes of this chapter, however, the most relevant form of climate is *safety climate*. Safety climate represents the priority and importance an organization places on safety. According to Zohar (2003), the most important antecedent of safety climate is likely to be the actions and attitudes of the top management group within an organization. The importance of safety climate can be seen in its link to actual behavior in organizations (Hofmann & Stetzer, 1996; 1998).

How might age interact with organizational safety climate to impact health in organizations? While this issue has not been examined in the occupational safety and health literature, we believe that in organizations where safety climate is poor, older employees may be at greater risk for work-related injuries compared to younger employees. This is largely due to the physical changes associated with aging that were discussed earlier in the chapter. For example, with the slow down of reaction time and speed of cognitive processing, older workers will very likely be more vulnerable to injury in a hazardous environment.

Another aspect of climate that may impact older employees, and which also has not received a great deal of attention, is simply the organizational climate with regard to older employees. Is the organizational climate such that older employees are treated with respect and dignity, or are they simply cast aside? Does the organization value the experience and wisdom of older employees? Is the organization willing to make adjustments in jobs when older employees reach a point when they may not be able to perform them as fast as younger employees? While research has not yet examined these questions in depth, we believe that organizational climates likely differ in this regard and that such differences impact older employees. It is possible, for example, that such climate differences impact what Pierce, Gardner, Cummings, and Dunham, (1989) termed Organization-Based Self-Esteem (OBSE) or "the self-perceived value that individuals have of themselves as organizational members acting within an organizational context" (p. 625). When the organizational climate toward older employees is negative, this may lead older employees to have low levels of OBSE. This is important because OBSE has been shown to be negatively related to both depression and physical health symptoms (Jex & Elacqua, 1999).

Occupational hazards and diseases. There is no reason to believe that older employees differ greatly from the general population in terms of responses to occupational hazards. People of all ages are vulnerable to diseases if they breathe in certain chemical agents, or work in dangerous conditions. However, according to Wegman and McGee (2004), older employees tend to be concentrated in a number of occupations that carry higher risk for biomechanical and other types of hazardous exposures. These include administrative support, production/craft/repair occupations, transportation and material moving, farming/forestry/fishing, private household services, protective services, and other services. As one might guess from this list of occupations, the risks are primarily in the areas of exposure to chemicals, being struck by heavy objects, exposure to violence, and repetitive motions.

INTERVENTIONS FOR IMPROVING
THE HEALTH OF OLDER EMPLOYEES

While understanding the impact of age on employee health is an important goal in and of itself, the primary reason for studying this issue is ultimately to take steps that will lead to improved health and safety of older employees. Furthermore, since this group represents the fastest growing segment of the population, it is an important overall occupational safety and health priority for organizations and society as a whole. Thus, in this final section we describe a number of interventions that can be used to increase the health and safety of older employees. Readers will note that several of the interventions described in this section could in fact be used to improve the health and safety of all employees regardless of age. Our emphasis, however, will be on using the intervention(s) for enhancing the health of older employees.

Job redesign. According to Morgeson and Campion (2003), jobs may be designed from a number of different perspectives, and these different perspectives are represented by different academic disciplines. According to Campion & Thayer (1987), these can be captured in four primary perspectives: *mechanistic, motivational, perceptual/motor,* and *biological.* The primary goal of the mechanistic approach to job design is to increase efficiency and decrease training time. The discipline most closely identified with this approach is industrial engineering.

The motivational approach is concerned with designing jobs in a way that maximizes outcomes such as employee motivation, job satisfaction, and job involvement. While there are many mechanisms for achieving these outcomes, according to this perspective, many focus on providing employees with greater control and discretion over how they schedule and perform their job tasks. The discipline that is most closely associated with the motivational approach is organizational psychology.

The perceptual-motor approach is concerned with designing jobs in a way that minimizes employees' information processing and sensory demands. This would involve analyzing what those demands are and designing the job in a way that either reduces those demands or provides employees with assistance in managing those demands. The discipline that is most closely associated with the perceptual-motor approach is human factors or engineering psychology.

Finally, the biological approach to job design is concerned with designing jobs in a way that maximizes employees' physical comfort. This typically involves analyzing the physical work environment for conditions that are likely to cause physical discomfort and to intervene to change these conditions. In many cases such conditions are (but are not limited to) repetitive motions, equipment that does not match the physical dimensions of employees, or work schedules that lead to fatigue and greater errors. The disciplines most closely associated with this approach are ergonomics and biomechanics.

Given these four approaches to job design, which are most relevant to the *redesign* of jobs to enhance the health and wellbeing of older workers? We believe that organizations wishing to enhance the health of their older workforce would not be well-served emphasizing the mechanistic approach in their job redesign efforts. This is because the focus on production efficiency may lead organizations to speed up work processes to a point that may be problematic for older employees. Also, this approach emphasizes simplification of work, something that may be detrimental to older employees, as they seem to react negatively to underutilization of skills (Mayes et al., 1991).

Job redesign that emphasizes the other three approaches in Campion's model, however, would appear to be beneficial to older employees. In the case of the motivational approach, increased control or discretion has been shown to provide health-related benefits to employees regardless of age (e.g., Spector, 1986). Thus redesigning jobs in this manner has the potential to benefit all employees.

The other two approaches to job design, however, may be particularly suited to older employees. Given the cognitive changes that are associated with aging, redesigning jobs by analyzing the information processing demands (e.g., the Perceptual Motor approach) would appear to especially benefit older employees. For example, redesigning jobs so that the information processing demands are reduced, or in such a way that employees are not required to process information as quickly, would appear to be particularly beneficial to older employees. The work environment could also be redesigned to make information easier to read, and perhaps steps could be taken to cut down on excessive noise if the job requires a high level of concentration.

Job redesign based on the Biological approach would also appear to be well-suited to the physical changes associated with aging. This might include an assessment of the physical demands of a job, ergonomic assessment of employees' work stations, or perhaps a consideration of work hours or schedules. Any job redesign intervention that enhances physical comfort would probably prove beneficial to older employees, due to the fact that age-related physical changes tend to increase the difficulty of performing physically demanding jobs or working difficult shifts (Kawada, 2002).

Organizational climate development. Changing any aspect of an organization is not easy; changing the climate or culture of an organization is especially difficult. Nevertheless, this does represent another potential way to enhance the health and wellbeing of older employees. What type(s) of changes in organizational climate would be most beneficial to older employees? Based on the earlier discussion of organizational climate, one would assume that pos-

JOB REDESIGN FOR OLDER EMPLOYEES

Although many jobs in today's economy require primarily cognitive effort, there are still many others that place physical demands on people. Examples of these types of jobs include firefighting, police work, construction, and nursing. Because of the physical demands, many people in these jobs tend to either retire at a fairly young age or end up in supervisory positions when they get older. Another option, however, would be to redesign jobs in order to make it possible for older employees to perform them. Considering the material on job redesign, how would you respond to the following questions?

1. What changes could be made in each of these jobs to make them less physically demanding?
2. Which of Campion and Morgeson's approaches to job design would be most useful in helping you redesign these jobs?
3. In redesigning jobs to decrease the physical demands, what are some of the things that would need to be taken into consideration?
4. Can you think of some jobs that simply could not be redesigned to make them less physically demanding?

itive changes in an organization's safety climate would benefit older employees, although younger employees would likely benefit as well. Previous research on safety climate (e.g., Zohar, 2003) has shown that the primary mechanisms for improving safety climate are actions and values of top management—that is, safety climate cannot be automatically changed.

The other type of climate that may impact older employees is the general organizational climate with regard to older employees, which was discussed earlier. This may involve developing greater awareness of the concerns of older employees, providing more training opportunities to older employees and more flexible career paths for older employees whose career trajectory has plateaued. Development of a more positive climate with regard to older employees has the potential to enhance older employees' (OBSE), which in turn may have positive effects on both mental and physical health (Jex & Elacqua, 1999). It is also possible that such a change in climate may help with the retention of younger employees, as they see that they will be treated well as they grow older.

Training to increase productivity and safety.   Another intervention that may enhance the health of older employees is training. According the Goldstein and Ford (2003), training is defined as "the systematic acquisition of skills, rules, concepts, or attitudes that result in improved performance in another environment" (p. 1). As applied to older employees, this may include training interventions to help older employees compensate for physical and/or cognitive changes associated with age. Training may also be used to increase younger employees' understanding of changes associated with increased age, and therefore may potentially increase empathy toward their older colleagues.

Another use of training may be to enhance older employees' adaptation to changes in work methods and technology. These issues certainly apply to employees of all ages, but may be particularly salient for older employees. This is because older employees may have been performing their jobs in a certain way for long periods of time, and thus adjusting to new methods or technology may be more challenging.

Rate of participation in training, however, might be slightly lower among older workers due to decreased self-efficacy for development (Maurer, 2001). Older workers may also experience less support for development, less opportunity for training, and feel less prepared to learn (Maurer, Weiss, & Barbeite, 2003), all challenges that must be overcome if training is to be helpful to older workers.

Health promotion.   Health promotion represents a number of activities that are designed to promote enhanced health and health behaviors among employees (Griffiths & Munir, 2003). The most common health promotion intervention in organizations is probably physical activity, but others such as nutritional counseling, smoking cessation, and weight loss programs are also quite common. While organizations may develop health promotion interventions for a variety of reasons, the most common is the goal of reducing organizational health care costs. The idea is that when employees become healthier they will have less need to utilize health services, and because of decreased use, health insurance premiums will go down.

While there is no evidence that health promotion should necessarily be targeted toward older employees, there are good reasons for why health promotion might be quite beneficial to this group. This is because the speed with which many physical changes associated with increased age occur depend on an individual's lifestyle and health habits. It has been well documented, for example, that individuals who are physically active throughout their lives will not age as quickly as those who are more sedentary (Griffiths, 1996). Other health habits such as eating a balanced diet and avoidance of smoking and excessive alcohol use will also slow the progression of the physical aging process.

From an organization's point of view, there are reasons why health promotion activities aimed at older employees may ultimately have more impact than the same activities aimed at younger employees. Specifically, since older people in general utilize health care services at a higher rate than younger employees, improving the health of older employees may have a much higher financial impact than improving the health of younger employees. This impact may be even greater considering that many organizations also pay at least a portion of the health insurance premiums of their retirees.

Legal interventions (antidiscrimination and wage/benefit protection). The primary piece of legislation that protects older employees is the Age Discrimination in Employment Act which was passed in 1967 and amended in 1978 and 1986. The primary purpose of this legislation was to prohibit employers from discrimination against older employees unless they could demonstrate that age was a "bonafide occupational qualification," or necessary for performing a particular job. Another objective of this law has been to prevent employers from singling out older employees when cutbacks or layoffs are necessary. This is unfortunately quite common because older employees tend to have higher salaries, and thus organizations stand to save more dollars in salary by letting them go.

The other major piece of legislation designed to protect older employees has been the Older Workers Benefit Protection Act, which was passed in 1990. This legislation protects older employees who are asked to sign waivers stating that they will not sue their employers if they are laid off. Under this act, older employees have 45 days to consider such waivers and up to 7 days to revoke them after signing.

Other then these two pieces of legislation, older employees may reap special benefits from pieces of employment legislation that cover all employees. Specifically, under the Americans with Disabilities Act which was passed in 1992, employers are required to make a "reasonable accommodation" for employees with disabilities who are able to perform major job functions. According to the ADA (1990), a disability is defined as: (a) a physical or mental impairment that substantially limits one or more major life activities of an individual, as, for example, walking, talking, seeing, hearing, or caring for oneself; (b) a record of such impairment; or (c) being regarded as having such an impairment. While the ADA was not created specifically for older workers, it may nevertheless help older workers who have performed work that has left them physically impaired. This is particularly the case due to the fact that many occupational injuries are cumulative over time (Schibye, Hansen, Sogaard, & Christensen, 2001). An older employee, for example, may perform a job that has caused damage to his or her hands due to repetitive motion injuries yet may not be ready or able to retire. Such an individual may be covered under the ADA if these cumulative trauma injuries have been sufficiently documented and/or have been shown to interfere with one or more major life activities.

The final type of legal intervention that may be used to enhance the health and wellbeing of older employees is actually a collection of interventions that come under the general umbrella of *income replacement*. Social security benefits, unemployment compensation, and worker's compensation are designed to provide income replacement for employees who may be unable to work. While these programs (with the possible exception of Social Security) were not specifically created for older workers, there may be certain instances when these might be especially beneficial for older employees. For example, if older employees are performing work that they find to be too physically demanding, they may be able to leave such work and collect unemployment benefits until they are able to secure less physically demanding work.

Worker's compensation programs provide compensation to employees who are injured while performing their jobs, or are at the work site. While all employees are covered under worker's compensation laws, these may be more beneficial to older employees for two reasons. First, older employees performing physically demanding work may be more vulnerable to injuries than younger employees. Second, it has been shown that compared to younger employees, older employees often take longer to recover from work-related injuries.

Overall, legal interventions have provided older workers with protection from unfair treatment and have supplied injured older employees with legal protection and financial support.

Employee assistance programs. Employee Assistance Programs (EAPs) represent a variety of organizational programs that are designed to help employees who are having a variety of problems, most typically mental health problems, substance abuse, and financial problems. The scope of EAPs varies considerably; some provide only referrals, while others may include on-site services such as mental health and financial counseling. The primary difference between an EAP and a wellness program is that wellness programs are much more focused on *prevention*, while an EAP is focused on employees who already have problems.

Like the other interventions described in this section, EAPs are not meant specifically for older employees. Nevertheless, it is possible for organizations to provide services within the context of EAPs that are more beneficial to older than younger employees. For example, through EAPs organizations may offer counseling to older employees who are considering early retirement. Organizations may also offer services to older employees who are going through difficult transitions such as children moving out of the home or death of a spouse.

CONCLUSIONS

If one views employee health as more than simply the "absence of physical disease," then organizations would be wise to consider the age of employees in their efforts to enhance employee health. As was shown in this chapter, employees bring a number of age-related changes with them to the workplace. To be sure, the rate of these changes will vary from employee to employee, but they will nevertheless occur for employees at all ages.

Given the changes that are associated with aging, what job and organizational conditions are most troublesome to older employees? A consistent theme in the literature is that, on average, older employees have the most difficulty with physically-demanding jobs. It has also been shown that older employees may have more difficulty than younger employees with jobs that require great amounts of cognitive resources, or require very rapid processing of information. Finally, because older employees typically have the highest income levels in organizations and may have limited employment prospects, they may find the possibility of layoffs much more stressful than their younger colleagues.

DIRECTIONS FOR FUTURE RESEARCH

While these would appear to be reasonable conclusions based on the currently available literature, we would hasten to add that the current research literature regarding age and occupational health is sparse. Thus, much more research is needed to document the job and organizational conditions that are most troublesome for older employees. Furthermore, such research should not only examine the vulnerability of older employees, but should also examine ways in which they may be more resilient than their younger colleagues. While older employees may have more difficulty with physically demanding jobs, it is certainly possible that they have experiences and coping resources that may enhance their capacity to handle many complex social situations in the workplace more effectively than younger employees.

In conducting future research on the impact of age on occupational health, we strongly recommend that close attention be paid to the research samples employed. This is particularly true when age is examined as a continuous variable. Given that most research on aging in the workplace is focused on age-related changes that occur as employees approach retirement, samples should include substantial numbers of research participants who are approaching retirement age. If samples include primarily younger and middle-aged employees, results may be misleading and not apply to older employees.

A final suggestion for future research would be to investigate job and organizational conditions that might moderate the relationship between age and health. Most occupational health research has examined age itself as a moderator variable (e.g., Mayes et al., 1991), but it is equally plausible that the effects of age could be moderated by other variables. For example, age and mental health might be negatively related when employees work in organizations that do not value or support older employees. In contrast, age and mental health might be positively related when employees work in organizations that value and support employees as the get older. This is obviously speculation, but certainly could be tested empirically.

IMPLICATIONS FOR PRACTICE

Based on research that has been done to date, what can organizations do to enhance the health and wellbeing of older workers? To a large extent, the answer to this question would be to do the same things that organizations would do to enhance the health and wellbeing of all employees. However, in the case of older employees, some special considerations need to be taken into account. For example, in redesigning jobs for older employees a special emphasis should be placed on reducing physical and/or cognitive processing demands. Other interventions such as climate change, training, health promotion, legal mandates, and employee assistance (all of which are commonly used in organizations) can also be tailored to the needs of older employees.

In conclusion, it is clear that older employees now represent a large percentage of the workforce worldwide, and this trend will likely continue. It is also the case that more and more employers have a vested interest in improving the health and wellbeing of their employees. Given these two trends, it is important for organizations to consider age in their efforts to enhance employee health. Such a consideration will result in a greater health of the overall workforce. Furthermore, given the time and loyalty older employees have often put into an organization, it is certainly the right and moral thing for organizations to do.

REFERENCES

Americans with Disability Act. (1990, July 26). PL 101-336, 104 Statute 327.
Aldwin, C. M., & Gilmer, D. F. (1999). Immunity, disease processes, and optimal aging. In J. C. Cavanaugh & S. K. Whitbourne (Eds.), Gerontology: Interdisciplinary perspectives (pp. 123–154). New York: Oxford University Press.
Arking, R. (1998). Biology of aging: Observations and principles. Sunderland, MA: Sinauer Associates.
Baddeley, A. (1992). Working memory. Science. 255, 556–559.
Baltes, P. B., & Lindenberger, U. (1997). Emergence of powerful connection between sensory and cognitive functions across the adult life span: A new window to the study of cognitive aging? Psychology and Aging, 12, 12–21.

Baron, R. M., & Kenny, D. A. (1986). The moderator-mediator variable distinction in social psychological research: Conceptual, strategic and statistical considerations. *Journal of Personality and Social Psychology, 51,* 1173–1182.

Boorse, C. (1975). On the distinction between disease and illness. *Philosophy and Public Affairs, 5,* 49–68.

Bunce, D., & Sisa, L. (2002). Age differences in perceived workload across a short vigil. *Ergonomics, 45,* 949–960.

Cavanaugh J. C., & Blanchard-Fields, F. (2002). *Adult development and aging.* Belmont, CA: Wadsworth Group.

Campion, M. A., & Thayer, P. W. (1987). Job design: Approaches, outcomes, and trade-offs. *Organizational Dynamics, 15,* 66–79.

Charatan, F. B. (1984). Some common psychiatric problems of aging employees. In S. F. Yolles, L. W. Krinsky, S. N. Kieffer, & P. A. Carone (Eds.), *The aging employee.* New York: Human Sciences Press.

Cherry, K. E., Park, D. C., Frieske, D. A., & Smith, A. D. (1996). Verbal and pictorial elaborations enhance memory in young and older adults. *Aging, Neuropsychology, and Cognition, 3,* 15–29.

Cristofalo, V. J., Tresini, M., Francis, M. K., & Volker, C. (1999). Biological theories of senescence. In V. L. Bengtson & K. W. Schaie (Eds.), *Handbook of theories of aging* (pp. 98–112). New York: Springer.

Currey, J. D., Brear, K., & Zioupos, P. (1996). The effects of ageing and changes in mineral content in degrading the toughness of human femora. *Journal of Biomechanics, 29,* 257–260.

Elder, G. H., & Johnson, M. K. (2003). The life course and aging: Challenges, lessons, and new directions. In R. A. Settersten, Jr. (Ed.), *Invitation to the life course: Toward new understandings of later life* (pp. 49–81). Amityville, New York: Baywood Publishing Company.

Fielding, R. A., & Meydani, M. (1997). Exercise, free radical generation, and aging. *Aging, 9,* 12–18.

Finch, C. E., & Seeman, T. E. (1999). Stress theories of aging. In V. L. Bengtson & K. W. Schaie (Eds.), *Handbook of theories of aging* (pp. 81–97). New York: Springer.

Gatz, M. (2000). Variations on depression in later life. In S. H. Qualls & N. Abeles (Eds.), *Psychology and the aging revolution* (pp. 239–254). Washington, DC: American Psychological Association.

Gatz, M., Kasl-Godley, J. E., & Karel, M. (1996). Aging and mental disorders. In J. E. Birren & K. W. Schaie (Eds.), *Handbook of the psychology of aging* (4th ed., pp. 365–382). San Diego, CA: Academic Press.

Goldstein, I. L., & Ford, J. K. (2002). *Training in organizations* (4th ed.). Belmont, CA: Wadsworth.

Griffiths, A. (1996). Employee exercise programs: Organizational and individual perspectives. In J. Kerr, A. Griffiths, & T. Cox (Eds.), *Workplace health: Employee fitness and exercise* (pp. 1–28). London: Taylor & Francis.

Griffiths, A., & Munir, F. (2003). Workplace health promotion. In D. A. Hofmann and L. E. Tetrick (Eds.), *Health and safety in organizations: A multilevel perspective* (pp. 316–340). San Francisco: Jossey-Bass.

Hansen, C. P. (1989). A causal model of the relationships among accidents, biodata, personality, and cognitive factors. *Journal of Applied Psychology, 14,* 81–90.

Hartley, A. A., & Little, D. M. (1999). Age-related differences in dual-task interference. *Journal of Experimental Psychology: General, 128,* 416–448.

Hasher, L., & Zacks, R. T. (1988). Working memory, comprehension, and aging: A review and a new view. In G. H. Bower (Ed.), *The psychology of learning and motivation* (Vol. 22, pp. 193–225). San Diego, CA: Academic Press.

Hayflick, L. (1996). *How and why we age* (2nd ed.). New York: Ballantine.

Hofmann, D. A., & Stetzer, A. (1996). A cross-level investigation of factors influencing unsafe behaviors and accidents. *Personnel Psychology, 49,* 307–339.

Hofmann, D. A., & Stetzer, A. (1998). The role of safety climate and communication in accident interpretation: Implications for learning from negative events. *Academy of Management Journal, 41,* 644–657.

Hofmann, D. A., & Tetrick, L. E. (2003). The etiology of the concept of health: Implications for "organizing" individual and organizational health. In D. A. Hofmann and L. E. Tetrick (Eds.), *Health and safety in organizations: A multilevel perspective* (pp. 1–28). San Francisco: Jossey-Bass.

Jansen, P. L. (2002). Liver disease in the elderly. *Best Practice and Research in Clinical Gastroenterology, 16,* 149–158.

Jex, S. M. (1998). *Stress and job performance: Theory, research, and implications for managerial practice.* Thousand Oaks, CA: Sage.

Jex, S. M., & Elacqua, T. C. (1999). Self-esteem as a moderator: A comparison of global and organization-based measures. *Journal of Occupational and Organizational Psychology, 72,* 71–81.

Kawada, T. (2002). Effect of age on sleep onset time in rotating shift workers. *Sleep Medicine, 3,* 423–426.

Khalil, Z., & Merhi, M. (2000). Effects of aging on neurogenic vasodilator responses evoked by transcutaneous electrical nerve stimulation: Relevance to wound healing. *Journal of Gerontology: Biological Sciences, 55,* 257–263.

Larson, J. S. (1999). The conceptualization of health. *Medical Care Research and Review, 56,* 123–136.

Lindenberger, U., & Baltes, P. B. (1994). Sensory functioning and intelligence in old age: A strong connection. *Psychology and Aging, 9,* 339–355.

Lisansky Gomberg, E. S., & Zucker, R. A. (1999). Substance use and abuse in old age. In I. H. Nordhus, G. R. VandenBos, S. Berg, & P. Fromholt (Eds.), *Clinical geropsychology* (pp. 189–204). Washington, DC: American Psychological Association.

Mauo, K., Kumagai, K., Tanaka, T., Yamagata, K., Shimizu, K., Nishida, Y., & Iimori, T. (1998). "Physiological" age as an outcome predictor for abdominal surgery in elderly patients. *Surgery Today, 28,* 997–1000.

Maurer, T. J. (2001). Career-relevant learning and development, worker age, and beliefs about self-efficacy for development. *Journal of Management, 27,* 123–140.

Maurer, T. J., Weiss, E. M., & Barbeite, F. G. (2003). A model of involvement in work-related learning and development activity: The effects of individual, situational, motivational, and age variables. *Journal of Applied Psychology, 88*(4), 707–724.

Mayes, B. T., Barton, M. E., & Ganster, D. C. (1991). An exploration of the moderating effect of age on job stressor-employee strain relationships. *Journal of Social Behavior and Personality, 6,* 389–308.

McArdle, A., Vasilaki, A., & Jackson, M. (2002). Exercise and skeletal muscle aging: Cellular and molecular mechanisms. *Aging Research Reviews, 1,* 79–93.

McDaniel, M. A., Schmidt, F. L., & Hunter, J. E. (1988). Job experience correlates of job performance. *Journal of Applied Psychology, 73,* 327–330.

Moody, H. R. (2002). *Aging: Concepts and controversies* (4th ed.). Thousand Oaks, CA: Sage.

Morgeson, F. P., & Campion, M. A. (2003). Work design. In W. C. Borman & D. R. Ilgen (Eds.), *Handbook of psychology: Industrial and organizational* (Vol. 12, pp. 423–452).

Park, D. C. (2000). The basic mechanisms accounting for age-related decline in cognitive function. In D. C. Park & N. Schwarz (Eds.), *Cognitive aging: A primer* (pp. 3–22). Philadelphia: Psychology Press.

Park, D. C., Smith, A. D., Morrell, R. W., Puglisi, J. T., & Dudley, W. N. (1990). Effects of contextual integration on recall of pictures by older adults. *Journal of Gerontology: Psychological Sciences, 45,* 52–57.

Parsons, T. C. (1972). Definitions of health and illness in the light of American values and social structure. In E. G. Jaco (Ed.), *Patients, physicians, and illness* (pp. 107–127). New York: Free Press.

Pedersen, W. A., Wan, R., & Matterson, M. P. (2001). Impact of aging on stress-responsive neuroendocrine systems. *Mechanisms of Aging and Development, 122,* 963–983.

Pierce, J. L., Gardner, D. G., Cummings, L. L., & Dunham, R. B. (1989). Organization-based self-esteem: Construct definition, measurement, and validation. *Academy of Management Journal, 32,* 622–648.

Prince, M. M. (2002). Distribution of risk factors for hearing loss: Implications for evaluating risk of occupational noise-induced hearing loss. *Journal of the Acoustical Society of America, 112,* 557–567.

Rhodes, S. R. (1983). Age-related differences in work attitudes and behavior: A review and conceptual analysis. *Psychological Bulletin, 93,* 328–367.

Rigler, S. K. (2000). Alcoholism in the elderly. *American Family Physician, 61,* 1710–1716.

Salthouse, T. A. (1991). *Theoretical perspectives on cognitive aging.* Hillsdale, NJ: Lawrence Erlbaum Associates.

Salthouse, T. A. (1993). Speed and knowledge as determinants of adult age differences in verbal tasks. *Journal of Gerontology: Psychological Sciences, 48,* 29–36.

Salthouse, T. A. (1996). The processing-speed theory of adult age differences in cognition. *Psychological Review, 103,* 403–428.

Schibye, B., Hansen, A. F., Sogaard, K., & Christensen, H. (2001). Aerobic power and muscle strength among young and elderly workers with and without physically demanding work tasks. *Applied Ergonomics, 32,* 425–431.

Seidman, M. D., Ahmad, N., & Bai, U. (2002). Molecular mechanisms of age-related hearing loss. *Ageing Research Reviews, 1,* 331–343.

Seitsamo, J., & Martikainen, R. (1999). Changes in capability in a sample of Finnish aging workers. *Experimental Aging Research, 25,* 345–352.

Sharpe, M., Chalder, T., Palmer, I., and Wessely, S. (1997). Chronic fatigue syndrome. A practical guide to assessment and management. *General Hospital Psychiatry, 19,* 185–199.

Sowers, M. F. (2001). Epidemiology of risk factors for osteoarthritis: Systemic factors. *Current Opinion in Rheumatology, 13,* 447–451.

Sparks, K., Cooper, C., Fried, Y., & Shirom, A. (1997). The effect of hours of work on health: A meta-analytic review. *Journal of Occupational and Organizational Psychology*, 70, 391–408.

Spector, P. E. (1986). Perceived control by employees: A meta-analysis of studies concerning autonomy and participation at work. *Human Relations*, 11, 1005–116.

Spector, P. E., & Jex, S. M. (1998). Development of four self-report measures of job stressors and strain: Interpersonal Conflict at Work Scale, Organizational Constraints Scale, Quantitative Workload Inventory, and Physical Symptoms Inventory. *Journal of Occupational Health Psychology*, 3, 356–367.

Spirduso, W. W., & MacRae, P. G. (1990). Motor performance and aging. In J. E. Birren & K. W. Schaie (Eds.), *Handbook of the psychology of aging* (3rd ed., pp. 183–200). San Diego: Academic Press.

Sverke, M., Hellgren, J., & Naswall, K. (2002). No security: A meta-analysis and review of job insecurity and its consequences. *Journal of Occupational Health Psychology*, 7, 242–264.

Vitiello, M. W. (1996). Sleep disorders and aging. *Current Opinions in Psychiatry*, 9, 284–289.

Wegman, D. H., & McGee (Eds.). (2004). *Health and safety needs of older workers*. Washington, DC: The National Academies Press.

Whitbourne, S. K. (1999). Physical changes. In J. C. Cavanaugh & S. K. Whitbourne (Eds.), *Gerontology: Interdisciplinary perspectives* (pp. 91–122). New York: Oxford University Press.

Zacks, R. T., Radvansky, G., & Hasher, L. (1996). Studies of directed forgetting in older adults. *Journal of Experimental Psychology: Learning, Memory, and Cognition*, 22, 143–156.

Zohar, D. (2003). The influence of leadership and climate on occupational health and safety. In D. A. Hofmann and L. E. Tetrick (Eds.), *Health and safety in organizations: A multilevel perspective* (pp. 201–232). San Francisco: Jossey-Bass.

11

Age and Technology for Work

Neil Charness, Sara Czaja, and Joseph Sharit

Adoption of technological systems is accelerating, particularly in the work place, at the same time that the workforce is aging. How can we design systems and training that will buttress the productivity of our aging workforce? We briefly examine trends in technology use as a function of age. We then present a framework for understanding how age can affect technology adoption and use and then outline age-related changes in perceptual, cognitive, and psychomotor functioning that have relevance to work activities. We discuss principles for the design of technological systems and for the design of training programs to accommodate an aging workforce. We also consider the newly developing area of telework. We close with the identification of research gaps and provide some practical guidelines for design for an aging workforce.

The nature of work has changed radically in developed countries over the past century. We have moved from a labor force that was employed primarily in physically challenging industries such as agriculture, manufacturing, and mining to one that is increasingly mentally challenging: service-sector work. The typical life course has also shifted from one where you worked until you died, usually in your sixth decade, to one where you work until you can retire, usually in your 60s, with death typically following one or two decades later. Accompanying the shift to a service-based economy has been the rapid rise of technology, mainly in the form of microchip technology. One amusing consequence of technology's rapid expansion, as a *New York Times* article pointed out some years ago, is that there are now more remote controls than people inhabiting American households. There are also more microprocessors than people in the world today.

Why worry about technology for work, particularly for older workers? As economists have known for years, productivity in the work place depends highly on capital investment. A fast-writing clerk with a quill, inkwell, and paper files cannot compete even with a slow-typing clerk who is trained and equipped with a database, e-mail, word processor, and printer. However, the training costs to use earlier office technology were probably considerably smaller than those necessary to use today's technology. Worker education and training thus become potential bottlenecks for assuring productivity increases as technology advances. Further, we are now experiencing, as other chapters in this volume have indicated, a rapidly aging labor force. Normative changes in perceptual, cognitive, and psychomotor abilities accompany increased age, and these can have an impact on work performance. For instance, learning rate slows with increased age, particularly for unfamiliar material. As a result, older adults can be expected to take between 50 percent and 100 percent more time to self-train on a new word processor (Charness, Kelley, Bosman, & Mottram, 2001).

Despite expected negative changes with increased age, there is little link between age and productivity measures (see the review by Salthouse & Maurer, 1996) suggesting that adaptation and acquired knowledge may protect older workers from any loss in productivity. However, the learning rate slowdown with age may become increasingly important in an economy where the pace of technology adoption is accelerating (Charness & Czaja, 2005).

Our chapter will first provide some definitions of aging and technology, and will then briefly examine some of the demographics relating to age and technology use. Next, we outline a framework for understanding how older adults interact with technology. We then look more specifically at how we can derive principles for selecting and designing technological artifacts to be useful for older workers. We also discuss a current trend of an increasing role for telework and its implications for our aging workforce. We close with a summary of recommendations for future research in this area and outline some practical implications for workplace and training design that are based on our existing knowledge of aging and work.

DEFINITIONS

Older Worker

We are all aging workers, so it is difficult to select a specific cut-off age for defining an *older worker*. However, the laws of the land can provide some guidelines. In the U.S., the Age Discrimination in Employment Act provides protection for adults 40 years of age and older (applying to or working in organizations with 20 or more employees: http://www.eeoc.gov/facts/age.html).

If we look at high performance environments, even earlier ages might define *older worker*. In many professional sports domains, for example, you are probably nearing (forced) retirement in your mid-30s. (The rise of a senior's tour in golf is a creative way to bypass age-related negative changes in skill in that domain.)

Given how many work settings are strongly visually constrained, and given that we typically become near sighted (presbyopic) in our early to middle 40s, requiring corrective lenses for near vision work, perhaps we can take age 45 as a reasonable cut-off. A recent National Research Council panel in the U.S. examined health and safety needs of older workers and adopted age 45 as their arbitrary cut-off point (Wegman & McGee, 2004).

One other caveat is worth considering when defining the older worker. Although work is usually equated with paid work, those who choose to stay out of the paid labor force by caring for children or older parents, who serve as unpaid volunteers, and who are unemployed at some point in time could all be considered as older workers, too. Finally, things blur even further when you consider part-time work, an increasingly popular option for those who have reached normal (pensionable) retirement age.

Technology

Trying to define technology is rather like shooting at a moving target. We are less concerned here with technology (one *Oxford English Dictionary* definition: a particular practical or industrial art) as with high technology which the OED defines as: "high-technology applied *attrib.* to a firm, industry, etc., that produces or utilizes highly advanced and specialized technology, or to the products of such a firm."

As this definition implies, we are looking at highly advanced and specialized products or processes. The manual typewriter was an incredible advance on paper and pen at its introduction, but would be a quaint-looking piece of technology (low technology) today compared to a computer equipped with word-processing software.

Given the ubiquity of embedded and nonembedded microprocessors in many devices today, a good first approximation definition of technology would be anything with a microprocessor, either in it, or controlling its function. A more function-oriented definition would be any device that serves as an information-processing system by accepting variable inputs and generating variable outputs. Such a definition would cover many devices found in the typical office workplace today: computers, monitors, fax machines, copying machines, scanners, telephone systems, networking equipment, printers, etc. Office work is not the only place where technology has advanced. A look at the instrument panel in a modern tractor shows how far farming has advanced from the days of animal-driven plows.

A new word, *gerontechnology*, was coined recently (e.g., see Charness, 2004) to encompass issues related to both age and technology. Another variant is *gerotechnology* (Burdick & Kwon, 2005). Gerontechnology is seen as: "The study of technology and aging for the improvement of the daily functioning of the elderly" (Bouma, 1992).

Technology Use by Age

One potential concern for older workers is whether they are up to date with technology. In general, older adults in the United States report lower use of technology than younger adults (Czaja et al., 2006) and are also far less likely to be users of computer technology and the Internet (Rainie & Packel, 2001; A nation online, 2002; The UCLA Internet report, 2003). Surveys in European countries have identified similar trends (Tacken, Marcellini, Mollenkopf, Ruoppila, & Széman, 2005).

Although, as some have noted, the older adult population is the fastest growing segment in terms of computer and Internet use, it is only because younger groups are approaching asymptote. A typical example is shown in Figure 11–1.

Even assuming the current rate of increase, many in the age 65 and older group will never catch up to other cohorts before they die. However, our interest is mainly in the comparison of older workers to younger workers, which corresponds roughly to the 50–64 age group versus the two younger ones. It is pretty clear that there is a very significant 10 to 20 percent gap in use.

Why are older adults, and by implication, older workers, less frequent users of technology such as computers and the Internet? Here we are forced to speculate a bit. It is helpful to consider the framework shown in Figure 11–2 that our research group, CREATE (Czaja, Sharit, Charness, Fisk, & Rogers, 2001), has adopted to understand age and technology use. Because this framework is aimed at understanding technology use rather than intention to use, it considers more factors than other models that focus on attitudinal components to technology acceptance, such as TAM2 (Venkatesh & Davis, 2000).

This framework notes that for successful interaction there must be a balance between the demands of a technological system and the capabilities of the intended user. Many factors can influence successful technology adoption. Broad classes include access, attitudes, motivation, ability, design, and training (Charness, 2003). Part of the reduced use of technology seen in older adults may be attributed to anxieties about and attitudes toward technology coupled with normative age-related declines in cognition that make using complex technology a more difficult task (Czaja et al., 2006). Another contributing factor may be the age-related perceptual and psychomotor changes that make interaction with such systems more challenging than in earlier years (e.g., night driving as a function of changes in vision).

For instance, as people age (age, education, technical experience box in Figure 11–2) movement precision (psychomotor component of the user) lessens and hence some older adults can have difficulty using a computer mouse (hardware interface). Substituting a different input device (e.g., light pen, speech recognition, changing the hardware interface), or providing *sticky*

Panel 1

Use a Computer by Age Group

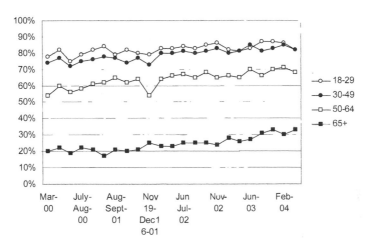

Panel 2

Go Online by Age Group

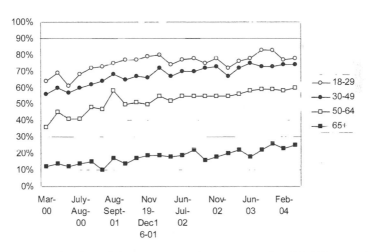

FIGURE 11-1. Panel 1. USA computer use by age group. Panel 2. USA go online by age group. Data from Pew Internet & American Life Project survey: March 2000 tracking survey. Retrieved July 30, 2005, from http://www.pewinternet.org/data.asp. The Pew Project bears no responsibility for the interpretations presented or conclusions reached based on analysis of the data.

229

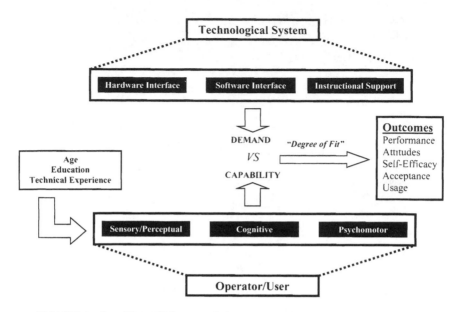

FIGURE 11-2. CREATE framework for understanding age and technology use.

menu items and lessening mouse acceleration (changing the software interface) may enable an older user to perform better with the technological system and increase its acceptability and usage. Only recently has much attention been paid to designing usable technology for older adults (Fisk, Rogers, Charness, Czaja, & Sharit, 2004).

In the next sections we provide an overview of changes with age that may affect work performance and the ability to use technology, and outline some principles for how to design technology products to avoid handicapping older workers. More detailed discussion can be found in Fisk et al. (2004).

OVERVIEW OF AGE-RELATED CHANGES
THAT MAY IMPACT WORK PERFORMANCE

Attention, Memory, Perception, Psychomotor

There is an abundance of knowledge regarding aging and abilities that is potentially useful in understanding the impact of aging on the performance of work-related tasks. However, caution must be exercised when generalizing from laboratory type studies to predict performance on real world tasks. The majority of studies concerned with age changes in component abilities are based on tasks that may have limited relevance to real world activities. Aging is also associated with a high degree of variability; people age differently so reliance on group averages may be misleading. Finally, studies that examine age changes in basic abilities such as working memory or speed of processing do not account for contextual variables such as experience with a particular task or the use of compensatory strategies such as reliance on memory aids.

Overall, it is fairly well established in the literature (e.g., Park & Schwartz, 2000) that many aspects of cognition such as working memory, selective attention, spatial cognition, processing speed, problem solving and reasoning tend to decline with age. In fact, many of these changes have relevance to work activities. This is especially true in today's technology-oriented work environment where workers are constantly confronted with the need to learn new skills or new ways of performing jobs to keep pace with developments in technology and changes in the way work is performed. In fact, potential problems with skill obsolescence and the need for retraining are major issues associated with the continued employment of older workers.

For example, age-related declines in working memory, the ability to keep information active temporarily while we process it or until we use it, may make it difficult for older people to learn new concepts or skills or recall complex operational procedures. Declines in attention capacity may make it difficult for an older person to perform concurrent activities or switch attention between competing displays of information. Older adults may also have problems selecting task targets or integrating information from crowded or complex displays or multiple information sources. Also, because older people tend to process information at a slower rate, highly paced work may also be unsuitable for older workers or it may take older workers longer to learn new skills. However, while these changes tend to occur with age, it is important to recognize that many declines in abilities have limited impact on real world task performance and that older workers are willing and able to learn new tasks and skills. In fact, recent studies (e.g., Czaja & Sharit, 1998; Czaja, Sharit, Ownby, Roth, & Nair, 2001; Sharit et al., 2004) have shown that older adults are quite willing and able to learn technology-based work tasks. However, as discussed later in this chapter, it is important that they are provided with access to training programs and that training programs are designed to accommodate the learning styles of older adults.

Aging is also associated with changes in motor skills, including slower response times, declines in the ability to maintain continuous movements, disruptions in coordination, loss of flexibility, and greater variability in movement (Rogers & Fisk, 2000). The incidence of chronic conditions such as arthritis also increases with age. These changes in motor skills may make it difficult for older people to perform tasks, such as assembly work that requires small manipulation, or to use current input devices, such as a mouse or keyboard.

Older adults also tend to have reduced strength and endurance. Generally, with age there is a gradual loss of muscle mass and muscles become weaker. Cardiac capacity and the time it takes to repair muscular damage also declines with age (Wegman & McGee, 2004). Clearly there is a great deal of variability in muscle groups, in types of muscular performance, and between individuals. However, in general older adults are less willing and able to perform physically demanding jobs.

In summary, there are a number of age-related changes in abilities that may have relevance to work. However, as we illustrate throughout this chapter, many age-related changes in abilities can be compensated for through training and good design practices. Unfortunately many designers of technology and interfaces have not considered the needs and preferences of older people. Furthermore, common myths that older people are less productive, and less able and less willing to work are not supported in the literature. In fact, most older people are interested in remaining in some form of productive work and there is very limited evidence to suggest that work performance declines with age.

Findings and Principles for Training, Retraining, and Instruction

The influx of technology into work settings has vast implications for worker training and retraining programs. Technology influences the types of jobs that are available by creating new jobs and opportunities for employment. Technology also changes the way in which jobs are performed and alters job content and job demands. Thus existing job skills and knowledge become obsolete and new knowledge and skills are required. Continuous changes in technology also imply that people will need to learn new systems and new activities at multiple points during their working lives. Workers not only have to learn to use technical systems, but they must also learn new ways of performing jobs. Issues of skill obsolescence and worker retraining are highly significant for older workers as they are less likely than younger workers to have had exposure to technology such as computers and expectations on the part of employers and older workers themselves that they (older workers) are less likely than younger workers to be successful in training programs (Hamil-Luker & Uhlenberg, 2002). As noted, a common myth about older workers is that they are unwilling and unable to learn. Generally, there is no support from studies the literature for this myth. Overall, the results of these studies indicate that older adults are, in fact, able to learn new forms of technology though they do so more slowly and sometimes with less success as a meta-analysis pointed out (Kubeck, Delp, Haslett, & McDaniel, 1996). However, in order for training and retraining programs to be successful, careful attention needs to be given to the design of these programs to ensure that they are suited to the learning needs and preferences of older people.

Important issues that need to be considered when designing training programs for older adults include pacing, the timing and amount of feedback, amount of practice, practice schedule, organization of the learning material, and design of support materials. For example, it is important to allow extra time for training older adults (1.5 to 2 times the training time expected for young adults). Feedback should always be provided as *unlearning* is particularly difficult for older adults. Feedback helps the learner correct mistakes and reinforces procedures and concepts. It is also important with respect to motivation. Thus both positive and negative (though constructive) feedback should be provided during training. Furthermore, traditional classroom type of instruction where typically a large amount of *declarative* knowledge concerning facts and concepts is imparted to the trainees prior to their performance of a task generally requires that a great deal of information be stored in memory. This may be especially difficult for older adults given age-related declines in working memory. Thus, when possible, an emphasis should be placed on a *learning-while-applying* approach that allows a person to process information while they are doing the task. Guided practice should also be given.

When presenting information to older learners, it is also important to promote consistency between the stimuli and the response requirements. For example, in learning a software application, if the appearance of an icon requires one type of response during some of the learning trials and a different response in other trials, the icon is not consistently being linked to a response. Training techniques that facilitate thinking about familiar concepts and relationships can also strengthen associations in memory and thereby improve retention. People often use analogies in forming their mental models. The benefit of providing analogies during training is that it allows the learner to use existing and familiar knowledge structures to better label and understand relationships among components of the task being learned. It is also important that training materials are well organized and that the reading level of all instructions and manuals matches the abilities of the user population. Illustrations that provide specific examples of the concepts and procedures can be useful. Finally, it is important to ensure that the training environment allows people to focus on the training materials and that distractions are minimized. Training programs must be given at convenient times and convenient locations.

Findings and Principles for Input/Output Devices

Most technological systems have input and output components to communicate with the user. For instance, a typical computer system has a keyboard and mouse as input devices and a screen and speakers as output devices. Efficient use of such devices depends on the user's vision, hearing, and dexterity, all of which typically change with age. See the review by Fozard and Gordon-Salant (2001).

Vision Changes

The major normative change with age in vision is loss of ability to change the focus of the lens of the eye to see near objects: presbyopia. Presbyopia typically occurs in the mid 40s and prompts most adults to get reading glasses or multifocal glasses if they already wear single lens glasses to correct near- or far-sightedness. Normal glasses might have been adequate for mid- and far-distance vision earlier in life, but now reading materials (e.g., newspapers, computer screens) are hard to see without additional correction. Often traditional reading glasses are not adequate for mid-distance vision (e.g., 40–60 cm to the target object), a distance typical for computer monitor placement or a car's instrument panel display. Special mid-distance computer glasses (or gradient lenses) may be a good solution.

Further, given changes in pupil size and in the optical media within the eye, less light is admitted to the back of the eye for transduction by the retina to neural impulses that travel to visual centers in the brain. A 65-year-old eye admits only about a third of the light that enters a young adult's eye. Thus, there is less light and correspondingly less contrast (e.g., for black print on a white background) available for older adults. Simply increasing light levels engenders other risks. Under high-intensity light conditions, older adults are more susceptible to masking of significant visual details by glare because of greater diffusion of light through the eye (due to loss of transparency in the optical media).

Such changes require that designers pay close attention to visual characteristics of work environments. For instance, print sizes less than 12 points should be avoided. Good contrast needs to be maintained between text and

Poor Design: Low Contrast 8 pt text	Good Design: High Contrast 14 pt text
This is not the way to present text to older workers. It uses small black type on a grey background.	This should provide sufficient contrast and size to enable easy reading by older workers.

FIGURE 11-3.   Case study of choice of display characteristics for text.

background. Black on white or white on black text is optimal, though this contrast guideline is violated frequently on many web sites as of this writing.

A nice feature of computer-based reading is that it is possible to adjust text size to improve legibility of print for older adults. However, too few users realize how to accomplish such changes, and poor design of web sites and browsers often makes it very difficult to change font sizes or override default settings for text. Similarly, as of this writing, the default size for images in popular videoconferencing software is sometimes too small for rapid and accurate identification of emotions (Roring, Hines, & Charness, accepted, a).

Hearing Changes

As we age, hair cells in the inner ear responsible for transducing sound may cease functioning. This loss is attributable both to lifelong exposure to noise in the environment as well as to normative aging processes. Men seem to be affected more than women. The end result is that we become impaired at detecting sounds, particularly high frequencies (high pitched). Such changes negatively impact speech perception sometimes by the mid to late 50s. Analogous to the case for vision, simply raising the intensity of sounds may not provide adequate compensation. Older adults are also more susceptible to masking by noise so that picking out voices in noisy environments becomes particularly challenging. Although hearing aids can help, current versions boost both signal and background noise, making them less effective in noisy environments.

Many warning signals are generated within frequency ranges that are difficult to perceive, even in quiet environments, by older listeners. A good example is a typical digital watch alarm. Therefore, important signals should be kept in a narrow frequency band (around 1000 Hz) and at a reasonable intensity (e.g., 65+ decibels) to ensure audibility.

Consequences for Technology Use

When such age-related impairments in vision and hearing are accompanied by modest changes in cognition and dexterity, problems can arise with typical computer input and output devices. A good example is the use of a mouse. A subset of older users, particularly novice users, have difficulty controlling cursor movement on a screen with movement of a mouse (Charness et al., 2001; Smith, Sharit, & Czaja, 1999) as in the case of easily acquiring small targets on a screen, or carrying out dragging and dropping operations. Double-clicking is often difficult because older adults have difficulty keeping the mouse from moving between clicks and thus the second click does not register as the second half of a double-click. One solution is to change the default parameters for the mouse (Worden, Walker, Bharat, & Hudson, 1997). Another strategy is to change to a different input device, such as a touch screen or light pen (Charness, Holley, Feddon, & Jastrzembski, 2004), though choice of device depends also on the type of task (Rogers, Fisk, McLaughlin, & Pak, in press).

On the other hand, some technological advances, such as the use of synthetic speech for output, may differentially handicap older workers who already have minor problems with normal speech perception (Roring, Hines, & Charness, accepted, b). Such output systems should be avoided until they show significant improvements, particularly for older listeners.

Some older adults are unfamiliar with a keyboard or relatively unskilled at typing. A potential solution is to make use of speech recognition software given that it seems to be equally effective for different age groups (Jastrzembski, Charness, Holley, & Feddon, 2005; Kalasky, Czaja, Sharit, & Nair, 1999).

In summary, advances in technology can compensate for age-related changes in older workers, though thoughtful design and choice of appropriate devices and default settings is necessary.

Findings and Principles for Software Interface

The software interface typically refers to the general operating procedures, menu design, display layout, system navigation, organization and amount of information, and design of help systems. Generally, there has been very little research examining the impact of the design of the software interface on the performance of older people. Given that there are age-related changes in cognitive processes, such as working memory and selective attention, it is highly likely that interface style (e.g., function keys vs. menus; amount and organization of information) will have a significant influence on the performance of older adults. In fact, the limited data that are available support this conclusion. The current cohort of older people may also have less experience with window operations or search engines or information search strategies. They may also have less information on where to turn for help or aids that are available to help them interact with computer or other technical systems.

In general, software interfaces that place minimal demands on working memory and spatial abilities are optimal for older adults. The information needed for performing a task or operation should be easily available and users should not need to rely on their memory to perform a task. Color coding and consistent placement of information is also beneficial. Complex operating procedures and inconsistencies in layout and design are also problematic. Furthermore, it is important to minimize clutter and organize information with natural groupings. Providing feedback about an activity or task completion and opportunities for error recovery is also important. The need for screen scrolling should also be kept to a minimum as should the opportunities for the user to *get lost* while searching for information. Thus, on-screen aids such as maps and history markers (if well designed) may also prove to be beneficial for older people.

The Future of Work: Telework, Part-time Work, Flexible Schedules

Telework, also referred to as telecommuting or flexiwork, has been defined as an "anytime-anyplace form of work" (Buessing, 2000) that has, in large part due to increases in networking capability and declines in the cost of technology, emerged as an important and attractive work option. As noted by the U.S. Office of Personnel Management (OPM; 2003) (http://www.telework.gov/), telework can be performed in a variety of settings that include the employee's residence, an office that is closer to the employee's residence than the employer's primary site (sometimes referred to as *satellite sites*), or some other acceptable location. There are also various possible telework schedules, including full-time and part-time work. Schedules can also be imposed on the degree to which teleworkers are required to physically report to the primary work site, ranging from a regular basis (such as once a week) to never. Similarly, training for the job that will be performed as telework can, at one extreme, be performed entirely at the primary work site, or at the other extreme, can be completely accomplished off-site using multimedia or other training arrangements.

Countless benefits of telework have been noted (Buessing, 2000; OPM, 2003) that encompass benefits to the employer, the worker, and the environment, and often to all three of these entities. Benefits include lower operational costs associated with space; a greater opportunity for recruiting part-time workers which, in addition to savings in office space, can also result in lower medical benefit costs; better job performance resulting from the ability to work in a more uninterrupted fashion; the ability to bind qualified personnel by giving them the opportunity to address personal responsibilities such as caregiving; reductions in commuting, which not only accommodates workers with disabilities for whom commuting is a burden but also plays a role in protecting the environment; and greater job satisfaction and thus an increased likelihood of lower absenteeism and turnover due to the greater flexibility teleworkers have in scheduling personal activities.

These purported benefits of telework should not be taken to suggest that telework is always a win-win proposition. Clearly, not all jobs are amenable to telework—many types of work require face-to-face interactions. Also, in addition to legal concerns (such as home safety), employers may be skeptical about their ability to adequately supervise teleworkers and concerned about the friction that may arise among other workers for whom telework is not a viable option. The prospects that telework may result in excessive burdens does not only apply to management—teleworkers may find themselves unable to meet performance quotas or objectives due to distractions arising from their home environments. Some of these issues indicate the need for formal telework programs that can inform employers about these concerns and provide a basis for resolving them (OPM, 2003).

The benefits of telework are especially relevant to older workers, especially older adults who are retired or near retirement. Many older adults have caregiving burdens or medical issues that make work at home convenient. Being able to work at one's own pace, and in the absence of direct scrutiny from managers, can also lower their anxiety levels. The economic realities of many older adults and the potential benefits to health and wellbeing of maintaining a productive lifestyle makes part-time flexible work arrangements particularly attractive to older workers, which telework easily accommodates.

From the standpoint of the employer, the crucial question is whether older workers can perform adequately as teleworkers, especially if the telework arrangement requires interacting with technology. An example of a job that can conceivably be performed exclusively as telework and that requires interaction with technology is a customer service representative who relies on search and retrieval of information from a company's database in formulating e-mail responses to customer queries. We simulated such a task for a fictitious company that sold media products such as computers, accessories, supplies, software, and books, through its on-line store (Sharit et al., 2004).

In this study, a total of 52 participants ranging in age from 50 to 80 years were recruited in two age groups: a *younger* older group (50–65 years) and an *older* older group (66–80 years). The information that the participants needed to access to respond to customer queries was contained in a database comprised of three primary sections: company policies and procedures, products, and customer and order information. The policies and procedures section consisted primarily of rule-based information grouped into ten categories. Associated with each of these categories were submenus for pursuing deeper searches. In contrast, the product and customer and order information sections were configured as more conventional relational databases. Participants were trained in groups of five or six, with each person sitting at his or her own workstation, and over the next four days they performed eight *work sessions*, two per day. In each work session, the task consisted of sequentially opening e-mails from a listing of 40 e-mails contained in an e-mail inbox window and responding to the customer's queries by navigating through the database and selecting the appropriate information corresponding to the customer's query or queries. The participants were informed that a *Wizard* would construct a formal e-mail reply letter based on the information they selected, much like the standard form letters sent by various institutions such as banks. Although the participants were told that they would not see these responses, it was emphasized that these reply letters could contain errors if information was missing, or if incorrect selections or more selections than necessary were made.

We specifically designed the interface with older users in mind. For example, we created a split-screen format that minimized memory demands by enabling the user to continually view the customer's e-mail while navigating the system in search for the appropriate information. We also provided a history function that allowed users to track which items of information they had already selected. The customer e-mails were varied to simulate different information-processing demands—some of the e-mails contained multiple as opposed to single queries, some required more diverse navigation through the database, and some were very wordy as opposed to being succinct.

A variety of performance measures were used to capture different aspects of performance, including the number of e-mails that were processed correctly (no wrong selections or additional selections over and beyond those that were warranted), average time spent searching for information per e-mail, and the efficiency of navigating for information in terms of navigational *moves*. In addition to these measures of performance, we also obtained measures on a large set of cognitive abilities and job-related attitudinal measures from instruments whose instructions were modified to conform to the nature of our study. These instruments included a work involvement questionnaire (Warr, Cook, & Wall, 1979), a work alienation questionnaire (Kanungo, 1982), a job motivation questionnaire (Warr et al.,1979), a modified version of the Minnesota Satisfaction Questionnaire (Weiss, Dawis, England, & Lofquist, 1967), and the Task, Job, and Role Characteristics module of the Michigan Organizational Assessment Questionnaire (Seashore, Lawler, Mirvis, & Cammann, 1982). Exit interviews were then conducted with each participant.

Although all the participants, but especially the older (66–80) participants had problems with *overselecting* information and to an extent with making incorrect selections, particularly for the more complex e-mails, for the most part the performance of the older group caught up with the younger (50–65) group, and there were indications from the analysis that this lag may have been due to the lesser prior experience the older group of people had with computers as compared to the younger group.

These findings indicate the importance during the early stages of training of ensuring that older workers are reasonably skilled and confident in using the technological tools—in this case, the computer-interactive tools— as well as the task procedures. Otherwise, cognitive resources that could immediately be directed toward developing a task mental model may instead be allocated to more peripheral concerns related to technology use. Most encouraging were

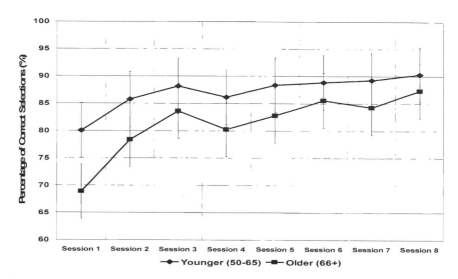

FIGURE 11-4. Percentage of correct selections.

the findings from the exit interviews that the vast majority of the participants
would welcome the opportunity to perform this type of work as telework, and
these findings were largely supported by the job motivation and job satisfaction data.

However, the data regarding abilities and performance did suggest the
need for design interventions that might prove to be beneficial to older adults,
particularly design aids that can help them focus their attention on what needs
to be done and keep track of multiple items of information. Overall, the findings from this study indicated that the older age group participants were able
to learn tasks that reflect the ability to adapt to the technically oriented work
environment.

Whether managers assume that older workers are capable of learning new
skills or meeting the challenges of jobs that rely on interacting with information technologies is an open question. The best we can do is to provide evidence that, with design configurations that minimize the deficits of older people, older workers can perform adequately with technological devices and
systems. A critical component in this equation is training. Assuming that many
older workers have poorer mental models than younger workers concerning
how technology works and thus how it can be used effectively and efficiently
to perform their jobs, different strategies of training will likely need to be
adopted for older populations of workers. These strategies would also benefit
all populations of workers who lack technological knowledge. However, as dis-

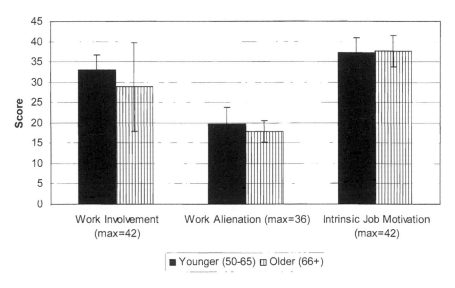

FIGURE 11-5. Work involvement and job motivation score.

cussed earlier, confronting new technology within the context of learning new work procedures is likely to provoke greater stress and anxiety in older adults, who are also inclined to have lesser degrees of confidence in learning new technologies. These considerations derive in part from declining cognitive abilities and the awareness by older adults of these declines, and argue for training strategies tailored to older workers.

Ergonomic considerations also require careful consideration when older workers are involved in telework jobs that require interacting with technological devices. The exit interviews from our study (Sharit et al., 2004) confirmed that the older participants were much more sensitive to work station design parameters. Although tasks such as information search and retrieval from a computer may not require large forces, even part-time telework using, for instance, a laptop at home, could result in many fine-grained repetitive movements which, if lighting, seating, and postures are being compromised, could prove annoying at the least and debilitating in the worst case. These considerations add additional burdens on management that, as implied earlier, may contribute to attitudes by companies against the adoption of telework, and represent another challenge in the design, implementation, and monitoring of telework performed by older workers.

Finally, although this discussion has focused on the potential for part-time customer service work involving information search and retrieval, there are other types of work requiring interfacing with technology that may be

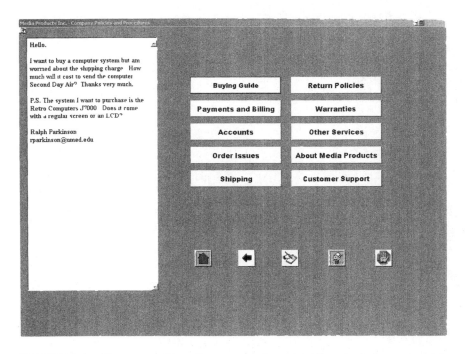

FIGURE 11–6.   Illustration of the split-screen configuration. The e-mail always remains in the left window during information search, and, in this screen the 10 submenus associated with the policies and procedures section of the database are contained in the right window. The icons enhance the user's navigation through the database.

amenable to telework, and even part-time telework. Thus we also need to explore the possible types of tasks involving the use of technology that are conducive to telework by older workers, and then convince management that with appropriate job and interface designs and training strategies, older workers can indeed make important work contributions.

Gaps in Knowledge Acquisition

People are generally more capable at adapting to new knowledge or devices when they have already heavily invested in precursor activities. Thus, learning version 7 of a software application is not as threatening if one is reasonably comfortable with version 6, than if one is unfamiliar with all previous versions of the application. That is, transitions are easier when the *gaps* are fewer. This holds true as well for older workers: if they have been transitioned well—that is, they are still very active in the knowledge and control loop—adapting to new technology, while perhaps still challenging in the face of cognitive declines, may not be problematic.

Unfortunately, with the rapid pace at which technology is being introduced into the workplace, many older workers are more likely to have gaps in knowledge, which makes it difficult for them to become facilitated with these devices. This is probably why managers are more inclined to hire younger workers for tasks with heavy technological demands—training requirements are fewer and more effective utilization of knowledge concerning the technology is expected. If our goal is to increase the prospects of incorporating older workers into our newer technological jobs, the issue of gaps in knowledge needs to be addressed. As was the case in the telework paradigm, older workers who need to be trained or retrained on jobs requiring facility with technologically-driven interfaces will likely require training strategies that are tailored to the gaps in knowledge that they possess, and particularly, training strategies that can most effectively close these gaps.

DIRECTIONS FOR FUTURE RESEARCH

The most rapidly growing portion of the workforce is adults ages 55–64, and there are also increased numbers of workers over the age of 65 (Toosi, 2004). However, despite the availability and willingness of older adults to remain in the workforce, or come out of retirement and reengage in work activities on either a full- or part-time basis, the literature indicates that older workers are not perceived as favorably as younger workers (Finkelstein, Burke, & Raju, 1995; Gordon & Arvey, 2004; Kite & Johnson, 1988; Kite, Stockdale, & Whitley, 2005; Perry, Kulik, & Bourhis, 1996). General perceptions by employers are that older workers are less flexible, less adaptive, less risky, and more forgetful than younger people. Many of these perceptions are based on a lack of knowledge about aging and more specifically about aging and work. This lack of knowledge stems from limited research on aging and work productivity, especially for today's jobs. Innovations in technology are creating fundamental changes in work such that there is an increased emphasis on cognition and information processing demands in a majority of work activities. Specifically, the introduction of technology across all work sectors serves to provide workers with greater access to greater amounts of information and the need to engage in problem solving and decision-making activities.

The increase in information-processing demands in work situations can be manifest in a number of different ways. Most importantly, the worker will be required to integrate much larger amounts of information. In addition, the need that often arises in modern technological workplaces for monitoring an array of automated processes increases demands on multitasking by requiring workers to access information from related work processes and to subsequently evaluate the effects of actions on these processes. There is also the assumption that new technologies will continue to become available at rapid paces, which will require that workers recognize the similarities and differences between new and previous technological tools and adapt accordingly. Finally, workers will continually need to learn new skills to keep abreast of changes in work demands and workplace technologies.

As we consider these technologically driven changes in the workplace, the important question concerns whether older workers can successfully adapt to work conditions that impose these types of cognitive demands. These issues suggest a number of directions for future research on aging and work. For instance, we know that older people demonstrate declines in various cognitive abilities, especially those that reflect speed of processing, problem solving, and multitasking. What we do not know is the extent to which declines in these abilities can be compensated for by job knowledge and experience or are modifiable by training or design interventions.

The current emphasis on lean manufacturing in industry exemplifies many of these considerations. In today's manufacturing environments, customized products need to be assembled quickly, requiring the ability to anticipate changes and make adjustments. The ability to work in teams is also critical, requiring integrating information from a number of different people as well as from multiple electronic formats (e.g., information displays) across various production processes. Workers in lean manufacturing enterprises must detect changes in orders, make corresponding changes in process plans and schedules, and always be ready to deal with shifting priorities. Implicit to these activities is the ability to interact efficiently with information technologies and other task-related technologies.

In the face of difficult or challenging demands, do older workers somehow compensate for decreased cognitive capabilities, perhaps by tailoring their work activities in a way to reduce the information-processing burdens? We also need to examine if they do so at the cost of work-related stress. Furthermore, we need to examine the extent to which experience and the increased skills in judgment that may accompany the accumulation of knowledge reduce the impact of cognitive declines, and the extent to which changes in processing speed and capacity represent a fundamental bottleneck that undermine an older worker's performance under challenging conditions. Research on these issues will probably need to examine closely the contexts under which older workers may be required to perform. A detailed analysis of work contexts will enable, for example, the identification of periods during which the task demands are likely to exceed the information-processing capacities of many older people, and the identification of demands for which compensation through knowledge and experience may not be afforded. Understanding the contextual elements of work will also enable us to understand how factors other than abilities, such as environmental distractions, influence the ability of older people to adapt to today's work environment.

There are also many questions that need to be addressed with respect to training. In particular, *e-learning* has become an important platform for job training for many companies and organizations, especially those that engage in telework. With respect to on-line learning, there are numerous issues regarding older workers that warrant investigation. For example, in training older workers do deficits in working memory abilities, attentional capacities, and technological knowledge diminish the capability of older people to learn new jobs through interaction with software routines? If research suggests that this concern is in fact well founded, the next logical research question is whether training interventions can circumvent these problems.

For example, in theory multimedia arrangements can reduce the memory load in learning, thus facilitating better integration of information and ultimately the development of mental models that are more conducive to successful task performance (Tardieu & Gyselinck, 2003). However, an open research issue is whether such arrangements actually impose even greater demands on the older learner. For instance, there is evidence suggesting that older people are less efficient at processing multiple sources of information than are younger people. We may also find that the potential utility of multimedia may be manifest only when we consider many other facets of the learning process, including issues related to practice schedules, motivation, and self-efficacy.

Finally, regardless of how many older adults adopt technology, there will always be a lag in technical expertise between younger and older workers due to the reality that a steady stream of new technologies will continue to emerge. Consequently, we should always expect to confront the issue of gaps in the technical knowledge of older workers as they attempt to reenter or become reassigned in the workforce. Thus, another important research issue concerns interventions that will provide the best opportunity for closing or bridging these gaps.

Practical Implications of What We Currently Know About Older Workers

Clearly there is a robust literature available on aging and basic abilities, training, and learning. At the same time, as discussed previously there are many unanswered questions regarding older workers. One of these questions is the potential implications of aging for the design of work environments, jobs, and training protocols. In other words, how can we apply what we know about aging to maximize the ability of older adults to remain productive in today's work environments?

Overall, we know that older people are both willing and capable of engaging in work activities and learning new skills, and that older workers can have high levels of domain knowledge and expertise. There is also little evidence to suggest that productivity declines with age. Furthermore, older workers tend to be more reliable; absenteeism rates are lower for older workers. However, we also know that there are changes in certain processes and abilities that occur as part of the aging process which have implications for design of work activities and work environments. For example, age-related declines in strength, stamina, and response speed have implications for job design such that jobs that are physically demanding or highly paced may be unsuitable for older workers. Flexible work schedules or alternative work arrangements such as working from home may also be preferred by older people, especially those who have some type of mobility impairment or caregiving responsibility. Work/rest schedules also need to be carefully evaluated for older workers as do the information-processing and time-sharing demands of tasks.

There are also perceptual and sensory changes that occur with age that have implications for the design of the ambient environment, displays, and instructional materials. Generally, levels of illumination need to be higher for older adults and potential sources of glare need to be minimized. Background noise should also be kept to a minimum and the use of high frequency alerting and warning signals should be avoided. Age-related changes in vision also have implications for the design of visual displays, Web sites, and written instructional materials. Careful consideration needs to be given to the size, contrast, and organization and of text, and clutter should be kept to a minimum. Age-related changes in motor skills and flexibility also have implications for the design of control and input devices such as a mouse or keyboard. Older adults, especially those with chronic conditions such as arthritis, may find it difficult to perform tasks or use devices that require fine motor coordination or repetitive movements.

Finally, there are age-related changes in cognition which have relevance to the design of training programs. Generally, self-paced training protocols are preferable by older adults, and it is important to allow extra time for training as well as more practice. Additionally, it is important to provide opportunities for the learner to be actively involved in the learning process and minimize demands on working memory. It is also important to ensure that older workers have access to training programs and are encouraged to engage in training activities.

These recommendations provide a brief summary of design guidelines to help accommodate older people in the workplace. There are other excellent sources of this material (e.g., Fisk et al., 2004). Perhaps the most important take home message is that older adults need to be considered as active, productive, and valuable members of today's workforce. As such, consideration needs to be given to their needs, preferences, and abilities. In most instances, systems and environments that are designed to accommodate older adults will benefit other user groups.

ACKNOWLEDGMENTS

This research was supported by the National Institute on Aging via grant NIA 1 PO1 AG17211–05, Project CREATE.

REFERENCES

A nation online: How Americans are expanding their use of the Internet (2002). US Department of Commerce study. Retrieved December 29, 2004, from http://www.ntia .doc.gov/ntiahome/dn/Nation_Online.pdf

Bouma, H. (1992). Gerontechnology: Making technology relevant for the elderly. In H. Bouma and J. A. M. Graafmans (Eds.), *Gerontechnology* (pp. 1–5). Amsterdam: IOS Press.

Buessing, A. (2000). Telework. In W. Karwowski (Ed.), *International encyclopedia of ergonomics and human factors* (pp. 1723–1725). London: Taylor & Francis.

Burdick, D. C., &. Kwon, S. (Eds.). (2005), *Gerotechnology: Research and practice in technology and aging—A textbook and reference for multiple disciplines.* NY: Springer.

Charness, N. (2003). Access, motivation, ability, design, and training: Necessary conditions for older adult success with technology. In N. Charness & K. W. Schaie (Eds.), *Impact of technology on successful aging* (pp. 15–27). New York: Springer.

Charness, N. (2004). Coining new words: Old (Greek) wine in new bottles? (Reply). *Gerontechnology, 3,* 52–53.

Charness, N., & Czaja, S. J. (2005). Adaptation to new technologies (7.13). In M. L. Johnson (General Editor). *Cambridge handbook on age and ageing* (pp. 662–669). Cambridge, UK: Cambridge University Press.

Charness, N., Holley, P., Feddon, J., & Jastrzembski, T. (2004). Light pen use and practice minimize age and hand performance differences in pointing tasks. *Human Factors, 46,* 373–384.

Charness, N., Kelley, C. L., Bosman, E. A., & Mottram, M. (2001). Word processing training and retraining: Effects of adult age, experience, and interface. *Psychology and Aging, 16,* 110–127.

Czaja, S. J., Charness, N., Fisk, A. D., Hertzog, C., Nair, S. N., Rogers, W. A., & Sharit, J. (2006). Factors predicting the use of technology: Findings from the Center for Research and Education on Aging and Technology Enhancement (CREATE). *Psychology and Aging, 21,* 333–352.

Czaja, S. J., & Sharit, J. (1998). Ability-performance relationships as a function of age and task experience for a data entry task. *Journal of Experimental Psychology: Applied, 4,* 332–351.

Czaja, S. J., Sharit, J., Ownby, R., Roth, D., & Nair, S. (2001). Examining Age Differences in Performance of a Complex Information Search and Retrieval Task. *Psychology and Aging, 16,* 564–579.

Czaja, S. J., Sharit, J., Charness, N., Fisk, A. D., & Rogers, W. (2001). The Center for Research and Education on Aging and Technology Enhancement (CREATE): A program to enhance technology for older adults. *Gerontechnology, 1*, 50–59.

Finkelstein, L. M., Burke, M. J., & Raju, N. S. (1995). Age discrimination in simulated employment contexts: An integrative analysis. *Journal of Applied Psychology, 80*, 652–663.

Fisk, A. D., Rogers, W. A., Charness, N., Czaja, S. J., & Sharit, J. (2004). *Designing for older adults: Principles and creative human factors approaches.* Boca Raton: CRC Press.

Fozard, J., & Gordon-Salant, S. (2001). Changes in vision and hearing with aging. In J. E. Birren & K. W. Schaie (Eds.), *Handbook of the psychology of aging,* (5th ed., pp. 241–266). San Diego: Academic Press.

Gordon, R. A., & Arvey, R. D. (2004). Age bias in laboratory and field settings: A meta-analytic investigation. *Journal of Applied Social Psychology, 34*, 468–492.

Hamil-Luker, J., & Uhlenberg, P. (2002). Later life education in the 1990s: Increasing involvement and continuing disparity. *Journal of Gerontology, 57B*, S324–S331.

Jastrzembski, T., Charness, N., Holley, P., & Feddon, J. (2005). Aging and input devices: Voice recognition is slower yet more acceptable than a lightpen. *Proceedings of the 49th Annual Meeting of the Human Factors and Ergonomics Society.* Orlando, FL.

Kalasky, M. A., Czaja, S. J., Sharit, J., & Nair, S. N. (1999). "Is speech technology robust for older populations?" *Proceedings of the 43rd Annual Meeting of the Human Factors and Ergonomics Society.* Santa Monica, CA.

Kanungo, R. B. (1982). *Work alienation: An integrated approach.* New York: Praeger.

Kite, M. E., & Johnson, B. T. (1988). Attitudes toward older and younger adults: A meta-analysis. *Psychology and Aging, 3*, 233–244.

Kite, M. E., Stokdale, G.D., & Whitley, B. E., Jr., (2005). Attitudes toward younger and older adults: An updated meta-analytic review. *Journal of Social Issues, 61*, 241–266.

Kubeck, J. E., Delp, N. D., Haslett, T. K., & McDaniel, M. A. (1996). Does job-related training performance decline with age? *Psychology and Aging, 11*, 92–107.

Park, D. C., & Swartz, N. (2000). *Cognitive aging: A primer.* Philadelphia, PA: Taylor & Francis.

Perry, E. L., Kulik, C. T., & Bourhis, A. C. (1996). Moderating effects of personal and contextual factors in age discrimination. *Journal of Applied Psychology, 81*, 628–647.

Rainie, L., & Packel, D. (2001). More online, doing more. 16 million newcomers gain Internet access in the last half of 2000 as women, minorities, and families with modest incomes continue to surge online. Retrieved December 29, 2004, from http://www.pewinternet.org/PPF/r/30/report_display.asp

Rogers, W., & Fisk, A. (2000). Human factors, applied cognition, and aging. In F. I. M. Craik & T. A. Salthouse (Eds.), *The handbook of aging and cognition.* Mahwah, NJ: Lawrence Erlbaum Associates.

Rogers, W. A., Fisk, A. D., McLaughlin, A. C., & Pak, R. (in press). Touch a screen or turn a knob: Choosing the best device for the job. *Human Factors.*

Roring, R. W., Hines, F. G., & Charness, N. (accepted, a). Age-related identification of emotions at different image sizes. *Human Factors.*

Roring, R. W., Hines, F. G., & Charness, N. (accepted, b). Age differences in identifying words in synthetic speech. *Human Factors.*

Salthouse, T. A., & Maurer, J. J. (1996). Aging, job performance, and career development. In J. E. Birren & K. W. Schaie (Eds.), *Handbook of the psychology of aging* (4th ed., pp. 353–364). New York: Academic Press.

Seashore, S. E., Lawler III, E. E., Mirvis, P. H., & Cammann, C. (1982). *Assessing organizational change: A guide to methods, measures, and practices.* New York: Wiley.

Sharit, J., Czaja, S. J., Hernandez, M., Yang, Y., Perdomo, D., Lewis, J. E., Lee, C. C., & Nair, S. (2004). An evaluation of performance by older persons on a simulated telecommuting task. *Journal of Gerontology: Psychological Sciences, 59B,* 305–316.

Smith, M. W., Sharit, J., & Czaja, S. J. (1999). Aging, motor control, and the performance of computer mouse tasks. *Human Factors, 41,* 389–396.

Tacken, M., Marcellini, F., Mollenkopf, H., Ruoppila, I., & Széman, Z. (2005). Use and acceptance of new technology by older people. Findings of the international MOBILATE survey: 'Enhancing mobility in later life.' *Gerontechnology, 3,* 126–137.

Tardieu, H., & Gyselinck, V. (2003). Working memory constraints in the integration and comprehension of information in a multimedia context. In H. van Oostendorp (Ed.), *Cognition in a Digital World.* Mahwah, NJ: Lawrence Erlbaum Associates.

The UCLA Internet report—"Surveying the Digital Future" 2003, UCLA Center for Communication Policy, Box 951586, Los Angeles, CA 90095-1586. Retrieved August 14, 2003, from http://www.ccp.ucla.edu/pdf/UCLA-Internet-Report-Year-Three.pdf

Toosi, M. (2004). Labor force projections to 2012: The graying of the U.S. workforce. *Monthly Labor Review, 127*(2), 37–57.

U. S. Office of Personnel Management. (2003) http://www.telework.gov/

Venkatesh, V., & Davis, F. D. (2000). A theoretical extension of the technology acceptance model: Four longitudinal case studies. *Management Science, 46,* 186–204.

Warr, P. (2000). Job performance and the ageing workforce. In N. Chmiel (Ed.), *Work and organizational psychology* (pp. 408–423). Malden, MA: Blackwell.

Warr, P., Cook, J., & Wall, T. (1979). Scales for the measurement of some work attitudes and aspects of psychological wellbeing. *Journal of Occupational Psychology, 52,* 129–148.

Wegman, D. H., & McGee, J. P. (Eds.) (2004). *Health and safety needs of older workers.* Washington, DC: National Research Council.

Weiss, D. J., Dawis, R. V., England, G. W., & Lofquist, L. H. (1967). *Manual for the Minnesota Satisfaction Questionnaire.* Minneapolis, MN: The University of Minnesota Press.

Worden, A., Walker, N., Bharat, K., & Hudson, S. (1997). Making computers easier for older adults to use: Area cursors and sticky icons. *Proceedings of CHI '97,* 266–271.

12

Aging and Work/Family Issues

Boris B. Baltes and Lindsey M. Young

This chapter explores work/family issues that are relevant to the aging of the population. As the population ages, the workforce itself is also aging, making it important to explore work/family issues across the life span. A review of the literature suggests older and younger workers differ both in the priorities they assign to work and family, as well as in their willingness to engage in coping behaviors to help balance the two domains. In addition, as the general population continues to age, more workers likely have the responsibility of caring for aging relatives. Thus, this chapter also reviews the many work/family issues uniquely resulting from these eldercare responsibilities. An overview of these topics and the practical implications of this line of research are provided. Gaps in the current literature that require future research are also discussed.

The rapid aging of the population in most industrialized countries reflects many factors such as the decline and stabilization of fertility rates since the birth of the baby boom generation, and, more importantly, an increase in life expectancy, and the entry of the large baby boom cohort into normal retirement age. In the United States it is estimated that the population over age 65 will rise from 13 percent now to 20 percent in 2050 and to 23 percent by 2100; and, similarly, the proportion over age 85 is expected to triple from less than 2 percent to 6.5 percent. This aging of the population will have two major effects on work/family issues. First, the aging of the population also means that the workforce will age. That is, the average age of the workforce will increase and older workers may have different work/family issues and needs than younger workers, and as a consequence, organizations and society may have to rethink how they help workers deal with balancing work and family. Thus, the first section of this chapter will focus on investigating work/family issues across the life span. Second, as the general population continues to age, the number of workers that will need to care for their aging relatives will also likely increase. This increase in eldercare responsibilities has implications for the study of work and family across the life span, and, further, the unique consequences of working and providing eldercare are many. Therefore, the second section of this chapter will be an in-depth discussion of eldercare issues as they relate to the balance between work and family.

DEFINING WORK AND FAMILY ISSUES

To most researchers work/family issues revolve around achieving a balance between these two facets of life. More specifically, most research has been conducted on work/family conflict. Work/family conflict occurs when the conflicting pressures between work and family become incompatible so that participation in one role is made more difficult because of participation in the other role (Greenhaus & Beutell, 1985). Managing the conflict (or alternatively, achieving a balance) between work and family has always been a challenge for employees; however, this challenge has increased as greater numbers of households change from single earner to dual earner. Conflict between work and family roles can be seen to have two facets: work interfering with family (WIF) and family interfering with work (FIW; Frone, Russell, & Cooper, 1992). Work interfering with family and/or family interfering with work conflicts occur when "(a) time devoted to the requirements of one role makes it difficult to fulfill requirements of another; (b) strain from participation in one role makes it difficult to fulfill requirements of another; or (c) specific behaviors required by one role make it difficult to fulfill requirements of another" (Greenhaus & Beutell, 1985; p. 76).

Work/family conflict models propose that conflict arises when the demands of one domain are incompatible with demands of the other domain (Adams, King, & King, 1996). Frone, et al. (1992) asserted that a reciprocal relationship between WIF and FIW conflicts exist based on the assumption that if work stressors (e.g., work pressure) begin to interfere with family obligations, these unfulfilled family obligations may then begin to interfere with work functions. The conflict that occurs between work and nonwork roles can be a source of stress, with physical and psychological outcomes for the individual. These outcomes have been shown to impact the work organization (e.g., burnout, reduced job satisfaction) as well as family relationships (e.g., marital and life satisfaction, child and adolescent adjustment) of the individual (e.g., Allen, Herst, Bruck, & Sutton, 2000; Frone, et al., 1992). In sum, work/family conflict can have a significant impact on the quality of both work and family life, and thus, it is of great interest to understand how and why work/family conflict occurs so that one can determine what type of individual level strategies and/or organizational support mechanisms can best help employees successfully balance work and family.

One of the largest potential causes of work/family conflict is the presence of children, especially young ones, and the extensive amount of childcare they require. However, the increase in the number of elderly individuals in the industrialized societies and the need for families to care for them has caused a new potential stressor that may become just as, or even more, important than childcare challenges, with respect to work/family conflict, in the future. In addition, as mentioned earlier, as the societies of the industrialized countries age, so will their workforces. Thus it is important to examine how this change may affect several issues central to work/family balance/conflict, as will be discussed later in detail.

OLDER EMPLOYEES AND WORK/FAMILY ISSUES

Though there is surprisingly little research on the topic, it seems incredibly important to investigate whether there are differences between older and younger workers in regards to how they experience and react to juggling the two domains of work and family. Specifically, in this section of the chapter, we will address three basic questions. First, what are the work/family issues across the life span and do older workers report more or less work/family conflict than younger workers? Second, are the type and/or amount of coping strategies used by older workers similar to younger workers? Third, do older workers need and/or desire different organizational policies/practices to help them deal with work/family issues?

Work/Family Issues Across the Life Span

The aging of the workforce will quite probably change the way organizations and the average worker view work/family issues. To date, there have been two central theoretical models with which one can form propositions about what this change may entail. The first model, referred to as the life-stages approach, relies on developmental stages that concern criteria such as family size and the developmental age of the oldest child. The second model concerns the emphasis that is placed on the career versus on the family by individuals across the lifespan.

Life stages. With respect to the developmental stages of individuals (and families) studies have demonstrated (e.g., Keith & Schafer, 1991; Schnittger & Bird, 1990) that an individual's life-cycle stage is associated with work and family role demands (i.e., potential for work/family conflict). Life-cycle stages refer to the variations in work and family role demands encountered during the life course (Aldous, 1978). It should be pointed out that life-cycle stages are not tied to chronological age (although the stages are correlated with age) but are distinctive role structures that separate them from other periods. The most commonly used conceptualization of the life-stage process revolves around a categorization system that is based on several criteria, first proposed by Duval and Hill (1948), which include; family size, the developmental age of the oldest child, and the work status of the breadwinners (Hill, 1986). Family size is divided into five categories: 1) stable stage, childless; 2) expanding stage, childbearing; 3) stable stage, childrearing; 4) contracting stage, launching; 5) stable stage, empty nest. The developmental age of the oldest child generates new stages within the expanding and stable childbearing stages of family size categories: 1) family with preschool children; 2) family with school age children; 3) family with adolescents; 4) family with young adults. Finally, work status of the breadwinners generates two additional stages within the stable empty nest stage: 1) family in the middle years; 2) family in the retirement phase. Using these criteria one can advance eight mutually exclusive categories of development:

1. Establishment stage (childless, newly married)
2. First parenthood (family with infant to 3 years)
3. Family with preschool children (oldest child 3–6 years of age)
4. Family with school children (oldest child 6–12 years of age)
5. Family with adolescents (oldest child 13–20 years of age)
6. Family as launching center (children begin to leave the home)
7. Family in middle years (postparental empty nest)
8. Family in retirement (breadwinners in retirement).

When one considers the life stages of working individuals, one would probably only want to use the first seven categories since life stage number eight involves retirement. With respect to work/family conflict, studies have shown that conflict between work and family increases as one enters into marriage and/or has children (Higgins, Duxbury, & Lee, 1994). However, research also suggests that as the age of the youngest child increases (i.e., as individuals/families move up thru the stages) the amount of work/family conflict experienced will decrease. Most job strain models (e.g., Karasek, 1979) would support the theory that work/family conflict should decrease as the age of the youngest child increases. Job strain models predict that stress will be the greatest in situations where employees have little or no control of the stressor. Since parents with younger children experience heavy and often unpredictable demands on their time (e.g., Hochschild, 2003), it is not surprising that they generally report the highest level of work/family conflict.

For example, Staines and O'Connor (1980) found work/family conflict to be related to the age of the youngest child in the home. Specifically, parents with children under 6 years of age reported higher levels of work/family conflict than parents of school-age children. An interesting study by Higgins et al.(1994), used the life-stage approach, and categorized individuals into three life-cycle stages; 1) families with preschool children, 2) families with young school-age children, and 3) families with adolescents. Using a large sample ($N = 3,616$) of Canadian public sector employees, they found that an individual's life stage was related to both work interfering with family and family interfering with work conflict. Specifically, for both men and women, levels of both types of work/family conflict were lower in the later life stages. It should be pointed out, however, that some gender differences were found in that while men reported lower levels of conflict in each successive life stage, women reported similar levels of work/family conflict in the early stages and then reported a large drop off in work/family conflict in later life stages.

In sum, the life-stages approach and most research seem to support the idea that work/family conflict will increase during the first few stages but then decrease as individuals move through the later life stages. Furthermore, since the life stages are correlated with age, one can also predict, and again research supports, the assertion that work/family conflict will show this same nonlinear relationship with age, and that those older individuals, who are in the later life stages, will experience less work/family conflict. One might also be tempted to assume that work/family conflict, and its negative outcomes, will be less of a concern to individuals and organizations in the future given the aging of the workforce. However, before one jumps to this conclusion, two things should be kept in mind. First, eldercare does not currently play into the criteria that are used to categorize an individual's life stage. As will be discussed in great detail later in the chapter, eldercare presents individuals with unique challenges in their struggle to balance work and family responsibilities. Eldercare responsibilities are not limited to younger workers, as older workers may also bear this responsibility. By including eldercare, one would essentially add another potential stressor to each life stage which would mean that the later stages of working individuals (i.e., stages 5, 6, and 7 of the current model) may not be as stress free as the original model predicts.

Furthermore, much of the research done on age and work/family conflict was done some years ago before eldercare became such a prominent issue. Thus, while current research suggests a nonlinear relationship between age and work/family conflict (i.e., WFC increases during the first few life stages, and then begins to decrease), future research including eldercare in the life stages model, may not replicate this nonlinear relationship. Second, as we will see below, while work/family conflict may decrease with age, that does not mean that the issue of balancing work and family is less important to older workers—the exact opposite actually appears to be the case.

Varying importance of work versus family.   Research has demonstrated that there does seem to be a shift in the importance individuals attribute to their career versus their family across the lifespan. Specifically, it appears as though younger employees focus more on their career than older employees (Evans & Bartolomé, 1984; Staudinger, 1996). Furthermore, when considering work/family conflict, younger workers focus more on the problems/challenges with their children than on their relationship with their significant others. This is not surprising given that young children are a large determinant of reported work/family conflict (e.g., Grandey & Cropanazano, 1999; Staines & O'Connor, 1980). Older employees, in contrast, report paying more attention to private life in general and to their marriages in particular. Not only does the importance given to work versus family seem to change over the life course, but it appears that importance given to balancing the two does, as well.

A series of interesting studies by Evans and Bartolomé (1979, 1981, 1984) presented evidence for the case that older employees show much "more sensitivity to the problems and opportunities present in their leisure and family lives" (p. 19; Evans & Bartolomé, 1984). In essence, balancing work and family life seems to take on more importance for older employees. Furthermore, the evidence from these studies also suggests that older employees, unlike younger employees, do not see work/family conflict as a given and undertake more coping strategies. It is interesting to note that Evans and Bartolomé also state that there are large individual differences in this process. Specifically, how employees perceived the relationship between work and family was important. In their studies they measured five possible relationships between work and family: 1) spillover, one affects the other in either a positive or negative way; 2) independence, they exist side by side and are independent; 3) conflict, work, and family are in conflict with one another; 4) instrumentality, one is primarily a means to obtain something desired in the other; and 5) compensation, one is a way for making up for what is lacking in the other. They found, for example, that older individuals who reported an instrumental orientation, used the new found emphasis on their private lives as a way for them to rationalize their perceived failure in their career goals. For these individuals, their new found emphasis on their family actually had negative affects on their private lives.

In sum, however, the research suggests that the shift in focus from work to family, along with an increased use of coping strategies to meet both sets of obligations, would lead to lower levels of work/family conflict in older workers. This proposition coincides with that of life-stages research and results in an overall conclusion that there is a life course for work/family conflict and, in general, it is one of decreasing conflict as workers enter their later years. However, since one main reason for this decrease in conflict is due to the fact that work/family balance takes on greater importance for individuals, it would appear as though organizations will still need to concern themselves with helping their employees balance work and family. Finally, it should again be pointed out, that the increasing prevalence of eldercare issues may push back the age by which work/family conflict begins to decline. Thus, future research on the life course of work/family conflict needs to focus on including eldercare both in theoretical models (i.e., developmental stages) as well as in empirical research.

Type and Use of Coping Strategies

As mentioned earlier, research indicates that older workers may be engaging in more coping behaviors than younger workers. Research that has focused more explicitly on coping styles and behaviors, with respect to handling work/family conflict, have, to date, relied on two main coping models. The first model is a typology that was proposed by Hall (1972) and includes strategies that can be categorized into three major types. Type 1 coping involves structural role re-definition and revolves around behaviors that would alter externally imposed expectations (e.g., utilizing social support, elimination of some activities). Type 2 coping involves personal role redefinition such as changing one's perception of what is expected of him/her in a given role (e.g., setting priorities). Type 3 coping entails reactive role behavior and in essence means that a person attempts to meet all role requirements simultaneously. While the first two coping types are considered positive in nature, the type 3 coping style would most often lead to negative outcomes (Hall, 1972).

A study by Schnittger and Bird (1990) measured coping behaviors using the Hall typology and examined whether the behaviors reported changed across the life stages mentioned earlier. The specific coping factors they measured included: 1) cognitive restructuring, 2) delegating, 3) limiting avocational activities, 4) subordinating career, 5) compartmentalizing, 6) avoiding responsibility, and 7) using social support. The results indicate that, on average, the amount of coping behaviors reported seemed to follow a positive linear relationship. Specifically, individuals reported increasing use of coping behaviors as they progressed through the life stages. However, it should be pointed out that this differed by the specific coping factor considered and by gender. For example, reported use of social support seemed to decline across the life stages and reported use of subordinating career was nonlinear in nature with the largest reported use in the middle life stages and smaller reported use in the early and late life stages.

The second coping model that has been presented in the work/family literature involves the use of adaptive behaviors and is entitled selection, optimization, and compensation (SOC). SOC was originally developed as a life-span model to explain successful adaptation to the loss of resources due to aging through adjustments in the use and allocation of resources (Baltes, 1997;

Baltes & Baltes, 1990; Freund & Baltes, 2002). Selection is primarily concerned with setting goals. Optimization refers to changes in the allocation and/or refinement of resources in order to achieve goals and compensation that occur when alternate means are used to maintain role functioning in the face of actual or anticipated decreased resources. A study by Baltes and Heydens-Gahir (2003) demonstrated that the use of SOC behaviors is related to perceived amounts of the job stressors and family stressors reported by individuals. More specifically, people who reported using SOC-related strategies also reported lower amounts of job and family stressors and subsequently lower levels of work/family conflict. Furthermore, the results indicated that the amount of SOC behaviors reported (especially behaviors related to work activities) were correlated with age. Specifically, older individuals reported increased use of SOC behaviors.

In sum, the empirical results using both types of coping models indicate that older employees report a higher use of coping behaviors. This finding is not surprising given that the research mentioned earlier on the changing importance of work versus family across the life course indicated that older workers reported being more concerned with balancing work and family, and using coping strategies should help one achieve that goal.

One interesting question that has not been addressed in detail, unfortunately, by the current research is whether there is an interaction between age and type of coping strategy used. That is, it is possible that while older employees report using more behaviors, this may differ when one considers the specific coping factors separately. Furthermore, do older employees become more efficient in their use of coping behaviors? The Schnittger and Bird (1990) article mentioned earlier did begin to examine this issue, but much more future research is needed on this topic.

Assistance in Dealing with Work/Family Issues

While employees use individual coping strategies to deal with work/family conflict, organizations have also attempted to help their employees deal with this issue. Policies and programs that organizations have implemented include on-site childcare, maternity and paternity leave, child sick days, and flexible scheduling, among many others. Family benefits provided by the organization are believed to assuage work/family conflict by enabling employees to have greater control over the work and family domains (Goff, Mount, & Jamison, 1990) and studies (Sinclair, Hannigan, & Tetrick, 1995; Warren & Johnson, 1995) have shown that the number of family benefits provided by the organization and used by the employee is negatively related to work/family conflict and strain, while positively related to employee attitudes about the support-iveness of the organization. However, older and younger employees are most probably quite differently affected by the implementation of various programs and policies, and thus, one can hypothesize that the aging of the workforce will change which programs and policies will positively affect the majority of an or-ganization's workforce.

For instance, on-site childcare will probably not be viewed as a major ben-efit to dealing with work/family issues for an older employee, while it may be of the utmost importance to a younger worker with young children. Furthermore, maternity and paternity leave will not be viewed by the majority of the em-ployees as an important benefit if an organization's workforce is made up of predominantly older employees. The increased occurrence of eldercare will mean that child sick days may become less important and the employees will consider eldercare sick days of greater importance. In the same vein, flexible work schedules and even the implementation of job sharing should be very attractive to older workers who seem to place a larger importance on the bal-ancing of work and family than younger workers. In sum, it would appear that the benefits offered to employees will have to be reconsidered and adjusted if an organization wants to be viewed as family friendly to its aging workforce.

Interestingly enough, policies put into place to attract and retain older workers may already be undertaking some of the adjustments that are needed. Many organizations are realizing that the impending workforce shortage, due to retirement of the baby boom generation, will mean that the retention of older workers will become very important. This is especially true for knowledge driven organizations where companies may lose their competitive edge because of this impending "brain drain" (Albright & Cluff, 2005). Thus, many com-panies (both private and public) as well as national governments are putting policies into place to both attract, but especially retain, older workers (Coates, Jarratt, & Mahaffie, 1990). These policies include phasing retirement, modi-fying retirement plans, modifying compensation plans, customizing benefits, job sharing, and redesigning the job. For example, the MITRE corporation has made its retirement benefits much more attractive (e.g., increased the employer contribution, instituted immediate vesting) to not only retain but also recruit older employees (Albright & Cluff, 2005). The MITRE Corpora-tion has also introduced a phased retirement plan where older workers can begin to decrease their work hours but still receive benefits. While these changes in company policies are meant to attract and retain older workers, they may also be having the unintended benefit of helping older workers bal-ance work and family. Given that the research suggests that achieving this goal is of greater importance to older workers, it would appear that many of the new policies mentioned herein are already making some of the adjustments that will be needed for an aging workforce to balance work/family issues.

Unfortunately, what older workers may want in terms of organizational benefits to help balance work and family can only be speculated on at this point since the research on this topic is almost nonexistent. Thus, future research needs to study what family-friendly benefits are most desired by older workers and which are most effective at reducing older employees' perceived work/family conflict.

In sum, it seems that there are differences between older and younger workers in terms of both the extent to which they experience work/family conflict, and in how they seek to manage the two domains. As previously mentioned, eldercare issues are likely becoming more prevalent and may influence the differences between older and younger workers' work-life balance. As discussed in the following section, there is an abundance of research that has investigated eldercare as it relates to the balance between work and family.

ELDERCARE

According to the AARP (1995), in 1986, about 6.1 million older individuals were having troubles with one or more of the activities required of them in their daily lives (e.g., bathing, eating, getting outside). In 1998, it was estimated that one quarter of the workforce served as eldercare providers (Bond, Galinsky, & Swanberg, 1998). Given the steady increase in the proportion of elderly, many of them needing daily assistance, it is likely that the number of working adults attempting to balance careers and eldercare responsibilities has also increased—a trend that is expected to continue to grow rapidly over the next decades. While the majority of research investigating balancing work and caregiving has focused on childcare (Neal, Chapman, Ingersoll-Dayton, & Emlen, 1993), researchers have begun to realize the importance of investigating eldercare issues as they relate to work, as is evident by the increased attention to the topic. The purpose of this section is to provide a synopsis of the research that has been conducted thus far involving the balance between work and eldercare responsibilities.

Balancing Work and Eldercare: Consequences of the Juggling Act

Guberman and Maheu (1999) suggest that without a proper balance between caregiving and work, one of the two spheres will be compromised. More specifically, not finding a proper balance between work and eldercare may jeopardize the quality of care that is given as well as the individual's standing within his/her organization. Research investigating the impact of working and providing eldercare has in fact indicated that participation in both domains leads to numerous negative consequences. Personal negative consequences include increased stress (e.g., Neal et al., 1993), increased work/family conflict (e.g., Hepburn, 1996) and other physical aliments such as anxiety, sleeping problems, and headaches (e.g., Wagner, 1987). Aside from individual consequences, a great deal of research has focused on investigating organizational consequences.

Organizational consequences. An abundance of evidence suggests that eldercare negatively impacts the amount of time that an individual spends at work (e.g., Dautzenberg, Diederiks, Philipsen, Stevens, & Vernooij Dassen, 2000; Enright & Friss, 1987; Gibeau & Anastas, 1989; Scharlach & Boyd, 1989; Singelton, 2000). For example, Enright and Friss (1987) found that 55 percent of working caregivers reported missing work, with the average absenteeism among these employees being 9 hours per month. Additionally, Singelton (2000) suggests that employees who provide eldercare lose approximately 4.8 million dollars in unpaid work, missed wages, and lost opportunities. Even when a caregiver is present at work, there is evidence suggesting that they are not performing to their maximum potential. To provide a few examples, Enright and Friss (1987) found that over half of employees also involved in eldercare felt that they sometimes worked more slowly because of worries brought on by the caregiving role. Further, care-giving employees report higher accident rates, lower productivity, and more use of their work time for personal phone calls (Dellmann-Jenkins, Bennett, & Brahce, 1994).

Potentially even more detrimental, past research has found that care-giving employees often have to rearrange their work schedules (e.g., Orodenker, 1990). Not only is altering work schedules often difficult for the employer, Orodenker (1990) found rearranging one's schedule in order to accommodate eldercare responsibilities to be a significant predictor of stress for the individual. In the worst case, employees are forced to abandon their jobs completely to pursue full-time care. Stone, Cafferata, and Sangl (1987) reported that 11 percent of caregivers have to leave their jobs entirely because of their eldercare demands. Such early abandonment of one's career may cause individuals to feel stressed, frustrated, and full of regret or even animosity toward their caregiver role or even toward the care recipient (e.g. Harris, Long, & Fujii, 1998).

As pointed out in Neal et al. (1993), there are many factors that likely contribute to the extent to which individuals experience negative consequences resulting from their participation in both work and eldercare roles. Such factors are discussed in the following section:

Gender. A great deal of research investigating the balance between work and eldercare has focused on exploring whether the consequences of these demands are different for men and women. Researchers have focused their attention toward this potential differential impact because women are typically seen as assuming the eldercare role to a greater extent than men. As indicated in a 1987 national survey, women have traditionally assumed the majority of the eldercare responsibilities (Stone et al., 1987). Further, research has suggested that working men reduce the amount of eldercare that they involve themselves in, while working women do not reduce their involvement in eldercare (Stoller, 1983). Thus, it stands to reason that working women may be impacted differently by eldercare than their working male counterparts.

Aside from the amount of care given by men and women, the type of care given to elders has been shown to be different according to gender. In 1985, Horowitz suggested that women tend to provide more domestic and personal care services, while such tasks as financial management are more evenly distributed between men and women caregivers. Similarly, Singelton (2000) suggests that while men partake in instrumental care activities such as lawn mowing, women tend to help with the activities of daily life (e.g., feeding, bathing, and clothing). Thus, the care that women tend to provide is not only more extensive, but also more time-consuming and more likely to interfere with their own daily activities (including work).

Additionally, research exploring gender differences suggests that women tend to experience negative consequences to a greater degree as a result of their caregiving role. For example, Buffardi, Smith, O'Brien, and Edwins (1999) found that women caregivers report more absenteeism from work and more general stress then their working and care-giving male counterparts. Further, while working men are more likely to reduce their caregiver role, working women are more likely to distance themselves from the organization through taking time off without pay, reducing their hours, and rearranging their work schedules. Such differences in coping with the competing demands of eldercare and work likely put women at a disadvantage in the workplace. In addition, several researchers have found women to experience greater levels of work/family conflict than their male counterparts (e.g., Gignac, Kelloway, & Gottlieb, 1996).

There are several explanations as to why women seem to be more negatively impacted by the balance of work and eldercare than men. One explanation is that working men receive more help from other individuals than their female counterparts, a notion that has been empirically supported by Enright (1991). A second explanation, also empirically supported, suggests that women have more of a tendency to view their care-giving role as a reflection of their self-worth (Abel, 1990). Such internalization likely causes them to make the caregiving role a greater part of their lives, decreasing their ability to balance this role with other obligations such as work.

While most research suggests that women are more negatively affected by juggling work and eldercare than men, there is also evidence suggesting otherwise. For example, a recent study found no differences between men and women eldercare providers and their levels of work/family conflict (Barrah, Shultz, Baltes, & Stolz, 2004). These authors suggest that new role exchanges between men and women are developing, with both men and women engaging in work and family roles. Further, Matthews and Rosenthal (1993) suggest that structurally, men have the potential to be involved in both work and eldercare into their late 50s, while the time of life that women are most likely to be involved in both work and eldercare is throughout their 40s. Thus, men have, on average, 10 more years of lifetime during which they have a high likelihood of dealing with work and eldercare issues than women. In other words, these authors suggest that there is actually greater potential for men to be dealing with issues of work and eldercare. Another qualitative study conducted by Harris et al. (1998) suggests that men have a difficult time with work and eldercare issues because it is less socially acceptable for them to take on the caregiver role. Thus, management and society in general are less understanding of and may even look down upon men involved in eldercare.

Ethnicity. As suggested by Neal et al. (1993), the research investigating ethnicity among employed caregivers of elders is extremely limited. However, a study conducted by Stone and Short (1990) did shed some light on this neglected area of research. In general, Stone and Short found that White caregivers of an elder were more likely to be employed than non-White caregivers. However, it is also suggested that White caregivers may be more likely to be employed in jobs that allow them flexibility to alter their schedules and responsibilities than non-Whites. Thus, while White individuals providing eldercare may be more likely to work than non-White caregivers, suggesting a greater struggle with work and care-giving balance; these individuals may also be better able to control their work situations and thus achieve better balance than their non-White counterparts. However, future research needs to further investigate the role of ethnicity in work and eldercare balance before any conclusions can be made.

This brief review of the research that has been conducted on ethnicity sheds light onto another potential factor that may influence work and eldercare balance. Specifically, the type of job that one holds, and the amount of time that one dedicates to the job, are also likely impact the relationship between work and eldercare.

Occupation/hours worked. Differences in workplace policy that stem from differences in the nature of the job likely influence the extent to which individuals can successfully balance work and eldercare. Higher-status jobs tend to allow for more flexibility and greater control and thus allow one more opportunity to attend to eldercare responsibilities (Archbold, 1983). In additional support of this notion, Guberman and Maheu (1999) suggest that the key element that makes juggling work and eldercare difficult is the instability of the situation. This instability can result from the needs of the recipient of care (as will be discussed later), from the instability of the family situation, but also from the instability of an individual's working environment. The higher up an individual's job position, the more control they likely have over their working environment, subsequently leading to successful balance. However, it is possible that higher-level jobs are more demanding, and thus more stressful. Thus future research should more explicitly examine the impact of job level on the balance between work and family.

Researchers have also investigated whether the actual amount of time an individual spends at work influences his/her ability to balance work and eldercare. Intuitively, one would suspect that the more time an individual spends at work, the harder it would be for him/her to attend to eldercare responsibilities. However, the research investigating time spent at work is not consistent with this intuition (Neal et al., 1993). To provide an example, Dautzenberg, Diederiks, Philipsen, Stevens, & Vernooij Dassen (2000) found that while full-time employees reported slightly more interference between work and eldercare, these differences were not significant. Further, another study found that hours worked did not affect role strain, nor did it impact the amount of time spent in eldercare activities over a 2-year period (Dautzenber et al., 2000). Thus, it would seem that hours worked has little impact on one's ability to balance work and eldercare, and the research supporting the influence of hours worked seems to suggest that the less an individual works, the harder it is to additionally deal with eldercare issues. Again, the research in this area is somewhat limited, thus further investigation is warranted.

Distance from recipient of care. Another factor that has been investigated regarding the impact of work and eldercare balance is the actual distance between the caregiver and the care recipient. In reviewing research, it was generally found that 8 to 13 percent of employed caregivers live with the elder they care for (Wagner, Creedon, Sasala, & Neal, 1987). On the surface, it would seem that living with the elderly person you care for could make work-elder balance both easier and more difficult. It is possible that by reducing the distance between the caregiver and the care recipient the stress of caring for multiple households and commuting/traveling would be reduced. However, living with the care recipient may also cause stress because it may be more difficult to control the extent to which one is involved in eldercare and more difficult to limit the time spent in caregiving activities.

Research investigating the physical distance between caregiver and care recipient have supported its negative impact and researchers have warned against caregivers and care recipients living together. More specifically, Horowitz (1985) concluded that sharing a household was associated with more demands on the caregiver's time, and more likelihood of work-caregiving conflict. However, a recent study by Joseph and Hallman (1996) found that the length of travel time to the elder significantly increased work interfering with family conflict. More specifically, respondents who were living with an elder reported much lower work interfering with family conflict scores than those respondents whose elderly relatives lived 31–120 miles away. These authors argue that by moving the elder into the home, individuals can have more control over the situation, subsequently reducing conflict between work and caregiving. As with many of the other factors already discussed, research on the subject of recipient location is mixed. Further research should focus on determining under what circumstances it is beneficial for the care recipient to live with the caregiver, and under what circumstances more distance would be appropriate.

Special care needs.   Several researchers have also investigated the nature of the care needed by the care recipient as a factor that impacts one's ability to balance work and caregiving. The premise behind this research is that certain kinds of elder disabilities and care requirements are more time consuming and more stressful than others. In particular, caring for an elder's daily functioning needs (e.g., bathing, dressing, and transportation) is particularly burdensome (Montgomery, Gonyea, & Hooyman, 1985). Other research has additionally found that caring for elders with cognitive as opposed to physical disabilities to be particularly difficult (e.g., Scarlach, 1989).

The number of care responsibilities that are required increase as the elder's ailments become more serious. Greater numbers of caregiving tasks performed are positively related with individuals' perceptions of work/family conflict (Gibeau & Anastas, 1989). Thus, as care becomes more difficult, caregivers find it more difficult to balance their work and family lives. Gibeau and Anastas further found the nature of the care required to predict work/family conflict. More specifically, the degree of an elder's limitations in daily activity, memory impairment, emotional health, and poor judgment were found to be significant predictors of work/family conflict for caregivers. Further, Stone and Short (1990) similarly found the nature of the tasks required by the caregiver and the number of hours the elder could be left alone to be predictors of the caregiver having to make special work accommodations. Recent research has continued to indicate that feelings of interference for an employed caregiver increase as an elder's health decreases and time spent in care increases (e.g., Dautzenberg et al., 1999).

In 1989, Scharlach conducted a study investigating the special issues associated with combining employment and eldercare for the cognitively impaired elderly. In general, those caring for a cognitively impaired elder reported more work/family conflict, greater personal stress, and more work absenteeism than those caring for a physically impaired elder. The sum of this research suggests that the state of the elder's health, and thus the time required of the caregiver, is an important variable to consider when investigating work and care balance.

While it seems clear that the nature of the elder's health relates to one's ability to balance work and eldercare, future research could further explore this relationship. For example, while cognitive disabilities seem to be more difficult to manage than physical disabilities, do a large number of physical disabilities equal the demand of a cognitive disability? Also, are the coping strategies that individuals use to deal with cognitive and physical disabilities of their older relatives different? Are there more resources in handling physical disabilities? If so, how can organizations and society better equip individuals to deal with cognitively impaired elderly? Thus, there are many questions that future researchers could continue to explore in order to better understand the relationship between the nature of the elder's condition and the caregiver's ability to balance work and care.

The sandwich generation.   A growing body of research has begun to explore what is typically referred to as *the sandwich generation*, or those individuals who are caring for both children and elders at the same time (Miller, 1981). In Miller's discussion of the sandwich generation, it was suggested that having multiple caregiver roles likely contributes to greater role conflict as individuals are struggling to identify themselves as parent, employee, son/daughter, homemaker, etc., all at the same time. While conceptually the struggle of balancing multiple caregiving roles was posited decades ago, it received very little empirical research attention (Neal et al., 1993). However, in more recent years, the importance of investigating the sandwich generation has been realized.

Generally, individuals are more likely to be sandwiched between work, childcare, and eldercare between the ages of 40–64, with a greater likelihood of being sandwiched occurring at the lower bound of this age range (Matthews & Rosenthal, 1993). In a discussion of the sandwich generation, Dellmann-Jenkins et al. (1994) suggest that the sandwich generation experiences more stress, greater emotional strain, tardiness, unscheduled days off, depression, anxiety, and sleeplessness than those individuals who are not sandwiched (i.e., working and caring for both children and elders). Aside from these serious individual consequences, research has begun to investigate the impact that dual caregiving roles may have on organizational functioning. For example, recent research has found sandwiched caregiving responsibilities to impact organizational productivity as well as organizational climate (Robinson, Barbee, Martin, Singer, & Yegidis, 2003).

However, while Buffardi et al. (1999) found multigenerational caregivers to have lower job satisfaction than those without caregiving roles, these researchers also found that this lower satisfaction could generally be accounted for by the sum of the decrease found for the single generation components (i.e., childcare and eldercare). In addition, Ward and Spitze (1998) found that marital satisfaction is generally maintained despite the stress being involved in multigenerational caregiving. Thus, while intuitively it would seem that those with the responsibilities of both elder and childcare are a unique population, research in this area is just beginning to grow. Therefore, the specific challenges and consequences of those in the sandwich generation are not completely understood.

What Can be Done to Help Individuals Cope with Eldercare?

Resources for individuals. In the research investigating the caregiving of the elderly, several variables have emerged as potential resources for individuals seeking to ease the burden of the caregiving role (Neal et al., 1993). For example, one potential resource that individuals may draw upon is the hiring of other individuals to help with care responsibilities. While this would likely reduce the time that individuals would have to spend in eldercare responsibilities, there are some down sides to this approach as well. First, individuals may experience guilt resulting from feeling that they are pushing their personal responsibilities off on someone unrelated to the situation (e.g., Harris et al., 1998). Second, hiring outside care is not an option for many individuals, as they do not have the extra money to hire outside help. In fact, Horowitz (1985) found lower-income caregivers to be more likely to live with the care recipient and to provide direct care and service to the individual, whereas those in higher socioeconomic classes were more likely to purchase services for help with eldercare, and to provide financial assistance for the elder.

An additional resource that may or may not be available to individuals caring for elders is the support of other family and friends. Research has supported the notion that caregiver stress reduces as support from friends and family increases (e.g., Montgomery et al., 1985), and for the notion that employed caregivers are better able to manage work when they have additional support (e.g., Scharlach, Sobel, & Roberts, 1991). Given this research, social support seems to be a valuable resource for individuals dealing with eldercare. While support from friends and family seems to be beneficial, as previously discussed, there is evidence suggesting that men typically seem to receive more outside help than women in dealing with eldercare issues (Enright, 1991). This differential social support may be because women are typically seen as assuming the caregiver role, so there may be a societal norm that a woman in this role knows what she is doing. However, when a man assumes this role, the natural reaction of others may be to assume that he needs help. Researchers need to further investigate the differences in social support received by men and women, and the causes and consequences of these differences.

Additionally, there is evidence suggesting that support from other family members may increase stress. A qualitative study conducted by Harris et al. (1998) suggests that the primary caregiver of an elderly parent may see the involvement of his/her siblings as meddling and intrusive, and even further, as insulting. Because, the care of an elder parent typically falls primarily on one of the children/siblings, it is important to fully understand the family dynamic involved with eldercare issues.

The organization's role. While Matthews and Rosenthal (1993) suggest that 80 percent of employers view eldercare as the employees' problem and largely ignore the issue, there seems to be an outcry among individuals dealing with these issues demanding organizations to be more understanding of their struggles. Several studies suggest that employees are asking for policies such as flextime, compressed workweeks, extended leave benefits (with eldercare in mind), and even for adult day care and support groups to aid them in balancing work and eldercare (e.g., Dellmann-Jenkins et al., 1994; Guberman & Maheu, 1999). While self-report data tends to indicate that such programs are helpful (Dellmann-Jenkins et al., 1994), organizations are only very slowly, if at all, beginning to implement such policies/benefits. Though many organizations are beginning to realize the multiple benefits of changes in scheduling policies (such as incorporating flextime), some other changes, such as adult day care, are lagging far behind. This is likely because scheduling policies have multiple tangible benefits to the organization, while spending money on adult day care and support groups initially seem less valuable (especially given Matthews and Rosenthal's assertion that 80 percent of employers do not care about eldercare issues).

However, there is some evidence of organizational change. For example, Neal et al. (1993) suggest more and more companies are beginning to offer long-term care insurance, and educational seminars directed toward caregivers of the elderly. But, as with anything, change is slow. Additionally, as Guberman and Maheu (1999) point out, not all of the impetus must lie with organizations. Government and society in general must also increase their interest in and attitudes toward eldercare issues.

It's Not All Bad: Beneficial Aspects of Work and Eldercare

Although the focus of this section has primarily dealt with the negative aspects of participating both in work and eldercare roles, there is evidence that this balancing act may have some benefits. For example, several researchers suggest and have supported the notion that employment buffers the negative consequences of eldercare (e.g., Orodenker, 1990; Scharlach, 1989). Or, in other words, by allotting individuals an escape from their eldercare responsibilities and providing them with money, employed caregivers can actually have lower stress than unemployed caregivers. Another positive consequence that can result from having both work and eldercare responsibilities is an increased feeling of confidence and accomplishment. For example, Dellman-Jenkins et al. (1994) suggest that individuals feel pride in their ability to juggle their work and care responsibilities. Future research should delve further into these possible positive spillover effects since it could have implications for individuals and organizations. For example, organizations may be able to change certain aspects of the work culture and/or environment to further bolster the feelings of confidence that the work environment may provide.

In sum, research on eldercare issues demonstrates: 1) that balancing work and eldercare is a difficult process and can cause large amounts of work/family conflict, 2) that individuals belonging to certain groups may endure more of the strain of eldercare because of societal norms (e.g., gender) or socioeconomic status; and 3) that organizations have been slow to respond to eldercare issues. Points one and three suggest that eldercare is a large challenge, and that this challenge can negatively affect individuals' family and work lives. And unfortunately, employees are not receiving much help from their employers in dealing with this issue. Given the fact that the amount of employees having to deal with eldercare will continue to increase over the next decades, this problem will only grow in magnitude, and, thus, future research on organizational (and governmental) level policies and programs that would help employees meet this eldercare challenge is sorely needed.

CONCLUSION

In summary, this chapter has touched on two of the main work/family issues surrounding the aging of industrialized societies as well as their workforces. First, it appears that work/family conflict does have a life course and that the priorities given to work versus family change as employees age. Additionally, while it seems older employees report lower levels of work/family conflict, this does not mean that achieving work/family balance becomes less important to them. In fact, older workers appear to value the balance between work and family life to a greater extent than younger workers, and are more willing to engage in coping behaviors to achieve this goal. Second, the responsibility to care for older relatives will continue to increase, which will likely mean an increase in the stressors that can cause work/family conflict for both younger and older workers. As mentioned, there are numerous negative individual and organizational consequences associated with eldercare. As reviewed in the next sections, there are several practical implications and promising areas for future research surrounding both work/family issues across the life span and eldercare.

IMPLICATIONS FOR PRACTICE

As discussed throughout the chapter, there are several practical implications of the aging of the population as it relates to the balance between work and family. First, research suggests that individuals put greater emphasis on achieving balance between the two domains as they progress through life. Thus, organizations should continue to put effort into assisting their employees with work/family conflict, no matter the employees' age. Further, as individuals age the family friendly benefits that are important to them likely also shift. For example, as workers age, eldercare may become of greater importance than childcare, and maternity or paternity leave likely becomes less important while retirement plans become more important. Given the growing need in the near future to retain and attract older workers, it appears that organizations will have to adopt new policies and programs that help employees achieve work/family balance.

In addition, as previously discussed, workers' eldercare responsibilities lead to several negative organizational outcomes. Thus, while not presently the case, assisting workers with their eldercare responsibilities should be of great concern to organizations. Research suggests that employees struggling with eldercare responsibilities are asking for organizational help in dealing with eldercare. Employees are beginning to ask their employers for everything from policies such as flextime (with eldercare in mind) to adult day care (e.g., Dellmann-Jenkins et al., 1994; Guberman & Maheu, 1999). Further, this review of the literature suggests that the work environment can actually serve as a buffer to the negative consequences of eldercare. Thus, by creating a work environment that encourages confidence and fosters accomplishment, the organization may also be enabling its employees to better cope with the pressures of eldercare.

DIRECTIONS FOR FUTURE RESEARCH

There is much research opportunity for the scholar interested in understanding the impact of aging on work/family issues. While suggestions for future research are made throughout the chapter, we will conclude our discussion of this topic by summarizing the many questions left unanswered.

As previously mentioned, there is relatively little literature investigating the differences between older and younger workers in regards to how they manage the two domains of work and family. To this end, we provide three potential avenues for future research. First, future research should focus on developing and testing a revised life-stages model. Research under the current model suggests work/family conflict to decline as individuals reach the later life stages. However, when categorizing individuals into various life stages, the current model does not include variables such as eldercare or grandparent responsibilities. Doing so would likely add additional stressors to the later life stages, subsequently leading to additional work-life balance challenges later in life. Second, current research suggests older workers utilize coping strategies to a greater extent than younger workers. However, future research should investigate whether there is an interaction between age and type of coping strategy used. More specifically, while older employees report using more behaviors, this may change when one considers the specific type of coping strategy utilized. Future research should more thoroughly examine individual coping strategies individuals of various ages utilize in dealing with work family conflict. A third suggestion for future research in the area of work/family issues across the life span involves further exploration of the organization's role. Much more research is needed investigating which specific family friendly benefits are most desired by and effective for older workers. Much of what can be assumed about what older workers may want is only speculation, and empirical research on this topic is very much needed.

Aside from broadly investigating work and family concerns across the life span, as the population ages the issues directly surrounding eldercare become increasingly important. While eldercare research is seemingly abundant, there are many avenues for future research. First, there is somewhat conflicting evidence regarding the differential impact eldercare has on women's and men's abilities to balance this responsibility with work. While most research suggests women to be more adversely affected, future research should further tease apart these differences. Similarly, very little research exists regarding potential ethnic differences in eldercare as it relates to work and family balance. Third, the fact that the actual amount of time an individual spends at work does not seem to influence his/her ability to balance work and eldercare seems very counter intuitive, and future research is needed to clarify this relationship and examine potential moderators that may explain this finding. Research has also been mixed on the extent to which distance between the caregiver and the care recipient is a stressor or a stress reliever; thus again, more research is needed. Moreover, while this body of research is increasing, further exploration of the specific challenges of the sandwich generation is also needed. Finally, researchers need to more thoroughly investigate the role of social support and of the organization in providing individuals with additional eldercare responsibilities.

REFERENCES

AARP. (1995). *American business and older workers: A road map to the 21st century.* Washington, DC: DYG, Inc.

Abel, E. K. (1990). Family care of the frail elderly. In E. K. Abel & M. K. Nelson (Eds.), *Circles of care: Work and identity in women's lives* (pp. 65–91). New York: State University of New York Press.

Adams, G. A., King, L. A., & King, D. W. (1996). Relationship of job and family involvement, family social support, and work/family conflict with job and life satisfaction. *Journal of Applied Psychology, 81*(4), 411.

Albright, W. D., & Cluff, G. A. (2005). Ahead of the curve: How MITRE recruits and retains older workers. *Journal of Organizational Excellence, Spring,* 53–63.

Aldous, J. (1978). *Family Careers.* New York: Wiley.

Allen, T. D., Herst, D. E. L., & Bruck, C. S., & Sutton (2000). Consequences associated with work-to-family conflict: A review and agenda for future research. *Journal of Occupational Health Psychology, 5,* 278–308.

Archbold, P. G. (1983). Impact of parent-caring on women. *Family Relations, 32,* 39–45.

Baltes, P. B. (1997). On the incomplete architecture of human ontogeny: Selection, optimization, and compensation as foundation of developmental theory. *American Psychologist, 52*(4), 366–380.

Baltes, P. B., & Baltes, M. M. (Eds.). (1990). *Successful aging: Perspectives from the behavioral sciences.* Cambridge, MA: Cambridge University Press.

Baltes, B. B., & Heydens-Gahir, H. A., (2003). Reduction of work/family conflict through the use of selection, optimization, and compensation behaviors. *Journal of Applied Psychology, 88,* 100–1018.

Barrah, J. L., Shultz, K. S., Baltes, B. B., & Stolz, H. K. (2004). Men's and women's eldercare-based work/family conflict: Antecedents and work-related outcomes. *Fathering, 2,* 305–330.

Bond, J. T., Galinsky, E., & Swanberg, J. E. (1998). *The 1997 national study of the changing workforce.* Families and Work Institute.

Buffardi, L. C., Smith, J. L., O'Brien, A. S., & Edwins, C. J. (1999). The impact of dependent-care responsibility and gender on work attitudes. *Journal of Occupational Health Psychology, 4,* 356–367.

Coates, J. F., Jarratt, J., & Mahaffie, J. B. (1990). *Future work.* San Francisco: Jossey-Bass.

Dautzenberg, M. G. H., Diederiks, J. P. M., Philipsen, H., Stevens, F. C. J., & Vernooij Dassen, M. J. F. J. (2000). The competing demands of paid work and parent care: Middle-aged daughters providing assistance to elderly parents. *Research on Aging, 22*(2), 165–187.

Dellmann-Jenkins, M., Bennett, J. M., & Brahce, C. I. (1994). Shaping the corporate response to workers with eldercare commitments: Considerations for gerontologists. *Educational Gerontology, 20*, 395–405.

Duval, E. M., & Hill, R. L. (1948). *Report of the committee on the dynamics of family interaction.* Washington, DC: National Conference on Family Life.

Enright, R. B. (1991). Time spent care giving and help received by spouses and adult children of brain-impaired adults. *The Gerontologist, 31*, 375–383.

Enright R. B., Jr., & Friss, L. (1987). *Employed caregivers of brain-impaired adults: An assessment of the dual role.* Final report submitted to the Gerontological Society of America. San Francisco: Family Survival Project.

Evans, P., & Bartolomé, F. (1979). Professional lives versus private lives: Shifting patterns of managerial commitment. *Organizational Dynamics, Spring*, 2–29.

Evans, P., & Bartolomé, F. (1981). *Must success cost so much?* New York: Basic Books.

Evans, P., & Bartolomé, F. (1984). The changing pictures of the relationship between career and family. *Journal of Occupational Behavior, 5*, 9–21.

Freund, A. M., & Baltes, P. B. (2002). Life-management strategies of selection, optimization, and compensation: Measurement by self-report and construct validity. *Journal of Personality and Social Psychology, 82*, 642–662.

Frone, M. R., Russell, M., & Cooper, M. L. (1992). Antecedents and outcomes of work/family conflict: Testing a model of the work/family interface. *Journal of Applied Psychology, 77*(1), 65–78.

Gibeau, J. L., & Anastas, J. W. (1989). Breadwinners and caregivers: Interviews with working women. *Journal of Gerontological Social Work, 14*, 19–40.

Gignac, M. A. M., Kelloway, E. K., & Gottlieb, B. H. (1996). The impact of care giving on employment: A mediation model of work/family conflict. *Canadian Journal on Aging, 15*(4), 525–542.

Goff, S. J., Mount, M. K., & Jamison, R. L. (1990). Employer supported childcare, work/family conflict and absenteeism: A field study. *Personnel Psychology, 43*, 793–809.

Grandey, A. A., & Cropanzano, R. (1999). The conservation of resources model applied to work/family conflict and strain. *Journal of Vocational Behavior, 54*, 350–370.

Greenhaus, J. H., & Beutell, N. J. (1985). Sources of conflict between work and family roles. *Academy of Management Review, 10*, 76–88.

Guberman, N., & Maheu, P. (1999). Combining employment and care giving: An intricate juggling act. *Canadian Journal on Aging, 18*(1), 84–106.

Hall, D. T. (1972). A model of coping with role conflict: The role behavior of college educated women. *Administrative Science Quarterly, 17*, 471–486.

Harris, P. B., Long, S. O., & Fujii, M. (1998). Men and eldercare in Japan: A ripple of change? *Journal of Cross-Cultural Gerontology, 13*, 177–198.

Hepburn, C. G. (1996). Eldercare responsibilities, interrole conflict, and employee absence: A daily study. *Journal of Occupational Health Psychology, 1*, 311–318.

Higgins, C., Duxbury, L., & Lee, C. (1994). Impact of life-cycle stage and gender on the ability to balance work and family responsibilities. *Family Relations, 43*, 144–150.

Hill, R. (1986). Life cycle stages for types of single parent families: Of family development theory. *Family Relations, 35*, 19–29.

Hochschild, A. (2003). Marriage, family, and economics: The time bind: When work becomes home and home becomes work. In J. M. Henslin (Ed.), *Down to earth sociology: Introductory readings* (pp. 379–389). New York: Free Press.

Horowitz, A. (1985). Family and care giving to the frail elderly. In M. P. Lawton & C. Maddox (Eds.), *Annual review of gerontology and geriatrics* (Vol. 5, pp. 194–246). New York: Springer.

Joseph, A. E., & Hallman, B. C. (1996). Caught in the triangle: The influence of home, work and elder location on work/family balance. *Canadian Journal on Aging, 15*(3), 393–412.

Karasek, R. (1979). Job demands, job decision latitude and mental strain: Implications for job redesign. *Administrative Science Quarterly, 24,* 285–307.

Keith, P., & Schafer, R. (1991). *Relationships and wellbeing over the life stages.* New York: Praeger.

Matthews, A. M., & Rosenthal, C. J. (1993). Balancing work and family in an aging society: The Canadian experience. In G. L. Maddox & M. P. Lawton (Eds.), *Focus on kinship, aging and social change.* New York: Using Co.

Miller, D. A. (1981). The "sandwich" generation: Adult children of the aging. *Social Work, 26,* 419–423.

Montgomery, R. J. V., Gonyea, J. G., & Hooyman, N. R. (1985). Care giving and the experience of subjective and objective burden. *Family Relations, 34,* 19–26.

Neal, M. B., Chapman, N. J., Ingersoll-Dayton, B., & Emlen, A. C. (1993). *Balancing work and care giving for children, adults and elders.* Newbury Park: Sage Publications.

Orodenker, S. Z. (1990). Family and care giving in a changing society: The effects of employment on caregiver stress. *Family and Community Health, 12,* 58–70.

Robinson, M. M., Barbee, A. P., Martin, M., Singer, T. L., & Yegidis, B. (2003). The organizational costs of caregiving: A call to action. *Administration in Social Work, 27,* 83–102.

Scharlach, A. E. (1989). A comparison of employed caregivers of cognitively impaired and physically impaired elderly persons. *Research on Aging, 11,* 225–243.

Scharlach, A. E., & Boyd, S. L. (1989). Care giving and employment: Results of an employee survey. *The Gerontologist, 31,* 778–787.

Scharlach, A. E., Sobel, E. L., & Roberts, R. E. L. (1991). Employment and caregiver strain: An integrative model. *The Gerontologist, 31,* 778–787.

Schnittger, M. H., & Bird, G. W. (1990). Coping among dual-career men and women across the family life cycle. *Family Relations, 39,* 199–205.

Sinclair, R. R., Hannigan, M., & Tetrick, L. E. (1995). Benefit coverage and employee attitudes: A social exchange perspective. In L. E. Tetrick & J. Barling (Eds.), *Changing employment relations: Behavioral and social perspectives* (pp. 163–185). Washington, DC: (publisher?).

Singleton, J. (2000). Women caring for elderly family members: Shaping non-traditional work and family initiatives. *Journal of Comparative Family Studies, 31,* 367–375.

Staines, G. L., & O'Conner, P. (1980). Conflicts among work, leisure, and family roles. *Monthly Labor Review, August,* 35–39.

Staudinger, U. M. (1996). Wisdom and the social-interactive foundation of the mind. In P. B. Baltes & U. M. Staudinger (Eds.), *Interactive minds: Life-span perspectives on the social foundation of cognition* (pp. 276–315). New York, NY: Cambridge University Press.

Stoller, E. P. (1983). Parental care giving by adult children. *Journal of Marriage and the Family, 45,* 851–858.

Stone, R., Cafferata, G. L., & Sangl, J. (1987). Caregivers of the frail elderly: A national profile. *The Gerontologist, 27,* 616–626.

Stone, R., & Short, P. F. (1990). The competing demands of employment and informal care giving to disabled elders. *Medical Care, 28,* 513–526.

Wagner, D. L. (1987). Corporate eldercare project: Findings. In M. A. Creedon (Ed.), *Issues for an aging America: Employees and eldercare: A briefing book* (pp. 25–29). Bridgeport, CT: University of Bridgeport, Center for the Study of Aging.

Wagner, D. L., Creedon, M. A., Sasala, J. M., & Neal, M. B. (1989). *Employees and eldercare: Designing effective responses for the workplace.* Bridgeport, CT: University of Bridgeport: Center for the Study of Aging.

Ward, R. A., & Spitze, G. (1998). Sandwich marriages: The implications of child and parent relations for marital quality in midlife. *Social Forces, 77,* 647–666.

Warren, J. A., & Johnson, P. J. (1995). The impact of workplace support on work/family role strain. *Family Relations, 44,* 163–169.

13

Examining Retirement from a Multi-level Perspective

Terry A. Beehr and Misty M. Bennett

As the baby-boomer population ages, the number of retirees and the proportion of society they represent will almost certainly increase to levels never before seen. It is thus now more important than ever to understand retirement. Because of the demographic trends, retirement and the effects it has on society stand to change dramatically, perhaps in some unforeseeable ways. In this chapter we take a multilevel approach to analyzing retirement by examining how retirement affects individuals, their families, organizations, and society at large. At each level of analysis, two key questions are asked: What influences or causes older workers to retire, and what does their retirement influence? These questions are answered by examining the current literature, as well as integrating information from different disciplines. Recommendations and directions for future research are also discussed.

Retirement is an increasingly important research issue for several disciplines in the social and behavioral sciences, and it is an important practical issue for the world. Its current importance is especially due to aging of the baby-boom cohort, those born in a 20-year or so period after the end of World War II (Hatcher, 2003). Due to a higher birth rate during that era than during the eras shortly before or after, this cohort is viewed as *large*. As the baby boomers aged, much political, social, and economic activity focused on them (increases in activities for them as children and later for their children, marketing to them as teens, increases in college enrollments, health and aging issues, and now impending retirements). Retirement is now *demanding* attention due to the baby-boom generation. In the U.S., there is a national debate about how to fund the retirements of this large cadre of people whose oldest members are approaching age 60, are thinking of retiring, and can expect to live for about 20 more years. Depending on the predictions of the particular politician, organization, or commentator, the coming decades pose anything from a need for minor adjustment to a national crisis for Social Security funding, but most people agree that something needs to be done.

In some disciplines focusing on the workplace (e.g., management, industrial and organizational psychology), little attention was paid to retirement research until the last decade or more, but gerontologists and sociologists, politicians, social planners, career counselors, and economists had been working in the area all along (Beehr, 1986). Although we now know quite a bit about what induces people to retire at a certain time and how they behave after retirement, there is still much we do not know. Better understanding of retirement can help us understand, predict, and plan for the potential effects of the baby boomers' aging on national and international economics and politics, on the organizations in which they currently work, and on the well-being of the generations that came before and will come after them.

Although the importance of retirement at this time in history seems clear, the conceptual and operational definition of retirement is unclear and debatable. Whereas retirement once meant that someone who has worked for a few decades suddenly quits paid employment altogether for the brief remainder of his or her life, that does not fit the retirement pattern of a great many older people in the U.S. today. For some time now, many retirees haven not fit this image of total withdrawal from the workforce and a short period of life thereafter, but writers have not taken notice of this until relatively recently. Many people ease into retirement by working part-time, by taking a different job, or by working for themselves after *retiring* from a career job that they held for a long period of time. The retiree may have a reduced commitment to work as a whole but still be a member of the economic workforce. This is sometimes labeled partial retirement (Beehr, 1986), and the jobs these retirees hold are known as bridge jobs (Feldman, 1994), because they provide the person a bridge between the commitment to a career job and a life of full retirement. In addition to our new awareness of the seeming oxymoron of working while retired, the other big change is that people often live for a much longer time after they retire than they did a half century ago.

THREE LEVELS OR PERSPECTIVES ON RETIREMENT

Examinations of retirement can take several approaches, and in this chapter we chose to describe retirement at three *levels*: retirement can affect or is affected by important variables at the level of the (1) individual retirees themselves, (2) employing organizations from which they retire, and (3) larger society.

At the individual level, researchers are interested in understanding the characteristics of individuals and their immediate situations that might make them more or less likely to retire and the degree to which individuals themselves are impacted by their retirement. Demographics, personalities, abilities, finances and health, as well as situational characteristics such as the individual's type of job and family situation, might influence his or her decision to retire. One possibility is that retirement is one form of a more global construct of withdrawal from the workplace, much like absenteeism and turnover (e.g., Hanisch & Hulin, 1991), and therefore the individual characteristics that predict absenteeism and turnover might also be the predictors of retirement decisions. This, however, is not the case (Adams & Beehr, 1998). Examples are easy and intuitive: Tenure (and age) tends to predict turnover and absenteeism negatively, but of course they actually predict retirement positively. Job satisfaction has usually been a negative predictor of turnover and absenteeism, but it is not a very good predictor of retirement at all. So retirement seems to have some unique characteristics as well as potential commonalities with other forms of withdrawal from work.

The organization or employer is the second level or perspective on retirement. Retirements do not occur randomly across all of the organization's employees; rather retirees are concentrated among a subset of the organization's employees (obviously older ones, among other things). Organizations might want more or fewer of their employees to retire, but what can they do to influence retirements? In the U.S., as a result of legal rulings based on the 1967 Age Discrimination in Employment Act and its 1978 and 1986 amendments, employers' previous policies of mandatory retirement based on age have been made illegal (Beehr, 1986), but actions, policies, and conditions provided by the employer can still affect people's retirement decisions (early retirement incentives or buyouts are only the most obvious and direct of these). It is often unclear whether the organization will be better or worse off for the loss of those who retire, and it is also uncertain what the organization can do about it.

In addition to examining retirement predictors and outcomes related to individuals and to organizations, the third perspective on retirement is that of the larger society. Societal variables also affect retirement decisions, and society is affected by large masses of retirements. Government is the agent of society, and it can pass and enforce laws affecting retirement. Examples cross many domains, including issues such as costs, taxes, voting, migration, health, and labor and unemployment statistics. The following section reviews what we know about retirement at the individual, organizational, and societal levels.

RESEARCH FINDINGS ABOUT RETIREMENT

Individuals and Retirement

Research has been conducted in many disciplines, including gerontology, clinical psychology, and counseling psychology to help understand the impact that retirement has on individuals. Retirement is a life-altering decision, often affecting individuals in ways that they may not have imagined. For instance,

individuals may be scared or apprehensive about changing the 40-hour work-
week to which they have become accustomed, and after retiring they may
experience boredom or lower life satisfaction (e.g., Ekerdt, Bosse, & Levkoff,
1985). Other individuals may view retirement as an exciting, positive experience, however, because many people have increased life satisfaction and are
able to engage in more leisure activities and spend positive time with their families (e.g., Earl, 2005). Adjustment to retirement has been shown to be affected
by many different factors and thus may vary from person to person. A study
of older couples found that adjustment to retirement is influenced by the context of the transition and several psychological factors such as control, anxiety,
and self-efficacy (Van Solinge & Henkens, 2005). Specifically, strong attachment to work (e.g., full-time jobs or long tenure), lack of control over the retirement transition, negative expectations about retirement (anxiety), and low
self-efficacy were all positive predictors of a difficult adjustment. However, this
study did not find strong results for couple effects, and thus it appears that retirement adjustment is a very individualized experience and may even differ
within married couples.

Why people retire. One of the key research issues in retirement is *why*
people retire. Variables offering answers include finances, spouse's work status,
pensions or social security income, and health, among others. Some of the
most frequently researched predictors of retirement factors are health, retirement income or expected income (which includes pensions, social security,
early retirement incentives, income from savings, and other retirement benefits), organizational variables such as organizational commitment, age, and
spousal influences. A study of faculty members' decisions to retire examined
various financial, personal, and institutional factors and found that salary, un-
capping of the retirement age, social security income, eligibility for full retirement benefits, early retirement incentives, other sources of income, preference
for leisure, teaching effectiveness, type of institution, and level of education
of faculty all had a significant effect on the decision to retire (Bahman, 2001).
With so many predictors factoring into the retirement decision, it becomes
immediately evident that the retirement decision truly is complex.

One issue that makes studying retirement difficult is that retirement is a
process that occurs over time rather than an event (Beehr, 1986). Although
we can think that retirement occurred at a certain time on a certain day, the decision to retire, planning for retirement, and anticipating and preparing for it
might have occurred over a period of years. Many retirement studies are cross-
sectional, however, measuring future retirement intentions rather than actual
retirement behaviors. That is, instead of studying the process over time, researchers can ask older employees to predict their own behaviors over time.
Here, one can legitimately ask whether people can and do accurately predict

their own retirement behavior. A study of 125 staff employees at a university sought to answer this question by measuring older employees' retirement expectations, intentions, and actions regarding the timing of retirement (Prothero & Beach, 1984). Expectations predicted intentions (78 percent correct predictions), and intentions predicted action (76 percent correct predictions). Results of this study substantiate the use of retirement intentions as a proxy for actual retirement behavior. Studies that thus measure retirement intentions are viable sources of information about retirement decisions.

Types of retirement. Contributing to the difficulty of understanding retirement are the numerous ways in which retirement can be categorized. For instance, many individuals do not fully retire; rather they transition into retirement by entering bridge employment or a period of partial retirement. Bridge employment (Shultz, 2003) or partial retirement (Beehr, 1986) occurs when older workers take employment after they retire from their main career, but before their complete withdrawal from the workforce (Feldman, 1994). Bridge employed individuals may continue employment in the same career but take a reduction in work hours, for example, or they may change careers. When viewed this way, bridge employment can make the retirement process seem like a continuum, with bridge employment serving merely as a transition point between full employment and retirement. Bridge employment is often a popular alternative to retirement for those who may still need the income or for those who simply enjoy working. In fact, bridge employment is often a very popular decision, because fewer than two fifths of household heads retire directly from their career, and over half partially retire at some point in their working lives (Ruhm, 1990). The simple career in which young adults obtain a job, keep it for about 40 years, and then leave the workforce is much less common than this recognizable stereotype would have it.

It is important, however, to consider bridge employment separately from full retirement, particularly when looking at what factors go into deciding to retire or take bridge employment. Bridge employment appears to be a separate behavior and should not be presumed to have the same characteristics as full retirement (e.g., Honig & Hanoch, 1985). For instance, a study of 2,771 workers from the Health and Retirement Study data found that voluntariness of retirement, anticipated financial reward, and job flexibility all significantly differentiated four types of retirement decisions: early retirement, continuing work, obtaining bridge employment in the same job, and obtaining bridge employment in a different job (Weckerle & Shultz, 1999). Those who were interested in obtaining more job flexibility were more likely to accept bridge employment. Those who continued employment did so mainly because of financial constraints and were less likely to be able to increase their work hours; thus their financial situation might be worsened.

Other research has focused specifically on the predictors of bridge employment. Kim and Feldman (2000) found that having working spouses, dependent children, good health, and organizational tenure were all positively related to accepting bridge employment, but age and salary were negatively related to accepting bridge employment. Other studies have compared work predictors with nonwork predictors of bridge employment. For instance, Bennett, Beehr, and Lepisto (2005) found that nonwork factors were more salient than work factors in predicting bridge employment. Specifically, psychological distress and role overload were found to be the strongest predictors of bridge employment. Clearly there are many factors that go into the decision to accept bridge employment, and research in this domain needs to continue as more people age and take bridge jobs.

In addition to bridge employment and partial retirement, there are still other ways to categorize retirement. Beehr (1986) also described retirement as voluntary versus involuntary, and early versus on-time. Early retirement is an interesting topic; much research is done on early retirement, although it is unclear exactly what that is. It can be defined as retirement taking place before a certain age (e.g., before the age of 65, the current age for receiving full social security benefits in the U.S.). Sometimes researchers studying early retirement simply use age of retirement as a continuous variable, correlating it with other variables to see how people who retire at younger ages are different from people who retire at older ages. This topic will be touched on later, considering early retirement incentives that organizations give and other factors that organizations might use to *push* workers into early retirement (note this could also be considered involuntary retirement).

Voluntary retirement means taking retirement of one's own volition, whereas involuntary retirement could either be forced on a person by the organization (e.g., through downsizing) or by other constraints (e.g., government laws). If we consider voluntariness to be perceptual, then still other factors such as poor health can make people feel forced to retire when they otherwise would wish to remain on their jobs. A distinct but somewhat related concept might be the so-called *push and pull* factors (e.g., Feldman, 1994; Hanisch, 1994). A push factor is usually something experienced as aversive, pushing one into retirement, such as poor health or difficulty with coworkers. These could easily make people feel they are forced to retire. A pull factor, on the other hand, is a positive factor that encourages one to retire, such as more time for leisure activities or time with one's family. A study of 992 early retirees from the Health and Retirement Study examined several push and pull factors and found that reports of push factors (poor health, inability to find work, dislike of work, health of a family member, employer's policy toward older workers, inability to get along with the boss, and feelings that one's work was not appreciated) were stronger correlates of voluntary versus involuntary retirement than pull factors were (Shultz, Morton, & Weckerle, 1998).

That study also provided evidence that involuntary retirement may be harmful to the individual. Specifically, those who retired voluntarily had higher life satisfaction scores and rated themselves as both physically and mentally healthier (although poor health might be a predictor of retirement as much as good health is a result of voluntary retirement) than those who retired involuntarily (Shultz et al., 1998). Regardless of how retirement is categorized, there are clearly many different factors that affect individuals' decisions to retire. Some researchers (e.g., Robertson, 2000) argue that traditional categorizations of retirement do not serve well for explaining the actual reasons that people retire; rather the decision to retire is too complex, complicated by ambiguity and multiple considerations at the individual, organizational, and societal level.

Adjustment/Outcomes of retirement. The complexity of the decision to retire is not surprising, however, considering that retirement reflects a very dramatic change in one's life. Developmental and counseling psychologists often examine the effects that retirement has on individuals after they retire. Because we are living longer than ever before, many people approaching retirement will continue to live for another 20 to 30 years or more. Retirement is thus a step to a new chapter in one's life. Interestingly, although much information is available on the decision to retire, there is less information, particularly in terms of an underlying framework, on what happens to individuals after they retire (Carter & Cook, 1995). A key question here of course is what happens to the individual's quality of life after they retire. Quality of life might be defined by examining several factors such as life or family satisfaction, physical and mental health, physical activity, leisure time, and retirement satisfaction, to name a few. In fact, these are some of the most commonly studied outcomes of retirement. To make understanding these outcomes more complex, there are many psychological and other factors that interact in the retirement-outcome relationship. For instance, a study of life satisfaction after retirement found that there were several correlates with life satisfaction; those who were less depressed, retired at an early age, were married (or had been married), had a college education, were active as a volunteer, were in good health, and who did not work part-time were more likely to be satisfied with their life after retirement (Tackett, 2001). A key variable that seems to be crucial to life satisfaction after retirement is health. People with impaired health will likely experience lower life satisfaction after they retire regardless of other factors (Schmitt, White, Coyle, & Rauschenberger, 1979).

An important question also is not just what happens to an individual immediately after they retire, but what effect retirement has on an individual years after they have retired, raising the issue of life after retirement as a process. Fortunately, there have been several longitudinal studies that have sought to answer this question. Individuals may find that their pre-retirement notions differ from what they experience when they first retire and that those feelings may change as more time passes. In retirement, individuals might not engage to the same degree in retirement activities that they had expected they would before they retired (Beehr & Nielson, 1995). Using data from the Normative Aging study, the life satisfaction and leisure activities of 293 male retirees were measured within the first three years of retirement at 6-month intervals (Ekerdt et al., 1985). Optimism was greatest for recent retirees and there was some temporary dysphoria during the second year of retirement. Other longitudinal studies have found that there is an adjustment period preceded by mild feelings of depression but alleviated some time after retirement. For instance, in a study of 56 Israeli men, pre-retirement interviews revealed the dominant view of retirement as uncertainty and crisis, as opposed to retirement as providing hope for change, as a continuation of life, or as a developmental transition (Nuttman-Shwartz, 2004). However, one year later, most of the men were happily occupied, with their stress dissipated. Although these two studies have somewhat contradictory results in that the earlier ratings of retirement feelings were positive for the first study and negative for the second, it still holds that feelings about retirement may change as years pass.

The good news about retirement is that it may not be as stressful as one might anticipate. In fact, Hankin, Bosse, and Spiro, III, (1999) assert that only 30 percent of retirees find retirement to be a stressful event. For others it is a positive experience in which people can take more time to enjoy doing the things that they like to do and spending time with the ones they love. Adjustment to retirement is not the same for everyone, however. It may not be that most people who retire will be happy because retirement is a role they have come to prefer at their life stage; a minority of older people, however, might not like the role of retiree. A study of employed, unemployed, and retired men and women examined their role preferences in relation to life satisfaction and affective well-being (Warr, Butcher, Robertson, & Callinan, 2004). Better well-being and higher life satisfaction were found for those who were in roles that they preferred, with role clarity (i.e., they understood the meaning and expectations of their roles) and opportunity for control both positively related to well-being and life satisfaction.

Effects of retirement on the individual's family. Aside from the individual retirees themselves, their families are also involved in their retirements. Retirement decision-making is not a wholly individual decision, because it affects other family members. Interestingly, one study found that the more involvement one has in their spouse's retirement decision, the less satisfied the retiring spouse is with retirement (Szinovacz & Davey, 2005). This was true for both men and women. Also, that longitudinal study found that retired spouses are less satisfied if their husband/wife remains employed. It may thus be that spouses want to spend more time with each other and that retirement will allow freedom of choosing times for various activities; therefore, spouses view retirement as a way to do that even though the other, retiring, spouse may not be ready yet. In fact, it has been noted that there is an increasing coincidence of spouses retiring at about the same time, despite the fact that the wives are usually younger and have less time in the workforce than their husbands (Gustman & Steinmeier, 2000). Both spouses being retired will enable couples to enjoy more leisure time and activities together. Another study found that retirees and their spouses both agreed that the spouse influenced the retirees' decision to retire, yet spouses perceive their role in the decision as less influential than retirees see their spouse's role in the decision (Smith & Moen, 1998). Spouses may thus have more influence on the retirement decision than they think. As a result, the retirees might try to take their spouse's welfare and wishes into account in making their decision to retire.

In terms of examining the effects that retirement has on families, it appears that there are some positive benefits. For instance, marital conflict has been studied with the idea that marital conflict may be a source of dissatisfaction after retirement. A study using the National Survey of Families and Households, however, found that husbands (but not wives) reported a decline in strong arguments when the wife retired (Szinovacz & Schaffer, 2000). Also, the husband's retirement increased the number of calm discussions. Couples do this, however, only when at least one spouse was strongly attached to the marriage. Another study found that husbands who stay physiologically relaxed and affectively positive during marital interaction (i.e., conflict) were happier 5 years later in retirement, although the findings did not hold for wives (Kupperbusch, Levenson, & Ebling, 2003). These findings suggest that retirement has a positive influence on marital communication and a negative influence on marital conflict.

Retirement and gender. Unfortunately, many studies (particularly older ones) that examined retirement used samples consisting of men only. Yet, on average there are many retirement-relevant differences between men and women (e.g., types of jobs, pay, and health or longevity). It is thus crucial that we examine retirement for women as well as men in order to determine if and how retirement differs for them—including making the decision to retire and subsequently adapting to retirement. For instance, some studies have found that women are more likely to accept bridge employment than men (e.g., Honig, 1985). Men may thus feel that they need to remain employed full-time longer, or they may simply be more inclined to fully retire after their working careers. In fact, there do seem to be differences in the decision to retire for men and women. A study of husbands' and wives' retirement behavior found that women were more likely to retire due to familial factors, economic resources, personal characteristics, and personal characteristics of their spouse, whereas familial and spousal characteristics did not have as strong an influence on the husband's retirement decision (Pienta, 2003). Family may also be a reason why women are more likely to accept bridge employment. If they must maintain employment due to economic reasons, yet they want (or need for health reasons) to spend more time with their family, then they may take a part-time bridge job.

The gender factor in making retirement decisions is more involved, however. Planning has been shown to be an important factor in retirement; in fact, those with no retirement plans are more likely to be in poorer physical health, have fewer resources, and have more obligations than those who had plans for retirement (Devaney & Kim, 2003). Regarding gender, women are less financially prepared for retirement than men and are less likely to use employer-sponsored retirement plans, although, contrary to expectations, financial self-efficacy did not account for this finding (Dietz, Carrozza, & Ritchey, 2003). While men are more likely to plan financially, however, women are more likely to engage in health, living arrangement, and psychological planning (Lee, 2003). Additionally, although differences in planning for retirement exist, findings are encouraging that there is help for those who are ill-prepared for retirement. Training programs such as job skills programs and managerial training could improve the financial situation of older workers (Devaney & Kim, 2003). This would help make them more economically secure in retirement, either because they have more money to fall back on or because they would be more able to find jobs after retirement, if necessary. Retirement training has even shown to increase retirees' internal locus of control, increasing their confidence in their ability to effectively handle the retirement transition (Valentine, 2003).

Organizations and Retirement

Besides the retiring individuals themselves, another constituent affected by retirement is the employing organization. Particularly as the baby boomers age, organizations will have to face large numbers of retirees, putting a strain on organizations and their employees to fill these gaps, as well as putting economic strain on the organization's pension fund. The strain would be greater if the organization's retirement plan is a defined benefit program, that is, it promises to pay retirees a certain amount of (e.g., monthly) money than if it is a defined contribution program into which the employer pays in a certain amount. Declining economic circumstances for the company make it more difficult for the company to keep paying its retirees the same amount of (defined benefit) pension money. The company promises no certain amount of money, however, for a defined contribution plan, making poor economic circumstances for the company less of a problem in theory (unless the company declares bankruptcy or has been dipping into its pension funds). In some ways, a large group of employees retiring could be looked at as downsizing if the organization decides not to replace them, which is more likely in poor economic times than in good. In this case, however, the downsizing is at the discretion of the employee, not the organization—assuming voluntary retirement only. Organizations that undergo downsizing often put more pressure on their employees to perform, increasing their role stressors (Moore, Grunberg, & Greenberg, 2004). The same may thus be true for younger workers left to fill the positions of the recently retired. If not using retirement as a reduction-in-force strategy, organizations may have to hire a large number of new employees to fill the positions left by older workers. Selection and training can be very expensive and do not guarantee that an employee will stay with the organization to make the contribution worthwhile. An additional issue that is increasing is early retirement. Many workers retire at younger ages than in past decades. But who is retiring and how does this affect the organization? Are the retiring workers outstanding employees whose absence can hurt the organization, or are they poor performers whom the organization can afford to lose?

These questions are important to organizations that wish to get rid of poorer performers or to offer incentives to retain their best employees. Because organizations have a vested interest in their employees, it behooves them to help their employees prepare for the retirement decision as well. There are, in fact, many things that organizations are doing to achieve these objectives. For instance, employer-provided health benefits have been shown to delay retirement until the age of eligibility but accelerate it after the age of eligibility (Gustman & Steinmeier, 1994). This clearly serves as an incentive for employees to remain employed until they reach a certain age. Some results show that these employer-initiated plans and pensions have a beneficial effect on early retirees.

For example, a study of 1,200 British men who had retired early in response to a pension policy or other company plan tended to be healthier and wealthier than the general British population and were satisfied with their early retirement experience (McGoldrick, 1983). Retirement planning programs are another benefit that organizations are increasingly offering to older workers. These programs are, in fact, becoming much more prevalent. A survey of 44 of the Fortune 100 companies revealed that 77 percent of the organizations had retirement preparation programs, and 82 percent of them made their programs available to all employees (Avery & Jablin, 1988). Unfortunately, there is little research on what the cost is to the organization and how effective these programs are in order to determine the true utility of these programs.

There has even been some investigation into the effect of early retirement incentives. One study examined early retirement plans in relation to individual and organizational retirement processes and found that early retirement plans often neglect some aspects of both individual and organizational retirement processes and are therefore less likely to be effective (Kiefer & Briner, 1998). Organizations are increasingly offering early retirement plans as part of their pension programs and are increasingly replacing defined benefit plans with defined contribution plans (Westerman & Sundali, 2005). In the hands of an uneducated investor, defined contribution plans are more risky than defined benefit plans for the individual, yet may be more fiscally beneficial for the organization. In addition, some individuals may take more risks with employer-sponsored retirement benefits than others (Dulebohn, 2002). Specifically, individuals who have higher incomes, participate in other plans, are younger, have a high propensity for general risk, a high self-efficacy of investments, and a good knowledge of investment principles tend to act more risky with defined contribution plans (Dulebohn, 2002). The interested reader should consult Feldman (2003) for more specific information on early retirement incentives.

Organizations affect retirement decisions in many other ways. For instance, working conditions such as difficult physical labor in performing one's job have been shown to impact early retirement behaviors (Blekesaune & Solem, 2005). In fact, working conditions have been shown to affect one's overall decision to retire, but they do not predict very clearly which type of retirement people will choose (Hyde, Ferrie, Higgs, Mein, & Nazroo, 2004).

The previous section identified several individual factors that are a part of the retirement decision-making process. Yet, organizational contexts and characteristics clearly have an impact on retirement as well. For instance, a study of the 1986–1989 General Motors United Auto Workers showed that those whose plants were going to be shut down sometime in the future were much more likely to accept early retirement than those whose plants were not going to shut down, regardless of individual characteristics such as age, physical health, and pension wealth (Hardy & Hazelrigg, 1999). Thus, organizational contexts may truly have a strong effect on an individual's decision to retire. Another study found that working conditions and individual characteristics had about equal overall impacts on the decision to retire, but it was unclear exactly what specific work characteristics had that effect (Beehr, Glazer, Nielson, & Farmer, 2000). Instead, a subjective judgment that the person was "tired of working" had the greatest predictive power.

The question remains as to how organizations can retain their best employees. Unfortunately, research has focused simply on what organizations do to retain any employee, without examining employees' performance records. Still, certain industries face an issue of retaining older employees, particularly in areas where large numbers of baby boomers will soon be retiring. The academic institution is one such area. Although the end of mandatory retirement led to some universities offering early retirement incentives to make room for new faculty, many are now faced with an impending loss of millions of faculty members from the baby boomer era (Sugar, Pruitt, Anstee, & Harris, 2005). It is unclear whether this is good or bad, but Sugar et al. (2005) suggest that this wave of retirement will pose two major concerns: 1) maintaining a balance between junior and senior faculty, and 2) designing and implementing retirement programs for older faculty members. This will obviously hold true in many other industries as well. Fortunately, for those organizations concerned with retaining employees, there may be help. Organizations can offer benefits that are not age-contingent, so that they will continue to be an incentive as the worker ages. Shkop (1982) also found that the availability of job modifications (e.g., perhaps reduction of difficult physical labor) would lead many older employees to remain employed in the company for a longer period of time. These job modifications may seem like a bridge job to older workers, enticing workers to remain employed for a "new job." Thus, organizations must be creative in finding ways to retain their best employees and make retirement a smoother transition for themselves and individuals. The hope is that future research will examine the effectiveness of these new programs and help organizations better understand how to retain their best employees.

Society and Retirement

Retirement obviously affects the lives of those individuals who retire, and it also can affect the organizations from which people retire; in addition, retirement affects and is affected by the nature of an entire society. Social changes typically lag behind the changes in life spans of a society's citizens (Herzog, Willis, & Weir, 2004). Life spans have been increasing for a long time, but the pace of this change is so slow that its effects might be difficult for us to see and fully comprehend. Older adults comprise an increasing proportion of society's population, and this could have a number of effects, but the baby boom, combined with increased longevity, has not yet played itself out. Living longer in part is accompanied by being healthier at older ages. People therefore can continue to work longer than earlier generations did. This has not yet been happening, however. Instead, the increasing life span has occurred alongside decreasing retirement ages (Szinovacz, 2003). These two factors combine to make retired life longer than it once was. We can ask whether these trends will continue, what forces they might exert on society, and what forces society might exert on them.

Societies and cultures help define our roles, and the role of retiree is no different. Retirement has the trappings of a social institution, a culturally accepted way that people of a certain status (age) can withdraw from the workforce (Szinovacz, 2003). That is, there are culturally based definitions of retirement, roles that retirees play, and rituals that accompany it. In America, the most explicit retirement rituals symbolize endings more than beginnings or processes of transitions. For example, they usually take place among people with whom one works (e.g., retirement parties and gold watches from the employer)—relationships that are ending rather than relationships that are beginning or changing.

Certain retirement behaviors show cultural conformity. For example, retirement ages in America have historically clustered around age 62 to 65 (Herzog et al., 2004; Szinovacz, 2003). Economic eligibility for retirement pensions of various sorts helps explain this clustering, but the decision to retire is not all based on economics. Some people say they just get tired of working (a variable in Beehr et al., 2000), and others seem to believe it is just "time" to retire. This could be due to cultural norms about when to retire (Beehr & Adams, 2003a). There does not need to be any retirement at all; people could work until they die—health and energy permitting. However, it is now a cultural norm that we should stop working at some point before death (Ekerdt, 2004).

There are also norms about the nature and role of retirement in society, and this is related to what retirees should do during their retirements. It could be a time of pure idleness, of uselessness, of enjoyed leisure activities, or of voluntary contribution to society. Compared to past views, Americans now tend to view retirement as a period of earned leisure (Beehr & Adams, 2003b), compared to a former time when it might have been viewed as a period of decline and relative uselessness. Many Americans approaching retirement indicate they expect and want to engage in various activities, including travel, visiting family, and sometimes bridge employment (e.g., Beehr & Nielson, 1995). We might speculate that retired life has become increasingly active as the age of retirement has declined and the longevity has increased, resulting in retirees who are healthier and more vigorous.

One retirement activity that could be useful for society is volunteer work. However, who and how many retirees will volunteer, and what will they volunteer to do? A study in Hong Kong found that retirees who were healthier, happier, and more educated were more likely to volunteer (Wu, Tang, & Yan, 2005). Because successive generations have tended to become more educated, older people today are more educated than ever before, and so this might be a promising sign for the future of volunteer work by retirees. On the other hand, a Finnish study reported that less educated people tended to think more about retiring (Elovainio, et al., 2005).

A global but important question is: how much retirement is good for society? Answers can be based on assumptions about the value one places on people's activities during retirement. For example, are retirees benefiting society in any way, such as through volunteer work, taking a constructive role in politics and government, taking on new and productive employment, and lending sage advice to younger people or babysitting with grandchildren? Alternatively they could be a nonproductive drain on society's resources or (especially among a very large cohort such as the baby boomers), voting in large numbers for policies that mainly help themselves. Government planners and others who try to answer the question regarding the proper amount of retirement for society usually focus on economics and productivity in deriving their answers. From this point of view, the best amount of retirement depends on phenomena such as the state of the economy and labor markets. If there is a shortage of workers, then fewer retirements might be better, but if there is a surplus of labor, more retirements would take older workers out of the jobs to make room for younger workers (e.g., Bhattacharya, Mulligan, & Reed, 2004). In addition, mass retirements might affect the supply of specific labor skills, such as managerial skills (Benest, 2005).

Another important question is who pays for retirement (Beehr & Adams, 2003b). Eventually, a society's productivity pays for it, indirectly. Nevertheless, the direct disperser of retirement money can be viewed as government, employer, employee, or others. Government can pay for retirement directly by providing pensions, which are of course derived from tax money; Social Security represents this source in the U.S. Employers can pay for retirement by providing pensions and health benefits for their retirees. The individual person can pay for his or her own retirement through savings and investments or by working again after retirement. Others (often relatives) can support the retiree financially. Depending on the source of retirement funding, we might expect the interests of that source to play a role in funding.

If individuals are the source (i.e., they fund their own retirements), then the savings and consumption patterns of employees as they age and of retirees are likely to be important determinants of the timing of retirement and the quality of retired life. Economics-oriented approaches assume that pay rates increase as people age, but people's productivity does not match that increase. Therefore, people get paid relatively less than they are worth when they are younger, but they get paid more than they are worth when they are older (Hatcher, 2003; Kim, 2003). Regarding retirees' consumption behavior, an assumption is that they wish to maintain the same level of consumption after retirement that they had before retiring. This leads to people saving more relative to their spending when they are younger and working and spending (consuming or dissaving) relatively more when they are older and retired (Herzog et al., 2004).

Regarding the timing of retirement, employees might leave their employment at the time when they have enough money to live on for the rest of their lives. Theoretically, rational-economic people might plan to spend their last dollar and take their last breath at the same moment—if they could only figure out when that moment would be! However, people's retirement activities deviate from the rational-economic assumptions. It is an often-repeated fact that the baby boomers are not saving at a rate that will allow their post-retirement consumption rate to be the same as their pre-retirement consumption rate (Hatcher, 2003). Savings, however, are typically consumed at a slower rate in retirement than the assumptions would predict (Herzog et al., 2004). There are probably several reasons why the economic-based predictions of retirement behavior are far from perfect. For example, (1) people never have full information (e.g. about how long they will live) and people know they do not have full information, (2) people often do not intend to spend all their money before they die (e.g., they may want to leave some for their children), and (3) retirement decisions, saving and spending are influenced by factors other than and in addition to economics. Health, the nature of the job, joint retirement decision-making with a spouse, the availability of health insurance, and individual differences are likely to affect the decision to leave the organization or the workforce.

To the extent that the person's organization or employer funds retirement, it must be kept in mind that, under capitalism, employers' primary operational goals usually do not include helping fund retirement (Greller & Stroh, 2003). To the extent that they do this, it is a secondary goal (e.g., part of civic responsibility) or a necessity (i.e., funding employees' retirements is necessary to obtain and keep a good workforce). Private sector employers' primary goal, one on which their very survival is contingent, is making money. Evidence for this is easily witnessed in news accounts about companies that are in some way reducing retirees' benefits or pensions due to economic difficulties or changing from defined benefit to defined contribution pension plans (Szinovacz, 2003). Defined contributions are often put into some kinds of financial markets (e.g., stock markets). In the U.S., the current federal administration is advocating something like this to replace all or part of Social Security. In addition, laws have made it easier for workers to start their own tax-free retirement accounts. In Australia, the government is also encouraging the baby boomers to invest in the stock market (Clark-Murphy & Soutar, 2002). This could lead to an economic-societal increase in stock prices in the short run, as the money put into demand for stocks increases at a greater rate than the supply of stocks; in the long run, however, if there is a baby-boom cohort who will all want to take their money out of the market at the same time, this could lead to declining stock prices later.

To the extent that organizations fund retirements of their former employees, they are helping society and families and making it less necessary for other entities to provide the funding; retirement funding by employers is unlikely ever to be all that is needed, however, because it will always be very uneven since some employers will be more able to provide it or will provide it better than others. Some organizations have offered phased retirement for their employees—that is, the employee is allowed in some way to work less as retirement approaches (perhaps part-time), as a way of easing into retirement. It is unclear whether the net effect of these opportunities is to get employees to retire earlier (i.e., to go from full- to part-time work before they would have actually retired) or later (i.e., to take part-time work at the time they otherwise would have fully retired; Greller & Stroh, 2003).

In economically developed societies, governments usually provide much of retirees' funding. Thus, there is a strong possibility for societies' retirement trends and governments to influence each other. Government policy can attempt to influence retirement rates, and retirement rates can affect a government's economics and policies (e.g., through its taxes and payouts; French, 2005). Government is the steward of a society's assets (Beehr & Adams, 2003a), and these assets include older people's skills, tax money, and productivity. In the U.S., the characteristics of the Social Security system programs may affect all of these. Because many societies are aging more rapidly than in past generations, there has been a great deal of economics-oriented discussion about what this means for society and what to do about it. Making the age of partial eligibility for Social Security 62 instead of 65 could have opened up jobs for younger people by inducing more retirements among older employees, thereby shrinking the labor pool and reducing unemployment (Szinovacz, 2003). Furthermore, there is a consensus among retirement experts that if older employees were to perceive that they would have good medical insurance during retirement, whether through the Social Security medical insurance programs or otherwise, this would encourage more retirements (Herzog et al., 2004). Yet, if a larger proportion of society is retired than in past years, presumably the productive work of a smaller proportion of society supports them economically. In the U.S., this could lead to higher Social Security taxes on those who are working, reduced benefits in some form to retirees, some combination of both, or neither (because Congress could simply decide to pay more out of the general fund, for example).

The U.S. is not unique in experiencing the economic pressure of retirements of an impending baby-boom generation. In Germany for example, where people have traditionally had relatively larger government payouts and smaller private (e.g., employer) pension payouts than in the U.S., the government feels pressure to reduce the amount of funding per retiree (Hungerford, 2003). Thus in any country, because it is thought that retirements can have large effects on society, government is likely to try to affect retirement decisions.

Government might decide it is good for society to induce older workers to work longer before retiring, so that the current workforce can more easily pay for the resulting smaller number of retirees. Congress recently raised the age of eligibility for receiving Social Security retirement funds for people of certain ages (i.e., the age of eligibility will be raised for people in future years). However, political discussions are still underway about additional changes. The U.S. government's banning of the mandatory retirement policies that many organizations had could also have had the effect of getting people to stay in the workforce longer, even though that was not the avowed purpose of the law. That law had little actual effect on retirements, however, because on the average, people had actually been retiring earlier anyway. It has also been estimated that eliminating mandatory retirement in Canada would also have little effect on the number of people in the labor force (Luchak, Fang, & Gunderson, 2004; Shannon & Grierson, 2004). The intent of the U.S. law was to prevent employers from discriminating against older workers by forcing them to retire—perhaps in order to avoid *overpaying* them (compared to their productivity, as noted earlier; Hatcher, 2003). Other ways that government can try to steward society's resources by affecting retirement ages include changing the amount of payout for Social Security recipients. According to economic models, an increase in payouts should cause people to retire closer to the age at which the payout eligibility could begin (Hatcher, 2003). When payouts are small, they have less effect, and when they are large, they have a greater effect on retirement decisions. It must be acknowledged, however, that when government makes retirement policy, data often do not drive politics (Herzog et al., 2004); instead, political decisions are often made based on other factors (e.g., ideology, expected effects on the next election), and then data are found, developed, or claimed to support the decisions.

In addition to individuals paying for their own retirements and employers or government paying for retirements, still other parties could fund one's retirement. Historically, the most likely parties to do this are members of the person's family. In former times in the U.S. when the economy was more agricultural than it is now, it was common for a grown child to receive ownership (formally or informally) of the family farm, and the retiring parent would continue to live there and be taken care of (including financially if necessary) by the child. In such cases, the parents might feel that they had supported their own retirements by working and accumulating wealth and material goods (e.g., farm, house, equipment), which then would support them in retirement. We might also view it, however, as the grown child's current labor now supporting the retired parent. In some ways, the current talk about the sandwich generation revives this image (Loomis & Booth, 1995; Riley & Bowen, 2005). This generation, partially due to the combined effects of longer lives and earlier retirements of their parents, sometimes takes care of the parents as well as taking care of their own children. The care for parents sometimes includes financial support. The extent to which offspring now financially support their parents' retirements is unknown, but it was probably more common in the U.S. a century ago. One expected effect of the Social Security Act of the 1930s was to free people from the burden of financially supporting their retired parents during the Great Depression, when it was difficult to support even oneself. Today, family members taking care of the elderly might be even more common in Eastern Asian countries, but one survey in Hong Kong concluded that middle-aged people are no longer sure that they can depend on their families to take care of them when they retire (Lee & Law, 2004).

One way that retirement can affect society is related to the migratory behavior of the retirees. While working, many older employees are closely tied to the geographic area where they have a job, but some people decide to move when they retire and have no work-related reason for staying in the same place. Much of this migration is from cooler to warmer climates (Longino, Perzynski, & Stoller, 2002), and in the U.S. in particular, it tends to be from the Northeast to the Southeast and from the Midwest to the Southeast, Southwest, and West (Longino et al., 2002). A similar phenomenon occurs in Europe (e.g., Casado-Diaz, Kaiser, & Warnes, 2004; Huber & O'Reilly, 2004). This probably occurs more among some specific groups of retirees than others: Those who are newer to retirement (and usually younger), the married and wealthy, or single male retirees are more likely to migrate (Casado-Diaz et al., 2004). Given the political geography in Europe, it usually means crossing national borders, although the implications of this have changed since the formation of the European Union. Some European destination countries are concerned about political and economic implications of such migration, and currently it seems as if the cross-border migrants will be granted more and better social policy rights if they have worked in the destination country for a while rather than moving there only after they have totally retired from the workforce (Ackers & Dwyer, 2004). In the U.S., it is easy to obtain full citizenship rights in a new state, and one might consider whether retirement migration, if large enough or concentrated enough geographically, might have an effect on voting patterns (Wright, Caserta, & Lund, 2003). For example, the North has tended to be politically more liberal than the South, and would large pockets of Northern retirees swing some Southern districts from right to left? Alternatively, will older migrants vote differently from the way they did when they were younger and in a different region? The answers are unknown. Aside from politics, regional economics may also be affected. Retirees can cause increases in local building booms, housing prices, and health care needs in specific areas; and these areas are often similar to some of the popular tourist areas (Casado-Diaz et al., 2004).

FUTURE DIRECTIONS FOR RESEARCH AND PRACTICE

As with any body of research, the literature on retirement leaves many questions unanswered. Many issues are simply under-researched, such as cross-national comparisons on retirement. Many more issues will need additional research as society changes. New public policies or demographic shifts such as the increasing retirement of the baby boomers will likely bring new questions about retirement into focus. In fact, these new changes may even affect the answers to old questions. For instance, research on the decision to retire is abundant, with many articles examining different factors. Yet as medical technology increases, health may no longer be as salient a factor for people of this age; or perhaps new technologies will make it more possible for older people to accept bridge jobs at home via telecommuting. The possibilities for the effect of these changes are endless and unpredictable. However, research on these areas must continue in order to allow a clearer understanding of retirement.

Although research on future issues will be useful, there are still many gaps in the current research that have left us with unanswered questions. For instance, there is an abundance of information on the effect of retirement on the individual, yet it is less clear what effect retirement has on one's spouse. There is even less literature on the effect of retirement on other family members (e.g., children who may be faced with eldercare issues after their parent retires). It is apparent that people's retirement decisions are not made overnight using only a small, simple set of criteria. There appear to be many factors in the decision, and one's family likely plays an important part in this decision. Retirement decisions are probably very different for those without children or a spouse.

To build on the organizational literature, attempts have been made to draw connections between retirement and turnover, as well as retirement and other organizational withdrawal behaviors. If these correlations existed, we could draw from the turnover and withdrawal literature to understand retirement behavior more. Unfortunately, evidence exists that the similarities between retirement and turnover, and retirement and other withdrawal behaviors, are few in number (Adams & Beehr, 1998; Rubenstein, 1995), suggesting some need for more research in this area.

One of the biggest gaps in the organizational literature is in measuring the effectiveness and utility of retirement training programs. Additionally, we need to examine which employees are retiring from organizations and what effect early retirement incentives or programs have on their intent to stay. For example, some programs might encourage poor performers to remain employed more than better performers. It is important to know the effects of these programs as organizations are implementing them at increasing rates. Additionally, the cost of early retirement incentives, financial or otherwise, to the organization is crucial to determine so that organizations may choose which programs would be best suited for their needs.

Finally, there are several issues in the literature on retirement that have simply not gotten the attention they deserved. One such issue is the effect of gender on retirement processes. Although some gender differences were examined in this chapter, many of the older studies involved samples of men only. More research needs to be done on how women make retirement decisions and on the effect that retirement has on them. Some evidence shows that there may very well be gender differences in predicting retirement decisions. For instance, a 6-year longitudinal study found that significant predictors of retirement for men were older age, lower education and occupational status, health limitations, and increased interactions with friends, while the only significant predictor of retirement for women was age (George, Fillenbaum, & Palmore, 1984). Another study of predictors of the decision to retire found that there were gender differences in the decision to retire, particularly when dependents lived in the household, when the health of one's spouse was a factor, and when one's spouse was retired (Talaga & Beehr, 1995). If there are gender differences in retirement, then it is essential that more studies examine these differences and include samples of women to determine exactly *how* men's and women's retirement processes differ.

Another final issue that is also under researched is cross-cultural or cross-national research. The majority of articles that deal with retirement decisions are from the United States, and for the international articles that have been written, it seems that certain countries or cities have been over sampled (e.g., Hong Kong, Great Britain, and France). More research in a variety of countries, particularly research comparing retirement at the societal level in different countries, would be helpful to understand the cultural influences that surround retirement. We are in an exciting time to study retirement, because there are many new issues arising and a large demographic shift quickly approaching. The effects of this shift will be interesting to observe and study.

CONCLUDING REMARKS

Retirement in the 21st century promises to be different, on average, from retirement in previous centuries. Retirement is no longer a short period of years after a long period of working, during which people have declined dramatically in activity and health. Today's retirees will experience relatively more bridge employment, longer periods of retirement with more activity, and longer periods of good health than the prior generations. Of course there is no threshold or cutoff point at which such a change occurred; instead, these trends began a long time ago, even though we only began to notice some of them (e.g., bridge employment) relatively recently. It is also hazardous to extrapolate trends far into the future, such as to the end or even to the middle of the 21st century. Fortunately, most of these changes seem positive, and we hope they continue. The trends can be altered, however, due to relatively unpredictable dramatic events (e.g., wars, economic depressions, widespread diseases, or aversive climate changes) or to more gradual changes. Currently, however, in economically developed countries, many older employees now anticipate a relatively long and enjoyable period of retirement.

REFERENCES

Ackers, L., & Dwyer, P. (2004). Fixed laws, fluid lives: The citizenship status of post-retirement migrants in the European Union. *Ageing and Society, 24,* 451–475.

Adams, G. A., & Beehr, T. A. (1998). Turnover and retirement: A comparison of their similarities and differences. *Personnel Psychology, 51,* 643–665.

Avery, C. M., & Jablin, F. M. (1988). Retirement preparation programs and organizational communication. *Communication Education, 37,* 68–80.

Bahman, B. (2001). Factors affecting faculty retirement decisions. *Social Science Journal, 38,* 297–305.

Beehr, T. A. (1986). The process of retirement: A review and recommendations for future investigation. *Personnel Psychology, 39,* 31–55.

Beehr, T. A., & Adams, G. A. (2003a). Concluding observations and future endeavors. In G. A. Adams & T. A. Beehr (Eds.), *Retirement: Reasons, processes, and results* (pp. 293–298). New York: Springer Publishing Company.

Beehr, T. A., & Adams, G. A. (2003b). Introduction and overview of current research and thinking on retirement. In G. A. Adams & T. A. Beehr (Eds.), *Retirement: Reasons, processes, and results* (pp. 1–5). New York: Springer Publishing Company.

Beehr, T. A., Glazer, S., Nielson, N. L., & Farmer, S. J. (2000). Work and nonwork predictors of employees' retirement ages. *Journal of Vocational Behavior, 57,* 206–225.

Beehr, T. A., & Nielson, N. L. (1995). Descriptions of job characteristics and retirement activities during the transition to retirement. *Journal of Organizational Behavior, 16,* 681–690.

Benest, R. (2005). It's a reality: The shrinking talent pool for local government managers. *Public Management, 85,* 14–18.

Bennett, M. M., Beehr, T. A., & Lepisto, L. R. (April, 2005). *Working after retirement: Predictors of bridge employment.* Paper presented at the annual meeting of the Society for Industrial and Organizational Psychology, Los Angeles.

Bhattacharya, J., Mulligan, C. B., & Reed, R. R., III. (2004). Labor market search and optimal retirement policy. *Journal of Economic Inquiry, 42,* 560–571.

Blekesaune, M., & Solem, P. E. (2005). Working conditions and early retirement: A prospective study of retirement behavior. *Research on Aging, 27,* 3–30.

Carter, M. T., & Cook, K. (1995). Adaptation to retirement: Role changes and psychological resources. *Career Development Quarterly, 44,* 67–82.

Casado-Diaz, M. A., Kaiser, C., & Warnes, A. M. (2004). Northern European retired residents in nine southern European areas: Characteristics, motivations and adjustment. *Ageing and Society, 24,* 353–381.

Clark-Murphy, M., & Soutar, G. N. (2002). What individual investors value: Some Australian evidence. *Journal of Economic Psychology, 25,* 539–555.

Devaney, S. A., & Kim, H. (2003). Older self-employed workers and planning for the future. *Journal of Consumer Affairs, 37,* 123–142.

Dietz, B. E., Carrozza, M., & Ritchey, P. N. (2003). Does financial self-efficacy explain gender differences in retirement saving strategies? *Journal of Women and Aging, 15,* 83–96.

Dulebohn, J. H. (2002). An investigation of the determinants of investment risk behavior in employer-sponsored retirement plans. *Journal of Management, 28,* 3–26.

Earl, B. T. (2005). *Effects of pre-retirement preparation on depression and quality of life in retirement for professional managerial males.* Dissertation.

Ekerdt, D. J. (2004). Born to retire: The foreshortened life course. *Gerontologist, 44,* 3–9.

Ekerdt, D. J., Bosse, R., & Levkoff, S. (1985). An empirical test for phases of retirement: Findings from the Normative Aging study. *Journal of Gerontology, 40,* 95–101.

Elovainio, M., Forma, P., Kivimaki, M., Sinervo, T., Sutinen, R., & Laine, M. (2005). Job demands and job control as correlates of early retirement thoughts in Finnish social and health care employees. *Work and Stress, 19,* 84–92.

Feldman, D. C. (1994). The decision to retire early: A review and conceptualization. *Academy of Management Review, 19,* 285–311.

Feldman, D. C. (2003). Endgame: The design and implementation of early retirement incentive programs. In G. A. Adams & T. A. Beehr (Eds.), *Retirement: Reasons, processes, and results* (pp. 83–114). New York: Springer Publishing Company.

French, E. (2005). The effects of health, wealth, and wages on labour supply and retirement behaviour. *Review of Economic Studies, 72,* 395–427.

George, L. K., Fillenbaum, G. G., & Palmore, E. B. (1984). Sex differences in the antecedents and consequences of retirement. *Journal of Gerontology, 39,* 364–371.

Greller, M. M., & Stroh, L. K. (2003). Extending work lives: Are current approaches tools or talismans? In G. A. Adams & T. A. Beehr (Eds.), *Retirement: Reasons, processes, and results* (pp. 115–135). New York: Springer Publishing Company.

Gustman, A. L., & Steinmeier, T. L. (1994). Employer-provided health insurance and retirement behavior. *Industrial and Labor Relations Review, 48,* 124–140.

Gustman, A. L., & Steinmeier, T. L. (2000). Retirement in dual-career families: A structural model. *Journal of Labor Economics, 18,* 503–545.

Hanisch, K. A. (1994). Reasons people retire and their relations to attitudinal and behavioral correlates in retirement. *Journal of Vocational Behavior, 45,* 1–16.

Hanisch, K. A., & Hulin, C. L. (1991). General attitudes and organizational withdrawal: An evaluation of a causal model. *Journal of Vocational Behavior, 39,* 110–128.

Hankin, C. S., Bosse, R., & Spiro, A., III. (1999). Assessment and treatment of retirement stress. In L. VandeCreek & T. L. Jackson (Eds.), *Innovations in clinical practice: A source book, 17* (pp. 49–63). Sarasota, FL: USource Press/Professional Resource Exchange, Inc.

Hardy, M. A., & Hazelrigg, L. (1999). A multilevel model of early retirement decisions among autoworkers in plants with different futures. *Research on Aging Special Issue: Multilevel Models, 21,* 275–303.

Hatcher, C. B. (2003). The economics of the retirement decision. In G. A. Adams & T. A. Beehr (Eds.), *Retirement: Reasons, processes, and results* (pp. 136–158). New York: Springer Publishing Company.

Herzog, A. R., Willis, R. J., & Weir, D. R. (2004). Research on aging. In J. S. House, F. T. Juster, R. L. Kahn, H. Schuman, & E. Singer (Eds.), *A telescope on society: Survey research and social science at the University of Michigan and beyond* (pp. 330–354). Ann Arbor: The University of Michigan Press.

Honig, M. (1985). Partial retirement among women. *The Journal of Human Resources, 19,* 613–621.

Honig, M., & Hanoch, G. (1985). Partial retirement as a separate mode of retirement behavior. *The Journal of Human Resources, 20,* 21–46.

Huber, A., & O'Reilly, K. (2004). The construction of Heimat under conditions of individualised modernity: Swiss and British elderly migrants in Spain. *Ageing and Society, 24,* 327–351.

Hungerford, T. L. (2003). Is there an American way of aging? Income dynamics of the elderly in the United States and Germany. *Research on Aging, 25,* 435–455.

Hyde, M., Ferrie, J., Higgs, P., Mein, G., & Nazroo, J. (2004). The effects of pre-retirement factors and retirement route on circumstances in retirement: Findings from the Whitehall II study. *Ageing and Society, 24,* 279–296.

Kiefer, T., & Briner, R. B. (1998). Managing retirement: Rethinking links between individual and organization. *European Journal of Work and Organizational Psychology, 7,* 373–390.

Kim, S. (2003). The impact of research productivity on early retirement of university professors. *Industrial Relations, 42,* 106–125.

Kim, S., & Feldman, D. C. (2000). Working in retirement: The antecedents of bridge employment and its consequences for quality of life in retirement. *Academy of Management Journal, 4,* 1195–1210.

Kupperbusch, C., Levenson, R. W., & Ebling, R. (2003). Predicting husbands' and wives' retirement satisfaction from the emotional qualities of marital interaction. *Journal of Social and Personal Relationships, 20,* 335–354.

Lee, W. K. M. (2003). Women and retirement planning: Towards the "feminization of poverty" in an aging Hong Kong. *Journal of Women and Aging, 15,* 31–53.

Lee, W. K. M., & Law, K. W. (2004). Retirement planning and retirement satisfaction: The need for a national retirement program and policy in Hong Kong. *Journal of Applied Gerontology, 23,* 212–233.

Longino, C. F., Jr., Perzynski, A. T., & Stoller, E. P. (2002). Pandora's briefcase: Unpacking the retirement migration decision. *Research on Aging Special Issue: Retirement Communities, 24,* 29–49.

Loomis, L. S., & Booth, A. (1995). Multi-generational caregiving and wellbeing: The myth of the beleaguered sandwich generation. *Journal of Family Issues, 16,* 131–148.

Luchak, A. A., Fang, T., & Gunderson, M. (2004). How has public policy shaped defined-benefit pension coverage in Canada? *Journal of Labor Research, 25,* 795–808.

McGoldrick, A. E. (1983). Company early retirement schemes and private pension scheme options: Scope for leisure and new lifestyles. *Leisure Studies, 2,* 187–202.

Moore, S., Grunberg, L., Greenberg, E. (2004). Repeated downsizing contact: The effects of similar and dissimilar layoff experiences on work and wellbeing outcomes. *Journal of Occupational Health Psychology, 9,* 247–257.

Nuttman-Shwartz, O. (2004). Like a high wave: Adjustment to retirement. *Gerontologist, 44,* 229–236.

Pienta, A. M. (2003). Partners in marriage: An analysis of husbands' and wives' retirement behavior. *The Journal of Applied Gerontology, 22,* 340–358.

Prothero, J., & Beach, L. R. (1984). Retirement decisions: Expectation, intention, and action. *Journal of Applied Social Psychology, 14*, 162-174.

Riley, L. D., & Bowen, C. P. (2005). The sandwich generation: Challenges and coping strategies of multigenerational families. *Family Journal: Counseling and Therapy for Couples and Families, 13*, 52-58.

Robertson, A. (2000). "I saw the handwriting on the wall": Shades of meaning in reasons for early retirement. *Journal of Aging Studies, 14*, 63-79.

Rubenstein, P. D. (1995). *The early retirement decision as a behavioral manifestation of organizational withdrawal.* Dissertation.

Ruhm, C. J. (1990). Bridge jobs and partial retirement. *Journal of Labor Economics, 8*, 482-501.

Schmitt, N., White, J. K., Coyle, B. W., & Rauschenberger, J. (1979). Retirement and life satisfaction. *Academy of Management Journal, 22*, 282-291.

Shannon, D., & Grierson, D. (2004). Mandatory retirement and older worker employment. *Canadian Journal of Economics, 37*, 528-551.

Shkop, Y. M. (1982). The impact of job modification options on retirement plans. *Industrial Relations, 21*, 261-267.

Shultz, K. S. (2003). Bridge employment: Work after retirement. In G. A. Adams & T. A. Beehr (Eds.), *Retirement: Reasons, processes, and results* (pp. 214-241). New York: Springer Publishing Company.

Shultz, K. S., Morton, K. R., & Weckerle, J. R. (1998). The influence of push and pull factors on voluntary and involuntary early retirees' retirement decision and adjustment. *Journal of Vocational Behavior, 53*, 45-57.

Smith, D. B., & Moen, P. (1998). Spousal influence on retirement: His, her, and their perceptions. *Journal of Marriage and the Family, 60*, 734-744.

Sugar, J. A., Pruitt, K., Anstee, J. L. K., Harris, S. G. (2005). Academic administrators and faculty retirement in a new era. *Educational Gerontology, 31*, 405-418.

Szinovacz, M. E. (2003). Contexts and pathways: Retirement as institution, process, and experience. In G. A. Adams & T. A. Beehr (Eds.), *Retirement: Reasons, processes, and results* (pp. 6-52). New York: Springer Publishing Company.

Szinovacz, M. E., & Davey, A. (2005). Retirement and marital decision making: Effects on retirement satisfaction. *Journal of Marriage and Family, 67*, 387-398.

Szinovacz, M. E., & Schaffer, A. M. (2000). Effects of retirement on marital conflict tactics. *Journal of Family Issues, 21*, 367-389.

Tackett, R. A. (2001). Correlates of life satisfaction after retirement. Dissertation.

Talaga, J. A., & Beehr, T. A. (1995). Are there gender differences in predicting retirement decisions? *Journal of Applied Psychology, 80*, 16-28.

Valentine, S. (2003). Training, retirement attitudes, and locus of control. *Psychology and Education: An Interdisciplinary Journal, 40*, 34-42.

Van Solinge, H., & Henkens, K. (2005). Couples' adjustment to retirement: A multi-actor panel study. Dissertation.

Warr, P., Butcher, V., Robertson, I., & Callinan, M. (2004). Older people's wellbeing as a function of employment, retirement, environmental characteristics, and role preference. *British Journal of Psychology, 95*, 297-324.

Weckerle, J. R., & Shultz, K. S. (1999). Influences on the bridge employment decision among older USA workers. *Journal of Occupational and Organizational Psychology, 72,* 317–329.

Westerman, J. W., & Sundali, J. (2005). The transformation of employee pensions in the United States: Through the looking glass of organizational behavior. *Journal of Organizational Behavior, 26,* 99–103.

Wright, S. D., Caserta, M., & Lund, D. A. (2003). Older adults' attitudes, concerns, and support for environmental issues in the "new west." *International Journal of Aging and Human Development, 57,* 151–179.

Wu, A. M. S., & Tang, C. S. K., & Yan, E. C. W. (2005). Post-retirement voluntary work and psychological functioning among older Chinese in Hong Kong. *Journal of Cross-Cultural Gerontology, 20,* 27–45.

14

In Search of a Unifying Paradigm for Understanding Aging and Work in the 21st Century

Kenneth S. Shultz and Gary A. Adams

The authors of the chapters that precede this culminating segment have admirably documented the extant research in their respective areas related to aging and work. The prior chapter authors have also quite convincingly laid the groundwork for future empirical and theoretical work within their given area. In addition, they have provided lucid guidance on practical concerns within their respective areas. Therefore, in this concluding chapter we will attempt to summarize the common themes that span the prior chapters by highlighting theoretical, methodological, and practice issues that cut across a variety of topics. In doing so, our goal is not to simply replicate what the previous authors have already so astutely summarized. Rather, our major objective is to provide the reader with a sense of the *big picture* with regard to both the current work, as well as future empirical, theoretical, and practice needs, related to the topic of aging and work, thus moving us toward a unifying paradigm for studying aging and work in the 21st century.

The preceding chapters in this book attest to the growing body of literature in the area of aging and work. As has been pointed out throughout this volume, the aging of the baby-boom cohort (those born between 1946 and 1964) is accelerating and will continue to accelerate the growth of the middle-aged and elderly populations, in both society at large as well as our workforce. However, as Alley and Crimmins point out early on, even after the last baby boomer is gone, both society and the workforce will continue to be older on average, both in terms of the median age and as a percentage of the population, than they are today due to lower fertility rates and increasing longevity. In addition, as Alley and Crimmins, as well as Jex, Wang, and Zarubin note, on average older individuals of today are healthier than in the past. While the baby boom cohort has sounded the alarm bells in terms of our need for more attention to aging, both in general and with regard to employment and retirement in particular, it is clear this is not a short term trend or phenomenon.

Hence, in this concluding chapter we will both summarize and integrate the key themes and ideas from across the chapters that precede us. We will also incorporate other relevant literature to support our ideas. In doing so, we will organize this chapter along three key foci: conceptual/theoretical, methodological, and practice issues. While we will attempt to integrate the current themes and ideas that cut across the chapters, we will also have our eyes clearly on the future in order to help set the stage for coming research, theorizing, and practice in the area of aging and work.

CONCEPTUAL/THEORETICAL ISSUES

A common thesis made across most of the chapters in this book is that perceptions matter. That is, how workers are viewed within, and outside of, organizations matters in terms of how competently they are perceived, how accepted they are, and to what extent they will continue to be valued members of organizations. Finklestein and Farrell spend a good portion of their chapter discussing the issue of perceptions in terms of older worker stereotypes and biases; however, it is a theme that cuts across most of the other chapters, at least implicitly, as well. For instance, Taylor and Geldhauser, and Goldberg describe how perceptions of older workers interact with negative perceptions of low-income workers, women, and certain ethnic groups. They suggest that this interaction among demographic characteristics exacerbates the negative effects any of these single variables have on a variety of employment-related outcomes. As another example, Maurer describes how perceptions of older workers held by others relate to training and development opportunities and outcomes. Importantly, he also notes that how older workers perceive themselves can affect these outcomes as well.

A number of chapters also attempt to answer the question, "what can be done about these perceptions" and offer a number of suggestions for changing the perceptions people have about older workers. Some suggest that in addition to active attempts to change perceptions, the realities of the labor market and sheer size of the aging workforce are also likely to influence perceptions held about older workers. Whether or not these will actually lead to more positive perceptions is an open question. Most of the research done on perceptions of aging and work has been bounded by the limits of the 20th century's relatively loose labor markets and "youngish population." We wonder what this research will have to say in the 21st century when organizations are more hard-pressed to find talented employees and when more than half of those in the workforce are over the age of 40. Clearly, the paradigm we use to conceptualize, theorize, and study perceptions of older workers held by others and themselves under these conditions will be different from what it has been in the past.

Another underlying conceptual theme that is incorporated into most of the chapters is the increasing diversity we are seeing in our aging workforce. For example, while men's labor force participation, particularly at older ages, showed a precipitous drop in the last century up until the mid-1980s, older women's labor force participation rates have continued to climb. In addition, minority group members continue to make up a larger and larger share of the workforce in a wide variety of occupations. So, while we have dedicated an entire chapter to the topic of diversity and aging at work (by Goldberg), the issue of diversity is prominent throughout the book. Much of the past research on aging and work, particularly in the United States, is based predominantly on white men, and so may not generalize to women and people of color.

For example, the findings of previous research discussed in the chapters on career issues (Feldman), occupational health (Jex, Wang, and Zarubin), work and family (Baltes and Young), and employee development and training (Maurer) issues in particular, may not be as relevant for women and minority workers as for white men. Therefore, any directions for both future research and practice must be evaluated with this limitation in mind. The evolving paradigm for studying aging and work in the 21st century clearly calls for more diverse samples of workers to be used. This diversity includes not only typical demographics such as race, ethnicity, and sex, but also wider age ranges than are typically used, as well as diversity across many of the contextual factors that will be discussed herein.

The need to incorporate contextual factors into the theorizing and study of aging and work is also a common implicit theme across chapters. Researchers sometime fail to consider that research participants' feelings, thoughts, and behaviors all take place within the broader context of their lives. This context includes individuals' current life circumstances, as well as their life-course history up to the current time. Factors such as changes in family structure (e.g., more blended families created through divorce, widowhood, remarriage, or adoptions), employment history, occupational health related changes (Jex et al.), as well as attitudes toward work (Barnes-Farrell and Matthews) and retirement (Beehr and Bennett), are examples of individual or micro-level contextual factors that influence aging and work. At the intermediate, or meso, level, organizational factors such as industry changes, attitudes towards older workers (Finkelstein and Farrell), employee training and development opportunities (Maurer), as well as pension and finances, provide a context for a host of aging and work related issues. Macro-level contextual factors such as the current labor market conditions, inflation rates, and the availability of governmental programs to assist older workers could all provide a context for employment and retirement related behaviors, attitudes, and feelings of workers as they age.

Another common theme that cuts across most of the chapters is the multidisciplinary nature of studying aging and work. Authors and researchers from a wide variety of disciplines, including sociology, economics, social work, psychology, demography, gerontology, and business, to name just a few, have studied aging and work. Each discipline, however, brings a unique perspective to the discussion. Even within a given discipline, different specialties may have different approaches and viewpoints. For example, within psychology, developmental, cognitive, counseling, and industrial/organizational psychologists have all examined aging and work issues. Thus, while the multidisciplinary nature of aging and work can make studying the area difficult and complex, particularly to the newcomer, it also makes the area of study much richer, as a wide variety of perspectives and theories are brought to bear on the assortment of topics covered within the field of aging and work.

For example, sociologists who study aging and work have examined the influence of group, organizational, and societal level factors on older workers' retirement-related decisions. Meanwhile, economists have focused on the economic incentives and disincentives to retire versus staying employed full-time. Psychologists, on the other hand, have continued to examine individual level predictors of retirement status. However, even within psychology different specialties are likely to examine different micro-level factors. For example, industrial/organizational psychologists are more likely to examine the predictive influence of constructs such as organizational attachment, job satisfaction, and work motivation on retirement-related behaviors. Developmental psychologists, however, typically focus on the individual's current life stage or career status. Counseling psychologists, on the other hand, tend to focus on the quality of current marital and workplace relationships or personality factors that may predict retirement timing and preparedness. Meanwhile, a cognitive psychologist may be more interested in how older individuals approaching retirement combine the overwhelming amount of information available to them in order to make a decision at all. Thus, a diversity of perspectives on a variety of work-related outcomes, including retirement decision-making, can only benefit from having a wide variety of perspectives and theorizing, to the extent that the diverse perspectives can be brought together in a unifying paradigm. However, a move to producing truly interdisciplinary, as opposed to simply multi-disciplinary, research will be needed in order to take full advantage of what each discipline and subdiscipline has to offer.

Cleveland and Lim, as well as Feldman, point out the need to look beyond typical personnel issues (e.g., hiring, appraising, training) when studying aging and work. Such topics have dominated the literature on aging and work in the past, and will continue to be important and deserving of research attention in the future. However, aging and work in the 21st century will bring an increased focus on career (Feldman), retirement (Beehr and Bennett), and related issues, as individuals look to extend their work-lives to match their increasing life spans. In addition, organizations and governments are also wondering what it will take to keep older workers in the workforce or attract them back into the workforce upon retiring from their career jobs. Organizations may be motivated by shrinking replacement labor pools, while both organizations and governments (local and federal) will be motivated by increasing pension liabilities to foster continued employment at older ages. Recent review (e.g., Shultz, 2003; Taylor, Shultz, & Doverspike, 2005) and empirical (e.g., Adams & Rau, 2004; Dendinger, Adams, & Jacobson, 2005; Loi & Shultz, in press; Rau & Adams, 2005) works by the present authors contribute to our understanding of why older adults seek employment. However, additional theoretical and empirical work is needed given the evolving landscape of aging and work.

Assuming workers do in fact stay in the workforce in one form or another longer than they do today, then a wide variety of other issues will also be in need of additional theoretical and empirical attention. For example, how best to create effective work groups and teams that will be made up of more diverse workers (Goldberg) will be critical. In addition, conceptions of career (Feldman) and retirement (Beehr and Bennett) are constantly evolving with the changing demographic mix of workers, as well as the changing nature of work itself. For example, Feldman discusses in his chapter the shift toward the protean career (see Hall, 2004) that has occurred over the last several decades—that is, a movement away from the organization deciding how an individual's career will unfold, to the need for individuals themselves to guide their own career (Sterns & Kaplan, 2003). How these changing conceptions will affect workers who stay or try to stay in the workforce longer than in the past is a critical issue that must be addressed.

A related conceptual shift is the gradual move away from the traditional tripartite view of the life course. That is, we spend the first one third of our life learning, the second working, and the third engaged in leisure pursuits (e.g., traditional retirement). Traditionally, work has been the largest component of the three, however, with more individuals seeking higher education and thus delaying full-time entry into the workforce, as well as increased longevity after retirement, the three segments have become much more comparable in length. However, theorists (e.g., Hagestad & Dannefer, 2001) have suggested that the traditional compartmentalization of learning, working, and leisure is slowly disappearing. Thus, we are likely to see the need for more lifelong learning and development (Maurer). In addition, instead of one, single lifelong cycle we may see a series of smaller cycles of learning, work, leisure, then retraining, new work roles, and new leisure pursuits. Accordingly, extending the average work-life of individuals will no doubt increase the need to engage in continuous learning and alter the balance of work, learning, and leisure at the end of the life-course. What implications might this shift have for theorizing about aging and work in the 21st century?

Successful aging at work is yet another underlying concept common to most of the chapters in this book. Hansson, DeKoekkoek, Neece, and Patterson (1997) adeptly summarized the literature on successful aging at work up to a decade ago. While we contemplated having a separate chapter on that topic for this book, in order to cover more recent research, we opted instead to have the individual chapter authors incorporate the concept throughout the book. Thus, a principal theme of most of the chapters in this book is that successfully aging at work encompasses a wide array of issues, from work and family balance (Baltes and Young), to employee development (Maurer), to occupational health (Jex et al). As a result, it is also an integrative concept, in that successful aging at work requires most, if not all, the topics covered in this book to be examined. However, as noted earlier, perceptions matter. Hence, how successful aging at work is defined for any given individual will depend on how he or she perceives the situation, as well as how he or she is perceived within the situation. Like many other concepts discussed in this book (e.g., retirement), what it means to successfully age at work in the 21st century will require new and evolving paradigms.

In summary, there are a host of conceptual and theoretical issues that need to be addressed as we search for a unifying paradigm for studying aging and work in the 21st century. We have briefly discussed several of the more ubiquitous topics (e.g., perceptions, diversity, contextual factors, successful aging), however, our list was not intended to be exhaustive. Rather, any unifying paradigm must focus on those concepts that touch on many, if not most, of the topic areas covered in the preceding chapters of this volume. We believe that these concepts that we have discussed do just that. In particular, the concept of successful aging at work is one that incorporates all of the previous chapters in one form or another. Thus, not only does the concept of successful aging focus us on what it means to successfully age at work, it also serves as a unifying framework for studying aging and work in the 21st century.

METHODOLOGICAL ISSUES

Addressing these conceptual and theoretical issues is fundamental to moving the area of aging and work forward. However, a wide variety of methodological concerns also need to be considered as we study aging and work in the 21st century, as it is the results of our present empirical endeavors that serve as the seeds for future theorizing. These methodological concerns can be placed into two broad categories. The first category concerns measurement and statistical-related issues. The second category relates to research design issues.

Measurement and statistical issues. A very basic measurement issue that surfaces immediately when studying aging and work is, what is the best way to define age? As Cleveland and Lim point out in their chapter, most studies have simply used chronological age when studying aging and work. This seems to make sense, just ask people how old they are. Why not? It's easy to measure and relatively noncontroversial. However, as Cleveland and Lim point out, there are a wide variety of alternative ways to define age. We can use functional age, relative age, and a host of other alternative definitions to define how old individuals feel, or are perceived, relative to other group members. Cleveland and Lim cite work showing differing results based on the definition of age used. Thus, how we measure age may well have implications for the theories we develop, as well as the results obtained in our empirical investigations when studying aging and work in the 21st century. Therefore, future work in the area may benefit greatly by using a variety of conceptualizations of age to determine their differential impact on an assortment of outcomes beyond Cleveland and Lim's discussion of aging and job performance.

A related measurement issue concerns who exactly is an older worker? A perusal of extant literature on almost any topic discussed in this book will produce a host of definitions of who qualifies as an older worker. In the United States, the Age Discrimination in Employment Act (ADEA) says that any person age 40 years old or older is covered under the ADEA, and hence, an older worker. However, the Older Americans Community Service Employment Program (Title V) specifies that individuals must be at least 55 years old (and low-income status) in order to be eligible for government assistance with employment and training-related concerns. The literature on workability of older workers that comes largely from the European community (see Snel & Cremer, 1994) typically uses age 45 or 50 as the cutoff to define workers as older workers. On a more personal note, on one's 50th birthday in the United States, we receive an application from the AARP (formerly known as the American Association of Retired Persons) inviting us into membership. The AARP is unmistakably seen as one of the leading advocates for "50+ workers" in the United States.

So, at what age should we set the lower-bound cutoff to distinguish older versus younger workers? Of course one avenue for dealing with this dilemma of where to set the cutoff is to not set any cutoff. While legislation and advocacy groups may need to set a somewhat arbitrary age cutoff to distinguish groups, researchers would be much better served by examining age as a continuous variable. In addition, shifting from comparing older versus younger workers, to examining age as a continuous variable, helps to shift the focus from age differences (fraught with a host of interpretation issues to be discussed below) to a focus on *aging* and work-related issues. However, we fully understand that policy makers and practitioners may not have the luxury of using a continuous age variable.

Related to the question of how to distinguish older workers from younger workers is where to set the upper-bound when defining older workers, or if there is even a need to set an upper-bound. Most of the research to date has focused on studying age across what was once considered *prime working years*— the ages between 20 and 60. However, as we noted earlier, an individual's work-life may well extend past the age of 60 and into later life. Examining age as a continuous variable will help remove and avoid the need for an arbitrary upper-bound. More than that, however, it will require that our paradigm for aging and work in the 21st century considers a broader array of concepts and issues than have been traditionally included in studies of aging and work. Some ideas for specific concepts might be gleaned from the literatures surrounding what some gerontologists refer to as the *third age*, with its focus on the time between when one no longer has the financial need for paid work and before morbidity limits one's activities (Weiss & Bass, 2002) or the *creative age*, with its focus on creativity and continued growth in the latter half of life (Cohen, 2000). Theory and research findings from the literature on productive aging (Morrow-Howell, Hinterlong, & Sherraden, 2001), which focuses sustaining contributions to work, community, and family, might also be consulted.

However, even with a focus on a continuous age variable, versus a dichotomous age variable, we still must be careful about focusing too much on age. *Age* (however defined) represents a fixed point in time, whereas *aging* represents a process that occurs over time. Accordingly, many of the contextual variables discussed herein exert their influence on the aging process, and vice versa, thus leading the same aged individuals to very different points on their life-course trajectories. As a result, we will obtain a much better picture of what happens as workers age, and thus, provide a much stronger foundation for theorizing about aging and work in the 21st century, when we focus on *aging* rather than *age* per se.

An additional measurement issue that arises with age is how best to statistically describe individuals as they age. We know that over the course of one's life there is an accumulation of life circumstances that provide for a wider set of life-course trajectories (Henretta, 2001; O'Rand, 2001). Thus, the variability on a host of psychological and work-related variables is likely to dramatically increase as we age. As a result, measures of central tendency, for example, will not describe individuals very well as they age. Consequently, we will need to develop alternative descriptive statistics to best describe our phenomenon of interest with regard to aging and work.

In addition, shifting from examining age differences to examining the aging process will require more sophisticated approaches to data analysis. For example, a move from simpler exploratory and confirmatory factor analytic measurement models to those that will allow researchers to evaluate factorial invariance/equivalence (and perhaps more interestingly variance/non-equivalence) over time. It will also be important to move from examining the relationships between age and a variety of work-related outcomes using correlations and regressions to more complex multivariate statistics, such as multilevel or growth curve modeling. These, along with ordinary time-series and latent transition analyses, will be required to capture the dynamic nature of such relationships (Zickar & Gibby, 2003).

Research design issues. Many of the issues that we will discuss will be familiar to the reader. However, assuming we do make the shift from studying age group differences (i.e., older versus younger workers) to studying aging at work in the 21st century, then a concomitant change from predominantly single administration cross-sectional to more sophisticated (e.g., longitudinal) research designs will also be required. However, modified cross-sectional designs, such as repeated cross-sectional designs, may be beneficial in teasing apart cohort versus generational differences (i.e., social change) that are impossible to decipher in traditional single administration cross-sectional studies (Firebaugh, 1997). Thus, cross-sectional designs can be beneficial with enhancements such as repeated administrations.

Longitudinal designs, however, are not a panacea for the shortcomings of single administration cross-sectional designs. All research designs have some shortcomings associated with them. Therefore, hybrid designs (e.g., such as multigroup, cross-lagged panel designs) are often needed to fully tease apart age, period, and cohort effects. The Health and Retirement Study (HRS; http://hrsonline.isr.umich.edu/) is a good example of combining samples and adding new cohorts to a cross-lagged panel design (http://hrsonline.isr.umich .edu/intro/dataflow.html) in order to isolate a wide variety of potential explanatory influences.

A related issue is the use of existing or archival data. Most psychologists are trained in the collection and analysis of original empirical data. Thus, most of the research cited in this book is based on the *single use data* model of conducting empirical research where data is collected at one point in time, analyzed, and then written up for publication. The researcher then moves on to designing another study and collecting more data to answer their next research question. However, as noted earlier, the study of aging and work is a multi-disciplinary effort. Thus, a perusal of studies from other disciplines, such as economics or sociology, is more likely to uncover the use of existing large-scale databases, such as the HRS already mentioned, in studying the various topics of aging and work discussed throughout this book. Hundreds of researchers have produced thousands of manuscripts based on the multiwave HRS data set. A perusal of the HRS web site (http://hrsonline.isr.umich.edu/papers/index.html) reveals a wide variety of papers regarding aging and work, including some of the topics discussed in this book. However, given the vast majority of HRS based research papers are written by researchers in fields other than psychology (e.g., economics, sociology, demography), much more could be done to examine the topics covered in previous chapters using data such as the HRS.

The nature of such large scale, multi-use data collection efforts, however, often necessarily requires the trade-off of sacrificing psychometric rigor for inclusiveness of topics. Thus, there tends to be a lot of breadth and less depth, particularly with regard to many of the psychological topics discussed in this volume (e.g., job satisfaction, work motivation, age bias, work and family concerns). As a result, it may be difficult to fully test many of the proposed relationships discussed in previous chapters using existing data from large-scale public use data sets. However, such archival data may be able to serve as *pilot data* for developing more comprehensive models of the phenomenon discussed throughout this text (Shultz, Hoffman, & Reiter-Palmon, 2005). In addition, researchers may be tempted to use age as a proxy for other variables that may not be readily available in the archival data set. For example, age may be used as a surrogate for job tenure. Doing so would lead to a host of interpretation issues. Therefore, researchers must be cautious about using age, or any variable for that matter, as a proxy for other variables not readily available in a given archival data set.

A related topic to reanalyzing existing data is the quantitative summary of previous empirical studies via meta-analytic techniques. In fact, there have been numerous meta-analytic studies examining the relationship between age and a variety of work-related variables. For example, Cleveland and Lim summarize several previous meta-analytic studies that have shown little to no relationship between age and job performance. In addition, Barnes-Farrell and Matthews also cite meta-analytic findings regarding differences between older and younger workers on outcomes such as job satisfaction and work motivation. Maurer, in his chapter, also cites meta-analytic findings regarding age differences in training performance. However, many of the other areas discussed in this book (e.g., career development, occupational health, retirement, work and family issues) are ripe for additional meta-analytical work. Nevertheless, as our discussion has already revealed, the examination of the simple bivariate relationship between age (even if measured continuously) and a variety of work-related phenomenon is unlikely to advance the field of aging and work very far beyond its current state. That is because it returns our focus to age differences, rather than focusing on the developmental processes that occur as we age across time.

Therefore, a better strategy would be to explore for variables that may mediate and/or moderate the relationship between age and work-related outcomes (e.g., Salthouse & Maurer, 1996). Maurer, Barnes-Farrell and Matthews, Baltes and Young, and Finkelstein and Farrell, all discuss in their respective chapters the need to examine for possible moderating and/or mediating variables between age and work-related outcomes. Doing so is not only methodologically advantageous, but will also lead to better theorizing. For example, as Cleveland and Lim note in their chapter, previous meta-analytic work examining the bivariate relationship between age and job performance has reported generally weak relationships. However, some researchers (e.g., Salthouse & Maurer, 1996; Shultz & Morton, 2000; Warr, 1994) have proposed the need to examine moderating factors in the relationship between age and job performance in order to examine the more intriguing question of how workers may adapt and actually perform their job differently from younger workers as they age. Thus, the focus is shifted to the more intriguing question of how older workers are able to maintain their performance as they age, despite the accumulation of age-related decrements.

Another methodological issue, hinted at under our discussion of contextual level variables, is the need to include multiple levels in our analyses. Psychologists have traditionally focused on the individual or micro level of analysis. For example, how is an individual's job performance, job satisfaction, physical health, or caregiver burden influenced by micro-level factors such as job demands, perceived work stress, or demographic status? However, the broader context in which these outcomes occur can provide additional explanatory power that is just not possible with a myopic micro-level focus. While traditionally psychologists have relied on related social science disciplines (e.g., sociology) to examine the macro-level factors, Hagestad and Dannefer (2001) have suggested that broader social science researchers have suffered from *microfication* in terms of their analysis—that is, an ever shrinking unit of analysis down to the individual or micro level. We hope it is clear that we are not advocating abandoning the micro level of analysis; nor are we recommending a shift to primarily macro-level analyses. Rather, it is the simultaneous examination of the multiple levels of analyses (Gilbert & Shultz, 1998–99) that will provide the rich explanatory context for best understanding aging at work in the 21st century.

The need for more cross- and multi-national research on aging and work is also evident. While most of the empirical literature cited in this book was conducted on samples from the United States [US], many other developed countries (e.g., most European Union [EU] countries, Japan) are also experiencing rapidly aging populations and workforces (Taylor, 2005; Usi, 1998). In fact, many EU countries have to face the issue of a ballooning elderly population before the US. As a result, literature on aging and work from the EU is increasing, as it is in the US. In addition, much of the research conducted by EU researchers is also more likely to be cross-national in nature, often including multiple EU nations. However, even more diverse cross-cultural samples that include fundamentally different economic structures and social mores may well provide additional insights and explanatory power with regard to the topics discussed throughout this book.

In summary, there are a wide variety of methodological concerns that need to be addressed if we are to hope to create a unifying paradigm for studying aging and work in the 21st century. These concerns encompass a broad swath of measurement, statistical, and research design issues. However, as with the conceptual and theoretical issues, our discussion of methodological concerns was meant to be representative rather than exhaustive. Our goal was to select a few topics that we believed could serve as unifying concerns that cut across a majority of topics covered in the previous chapters in this book. Thus, how we define and measure age for example, will influence research in almost every topic covered in this book. In addition, how we design our studies, whom we collect data on, and how we analyze our data, will all influence our research results and the conclusions we draw from our studies. Thus, it is critical that we examine carefully the methodological concerns discussed in this section if we are move forward in our search for unifying paradigm for studying aging and work in the 21st century.

PRACTICE ISSUES

Many applied fields, such as industrial/organizational psychology, use as a guiding principle the scientist/practitioner model—that is, high-quality science leads to cutting-edge practice, while current practice needs to inform rigorous science. As a result, the scientist/practitioner model requires a synergy between science (i.e., empirical and theoretical research) and applied practice. We have seen this synergy in several areas in industrial/organizational psychology, as demonstrated in the Society for Industrial and Organizational Psychology's (SIOP's) Professional Practice and Frontiers series of books, where academic-based researchers and applied practitioners work together to create cutting-edge knowledge in the field. Thus, with the scientist/practitioner model as a backdrop, we discuss several practice issues that cut across many of the chapters in this book. Our goal in doing so is to further move us toward a unifying paradigm for studying aging and work in the 21st century.

A key practice issue that is common to all the topics discussed throughout this book is the various moving targets one encounters when studying aging and work. For example, the changing nature of work itself has made the issues of employee development (Maurer), job performance (Cleveland and Lim), older worker attitudes (Barnes-Farrell and Matthews), and career development (Feldman), to name just a few, increasingly difficult to study. The nature of jobs, the work environment, and what defines a career (Feldman) are continually shifting. For example, technological advances (Charness et al.), offshoring of jobs, and the burgeoning well-educated, English-speaking labor forces abroad will change how we view work in the coming years. These issues, along with older workers' physical (e.g., increasing obesity rates) and mental (e.g., increasing job stress) health (Jex et al.), will also impact older workers' ability to work at upper ages. Similarly, how we define retirement (Beehr and Bennett) and who is retired is also a moving target. Thus, it is becoming increasingly challenging to study these topics with the changing nature of work and the work environment.

Another practice issue that encompasses most of the chapters in this book is the need to examine the utility of many of the suggestions for practice provided by the chapter authors. For example, what is the cost/benefit of implementing a new performance assessment system (Cleveland and Lim), employee development program (Maurer), retirement planning program for low-income elderly workers (Taylor and Geldhauser), or a family-friendly eldercare program (Baltes and Young)? It is one thing to make general recommendations that sound good. It is entirely another to show that there is a real return on investment (ROI) for implementing such programs. While some programs may be easier to quantify than others, Cascio (2000) provides numerous examples of concepts that initially may have seemed difficult, if not impossible, to quantify (e.g., sexual harassment), where an estimate of the concept's utility (e.g., dollar value) was ultimately obtained and subsequently used to justify its importance.

Beyond demonstrating the utility of specific programs aimed at better managing an aging workforce for a particular organization, practitioners may also want to demonstrate that *bundles* of these types of practices can influence organizational performance—that is, to argue that sets of mutually reinforcing practices (for example those aimed at attracting, developing, and designing work for aging workers) impact not just individual performance, but also more macro-level indicators of organizational performance. Until more research in this area is conducted, such an argument could be based on work done in the area of strategic human resources management that has stressed the importance of aligning HR practices with business strategy (e.g., Guthrie, Spell, & Nyamori, 2002) and demonstrating their impact on organizational performance (e.g., Becker & Huselid, 1998; Subramony, Adams, Webster, & Bentz, 2006; Wright, Gardner, Moynihan, & Allen, 2005).

While we encourage the use of utility analysis and other forms of research evidence to make the case for adopting some of the practices and policies recommended throughout the various chapters, we are also well aware of the limitations of such rational approaches. Utility analysis has long been touted in industrial/organizational psychology as a key ally in the effort to influence organizational decision makers and politicians. However, many have questioned how much influence such quantification has on decision makers (e.g., Johns, 1993; Whyte & Latham, 1997). As a result, a key practice issue becomes how best to receive support and funding for the practice recommendations proposed throughout this book. We concur with Subramony et al.'s (2006) assertion that it is essential to consider the constraints on organizational decision- and policy-maker's decision-making processes when making adoption/rejection decisions and the tendency for policies to gain favor when it can be shown that they are being adopted by other organizations.

At the broader policy level, much work still needs to be done to adequately inform societal-level decision makers with regard to the employment of older workers. Papers by Burkhauser and Quinn (1997), Burtless and Quinn (2001), and Shultz, Sirotnik, and Bockman (2000) have outlined numerous macro-level strategies to shift us from anti, and neutral, older-worker policies to pro older-work policies. For example, Burkhauser and Quinn discuss the need for changes to current pension penalties for older workers who wish to continue working for the same employer they are eligible to collect a pension from (Feldman). In addition, the ability to prorate fringe benefits, such as eldercare subsidies (Baltes and Young) based on the number of hours worked, may encourage many older workers, who desire primarily part-time work, to remain or return to the workforce.

Shultz et al. (2000) suggested offering tax credits to both employers and older workers for training targeted to older workers. Additional incentives in the form of need-based tuition waivers or tuition subsidies targeted at older workers wishing to update their skills to remain in, or return to, the workforce were also suggested. Shultz et al. also recommend increased government funding for applied research, such as demonstration projects, targeted to low-income older workers and job seekers (Taylor and Geldhauser) to assist with their retirement planning and assessment of training needs. These are but a few of the many pro older-worker policies delineated by these authors that relate to much of what is discussed throughout this book. Thus, any unifying framework developed must include not only an interdisciplinary perspective, but also a diversity of approaches (e.g., applied versus basic) to both research and practice, as well as an investigation of the phenomena discussed throughout the book at multiple levels of analysis, including individual, organizational, and societal levels.

In summary, a plethora of practice concerns will face individuals, employers, governments, and societies at large as our population, and workforce, continues to age. We have chosen to highlight several of the more prominent practice issues. However, many more exist, and new ones not yet known will no doubt be created as the working-age population in the developed world continues to age. Thus, if we are to truly move the field of aging and work forward, we must examine not only theoretical and methodological issues, but also practice issues.

IS A UNIFYING PARADIGM DESIRABLE? POSSIBLE? PREMATURE?

The title of this chapter reflects our search for a unifying paradigm for understanding aging and work in the 21st century. In summarizing the key issues of the earlier chapters, we attempted to identify some of the important theoretical issues that new paradigm must address, as well as some of the more prominent methodological and practical issues any new paradigm must confront. However, the reader will note that we stop short of actually suggesting what this new paradigm will be. Rather we leave you, the reader, with some questions. Is a unifying paradigm desirable or even necessary? Alternatively, would a single paradigm for the study of aging and work serve to limit the type of questions and approaches researchers, practitioners, and policy makers pursue? Is a unifying paradigm even possible? On the other hand, are the issues, approaches, problems, and solutions just too diverse to organize under a single framework? Given that it is just now the start of the 21st century, could it be that a unifying paradigm would be simply premature?

REFERENCES

Adams, G. A., & Rau, B. L. (2004). Job seeking among retirees seeking bridge employment. *Personnel Psychology, 57,* 719–744.

Becker, B., & Huselid, M. (1998). High performance work systems and firm performance: A synthesis of research and managerial implications. *Research in Personnel and Human Resources, 16,* 53–101.

Burkhauser, R. V., & Quinn, J. F. (1997). *Pro-work policy proposals for older Americans in the 21st century.* Policy Brief No. 9, Maxwell School for Citizenship and Public Affairs, Syracuse University, Syracuse, New York.

Burtless, G., & Quinn, J. F. (2001). Retirement trends and policies to encourage work among older Americans. In P. P. Budetti, R. V. Burkhauser, J. M. Gregory, & H. A. Hunt

(Eds.), *Ensuring health and income security for an aging workforce* (pp. 375–415). Kalamazoo, MI: W.E. Upjohn Institute for Employment Research.

Cascio, W. F. (2000). *Costing human resources: The financial impact of behavior in organizations* (4th ed.). Cincinnati, OH: South-Western College Publishing.

Cohen, G. D. (Ed.). (2000). *The creative age.* New York: HarperCollins.

Dendinger, V. M., Adams, G. A., & Jacobson, J. D. (2005). Reasons for working and their relations to retirement attitudes, job satisfaction, and occupational self-efficacy of bridge employees. *International Journal of Aging and Human Development, 61, 21–35.*

Firebaugh, G. (1997). *Analyzing repeated surveys.* Sage University Paper Series on Quantitative Applications in the Social Sciences, Series No. 07-115. Thousand Oaks, CA: Sage.

Gilbert, G. A., & Shultz, K. S. (1998–99). Multilevel modeling in industrial and organizational psychology. *Current Psychology, 17, 287–300.*

Guthrie, J., Spell, C. S., & Nyamori, R. O. (2002). Correlates and consequences of high involvement work practices: The role of competitive strategy. *International Journal of Human Resource Management, 13, 183–197.*

Hagestad, G. O., & Dannefer, D. (2001). Conceptions and theories of aging: Beyond microfication in social science approaches. In R. H. Binstock & L. K. George (Eds.), *Handbook of Aging and the Social Sciences, 5th ed.* (Ch. 1, pp. 3–21). San Diego, CA: Academic Press.

Hall, D. T. (2004). The protean career: A quarter-century journal. *Journal of Vocational Behavior, 65, 1–13.*

Hansson, R. O., DeKoekkoek, P. D., Neece, W. M., & Patterson, D. W. (1997). Successful aging at work: Annual review, 1992–1996: The older worker and transitions to retirement. *Journal of Vocational Behavior, 51, 202–233.*

Henretta, J. C. (2001). Work and retirement. In R. H. Binstock & L. K. George (Eds.), *Handbook of Aging and the Social Sciences, 5th ed.* (Ch. 14, pp. 255–271). San Diego, CA: Academic Press.

Johns, G. (1993). Constraints on the adoption of psychology-based personnel practices: Lessons from organizations. *Personnel Psychology, 46, 569–593.*

Loi, J., & Shultz, K. S. (in press). Why older adults seek employment: Differing motivations among subgroups. *Journal of Applied Gerontology.*

Morrow-Howell, N., Hinterlong, J., & Sherraden, M. (Eds.) (2001). *Productive aging: Concepts and challenges.* Baltimore: Johns Hopkins Press.

O'Rand, A. M. (2001). Stratification and the life course: The forms of life-course capital and their interrelationships. In R. H. Binstock & L. K. George (Eds.), *Handbook of Aging and the Social Sciences, 5th ed.,* (Ch. 11, pp. 197–213). San Diego, CA: Academic Press.

Rau, B. L., & Adams, G. A. (2005). Attracting retirees to apply: Desired organizational characteristics of bridge employment. *Journal of Organizational Behavior, 26, 649–660.*

Salthouse, T., & Maurer, T. (1996). Aging, job performance, and career development. In J. Birren & K. Schaie (Eds.) *Handbook of the psychology of aging* (4th ed., pp. 353–364). San Diego, CA: Academic Press.

Shultz, K. S. (2003). Bridge employment: Work after retirement. In G. A. Adams & T. A. Beehr (Eds.), *Retirement: Reasons, processes, and results,* (Ch. 9, pp. 214–241). New York: Spring Publishing Company.

Shultz, K. S., Hoffman, C. C., & Reiter-Palmon, R. (2005). Using archival data for I-O research: Advantages, pitfalls, sources, and examples. *The Industrial-Organizational Psychologist, 42*(3), 31–37.

Shultz, K. S., & Morton, K. R. (2000). Successful Aging at Work: How do older workers adjust? *Southwest Journal of Aging, 16*(2), 63–72.

Shultz, K. S., Sirotnik, B. W., & Bockman, S. E. (2000). An aging workforce in transition: A case study of California. *Southwest Journal of Aging, 16*(2), 9–16.

Snel, J., & Cremer, R. (Eds.) (1994). *Work and aging: A European perspective.* London, UK: Taylor & Francis.

Sterns, H. L., & Kaplan, J. (2003). Self-management of career and retirement. In G. A. Adams & T. A. Beehr (Eds.), *Retirement: Reasons, processes, and results.* (pp. 188–213). New York: Springer Publishing Company.

Subramony, M., Adams, G. A., Webster, J., & Bentz, K. (2006, August). *Human resources management practices and business performance: A meta-analytic investigation.* Paper presented at the annual meeting of the Academy of Management, Atlanta, Georgia.

Taylor, M. A., Shultz, K. S., & Doverspike, D. (2005). Recruiting and retaining talented older workers. In P. T. Beatty & R. M. S. Visser (Eds.), *Thriving on an aging workforce: Strategies for organizational and system change.* Malabar, FL: Krieger Publishing Company.

Taylor, P. (2005). *The ageing European workforce.* Issue Brief Vol. 2, No. 5, from the Alliance for Health & the Future at the International Longevity Centre. Available on the Internet from http://www.ilcusa.org/_lib/pdf/Aging%20Workforce.pdf

Usi, C. (1998). Gradual retirement: Japanese strategies for older workers. In K. W. Schaie & C. Schooler (Eds.), *Impact of work on older adults.* (Ch. 2, pp. 45–84). New York: Spring Publishing Company.

Warr, P. B. (1994). Age and employment. In H. C. Triandis, M. D. Dunnette, & L. M. Hough (Eds.), *Handbook of industrial and organizational psychology* (Vol. 4, pp. 485–550). Palo Alto, CA: Consulting Psychologists Press.

Weiss, R. S., & Bass, S. A. (Eds.). (2002). *Challenges of the third age: Meaning and purpose in later life.* New York: Oxford.

Whyte, G., & Latham, G. (1997). The futility of utility analysis revisited: When even an expert fails. *Personnel Psychology, 50,* 601–611.

Wright, P., Gardner, T., Moynihan, L., & Allen, M. (2005). The relationship between HR practices and firm performance: Examining Causal Order. *Personnel Psychology, 58,* 409–446.

Zickar, M. J., & Gibby, R. E. (2003). Data analytic techniques for retirement research. In G. A. Adams & T. A. Beehr (Eds.), *Retirement: Reasons, processes, and results* (pp. 264–292). New York: Spring Publishing Company.

Author Index

A

Abel, E. K., 263, 272
Abraham, J. D., 120, 121, 131
Ackerman, P. L., 114, 122, 131, 133, 153, 155, 160
Ackers, L., 295, 298
Adams, G. A., 39, 45, 154, 159, 252, 272, 279, 290, 291, 293, 296, 298, 307, 316, 317, 318, 319
Ahmad, N., 204, 222
Albrecht, J. W., 183, 195
Albrecht, R. A., 58, 68
Albright, W. D., 259, 272
Alderfer, C. P., 181, 195
Aldous, J., 253, 272
Aldwin, C. M., 205, 219
Alexander, L. B., 141, 161
Alexander, R. A., 110, 111, 115, 136
Allen, M., 316, 319
Allen, T. D., 25.20, 55, 67, 119, 131, 188, 195, 272
Altschuler, J., 153, 159
Alvarez, M. G., 76, 78, 86, 95, 103
Anastas, J. W., 261, 265, 273
Anderson, N. H., 63, 66
Anderson, S. E., 148, 160
Anderson, S. G., 35, 45
Andrews, K., 165, 167, 169, 170, 171, 173, 175, 176
Anstee, J. L. K., 289, 301
Arad, S., 120, 135
Archbold, P. G., 264, 272
Aries, P., 169, 175
Arkes, H., 123, 131
Arking, R., 203, 219
Armstrong, P. S., 30, 31, 45
Arthur, M. B., 179, 184, 193, 195
Artt, S., 111, 112, 133
Arvey, R. D., 53, 60, 64, 66, 68, 74, 76, 78, 87, 88, 89, 90, 95, 100, 105, 155, 159, 168, 176, 243, 248

Ashman, O., 99, 104
Atwater, L. E., 61, 66, 125, 131
Au, W. T., 123, 134
Austin, J. T., 187, 195
Austrom, G., 30, 45
Avery, C. M., 287, 298
Avery, D., 60, 66
Avolio, B. J., 54, 66, 71, 76, 78, 84, 87, 103, 115, 116, 117, 118, 131, 136

B

Backman, L., 121, 132
Baddeley, A., 203, 219
Bahman, B., 280, 298
Bai, U., 204, 222
Bailey, L. L., 131
Bailey, W. C., 34, 49
Baltes, B. B., 258, 263, 272
Baltes, M. M., 120, 121, 131, 258, 272
Baltes, P. B., 120, 121, 131, 166, 176, 182, 195, 204, 219, 221, 257, 258, 272, 273
Banaji, R. B., 81, 97, 106
Bandura, A., 169, 175
Barak, B., 110, 111, 131
Barbee, A. P., 267, 274
Barbeite, F. G., 149, 150, 161, 170, 177, 215, 221
Barling, J., 32, 47
Barnes-Farrell, J. L., 118, 131, 140, 146, 159
Barnett, W. P., 186, 196
Barnsley, J., 65, 71
Barnum, P., 52, 56, 57, 66
Baron, R. M., 209, 220
Barrah, J. L., 263, 272
Barrett, G. V., 76, 78, 84, 87, 103, 115, 136
Bartel, A. P., 20, 21
Bartolomé, F., 256, 273
Barton, M. E., 208, 210, 213, 219, 221
Bass, S. A., 310, 319
Baum, S. K., 111, 131
Baxter, J. C., 78, 86, 89, 98, 105

321

Beach, L. R., 281, *301*
Beatty, R. W., 125, *134*
Becker, B., 316, *317*
Becker, P. E., 59, 66
Bedeian, A., 140, *159*
Beedon, L., 27, 28, 29, *45, 48, 49*
Beehr, T. A., 123, *131,* 184, 188, 189, 190, 191, *195, 197,* 278, 279, 280, 281, 282, 284, 288, 290, 291, 293, 296, 297, 298, *301*
Bégat, I., 150, *159*
Bellusci, S. M., 115, *132*
Bem, S. L., 59, 66
Ben-Sira, D., 166, *177*
Benecki, T. J., 75, 78, 84, *104*
Benest, R., 291, *298*
Bennett, J. M., 261, 266, 268, 269, 270, *273*
Bennett, M. M., 282, *298*
Bennett, N., 122, *133*
Bennett, R. J., 122, *135*
Bentz, K., 316, *319*
Berger, P. K., 60, 69
Berman, A. H., 60, 66
Bernstein, J., 27, 40, *45*
Beutell, N. J., 252, *273*
Beyerlein, M., 127, *133,* 149, *160*
Bharat, K., 233, *249*
Bhattacharya, J., 291, *298*
Biernat, M., 81, 82, *103*
Bird, C. P., 78, 94, *103*
Bird, G. W., 253, 257, 258, *274*
Blake-Beard, S., 59, 69
Blanchard-Fields, F., 203, 205, *220*
Blekesaune, M., 288, *298*
Bluck, S., 184, *196*
Blumer, C., 123, *131*
Bobo, L., 81, 82, *103*
Bockman, S. E., 316, *319*
Boerlijst, J., 168, *175*
Bokemeier, J. L., 152, *161*
Bolino, M. C., 182, 184, 192, *195*
Bond, J. T., 260, *272*
Bond-Huie, S. A., 32, *45*
Boorse, C., 200, *220*
Booth, A., 294, *300*
Bordieri, J. E., 76, *104*
Borgatta, E. F., 52, 58, 63, 66
Borges, F. N., 115, *132*
Borman, W. C., 113, 115, 118, 119, 124, 128, 129, *131, 133*
Bosman, E. A., 226, 233, *247*
Bosse, R., 280, 284, *299*

Bouma, H., 227, *247*
Bound, J., 18, *21*
Bourhis, A. C., 42, 48, 59, 61, 69, 78, 84, 90, 91, *107,* 243, *248*
Bourne, A., 125, *136*
Bourne, B., 140, 141, *159*
Bowen, C., 54, 66
Bowen, C. P., 294, *301*
Bowling, N. A., 123, *131,* 184, 189, 190, 191, *195*
Boxley, R. L., 111, *131*
Boyd, S. L., 261, *274*
Bradford, W. D., 38, *45*
Brahee, C. I., 261, 266, 268, 269, 270, *273*
Braithwaite, V., 101, *103*
Brear, K., 204, *220*
Brett, J. M., 187, *197*
Brett, M. J., 56, *70*
Bretz, R. D., 60, *70*
Brewer, M., 59, 66
Brief, A. P., 101, *103*
Brigham, J. C., 76, *104*
Briner, R. B., 288, *300*
Brkljacic, T., 118, *133*
Brougham, R., 31, 39, *46*
Bruck, C. S., 252, *272*
Brymer, R. A., 147, *160*
Buckley, R. M., 54, *70*
Buessing, A., 237, *247*
Buffardi, L. C., 262, 267, *272*
Bunce, D., 207, *220*
Burch, P., 53, 66
Burdick, D. C., 227, *247*
Burke, M. J., 53, 67, 74, 78, 87, 88, 89, 91, 93, 100, *104,* 165, *176,* 243, *248*
Burkhauser, R. V., 10, 13, 14, 16, 17, 18, 20, 22, 23, 316, *317*
Burtless, G., 316, *317*
Busse, E., 63, 66
Butcher, V., 284, *301*
Butrica, B. A., 41, 42, *45*
Butterfield, D. A., 54, 59, 69
Byosiere, P., 182, *196*
Byrne, Z., 147, *159*
Bytheway, B., 95, 101, *103*

                                   C

Cafferata, G. L., 261, 262, *275*
Cahill, K., 16, *23*
Caldwell, D. F., 186, *196*

Caldwell, S. D., 151, 159
Callahan, J. S., 172, 175
Callinan, M., 284, 301
Cammann, C., 239, 249
Campbell, J. P., 110, 112, 113, 114, 118, 119, 124, 128, 131
Campion, M. A., 212, 220, 222
Cannings, K., 52, 58, 68
Capowski, G., 165, 168, 175
Capwell, D. R., 142, 160
Carlson, D. S., 147, 160
Carlucci, C. A., 76, 104
Carnazza, J., 183, 195
Carpenter, B., 53, 70
Carrozza, M., 286, 299
Carstensen, L. L., 145, 151, 159
Carter, M. T., 283, 298
Carter, S., 31, 39, 46
Casado-Díaz, M. A., 295, 298
Cascio, W. F., 54, 69, 115, 116, 134, 189, 195, 318
Caserta, M., 295, 302
Catalano, M., 184, 197
Cavanaugh, J. C., 203, 205, 220
Chachere, J. G., 126, 132
Chalder, T., 206, 222
Chan, A. W., 78, 84, 92, 93, 94, 95, 98, 99, 103
Chan, S., 17, 22
Chang, S., 59, 66
Chapman, N. J., 260, 261, 263, 264, 266, 267, 268, 274
Charatan, F. B., 208, 220
Charles, S. T., 145, 159
Charness, N., 226, 227, 228, 230, 235, 236, 247, 248
Chasteen, A. L., 85, 94, 103
Chayet, E. F., 124, 137
Chen, H., 18, 22
Cherry, K. E., 204, 220
Chi, I., 31, 45
Chiu, W. C. K., 78, 84, 92, 93, 94, 95, 98, 99, 103
Choi, B. C. K., 115, 132
Choi, N. G., 30, 41, 45
Chou, K. L., 31, 45
Chown, S. M., 165, 176
Christensen, H., 216, 222
Christoffolete, M. A., 115, 132
Chuang, A., 148, 161
Church, A. H., 125, 132
Clancy, M., 76, 78, 84, 98, 104
Clark, A., 142, 144, 159
Clark, R. L., 13, 22

Clark-Murphy, M., 292, 298
Clemons, T., 78, 87, 89, 96, 106
Cleveland, J. N., 55, 59, 60, 61, 66, 67, 70, 78, 84, 90, 93, 103, 107, 110, 112, 113, 121, 124, 125, 126, 132, 134, 135, 141, 147, 159, 169, 170, 175
Cluff, G. A., 259, 272
Coates, J. F., 259, 272
Cockerill, R., 65, 71
Cohen, D. J., 40, 41, 45
Cohen, G. D., 310, 318
Collins, R. W., 117, 132
Collins, S. M., 60, 67
Colonia-Willner, R., 118, 132
Colquitt, J. A., 163, 175
Connor, C. L., 76, 78, 86, 95, 103
Conroy, D., 169, 177
Cook, J., 239, 249
Cook, K., 38, 48, 283, 298
Cook, T. C., 52, 67
Cooper, C. L., 141, 162, 210, 223
Cooper, M. L., 252, 273
Corter, D. A., 53, 67
Cotton, J. L., 55, 70
Cox, T. H., 55, 67
Coyle, B. W., 283, 301
Cozzarelli, C., 26, 42, 46
Craft, J. A., 75, 78, 84, 104
Credé, M., 77, 78, 85, 86, 95, 101, 107
Creedon, M. A., 264, 275
Cremer, R., 309, 319
Crew, J. C., 59, 67, 75, 78, 95, 104
Crimmins, E. M., 16, 19, 22, 23
Cristofalo, V. J., 202, 220
Cropanzano, R., 147, 159, 256, 273
Cross, T., 172, 175
Cuddy, A. J. C., 41, 46, 80, 82, 93, 97, 98, 104
Cumming, E., 58, 67
Cummings, L. L., 211, 222
Cunningham, J. B., 140, 159
Currey, J. D., 204, 220
Czaja, S. J., 113, 114, 116, 129, 132, 135, 190, 195, 226, 228, 230, 231, 233, 235, 236, 238, 241, 247, 248, 249, 1173

D

Dalton, G., 168, 177
Damush, T. M., 30, 45, 46
Danigelis, N. L., 30, 46

Dannefer, D., 308, 313, *318*
Darrow, C., 58, 69
Dasgupta, N., 99, *104*
Dautzenberg, M. G. H., 261, 264, 266, *272*
Davey, A., 38, *48*, 285, *301*
Davies, J., 168, *175*
Davies, S., 41, *46*
Davis, F. D., 228, *249*
Davison, S., 123, *136*
Dawis, R. V., 239, *249*
Deaux, K., 60, 68
Dedrick, E. J., 78, 86, 99, *104*
DeFiore, J., 53., 67
Deimler, J. D., 116, *133*
DeKoekkoek, P. D., 116, 117, 120, 129, *133*, 308, *318*
Delery, J. E., 188, *196*
Dellmann-Jenkins, M., 261, 266, 268, 269, 270, *273*
Delp, N. D., 171, *176*, 190, *196*, 232, *248*
Dendinger, V. M., 154, *159*, 307, *318*
Denton, M., 41, *46*
Derbin, V., 111, 112, *133*
Devaney, S. A., 286, *298*
DeViney, S., 38, *48*, 140, 146, *160*
DeVore, C. J., 128, *135*
Dick, J., 152, *162*
Diederiks, J. P. M., 261, 264, 266, *272*
Dietz, B. E., 286, *299*
Digman, J. M., 182, *195*
DiMaggio, P., 191, *197*
DiTomaso, N., 52, 56, 57, *66*
Dittman, M., 32, *46*
Dixon, R. A., 121, *132*, 166, *176*
Dobbins, G. H., 54, 69, 78, 86, *104*, *106*
Doctors, S. I., 75, 78, 84, *104*
Doering, M., 127, *132*, 165, *175*, xiii
Doeringer, P. B., 181, 182, 191, *195*
Doerpinghaus, H. I., 141, 150, *160*
Dohm, A., 20, *22*
Donald, I., 141, *162*
Donlon, M. M., 99, *104*
Donohue, J. M., 153, *160*
Donovan, M. A., 120, 128, *135*
Doorewaard, H., 154, *159*
Dorsett, J. G., 121, *136*
Douthitt, S. S., 188, *195*
Doverspike, D., 32, *48*, 110, 111, *136*, 307, *319*
Dovidio, J. F., 59, 67, 76, *104*
Dreher, G. F., 55, 67
Drehmer, D. E., 76, *104*

Dudley, W. N., 204, *222*
Dulebohn, J. H., 38, 46, 288, *299*
Dull, V., 59, 66
Duncan, C., 78, *106*
Dunham, R. B., 211, *222*
Dunn, A., *46*
Dunnette, M. D., 94, *105*
Durick, M., 141, *160*
Duval, E. M., 254, *273*
Duxbury, L., 254, 255, *273*
Dwyer, P., 295, *298*
Dye, D. A., 115, *132*

E

Eagly, A. H., 54, 67
Earl, B. T., 280, *299*
Easterby-Smith, M., 168, *175*
Easterlin, R. A., 13, *22*
Eastman, L., 168, *177*
Ebling, R., 285, *300*
Eby, L. T., 188, 192, *195*, *196*
Edin, P. A., 183, *195*
Edwards, C., 56, 67
Edwins, C. J., 262, 267, *272*
Einbender, S., 53, *71*
Ekamper, P., 78, 92, 98, *107*
Ekerdt, D. J., 140, 146, *160*, 280, 284, 290, *299*
Elacqua, T. C., 211, 214, *221*
Elder, G. H., 203, *220*
Elias, M. F., 54, 67
Elias, P. K., 54, 67
Ellefsen, B., 150, *159*
Elman, C., 28, *46*
Elovainio, M., 290, *299*
Emlen, A. C., 260, 261, 263, 264, 266, 267, 268, *274*
England, G. W., 239, *249*
Enright, R. B., Jr., 261, 262, 268, *273*
Erez, M., 180, 185, 186, 187, 188, *196*
Ettner, S. L., 30, *46*
Evans, D. R., 30, *46*
Evans, P., 256, *273*
Eysenk, M. W., 181, *195*

F

Fair, S., 114, *135*
Fang, T., 294, *300*

Farh, J. L., 54, 69, 78, 106
Farmer, S. J., 288, 290, 298
Farr, J. L., 115, 120, 132, 168, 176
Farrell, A., 31, 39, 46
Feagin, C. B., 59, 67
Feagin, J. R., 59, 67
Featherman, D. L., 120, 132
Feddon, J., 236, 248
Fedor, D. B., 151, 159
Feinberg, B., 184, 186, 193, 196
Feldman, D. C., 141, 150, 160, 179, 180, 181,
    182, 184, 187, 189, 191, 192, 194, 195, 196,
    278, 281, 282, 288, 299, 300
Feldon, J., 247
Ference, T. P., 183, 195
Ferguson, R. F., 26, 40, 46
Ferreira, R. M., 115, 132
Ferrie, J., 288, 300
Ferris, G. R., 78, 106, 126, 132, 140, 142, 159, 160
Festa, R. M., 78, 90, 103, 112, 121, 132
Ffusilier, M. R., 78, 96, 104
Field, H., 54, 69
Fielding, R. A., 204, 220
Fillenbaum, G. G., 297, 299
Finch, C. E., 202, 220
Finegold, D., 147, 160
Finkelstein, L. M., 52, 53, 55, 56, 61, 65, 67, 74,
    76, 78, 84, 87, 88, 89, 90, 91, 93, 98, 100,
    102, 104, 107, 165, 176, 243, 248
Firebaugh, G., 311, 318
Fischer, F. M., 115, 132
Fisher, T. D., 78, 94, 103
Fisk, A. D., 228, 230, 231, 236, 246, 247, 248
Fiske, S. T., 41, 46, 73, 75, 76, 77, 79, 80, 81, 82,
    82, 83, 87, 88, 93, 97, 98, 101, 104
Flanagan, R. J., 55, 67
Folsom, A. R., 52, 67
Foltman, E., 170, 177
Ford, J. K., 215, 220
Forma, P., 290, 299
Forte, C. S., 165, 176
Forteza, J. A., 92, 104
Fosuum, J., 168, 176
Fox, J. B., 153, 160
Fozard, J., 234, 248
Francis, M. K., 202, 220
Franken, R. E., 75, 104
French, E., 293, 299
Freund, A. M., 258, 273
Fried, Y., 210, 223
Friedman, S., 18, 22

Frieske, D. A., 204, 220
Friss, L., 261, 273
Frone, M. R., 252, 273
Fujii, M., 261, 263, 267, 268, 273
Fujioka, Y., 59, 70
Fullerton, H. N., Jr., 18, 22, 51, 52, 67

G

Gaertner, S. L., 59, 67, 76, 104
Galinsky, E., 260, 272
Gall, T. L., 30, 46
Gangaram, S., 149, 161
Gansrer, D. C., 208, 210, 213, 219, 221
Gardner, D. G., 211, 222
Gardner, T., 316, 319
Garris, J. M., 30, 32, 48
Garstka, T. A., 86, 105
Garta, M. L., 56, 70
Gatz, M., 145, 159, 205, 206, 220
Gendell, M., 15, 22
George, L. K., 297, 299
George, P., 54, 67
Gerhart, B., 60, 70
Geyer, M. D., 124, 136
Geyer, P. D., 141, 142, 153, 160, 161
Gibby, R. E., 311, 319
Gibeau, J. L., 261, 265, 273
Gibson, D., 101, 103
Gibson, J., 55, 71
Gibson, K. J., 75, 104
Gibson, R., 57, 70
Gignac, M. A. M., 262, 273
Gilbert, G. A., 313, 318
Gilbert, G. R., 117, 132
Gilbert, P. R., 152, 162
Giles, H., 87, 91, 97, 98, 102, 105, 106
Gilmer, D. F., 205, 219
Gist, M., 171, 176
Girtleman, M., 27, 40, 45
Glass, J. C., 33, 46
Glazer, S., 288, 290, 298
Glick, P., 61, 67
Glisson, C., 141, 160
Godsky, E., 56, 68
Goebel, B. L., 101, 105
Goedhart, W. J. A., 115, 133
Goff, S. J., 258, 273
Goldberg, C., 52, 53, 55, 56, 59, 61, 65, 67, 68,
    70, 74, 78, 83, 90, 93, 107, 116, 121, 123, 135

Goldenberg, J. L., 81, 82, 97, 100, *106*
Goldstein, I. L., 215, *220*
Goncalves, M. B., 115, *132*
Gonyea, J. G., 265, 267, *274*
Goodman, J. C., 33, *46*
Gordon, R. A., 60, 64, 68, 74, 76, 78, 86, 87, 88, 89, 90, 95, 98, 100, *105*, 243, *248*
Gordon-Salant, S., 234, *248*
Gottfredson, M., 124, *132*
Gottlieb, B. H., 262, *273*
Gould, R., 53, *66*
Goulet, L. R., 147, *160*
Grable, J. E., 37, *47*
Graf, P., 182, *195*
Grandey, A. A., 256, *273*
Granovetter, M., 191, *195*
Green, S. G., 148, *160*
Greenberg, E., 287, *300*
Greenberg, J., 81, 82, 97, 100, *106*
Greenhaus, J. H., 252, *273*
Greenspan, A., 29, *46*
Greenwald, A. G., 99, *104*
Greller, M. M., 151, 152, *160*, 162, 163, 169, *176*, 292, 293, *299*
Grierson, D., 294, *301*
Griffith, R. W., 141, *162*
Griffiths, A., 115, 117, 118, 123, *133*, *136*, 215, *220*
Gruber, J., 17, *22*
Grunberg, L., 287, *300*
Grzywacz, J., 30, *46*
Guberman, N., 260, 264, 268, 270, *273*
Guerriero-Austrom, M., 30, *46*
Gunderson, M., 294, *300*
Gupta, N., 188, *196*
Gurtman, M. B., 101, *106*
Gustman, A. L., 285, 287, *299*
Guthrie, J., 316, *318*
Guzzo, R. A., 181, *195*
Gyselinck, V., 245, *249*

H

Habermas, T., 184, *196*
Hackett, R. D., 122, *133*
Haefner, J. E., 78, 96, *105*
Hagedoorn, M., 150, *162*
Hagestad, G. O., 97, 98, 99, *105*, 308, 313, *318*
Hall, D. T., 144, *160*, 163, *176*, 257, *273*, 307, *318*
Hall, M. J., 125, *137*

Hallman, B. C., 265, *274*
Hamil-Luker, J., 232, *248*
Hamilton, D. L., 80, 86, *105*
Hamilton, R. F., 127, *137*
Hanisch, K. A., 187, *195*, 279, 282, *299*
Hankin, C. S., 284, *299*
Hannigan, M., 258, *274*
Hanoch, G., 281, *300*
Hansen, A. F., 216, *222*
Hansen, C. P., 207, *220*
Hansson, R. O., 116, 117, 120, 121, 129, *131*, *133*, *318*
Hansvick, C. L., 165, *176*
Hardy, M. A., 55, 68, 288, *299*
Harma, M., 115, *133*
Harris, P. B., 261, 263, 267, 268, *273*
Harris, R. M., 116, *133*
Harris, S. G., 289, *301*
Hartley, A. A., 207, *221*
Hasher, L., 204, *221*, *223*
Haslett, T. K., 171, *176*, 190, *196*, 232, *248*
Hassell, B. L., 76, 78, 94, 98, 100, *105*, 189, *196*
Hatcher, C. B., 277, 291, 292, 294, *299*
Havighurst, R. J., 58, 63, *68*
Hayflick, L., 202, *221*
Hayslip, B., Jr., 127, *133*, 149, *160*
Hayward, M. D., 18, 19, *22*
Hazelrigg, L., 288, *299*
Healy, M. C., 123, *133*
Heckhausen, J., 31, 49, 121, *135*, 146, *160*, 166, *176*
Hedge, J. W., 129, *133*
Hellgren, J., 210, *223*
Hendrick, J., 154, *159*
Hendrie, H. C., 30, *45*, *46*
Heneman, H. G., 155, *160*
Henkens, K., 20, *23*, 78, 92, 98, *107*, 126, *133*, 280, *301*
Henretta, J. C., 19, *22*, 311, *318*
Henry, W., 58, *67*
Hepburn, C. G., 261, *273*
Hermans, H. J. M., 183, *196*
Hermsen, J. M., 53, *67*
Hernandez, M., 114, *135*, 231, 238, 241, *249*
Herold, D. M., 151, *159*
Heron, A., 165, *176*
Hershey, D. A., 31, 33, 38, 39, *39*, *46*
Herst, D. E. L., 25, 20, *272*
Hertzog, C., 228, *247*
Herzberg, F. I., 142, *160*
Herzog, A. R., 289, 290, 291, 292, 293, 294, *299*

Hesketh, B., 120, *133*
Heydens-Gahir, H. A., 258, *272*
Heywood, J. S., 55, 68
Higginbottom, S. F., 32, 47
Higgins, C., 254, 255, *273*
Higgins, K. D., 76, 78, 84, 98, *104*
Higgs, P., 288, *300*
Hill, E. T., 16, *22*
Hill, R., 254, *273*
Hill, R. L., 254, *273*
Hillman, D. J., 116, *133*
Hines, F. G., 235, 236, *248*
Hinterlong, J., 310, *318*
Hirsch, B. T., 55, 68
Hirschi, T., 124, *132*
Hitt, M. A., 78, 96, *104*
Ho, J. M. C., 123, *134*
Ho, L., 55, 68
Hoare, S., 125, 126, *137*
Hochschild, A., 254, *274*
Hoffman, C. C., 312, *319*
Hofmann, D. A., 199, 211, *221*
Holley, P., 235, 236, 247, *248*
Holman, J., 101, *103*
Holtom, B. C., 180, 185, 186, 187, 188, *196*
Holzer, H. J., 41, *46*
Hong, B. E., 36, *47*
Honig, M., 281, 285, *300*
Hooyman, N. R., 265, 267, *274*
Horowitz, A., 265, 267, *274*
Hosoda, M., 52, 57, 58, 59, 60, 61, 65, 68
Huber, A., 295, *300*
Huber, F. N., 80, 87, 97, *106*
Hudson, S., 233, *249*
Huffcutt, A., 54, 68
Hulin, C. L., 279, *299*
Hummer, R. A., 32, *45*
Hummert, M. L., 86, 96, 97, 101, *105*
Hungerford, T. L., 293, *300*
Hunt, M. O., 42, *47*
Hunter, J. E., 54, 70, 118, *133*, 207, *222*
Hunter, R. F., 118, *133*
Huselid, M., 316, *317*
Hyde, M., 288, *300*
Hyland, D. T., 116, *133*

I

Iams, H. M., 41, *45*
Iimori, T., 203, *221*

Ilgen, D., 168, *176*
Ingersoll-Dayton, B., 260, 261, 263, 264, 266, 267, 268, *274*
Intrieri, R., 85, *105*
Isabella, L., 169, *176*
Isaksson, K., 146, 149, *160*
Ishio, Y., 55, 68
Iskra-Golec, I., 118, *133*

J

Jablin, F. M., 287, *298*
Jackson, L. A., 94, *105*
Jackson, M., 204, *222*
Jacobs, E. E., 11, 12, 14, 15, *22*
Jacobs, R. R., 54, 66
Jacobs-Lawson, J. M., 30, 32, 38, *46*
Jacobson, J. D., 154, *159*, 307, *318*
James, E. H., 56, 68
Jamison, R. L., 258, *273*
Jansen, P. L., 205, *221*
Jardee, T. H., 75, 78, 83, *107*
Jarratt, J., 259, *272*
Jastrzembski, T., 236, 247, *248*
Jenkins, G. D., 188, *196*
Jerdee, T. H., 59, 70, 75, 78, 95, *107*, 165, 166, 167, *177*
Jex, S. M., 210, 211, 214, *221*, *223*
Jivan, N., 40, *47*
Johansson, G., 146, 149, *160*
Johns, G., 123, *134*, 316, *318*
Johnson, B. T., 42, *47*, 76, 87, 88, 89, 93, 96, 97, 99, *104*, *105*, 126, *134*, 164, *176*, 243, *248*
Johnson, D., 127, *133*, 149, *160*
Johnson, J. W., 113, 119, 120, 128, *133*
Johnson, M. K., 203, *220*
Johnson, P. J., 258, *275*
Johnson, R. L., 31, *47*
Johnson, R. W., 42, *45*
Joo, S., 37, *47*
Joseph, A. E., *274*
Joshi, A., 148, *161*
Judge, T. A., 126, *132*

K

Kacmar, K. M., 140, 142, 147, *159*, *160*
Kahn, R. L., 63, 70, 182, *196*
Kaiser, C., 295, *298*

Kalasky, M. A., 236, 248
Kalavar, J. M., 95, 105
Kaliterna, L., 118, 133
Kalleberg, A. L., 141, 152, 160, 161
Kanfer, R., 122, 133, 153, 155, 160
Kanter, R. M., 63, 68
Kanungo, R. B., 239, 248
Kaplan, J., 307, 319
Karasek, R., 254, 274
Karel, M., 206, 220
Kasl, S. V., 31, 48
Kasl-Godley, J. E., 206, 220
Kastenbaum, R., 111, 112, 133
Katz, A., 40, 47
Kauffman, S., 141, 161
Kaufman, B. E., 55, 65, 68
Kausler, B. C., 51, 68
Kausler, D. H., 51, 68
Kawada, T., 208, 213, 221
Kay, E. J., 116, 133
Kaye, L. W., 141, 161
Keith, P., 253, 274
Kelley, C. L., 226, 233, 247
Kelloway, E. K., 32, 47, 262, 273
Kelly, H. H., 180, 196
Kelly, J. A., 85, 105
Kenny, D. A., 209, 220
Khalil, Z., 204, 221
Kidwell, R. E., 122, 133
Kiefer, T., 288, 300
Kiker, D. S., 172, 175
Kilpatrick, B. B., 33, 46
Kilry, K. M., 187, 196
Kim, H., 286, 298
Kim, J. E., 31, 34, 47
Kim, S., 179, 182, 187, 189, 191, 196, 282,
    291, 300
Kimberly, J. R., 179, 190, 197
Kindelan, A., 66, 68
King, D. W., 252, 272
King, L. A., 252, 272
Kinnunen, U., 147, 161
Kinsella, K., 8, 22
Kirchner, W. K., 94, 105
Kirkman, B. L., 140, 161
Kite, M. E., 42, 47, 60, 68, 75, 76, 79, 80, 87, 88,
    89, 93, 95, 96, 97, 99, 105, 126, 134, 164,
    176, 243, 248
Kivimaki, M., 290, 299

Kizilos, M. A., 141, 162
Klein, E., 58, 69
Kleiner, B. H., 59, 66
Klonsky, B. G., 54, 67
Knoke, D., 55, 68
Kogan, N., 75, 76, 78, 85, 105, 106
Kolb, P. J., 52, 57, 68
Kong, S. X., 147, 161
Konovsky, M., 120, 134
Konrad, A., 52, 55, 56, 58, 61, 65, 67, 68
Koopman-Boyden, P. G., 157, 161
Korman, A., 183, 195
Kowalewski, B., 53, 67
Kozlowski, S., 168, 176
Kram, K., 169, 176
Krause, N., 31, 47
Krefting, L. A., 60, 69
Krieger, J. L., 80, 97, 106
Kristof, A. L., 186, 196
Krueger, P. M., 32, 45
Kruger, A., 183, 196
Kubeck, J. E., 171, 176, 190, 196, 232, 248
Kulik, C. T., 42, 48, 78, 84, 90, 107, 243, 248
Kumagai, K., 203, 221
Kupperbusch, C., 285, 300
Kwon, S., 227, 247

                                 L

Lachman, M. E., 31, 49
Lacy, W. B., 152, 161
Laine, M., 290, 299
Lakhdari, M., 150, 162
Lammlein, S. E., 129, 133
Landau, J., 55, 69
Landy, F. J., 59, 60, 67, 78, 84, 90, 103,
    116, 134
Lane, J. I., 41, 46
Langer, E., 93, 106
Larsen, Z. P., 118, 133
Larson, J. S., 201, 221
Latham, G., 316, 319
Latimer, S., 169, 177
Lau, V. C., 123, 134
Law, K. W., 295, 300
Lawler, E. E., III, 239, 249
Lawrence, B. S., 55, 69, 78, 81, 90, 91, 99, 106,
    110, 112, 121, 134, 169, 178

Lawrence, C., 56, 69
Leana, C. R., 182, 195
Leavitt, J., 26, 47
Lee, C., 254, 255, 273
Lee, C. C., 114, 135, 231, 238, 241, 249
Lee, J. A., 78, 87, 89, 96, 106
Lee, R., 10, 22
Lee, T. W., 180, 185, 186, 187, 188, 196
Lee, W. K. M., 286, 295, 300
Lehman, M., 123, 133
LePine, J. A., 163, 175
Lepisto, L. R., 282, 298
Levenson, R. W., 285, 300
Leviatan, U., 152, 161
Levin, W. C., 75, 78, 106
Levine, P. B., 13, 17, 22
Levinson, D., 58, 69
Levinson, M., 58, 69
Levitsky, M., 115, 132
Levkoff, S., 280, 284, 299
Levy, B. R., 81, 93, 97, 99, 104, 106
Levy, P. E., 125, 134
Lewis, J. E., 135 114, 231, 238, 241, 249
Lewis, P., 54, 69
Lewis, W. R., 140, 159
Leyens, J. P., 81, 88, 106
Liao, H., 148, 161
Lichtenwalter, S., 26, 28, 47
Liden, R. C., 52, 56, 57, 66, 78, 106, 126, 132
Lightfoot, E., 32, 36, 47
Lin, T. R., 54, 69, 78, 106
Lindenberger, U., 204, 219, 221
Lingafelter, T., 26, 47
Lingl, A., 120, 134
Linville, P. W., 81, 94, 106
Lisansky Gomberg, E. S., 206, 221
Little, D. M., 207, 221
Litzelman, D. K., 76, 78, 86, 95, 103
Lloyd, R. D., 115, 132
Locke-Connor, C., 78, 86, 94, 96, 106
Loewentheil, N., 26, 47
Lofquist, L. H., 239, 249
Loi, J., 307, 318
Lombardo, M., 168, 177
London, M., 120, 125, 134, 137
Long, S. O., 261, 263, 267, 268, 273
Longino, C. F., Jr., 295, 300
Loomis, L. S., 294, 300
Lorence, J., 148, 161

Loretto, W., 78, 106
Loscocco, K. A., 141, 152, 160, 161
Luchak, A. A., 294, 300
Lucht, N., 59, 70
Lui, L., 59, 66
Lum, Y. S., 32, 36, 47
Lund, D. A., 295, 302
Lyness, K., 55, 69
Lyon, P., 76, 78, 95, 99, 106

M

MacDonald, L., 157, 161
MacEwen, K. E., 32, 47
MacGregor, J., 140, 159
MacNeil, R. D., 166, 176
Macpherson, D. A., 55, 68
MacRae, P. G., 204, 223
Maddox, G., 63, 66
Magafas, A. M., 166, 176
Mahaffie, J. B., 259, 272
Maheu, P., 260, 264, 268, 270, 273
Makhijani, M. G., 54, 67
Manis, M., 81, 82, 103
Marcellini, F., 228, 249
Martens, A., 81, 82, 97, 100, 106
Martikainen, R., 208, 222
Martin, M., 267, 274
Martins, S. E., 115, 132
Martocchio, J. J., 122, 134
Matterson, M. P., 202, 222
Matthews, A. M., 263, 266, 268, 274
Matthews, R., 140, 159
Maume, D. J., 56, 69
Mauno, S., 147, 161
Mauo, K., 203, 221
Maurer, T. J., 42, 49, 55, 69, 76, 79, 84, 108,
    110, 116, 118, 121, 135, 148, 149, 150, 161,
    164, 165, 166, 167, 168, 169, 170, 171, 172,
    173, 174, 175, 176, 177, 178, 215, 221, 226,
    249, 313, 318
Mausner, B., 142, 160
May, D. R., 140, 162
Mayes, B. T., 208, 210, 213, 219, 221
Mayr, U., 145, 151, 159
Mazerolle, M. J., 149, 161
McArdle, A., 204, 222
McCain, B. E., 123, 134

McCall, M., 168, 177
McCann, R., 87, 91, 102, 106
McCauley, C. D., 168, 177
McClary, A. M., 111, 136
McCloy, R. A., 110, 112, 113, 114, 118, 119, 124, 128, 131
McDaniel, M. A., 54, 66, 115, 116, 117, 123, 131, 132, 133, 136, 171, 176, 190, 196, 207, 222, 232, 248
McEvoy, G. M., 54, 69, 115, 116, 134
McFarlin, D. B., 140, 161
McGee, J. P., 211, 223, 227, 232, 249
McGoldrick, A. E., 287, 300
McIntosh, B. R., 30, 46
McKee, B., 58, 69
McLaughlin, A. C., 236, 248
McNally, J., 28, 47
McNamara, T. K., 40, 41, 47
Mein, G., 288, 300
Meir, E., 184, 197
Mercer, W. M., 167, 177
Merhi, M., 204, 221
Methany, W., 127, 133, 149, 160
Meydani, M., 204, 220
Miele, M., 60, 68
Miene, P. K., 79, 99, 102, 107
Miklos, S., 125, 136, 144, 162
Miller, C., 127, 133, 149, 160
Miller, D. A., 274
Miller, H. E., 53, 66
Mirvis, P. H., 144, 160, 163, 176, 239, 249
Mischel, W., 181, 196
Mitchell, O. S., 13, 17, 22
Mitchell, T. R., 180, 185, 186, 187, 188, 196
Moen, P., 30, 31, 32, 34, 38, 47, 48, 59, 66, 70, 285, 301
Mohrman, 147, 160
Mollenkopf, H., 228, 249
Mone, E. M., 120, 134
Montgomery, L., 78, 90, 103, 112, 121, 132
Montgomery, R. J. V., 265, 267, 274
Moody, H. R., 199, 222
Moon, M., 13, 22
Moore, S., 287, 300
Mor-Barak, M., 152, 154, 161
Morgeson, F. P., 212, 222
Morin, L., 150, 162
Morrell, R. W., 204, 222
Morris, M. G., 149, 161
Morrison, A., 168, 177

Morrison, E. W., 179, 196
Morrow, J. E., 168, 177
Morrow-Howell, N., 310, 318
Morse, C. W., 171, 177
Morton, K. R., 146, 162, 183, 197, 283, 301, 313, 319
Motowidlo, S., 59, 69, 113, 118, 119, 124, 128, 131
Mottram, M., 226, 233, 247
Mount, M. K., 125, 134, 258, 273
Mowen, J. C., 38, 46
Moynihan, L., 316, 319
Mulligan, C. B., 291, 298
Munir, F., 215, 220
Munnell, A. H., 40, 47
Murphy, K. R., 118, 125, 134
Murray, B., 38, 46
Mutran, E. J., 30, 48

N

Nair, S. N., 228, 231, 236, 238, 241, 247, 248, 249
Nason, S. W., 141, 162
Naswall, K., 210, 223
Nazroo, J., 288, 300
Neal, A., 120, 133
Neal, M. B., 260, 261, 263, 264, 266, 267, 268, 274, 275
Near, J. P., 119, 136
Neece, W. M., 116, 117, 120, 129, 133, 308, 318
Nelson, C., 61, 67
Nelson, T. D., 74, 106
Nelson, T. E., 81, 82, 103
Nesselroade, J. R., 145, 151, 159
Netz, Y., 166, 177
Neuberg, S. L., 80, 87, 104
Neugarten, B., 63, 68
Neukam, K. A., 30, 33, 46
Ng, T. W. H., 192, 196
Nichols, T., 141, 161
Nicholson, N., 123, 134
Nielson, N. L., 284, 288, 290, 298
Nishida, Y., 203, 221
Nkomo, S. M., 55, 67
Noe, R., 55, 69, 163, 175
Norton, M. I., 41, 46, 80, 93, 104
Nussbaum, J. F., 80, 87, 97, 106
Nuttman-Shwartz, O., 284, 300
Nyamori, R. O., 316, 318

O

O'Brien, A. S., 262, 267, 272
O'Conner, P., 254, 256, 274
Offerman, L., 171, 177
Ohanian, L., 13, 22
Ohlott, P. J., 168, 177
Ohs, J. E., 80, 87, 97, 106
Oles, P. K., 183, 196
O'Neill, R., 59, 69
Ones, D. S., 122, 136
Oppler, S. H., 110, 112, 113, 114, 118, 119, 124, 128, 131
O'Rand, A. M., 19, 22, 27, 28, 40, 46, 47, 311, 318
O'Reilly, C. W., 123, 134, 169, 178, 186, 196
O'Reilly, K., 295, 300
Organ, D. W., 119, 120, 134, 136
Orodenker, S. Z., 261, 269, 274
Osawa, M. N., 36, 47
Ostroff, C., 184, 186, 193, 196
Oswald, A., 142, 144, 159
Ownby, R., 231, 247

P

Packel, D., 248
Pager, D., 56, 68
Pak, R., 236, 248
Palmer, I., 206, 222
Palmore, E. B., 297, 299
Pandey, S., 40, 49
Paradise, C., 168, 176
Park, D. C., 85, 94, 103, 115, 117, 135, 203, 204, 220, 222, 231, 248
Park, K. S., 28, 47
Parlamis, J. D., 74, 91, 92, 93, 107
Parra, L., 140, 162
Parsons, T. C., 201, 222
Pasupathi, M., 145, 151, 159
Patterson, D. W., 116, 117, 120, 129, 133, 308, 318
Peck, R., 58, 69
Pedersen, W. A., 202, 222
Penner, L. A., 119, 131
Penner, R. G., 42, 48
Pennington, J., 165, 178
Perdomo, D., 114, 135, 231, 238, 241, 249
Perdue, C., 101, 106

Perkins, A. J., 30, 45, 46
Perkins, K., 27, 48
Perrewe, P. L., 76, 78, 94, 98, 100, 105, 189, 196
Perry, E. L., 42, 48, 52, 55, 56, 59, 61, 63, 65, 67, 69, 74, 78, 80, 84, 90, 91, 92, 93, 98, 99, 106, 107, 243, 248
Perry, J. S., 75, 78, 96, 107
Perun, P., 42, 48
Perzynski, A. T., 295, 300
Peterson, R. O., 142, 160
Pfeffer, J., 112, 123, 134, 135
Philipsen, H., 261, 264, 266, 272
Piasecki, M., 127, 136
Pienta, A. M., 286, 300
Pierce, J. L., 211, 222
Pioncus, L. B., 76, 104
Pitt-Catsouphes, M., 109, 135
Pitts, M. J., 80, 87, 97, 106
Plamondon, K. E., 120, 128, 135
Pogash, R., 127, 136
Pollard, D., 76, 78, 95, 99, 106
Pond, S. B., 141, 142, 161
Post, G. M., 127, 136
Postma, S., 150, 162
Powell, G. N., 54, 59, 69
Prewett-Livingston, A., 54, 69
Price, R., 168, 177
Prieto, J. M., 92, 104
Prince, M. M., 204, 222
Prothero, J., 281, 301
Pruitt, K., 289, 301
Puglisi, J. T., 204, 222
Pulakos, E. D., 120, 128, 135
Purcell, P. J., 14, 15, 18, 23

Q

Quick, H., 30, 32, 38, 48
Quinn, J. F., 10, 13, 14, 16, 17, 18, 20, 22, 23, 316, 317

R

Radvansky, G., 204, 223
Rafuse, N. E., 55, 69, 167, 171, 172, 174, 176
Ragins, B. R., 55, 70
Rainie, L., 248

Raju, N. S., 53, 67, 74, 78, 87, 88, 89, 91, 93, 104, 165, 176, 243, 248
Ramos, C. I., 166, 176
Rankin, B., 41, 48
Rau, B. L., 39, 45, 307, 317, 318
Rauschenberger, J., 283, 301
Raza, S. M., 53, 70
Rebok, G., 171, 177
Reck, M., 115, 132
Redman, T., 78, 84, 92, 93, 94, 95, 98, 99, 103
Reed, R. R., III, 291, 298
Reid, S. A., 97, 98, 105
Reilly, A. H., 56, 70, 187, 197
Reiter-Palmon, R., 312, 319
Reitzes, D. C., 30, 48
Remery, C., 78, 92, 98, 107
Renaud, S., 150, 162
Reynolds, C. A., 145, 159
Reynolds, S., 39, 48
Reynolds, S. L., 16, 22, 23
Rhodes, S. R., 127, 132, 135, 140, 141, 142, 144, 146, 152, 162, 165, 175, 208, 222, xi, xiii
Rhoton, L., 55, 67
Richardson, V., 187, 196
Ridley, N., 39, 48
Rigler, S. K., 206, 222
Riley, L. D., 294, 301
Ringseis, E. L., 115, 120, 132
Riordan, C. M., 141, 162
Ritchey, P. N., 286, 299
Rix, S. E., 14, 23, 29, 48
Robbins, M. A., 54, 67
Robbins, N., 168, 176
Roberts, R. E. L., 267, 274
Robertson, A., 283, 301
Robertson, I., 284, 301
Robie, C., 140, 162
Robinson, M. M., 267, 274
Robinson, O., 56, 67
Robinson, S. L., 122, 135
Rogers, R. G., 32, 45
Rogers, W. A., 228, 230, 231, 236, 247, 248
Roos, P. A., 56, 70
Roring, R. W., 235, 236, 248
Rosen, B., 59, 70, 75, 78, 83, 95, 107, 165, 166, 167, 170, 171, 176, 177
Rosenfeld, R. A., 41, 48
Rosenkoetter, M. M., 30, 32, 48
Rosenthal, C. J., 263, 266, 268, 274
Roth, D., 231, 247

Roth, P., 54, 68
Rothbaum, F., 85, 94, 107
Rousseau, D. M., 179, 184, 193, 195
Rowe, J., 63, 70
Rozelle, R. M., 78, 86, 89, 98, 105
Rubenstein, P. D., 296, 301
Ruderman, M. N., 168, 177
Ruhm, C. J., 19, 23, 281, 301
Rumery, S. M., 118, 131
Ruoppila, I., 228, 249
Rupp, D. E., 77, 78, 85, 86, 95, 101, 107, 147, 159
Rush, M. C., 119, 136
Russell, M., 252, 273
Ryan, A. M., 140, 162
Ryan, E., 166, 177
Ryan, K., 120, 134
Ryan, M. M., 11, 12, 14, 15, 22
Rynes, S. L., 60, 70

S

Saarnio, D. A., 166, 177
Sabatini, P., 111, 112, 133
Sablynski, C. J., 180, 185, 186, 187, 188, 196
Sackett, P. R., 122, 128, 135
Sager, C. E., 110, 112, 113, 114, 118, 119, 124, 128, 131
Saito, Y., 16, 22, 23
Salthouse, T. A., 52, 63, 70, 110, 111, 116, 118, 121, 135, 168, 170, 172, 177, 178, 203, 207, 222, 226, 249, 313, 318
Sangl, J., 261, 262, 275
Sasala, J. M., 264, 275
Scandura, T. A., 179, 196
Schabracq, M., 75, 79, 87, 108, 169, 177
Schadron, G., 81, 88, 106
Schafer, R., 253, 274
Schaffer, A. M., 285, 301
Schaie, K. W., 117, 135
Scharlach, A. E., 261, 265, 267, 269, 274
Schein, E. A., 184, 192, 196
Schibye, B., 216, 222
Schippers, J., 78, 92, 98, 107
Schmeider, R., 140, 162
Schmidt, F. L., 54, 70, 207, 222
Schmitt, N., 283, 301
Schneider, B., 60, 70
Schnitger, M. H., 253, 257, 258, 274

Schoenbaum, M., 18, *21*
Schulman, M. D., 30, 31, *45*
Schulz, R., 121, *135*, 146, *160*
Schuster, M., 127, *132*, 165, *175*, *xiii*
Schwarz, N., 85, 94, *103*
Schwoerer, C., 140, *162*, 171, *176*
Scott, J., 35, *45*
Scott, J. P., 34, *49*
Scullen, S. E., 125, *134*
Seashore, S. E., 239, *249*
See, S., 166, *177*
Seeman, T. E., 202, *220*
Seidman, M. D., 204, *222*
Seitsamo, J., 208, *222*
Severinsson, E., 150, *159*
Sewell, C., 78, 87, 95, *107*
Shaner, J. L., 86, *105*
Shannon, D., 294, *301*
Shapiro, D. L., 140, *161*
Sharit, J., 113, 114, 129, *135*, 190, 195, 228,
    230, 231, 233, 236, 238, 241, *247*, *248*, *249*
Sharpe, M., 206, *222*
Shaw, J. D., 188, *196*
Shearer, R. L., 121, *135*
Shelton, F. C., 75, 76, 78, *106*
Shepard, J. M., 152, *161*
Sherman, R. H., 37, *48*
Sherman, S. J., 80, 86, *105*
Sherraden, M., 310, *318*
Shimizu, K., 203, *221*
Shin, Y., 184, 186, 193, *196*
Shinar, E. H., 60, 64, *70*
Shirom, A., 210, *223*
Shivers, S. L., 148, *160*
Shkop, Y. M., 75, 78, 84, *104*, 289, *301*
Shore, L. M., 53, 55, 59, 61, 65, 67, 68, *70*, 74,
    78, 83, 90, 93, *107*, 110, 112, 116, 121, 123,
    126, *132*, *135*, 141, 147, *159*, 169, 170, *175*
Short, P. F., 263, 265, *275*
Shultz, K. S., 19, *23*, 32, *48*, 146, *162*, 183, *197*,
    263, *272*, 281, 283, *301*, *302*, 307, 312, 313,
    316, *318*, *319*
Sicherman, N., 20, *21*
Simon, R., 168, *177*
Simpson, P., 152, *160*
Simpson, P. A., 151, *162*
Sinclair, R. R., 258, *274*
Sinervo, T., 290, *299*
Singer, M. S., 78, 87, 95, *107*
Singer, T. L., 267, *274*

Singh, P., 147, *160*
Singleton, J., 261, 262, *274*
Sirotnik, B. W., 316, *319*
Sisa, L., 207, *220*
Siu, O., 141, *162*
Slotterback, C. S., 166, *177*
Smeeding, T. M., 13, *22*
Smith, A., 59, *70*
Smith, A. D., 204, *220*, *222*
Smith, C. A., 119, *136*
Smith, D. B., 30, *48*, 59, *70*, 285, *301*
Smith, J. L., 262, 267, *272*
Smith, K. E., 42, *45*
Smith, M. W., 233, *249*
Smith, P., 140, *162*
Smith Wagner, L., 75, 79, 80, 95, *105*
Smither, J. W., 125, *134*
Smola, K. W., 144, 153, *162*
Smyer, M. A., 109, *135*
Snape, E., 78, 84, 92, 93, 94, 95, 98, 99, *103*
Snel, J., 309, *319*
Snyder, M., 79, 99, 102, *107*
Sobel, E. L., 267, *274*
Sogaard, K., 216, *222*
Solem, P. E., 288, *298*
Sonnenfeld, J. A., 179, 190, *197*
Sorensen, J. B., 60, *70*
Sorensen, K. L., 192, *196*
Soutar, G. N., 292, *298*
Sowers, M. F., 205, *222*
Sparks, K., 210, *223*
Spector, P. E., 140, 141, 145, *162*, 210,
    213, *223*
Spell, C. S., 316, *318*
Spiegel, P. E., 32, *48*
Spirduso, W. W., 204, *223*
Spiro, A., III, 284, *299*
Spitze, G., 267, *275*
Spokane, A. R., 184, *197*
Spreitzer, G. M., 141, 147, *160*, *162*
Spurr, S. J., 56, *70*
Stagner, R., 165, 167, 168, *177*
Staines, G. L., 254, 256, *274*
Staudinger, U. M., 256, *274*
Stauffer, J. M., 54, *70*
Steger, J., 121, *135*
Steinberg, S., 60, *70*
Steinmeier, T. L., 285, 287, *299*
Steitz, J. S., 111, *136*
Stern, B., 111, *131*

Stern, S. M., 23
Sterns, H. L., 110, 111, 115, 117, 121, 125, 136,
    144, 162, 307, 319
Stetzer, A., 211, 221
Steuerle, E., 42, 45, 48
Stevens, A. H., 17, 22
Stevens, F. C. J., 261, 264, 266, 272
Stewart, A. J., 59, 70
Stilwell, D., 78, 106
Stockdale, G. D., 42, 47, 76, 87, 88, 89, 93, 96,
    97, 99, 105, 126, 134, 164, 176, 243, 248
Stoller, E. P., 30, 48, 57, 70, 262, 275, 295, 300
Stoller, M. A., 30, 48
Stolz, H. K., 263, 272
Stone, D. L., 52, 57, 58, 59, 60, 61, 65, 68
Stone, R., 261, 262, 263, 265, 275
Stone-Romero, E. F., 52, 57, 58, 59, 60, 61,
    65, 68
Stoner, J. A. F., 183, 195
Stones, I. M., 115, 132
Streufert, S., 127, 136
Stroh, L. K., 56, 70, 151, 160, 162, 163, 169,
    176, 187, 197, 292, 293, 299
Sturman, M. C., 150, 162
Subramony, M., 316, 319
Sugar, J. A., 289, 301
Sugur, N., 141, 161
Sullivan, L. A., 94, 105
Sun, M., 38, 46
Sundali, J., 288, 302
Sundstrom, M., 183, 195
Sutinen, R., 290, 299
Sutton, C. D., 144, 153, 162
Sutton, M., 252, 272
Sverke, M., 210, 223
Swanberg, J. E., 260, 272
Swartz, N., 231, 248
Sweeney, P. D., 140, 161
Swim, J. K., 54, 66
Swody, C. A., 118, 131
Szafran, R. F., 16, 23
Széman, Z., 228, 249
Szinovacz, M. E., 38, 48, 285, 289, 290, 292,
    293, 301

Tagler, M. J., 26, 42, 46
Talaga, J. A., 188, 197, 297, 301
Tan, A., 59, 70
Tanaka, T., 203, 221
Tang, C. S. K., 290, 302
Tang, T. L. P., 152, 162
Taniguchi, H., 41, 48
Tanner, J., 65, 71
Tardieu, H., 245, 249
Tasiran, A. C., 141, 161
Taylor, M. A., 32, 48, 307, 314, 319
Taylor, P., 75, 107, 319
Taylor-Carter, M. A., 38, 48
Teixeira, L. R., 115, 132
Tetrick, L. E., 199, 221, 258, 274
Tharenou, P., 169, 177
Thayer, P. W., 212, 220
Thomas, D. A., 55, 71
Thomas, K. M., 60, 71
Thompson, D. E., 55, 69
Thompson, L., 123, 136
Thompson, P., 168, 177
Tinsley, H. E. A., 184, 197
Tobin, S., 63, 68
Toosi, M., 13, 23, 51, 52, 67, 249
Tosi, H., 53, 71
Tosti-Vasey, J. L., 121, 137
Tower, R. B., 31, 48
Tresini, M., 202, 220
Triadis, H. C., 79, 95, 96, 108
Trupin, L., 17, 23
Tsui, A., 169, 178
Tucker, F. D., 170, 178
Turner, J. C., 81, 82, 108
Turner, M. J., 34, 49
Turnley, W. H., 141, 150, 160
Tyson, L. D., 34, 49

                        U

Uhlenberg, P., 97, 98, 99, 105, 232, 248
Useem, M., 191, 197
Usi, C., 314, 319

            T   V

Tacken, M., 228, 249   Valentine, S., 152, 162, 286, 301
Tackett, R. A., 283, 301   Valentine, W. R., 152, 162

Valenzi, E., 117, 132
Van Dalen, H. P., 20, 23
Van Horn, C. E., 39, 48
Van Solinge, H., 280, 301
VanFleet, D. D., 61, 66
Vanneman, R., 53, 67
VanYperen, N. W., 150, 162
Varney, T. L., 75, 78, 96, 107
Vasılaki, A., 204, 222
Vecchio, R. P., 126, 136
Velkoff, V. A., 8, 22
Venkatesh, V., 149, 161, 228, 249
Veres, J., 54, 69
Verhaeghen, P., 170, 178
Vernoon Dassen, M. J. F. J., 261, 264, 266, 272
Verschuren, P., 154, 159
Vilhuber, L., 41, 46
Viswesvaran, C., 122, 136
Vitıello, M. W., 206, 223
Vodanovich, S. J., 77, 78, 85, 86, 95, 101, 107
Volker, C., 202, 220
von Eye, A., 85, 105
Voon, C. P., 28, 47
Voros, R. S., 116, 133
Vroman, S. B., 183, 195
Vrugt, A., 75, 79, 87, 108

W

Wagner, D. L., 261, 264, 275
Wagner, S. L., 119, 136
Waidmann, T., 18, 21
Waite, L. J., 8, 15, 23
Waldman, D. A., 54, 66, 71, 115, 116, 117, 118, 131, 136
Waldrop, J., 23
Walker, A., 75, 107
Walker, N., 233, 249
Wall, T., 239, 249
Wallace, M. J., 60, 69
Walsh, D. A., 31, 39, 46
Walsh, P., 76, 78, 86, 95, 103
Walsh, R. P., 78, 86, 94, 96, 106
Walters, G. D., 124, 136
Wan, R., 202, 222
Wanek, J. E., 122, 135
Ward, A. J., 179, 190, 197
Ward, R. A., 267, 275

Waring, E. J., 124, 137
Warnes, A. M., 295, 298
Warr, P. B., 114, 115, 116, 117, 120, 122, 123, 125, 126, 136, 137, 142, 143, 144, 159, 162, 165, 170, 178, 185, 197, 239, 249, 284, 301, 313, 319
Warren, J. A., 258, 275
Warren, N. C., 155, 159
Watane, C., 55, 71
Weatherly, E. W., 141, 162
Weathers, R., 16, 23
Webster, J., 316, 319
Weckerle, J. R., 146, 162, 183, 197, 281, 283, 301, 302
Wegman, D. H., 211, 223, 227, 232, 249
Wei, X., 55, 68
Weir, D. R., 289, 290, 291, 292, 293, 294, 299
Weisburd, D., 124, 137
Weiss, D. J., 239, 249
Weiss, E. M., 42, 49, 76, 79, 84, 108, 149, 150, 161, 164, 165, 167, 169, 170, 171, 173, 175, 176, 177, 178, 215, 221
Weiss, H. M., 101, 103
Weiss, R. S., 310, 319
Welchman, R., 56, 67
Weller, C. E., 47
Wessely, S., 206, 222
Westerman, J. W., 288, 302
Whitbourne, S. K., 205, 206, 223
White, A. T., 140, 145, 162
White, J. K., 283, 301
White, P. J., 78, 106
Whitley, B. E., Jr., 42, 47, 76, 87, 88, 89, 93, 96, 97, 99, 105, 126, 134, 164, 176, 243, 248
Whyte, G., 316, 319
Wilkinson, A. V., 26, 42, 46
Williams, A. P., 65, 71
Williams, J. R., 125, 134
Williams, L., 170, 177
Williamson, J. B., 40, 41, 47
Willis, R. J., 289, 290, 291, 292, 293, 294, 299
Willis, S. L., 121, 137
Wilson, G., 20, 23
Wise, D. A., 17, 22, 23
Wise, P. G., 60, 71
Wohlers, A. J., 125, 137
Woodall, J., 56, 67
Worden, A., 233, 249
Wray, L. A., 19, 22
Wrenn, K., 166, 178

Wright, J. D., 127, *137*
Wright, P., 316, *319*
Wright, S. D., 295, *302*
Wrosch, C., 31, 49
Wu, A. M. S., 290, *302*
Wu, K. B., 27, 28, 29, 45, 49

Y

Yamagata, K., 203, *221*
Yammarino, F. J., 125, *131*
Yan, E. C. W., 290, *302*
Yang, Y., 114, *135*, 231, 238, 241, *249*
Yeatts, D., 127, *133*, 149, *160*
Yegıdıs, B., 267, *274*
Yelin, E. H., 17, *23*

Youtz, M., 168, *176*
Yzerbyt, V. Y., 81, 88, *106*

Z

Zacks, R. T., 204, *221*, *223*
Zenger, T., 169, *178*
Zerbe, W. J., 75, *104*
Zhan, M., 35, 40, 45, 49
Zickar, M. J., 311, *319*
Zion, C., 61, 67
Zioupos, P., 204, *220*
Zohar, D., 210, 214, *223*
Zucker, R. A., 206, *221*
Zukin, S., 191, *197*
Zweers, M., 150, *162*

Subject Index

A

Absenteeism, 122–123
Absolute *versus* relative decisions, in age bias, 88–89
Accidents, 115–116
Accountability, in age bias, 89–90
Adaptive performance, 120–122
Additive effects, belonging to two or more disadvantaged groups, 56–58
Affective component
  attitude, 76
  connection to discrimination, 85–86
Age bias
  communication patterns, 87
  constraint on entry into alternative career, 188–190
  everyday interactions, 102
  expanded view of, 2, 73–108, 78–79t
  explicit *versus* implicit, 101
  future research, 100–103
  illusory correlation, 86–87
  measurements used, 100–101
  mediators for, 83–87
  moderators for, 87–96
  motivators for, 79–83
  rater issues, 93–95
  selected overview of bias research, 80–81t
  solutions for, 96–100
  specific or general bias, 101
  tripartite view, 75–77, 78–79t
  types, 101–102
Age Discrimination in Employment Act (ADEA) of 1967, 111, 216
Age-satisfaction relationship, 142–143
Aging. *see also* Older workers
  changes in population composition, 7–11, 8t, 9f
  changing abilities related to, 230–243
  conceptions of age, 110–112
  demography, 7–23

effects on work outcomes, 53–56
employee development and training issues, 3, 163–178
employee performance and, 3, 109–137
  measurements used in bias, 100–101
  methodological issues, 309–314
  occupational health and, 4, 199–222
  physical and cognitive changes, 202–206
  practice issues, 314–317
  research design issues, 311–314
  technology for work and, 4, 225–249
  unifying paradigm for understanding, 5, 303–319
  work attitudes and, 3, 139–162
  work behavior and, 206–209
  work motivation and, 150–154
  work/family issues, 4–5, 251–275
Aging workforce, 11–15. *see also* Older workers
  directions for future research, 21, 65–66
  diversity issues for, 2, 51–71
  historical trends in participation, 13–15, 14–15f
  influences on the age structure, 15–20
  interactive model, 58–59
  person-based measures, 111–112
  population pyramids by age and gender, 12f
American Association of Retired Persons (AARP), Roper survey, 29
Attention, changes with aging, 230–232
Attitude components, 75
Attributions, older workers, 86

B

Baby boomers, financial planning and, 32–35
Behavioral component, attitude, 76
Bias holder, what can be done, 97
Biological and gerontological perspectives on aging, 202–203
Blatant bias, 77

Boundary spanning responsibilities, 186
Bridge employment, 181
    career embeddedness effects, 191–192
    effects on age structure of the workforce, 19
Bureau of Labor Statistics, 51–52

C

Career change
    constraints on entry into alternative careers,
        188–190
    construct of, 180–181
    motivation in older workers, 181–184
    sacrifices, 187–188
Career embeddedness, 185–186
    anchors and, 192–193
    hanging-on process, 193
    retirement and bridge employment, 191–192
    senior executives, 190–191
Career mobility and stability, 4, 179–197
Career stability and embeddedness, 184–190
    directions for future research, 190–193
    implications for practice, 193–194
Careers, definition, 180
Census Bureau, definition of poverty, 26
Change and development, work attitudes
        toward, 148–149
Chronological age, 111
Classic Model of performance, 113
Cognitive ability changes with aging, 203–204
    at work, 207
Cognitive busyness, in age bias, 90
Cognitive component, attitude, 75
Commission on Behavioral and Social Sciences
        and Education, 26
Committee on National Statistics, 26
Communication patterns, in age bias research, 87
Community involvement, alternative careers
        and, 192
Computers, use by older workers, 228–230, 229f
Constructs
    career change, 180–181
    operational definitions of age, 156
Context
    age bias, 87–92
    age measures based on, 112
    organizational citizenship behavior,
        119–120
Context-based age measures, 112
Coping strategies, 257–258

Country/culture
    effects on ageism at work, 92–93
    what can be done about age bias, 99–100
CREATE, technology use, 228, 230f

D

Demographic transition, population aging
        and, 8
Demography, aging and work, 1–2, 7–23
Dependency ratios, population aging and, 10
Developmental job experiences
    access to, 168–169
    participation rates and performance,
        170–172
Diversity
    effects on age structure of the workforce,
        18–19
    issues for an aging workforce, 2, 51–71
Double jeopardy
    belonging to two or more disadvantaged
        groups, 56–58
    person stereotypes and, 59

E

Economic conditions, effects on age structure of
        the workforce, 17
Economic imperative, studying low-income
        workers, 30–32
Education, effects on age structure of the
        workforce, 16
Eldercare
    balancing work with, 260–267
    directions for future research, 270–272
    distance from recipient of care, 264–265
    occupation/hours worked and, 264
    organizational consequences, 261–262
    practice issues, 270
    special care needs, 265–266
    what can be done to help, 267–268
Elderly dependency ratios, effects on pay-as-
        you-go entitlement programs, 10, 11f
Employee assistance programs (EAPs), 217
Employee benefits, sacrifice in career change,
        187–188
Employee development
    aging workforce, 3, 163–178
    directions for future research, 172–174

implications for practice, 174–175
situational influences, 164–169
Employee health, 200–201
Employment, continued availability for older
    workers, 39–42
Employment decisions, older female and
    minority employees, 62f
Ethnicity. see also Racial differences
    eldercare and, 263
Executive attitudes, effect on opportunities for
    older workers, 42
Experience and expertise, in older workers, 207

                            F

Facet satisfaction, age and, 141–142
Family issues
    across the life span, 253–257
    aging and work, 4–5, 251–275
    assistance in dealing with, 258–260
    career change and, 188
    defining work and family, 252–253
    effects of retirement, 284–285
    work versus family, 255–257
Female labor force participation, effects on age
    structure of the workforce, 16
Fertility declines, population changes and, 8–9
Finances, effects on well being, 30–31
Financial planning
    behavior of boomers, 32
    improvement for low-income workers, 37–42
    lack of information on, 34
    lack of money for investment, 35
    in low-income groups, 32–33
    no access to formal planning programs, 35
    understanding impediments to, 33–35
Financial stress, attitudes toward retirement
    and, 30
Fit
    in career embeddedness, 186–187
    lack of, occupational change and, 184
    lifestyle, 187
Flexiwork, 237–242
Functional (biological) age, 111

                            G

Gender. see also Older women
    declining participation in workforce, 13–15,
        14–15f

differences in aging effects, 52–53
directions for future research in job
    matching, 65–66
effects on work outcomes, 53–56
eldercare and, 262–263
female labor force participation, 16
interactive model, 58–59
poverty and, 28
retirement and, 285–286
retirement planning behavior and, 33
Gerontechnology (gerotechnology),
    definition, 227
Goal setting, in retirement planning, 38

                            H

Hall typology, coping behaviors, 257
Hanging-on process, career embeddedness
    and, 193
Health
    effects on age structure of the workforce,
        16–17
    environmental perspective, 201
    in low-income workers, 31–32
    traditional medical perspective, 200
    wellness perspective, 201
Health and Retirement Study (HRS), 311–312
Health promotion, for older workers, 215–216
Health-related performance indicators, 115
Hearing changes, effects on technology for
    older workers, 235–236
Homeostasis, 202

                            I

Illusory correlation, in age bias research,
    86–87
Income
    importance in well being, 30–32
    perceived adequacy of, 30
Individual characteristics, age-related,
    169–170
Individual-level factors, motivation for
    career change, 181–182
Individuating information, in age bias, 87–88
Institutional barriers, opportunities for older
    workers, 42
Instruction in technology, issues for older
    workers, 232–233

Internet
  financial planning resources, 37
  use by older workers, 228–230, 229f

J

Job characteristics and stressors, effects on older
    workers, 209–210
Job context, age bias in, 90–91
Job embeddedness, 185
Job involvement, 146–148
Job level factors, motivation for career change,
    182–183
Job performance
  age, gender, and race effects, 54–55
  implications for future research, 127–129
  implications for practice, 129–130
Job redesign, for older employees, 212–214
Job satisfaction, age and, 140–141
Job stereotypes, 61, 62f

K

Knowledge acquisition, gaps for older workers,
    242–243

L

Labor market realities, older female and
    minority employees, 62f
Legal age, 111
Legal barriers, opportunities for older workers, 42
Legal interventions, for older workers, 216–217
Leisure activities, in low-income workers, 31–32
Life course perspective on aging, 203
Life stages, work/family issues, 253–255
Lifestyle fit, 187
Links, in career embeddedness, 185–186
Low wage work, definition, 27
Low-income older workers. see also Aging;
    Aging workforce; Older workers, 2, 25–49
  continued employment and, 39–42
  definition, 26–27
  directions for future research, 43–44
  economic imperative for studying, 28–29
  financial planning behavior, 32–33
  improving financial planning for, 37–42

lack of education, 40–41
psychological imperative for studying, 30–32
suggestions for job seekers, 43

M

Market changes, effects on age structure of the
    workforce, 20
Medicare, effects of increasing elderly
    dependency ratios, 10
Memory, changes with aging, 230–232
Mental health changes with aging, 205–206
  at work, 208–209
Middle-aging workforce, 13
Minorities. see also Ethnicity; Racial differences
  directions for future research in job
      matching, 65–66
  employment consequences for, 56–57
Mobility and compensation, age, gender, and
    race effects, 55–56
Morality declines, population changes and,
    8–9
Multi-source and team-based measures of
    performance, 125–127

N

National Research Council, 26

O

Occupation, eldercare and, 264
Occupational hazards and diseases, effects on
    older workers, 211–212
Occupational health
  aging and, 4, 199–222
  future research, 218–219
  implications for practice, 219
Occupation-level factors, motivation for career
    change, 183–184
Older women
  employment consequences for, 56–57
  summary model and implications for practice,
      61–65, 62f
Older workers. see also Aging; Aging workforce;
    Low-income older workers
  aging and work/family issues, 4–5, 251–275

assistance in dealing with work/family issues, 258–260

barriers to entry into alternative careers, 188–190

benefits of telework, 237-242, 240f, 241f

better off or easier to please, 143–145

career mobility and stability, 4, 179–197

conceptual/theoretical issues of perception, 304–308

coping strategies, 257–258

definition, 226–227

effects of workplace exposures on, 209–211

eldercare and, 260–269

gaps in knowledge acquisition, 242–243

hanging-on process, 193

interventions for improving health, 212–218

methodological issues, 309–314

motivation for career change, 181–184

participation rates in developmental activities, 170–172

possible discriminatory treatment, 167–168

reactions to organizational treatment, 150

research on everyday interactions, 102

retirement as a psychological option for, 145–146

sacrifice in career changes, 187–188

specific or general bias, 101

stereotypes about learning and development behavior, 164–166

what can be done about age bias, 97–98

what is old?, 100–101

Online. see Internet

Organization change, definition, 180

Organization context, age bias in, 91 –92

Organization for Economic Co-operation and Development, 42

Organizational barriers, opportunities for older workers, 42

Organizational citizenship behavior (OCB), 119–120

age and predictors of, 119–120

Organizational climate

development for older workers, 213–214

effects on older workers, 210–211

Organizational commitment, 146–148

Organizational deviant behaviors, 122–125

Organizational entry, age, gender, and race effects, 53–54

Organizations

age-related reactions to treatment by, 150

eldercare and, 261–262

employee age and performance in, 3, 109–137

perspectives on retirement, 278–279, 286–289

role in eldercare, 268

what can be done about age bias, 98–99

Overt destruction, 123–124

P

Panel on Poverty and Family Assistance, 26

Pension availability, effects on age structure of the workforce, 17-18

Perception

changes with aging, 230–232

conceptual/theoretical issues, 304–308

Person stereotypes, 59–60, 62f

Person-based measures of age, 111–112

Person-group fit (P-G), 186

Person-job fit (P-J), 186

Person-organization fit (P-O), 186

Physical and functional changes with aging, 204–205

Physical changes, at work, 207–208

Policy environment, effects on age structure of the workforce, 20

Population

changes in composition, 7–11, 8t, 9f

percent aged 65 and over, 8t

pyramids by age and gender, 9f, 12f

Poverty

definition, 26

older Americans and, 27

prevalence of, 27–32

Practice issues

aging research, 314–317

career stability and embeddedness, 193–194

eldercare, 270

employee development, 174–175

job performance, 129–130

minorities, 61–65, 62f

retirement, 295–297

task performance, 129–130

training, 174–175

work attitudes, 155–158

Promotability, age, gender, and race effects, 55–56

Prototype matching, 61

Proximal context factors, age and, 125–127
Psychological imperative, studying low-income workers, 30–32
Psychomotor skills, changes with aging, 230–232

R

Racial differences. *see also* Ethnicity; Minorities
    effects of aging on employment consequences, 52–53
    effects on work outcomes, 53–56
    interactive model, 58–59
    poverty and, 28
Rate-of-living theory, 202
Rater, in age bias, 93–95
Research design issues, study of aging, 311–314
Retirees, perspectives on retirement, 278–286
Retirement
    adjustment/outcomes, 283–284
    attitudes toward, 30
    career embeddedness and bridge employment, 191–192
    continued work after, 181, 189t
    effects on family, 284–285
    future directions for research and practice, 295–297
    gender and, 285–286
    multi-level perspective, 5, 277–302
    planning, 32
    as a psychological option for older workers, 145–146
    timing, 15
    types, 281–283
Retirement planning
    active *versus* passive involvement, 38–39
    content of programs, 37–38
Retraining, issues for older workers, 232–233

S

Sandwich generation, caring for children and elders at the same time, 266
Satellite sites, telework, 237
Selection, optimization, and compensation (SOC), coping behaviors, 257
Senate Committee on Aging, 2005, 29

Senior executives, career embeddedness of, 190–191
Situational influences, employee training and development, 164–169
Skills training and education, lack in older low-income workers, 40
Social limitations, view of older low-income workers, 41–42
Social Security
    effects of increasing elderly dependency ratios, 10
    inadequacy of, 28–29
    over reliance by low-income groups, 29, 34
Social support
    financial hardship in older adults and, 31
    older worker access to, 168–169
Social workers, effect on opportunities for older workers, 42
Society, perspectives on retirement, 278–279, 289–295
Software interface, for older workers, 236–237
Special populations, work motives and values, 154
Stereotypes
    job, 61, 62f
    older workers' learning and development, 164–166
    person, 59–60, 62f
    possible discriminatory treatment, 167–168
    use to explain discrimination, 83–85
    view of older low-income workers, 41–42
Subjective (personal or perceived) age, 111
    task performance and, 118
Subtle bias, 77

T

Target, in age bias, 95–96
Target demographics, older female and minority employees, 62f
Task interdependence, 186
Task performance, 113–118, 114t
    accidents, 115–116
    adaptive, 120–122
    age and objective, 113–115
    age and predictors of, 117–118
    age and subjective ratings of, 116–117

contextual, 119–120
health-related indicators, 115
implications for future research, 127–129
implications for practice, 129–130
subjective age and, 118
Team performance, 127
Technology
age and, at work, 4, 225–249
barrier to entry into alternative career, 190
definition, 227
directions for future research, 243–245
effects on age structure of the workforce,
19–20
hearing changes and, 235–236
input/output device issues for older workers,
233–234
instruction for older workers, 232–233
practical implications of what we know
about older workers, 245–247
retraining issues for older workers, 232–233
software interface for older workers, 236–237
training issues for older workers, 232–233
use by older workers, 228–230, 229f
vision changes and, 234–236, 234f
Telecommuting, 237–242
Telework, 237–242, 240f, 241f
Theft, 123–124
Training
access to, 168–169
age, gender, and race effects, 55
development and, aging workforce, 3, 163–178
directions for future research, 172–174
discrimination in access to in an alternative
career, 188–190
increase productivity and safety, 215
issues for older workers, 232–233
situational influences, 164–169
Tripartite view, age bias, 75–77, 78–79t
Turnover, 123

W

White-collar crime, 123–124
Work attitudes
age and, 3, 139–162
job involvement and organizational
commitment, 146–148
retirement as a psychological option for
older workers, 145–146
suggestions for implementation and
policy, 157
toward change and development,
148–149
unifying paradigm for understanding
aging, 5, 303–319
Work behavior, effects of age, 206–209
Work motivation
age and, 150–151
processes, 155
Work motives and values
aging and, 151–154
special populations, 154
Work performance
age linkages with, 112–127
construct explication and, 112–113
emerging domain of, 114t
employee aging and, 3, 109–137
multi-source and team-based measures,
125–127
Work-based theories of aging, 156
Worker age, as a focal issue, 155–156
Workforce. see Aging workforce; Older workers,
Low-income older workers
Working poor, 26
Working-poverty trap
Workplace, age bias in, 73–108
Workplace exposures, effect on older workers,
209–211
World Health Organization (WHO), wellness
perspective, 201

V

Vision changes, effects on technology for older
workers, 234–236, 234f

Y

Youth dependency ratios, 10, 11f